中国残疾人事业统计年鉴

China Statistical Yearbook on the Work for Persons with Disabilities

2015

（总第14期 No. 14）

中国残疾人联合会 编

China Disabled Persons' Federation

图书在版编目（CIP）数据

中国残疾人事业统计年鉴. 2015 : China Statistical Yearbook on the Work for Persons with Disabilities : 汉、英 / 中国残疾人联合会编. -- 北京 : 中国统计出版社, 2015.8
ISBN 978-7-5037-7525-3

Ⅰ. ①中… Ⅱ. ①中… Ⅲ. ①残疾人－社会福利事业－统计资料－中国－2015－年鉴－汉、英 Ⅳ.①D669.69-66

中国版本图书馆 CIP 数据核字(2015)第 185501 号

中国残疾人事业统计年鉴-2015
China Statistical Yearbook on the Work for Persons with Disabilities

作　　者/中国残疾人联合会
责任编辑/王振宇
封面设计/王　鹏
出版发行/中国统计出版社
通信地址/北京市丰台区西三环南路甲 6 号　邮政编码/100073
电　　话/邮购（010）63376909　书店（010）68783171
网　　址/http://www.zgtjcbs.com
印　　刷/河北天普润印刷厂
经　　销/新华书店
开　　本/880×1230mm　1/16
印　　张/20　8 彩页
字　　数/620 千字
版　　别/2015 年 8 月第 1 版
版　　次/2015 年 8 月第 1 次印刷
定　　价/180.00 元

如有印装差错，由本社发行部调换。

《中国残疾人事业统计年鉴-2015》
编委会和编辑工作人员

编委会

编辑工作人员

编者说明

《中国残疾人事业统计年鉴-2015》系统收录了全国和各省、自治区、直辖市2014年残疾人工作各方面的统计数据，是一部全面反映中国残疾人事业发展的资料性年刊。

本书内容由六部分组成：第一部分为主要指标数据图；第二部分为2014年中国残疾人事业发展统计公报；第三部分为综合统计资料，是历年统计情况的综合反映；第四部分为2014年度分省统计资料，记录2014年各省任务指标执行情况和全国汇总情况；第五部分为分省统计报告，包括全国31个省（自治区、直辖市）、新疆生产建设兵团和黑龙江垦区的残疾人事业统计公报；第六部分为附录，介绍中国残疾人事业统计有关的政策法规文件。

本年鉴涉及的全国性统计数据均不包括香港、澳门特别行政区和台湾省数据。

本年鉴是根据各地残联报送的统计年报和部分专项业务项目统计结果编制而成。表格中"空格"表示该项统计指标数据不足本表最小单位数、数据不详或无该项数据。

2015年7月

目　录

Contents

第一部分　主要数据图

Part Ⅰ　Charts

第二部分　统计公报与专文
Part Ⅱ　Communiqué and Reports

第三部分　综合统计资料
Part Ⅲ　Comprehensive Statistical Data

第四部分　分省统计资料
Part Ⅳ　Statistical Data of Provinces

康　复
Rehabilitation

教　育

Education

就　业

Employment

社会保障

Social Security

扶　贫

Poverty Alleviation

1 主要数据图

Charts

图-1 “十二五”期间累计得到不同程度康复的残疾人

Chart1 PWDs Receiving Rehabilitation Service during the 12th Five-year Planning Period

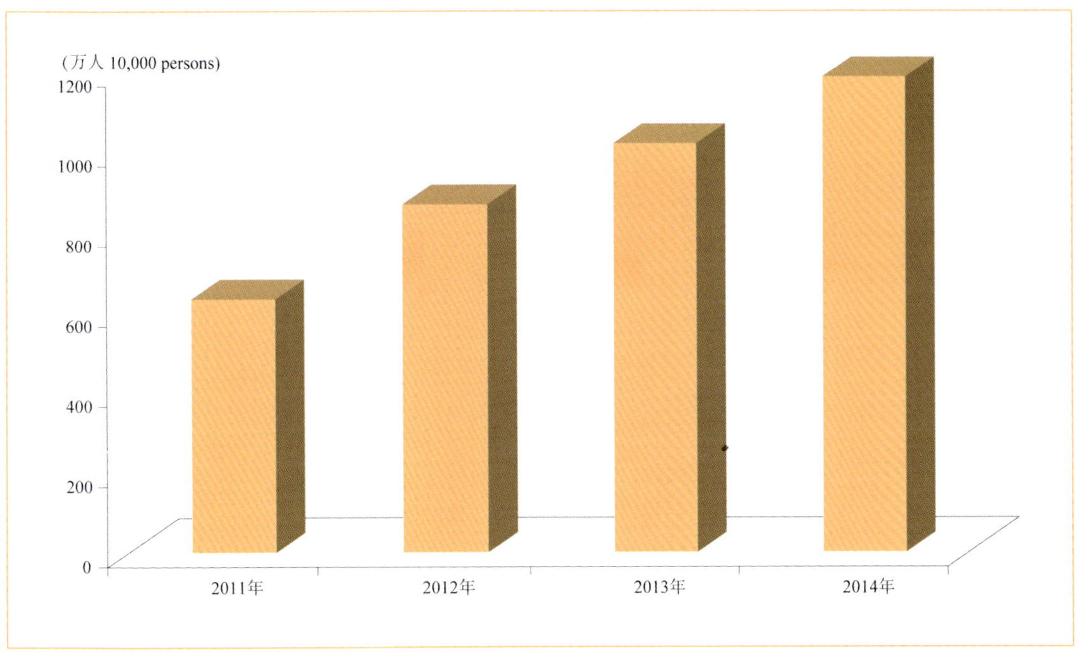

图-2 2011-2014年开展社区康复服务的县（市、区）

Chart2 Counties and Cities Where CBR has been Conducted during 2011-2014

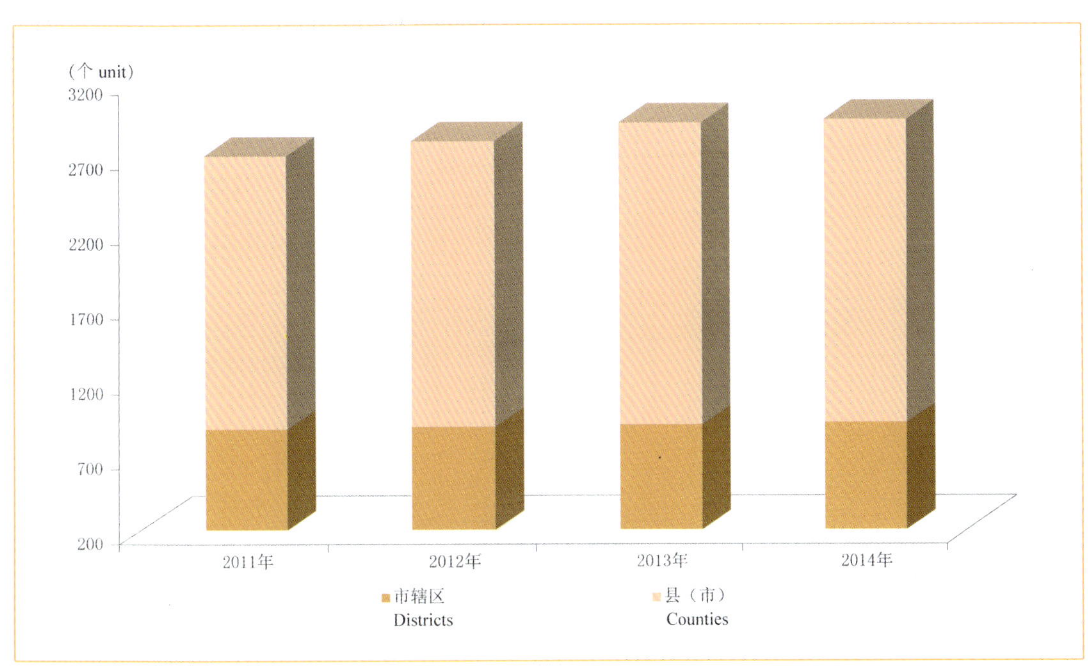

图-3 2011-2014年残疾儿童康复主要工作完成情况

Chart3 Rehabilitation for Children with Disabilities during 2011-2014

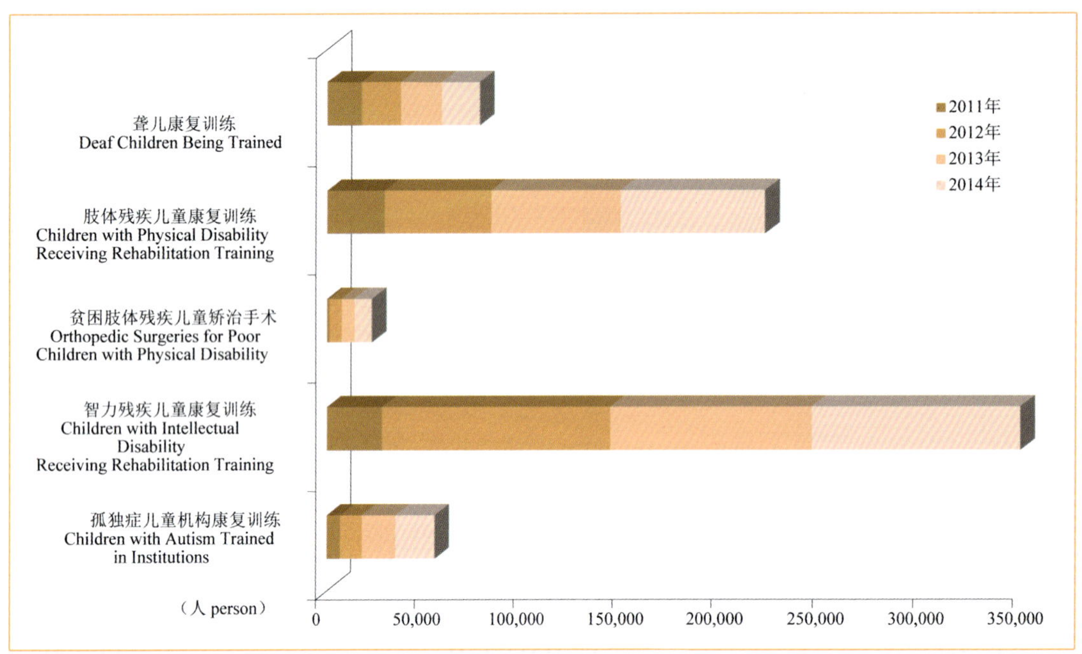

图-4 2011-2014年假肢与矫形器装配情况

Chart4 Artificial Limbs and Orthotic Devices Fitted during 2011-2014

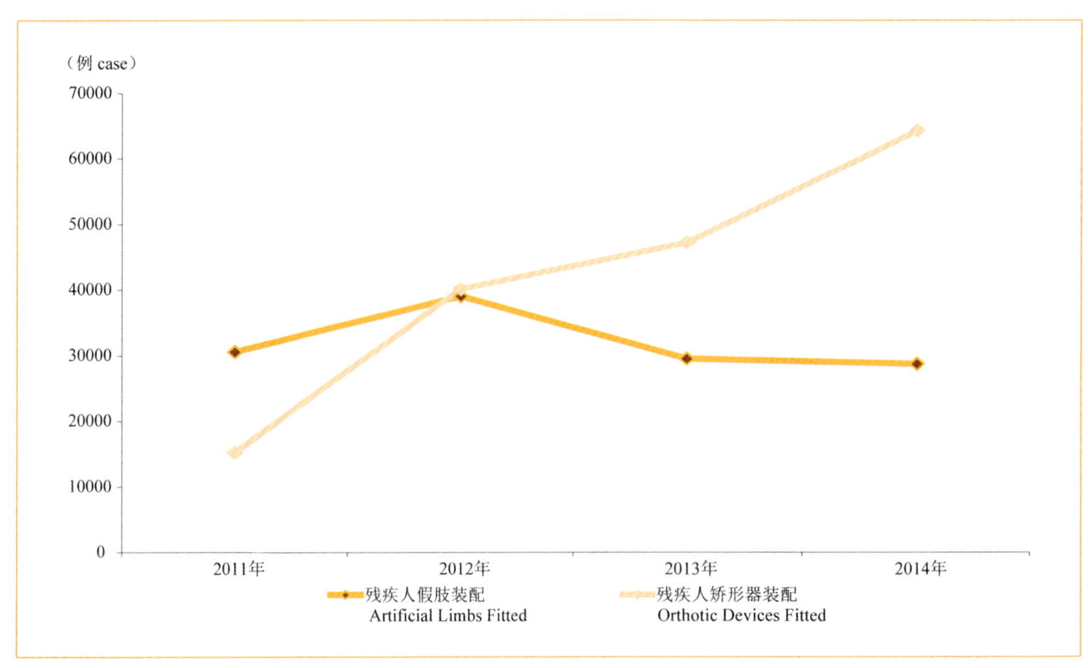

图-5 2011-2014年高等院校录取残疾考生情况

Chart5 Admission of Disabled Students by Higher Educational Institution during 2011-2014

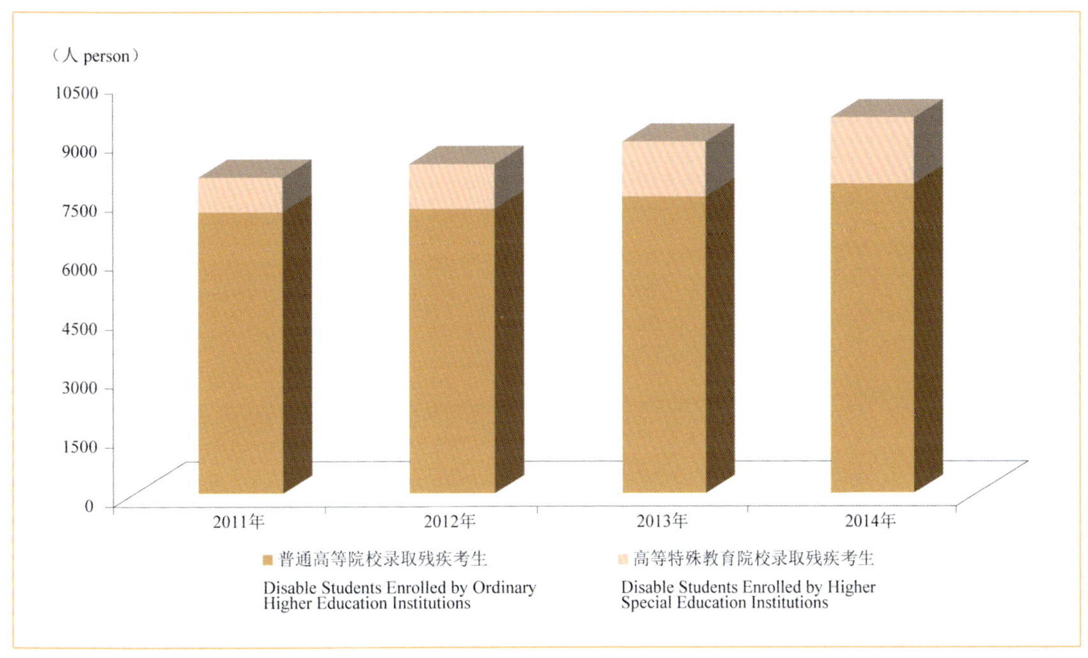

图-6 2014年城镇残疾人新安排就业情况

Chart6 Newly-added Employment of Disabled Persons in Urban Areas in 2014

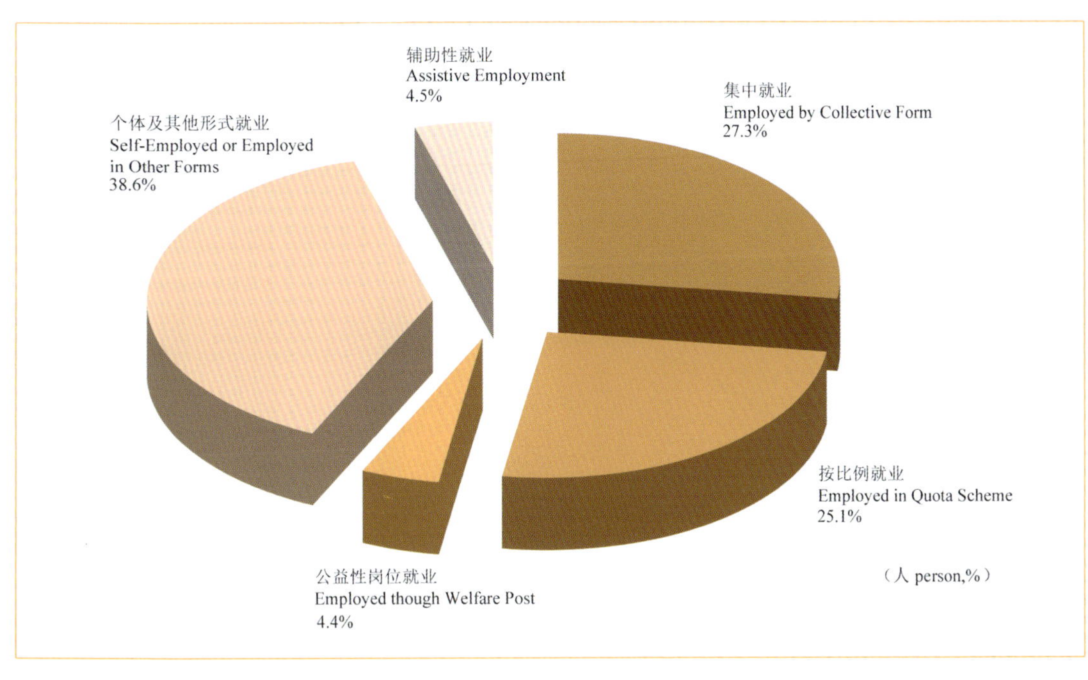

图-7 2011-2014年度盲人按摩人员培训情况

Chart7 Massage Training for Blind Persons during 2011-2014

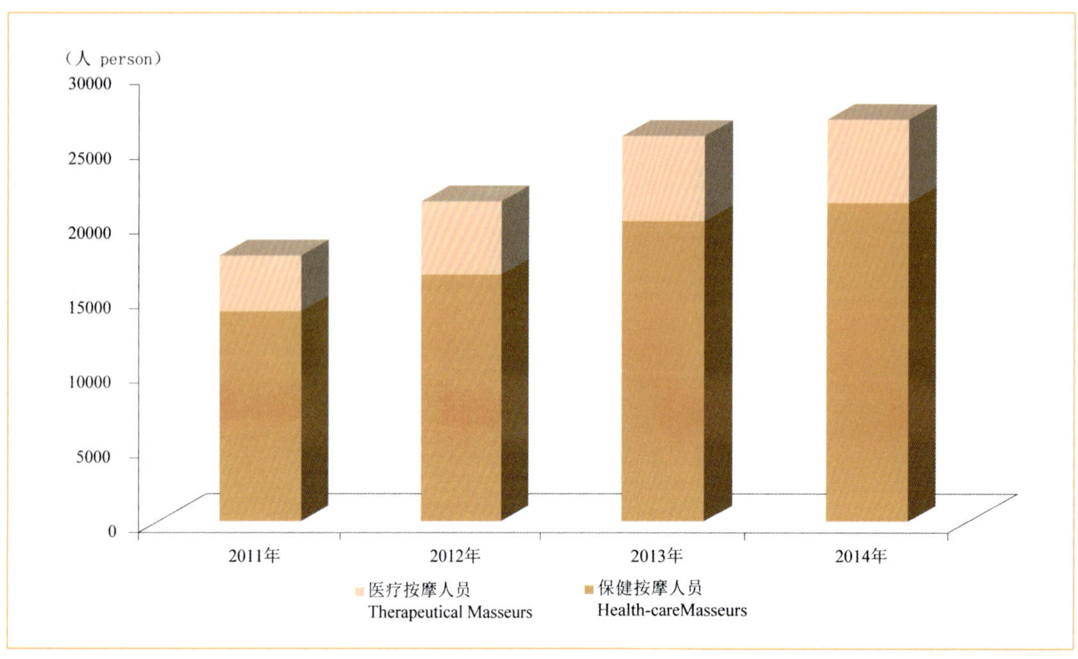

图-8 2011-2014年残疾人获得护理补贴和生活补贴情况

Chart8 PWDs Receiving Care Subsidies and Living Allowances during 2011-2014

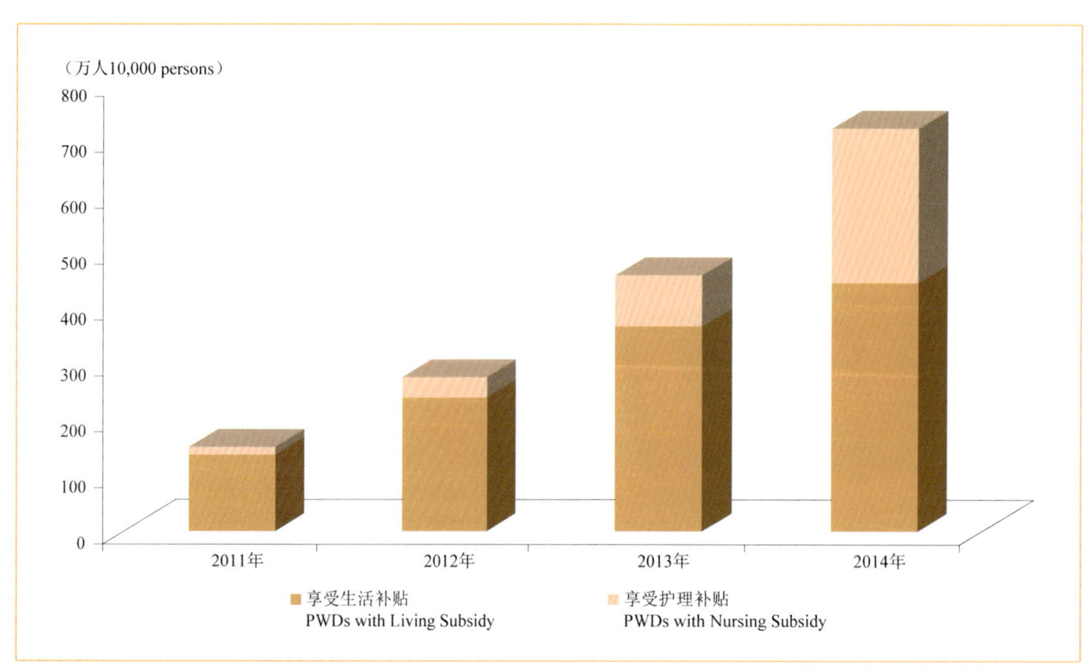

图-9 2011-2014年残疾人接受托养服务情况

Chart9 PWDs Receiving Fostering Serviceduring 2011-2014

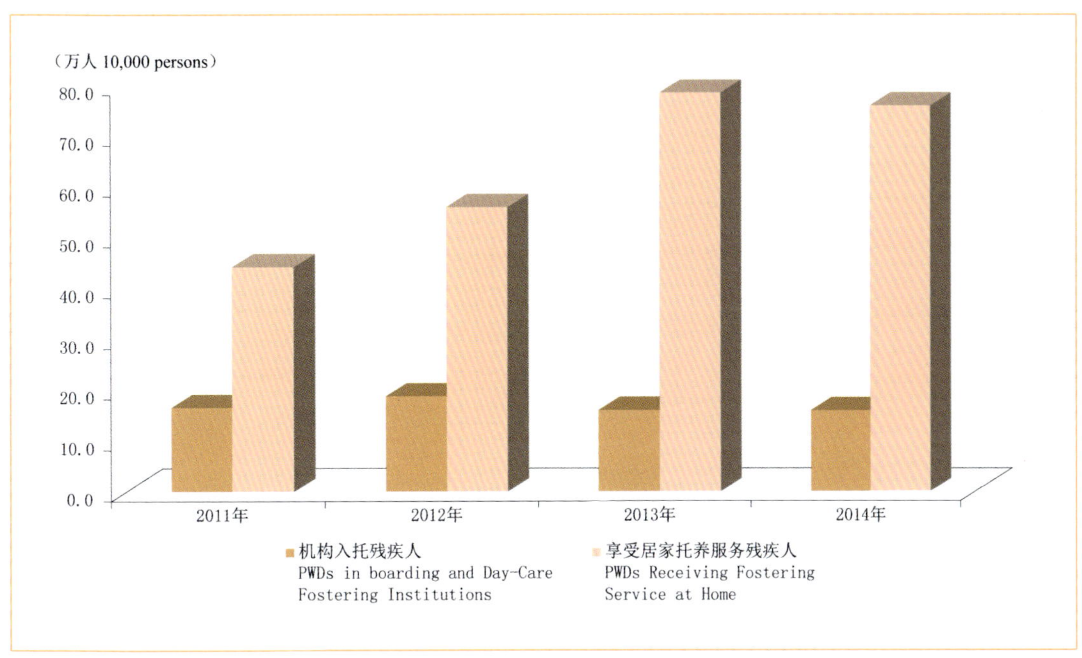

图-10 2011-2014年农村贫困残疾人扶持情况

Chart10 Supported by Poverty Alleviation Projects for Poor PWDs in Rural Areas during 2011-2014

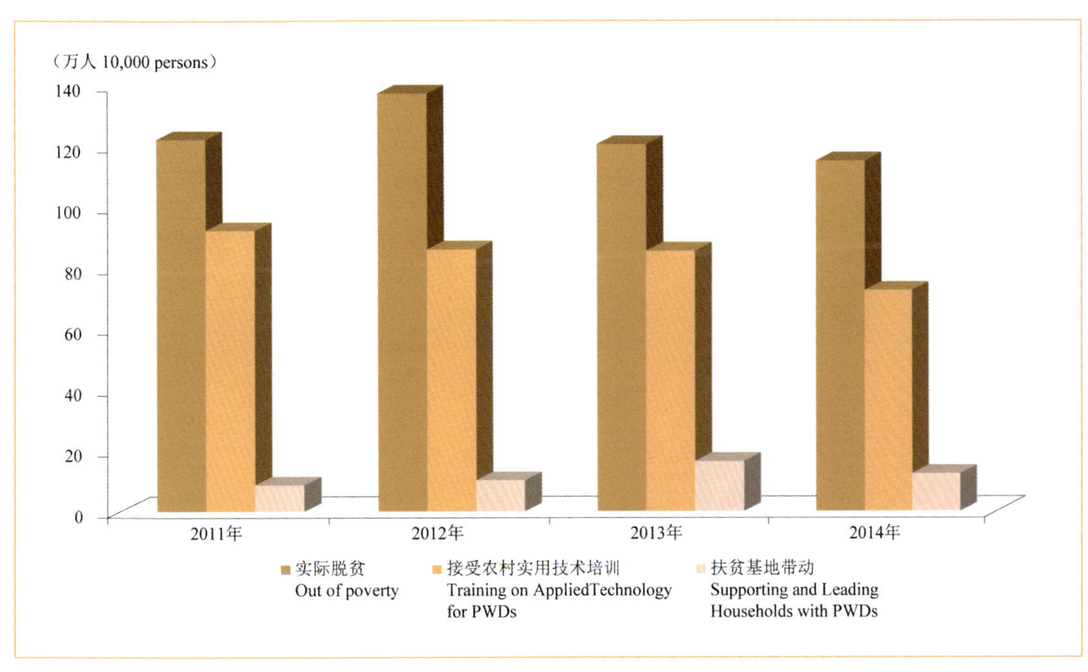

图-11 2011-2014年农村贫困残疾人危房改造情况

Chart11 House Renovation for Poor PWDs in Rural Areas during 2011-2014

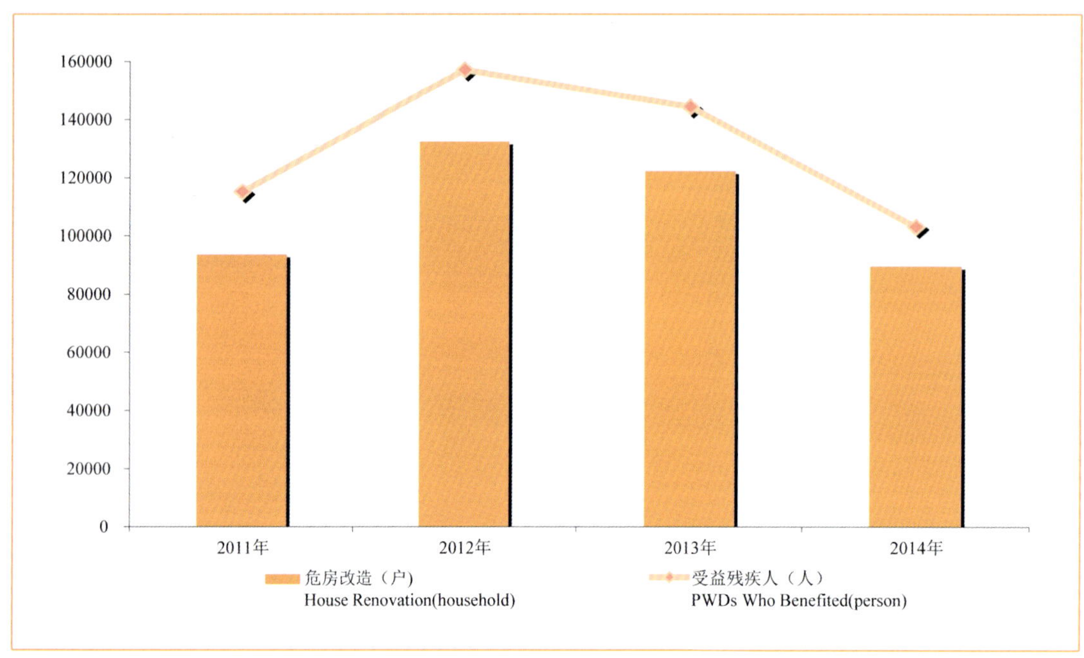

图-12 2011-2014年省、市两级残疾人宣传栏目开展情况

Chart12 Propaganda Columns for PWDs at Provincial and City Level during 2011-2014

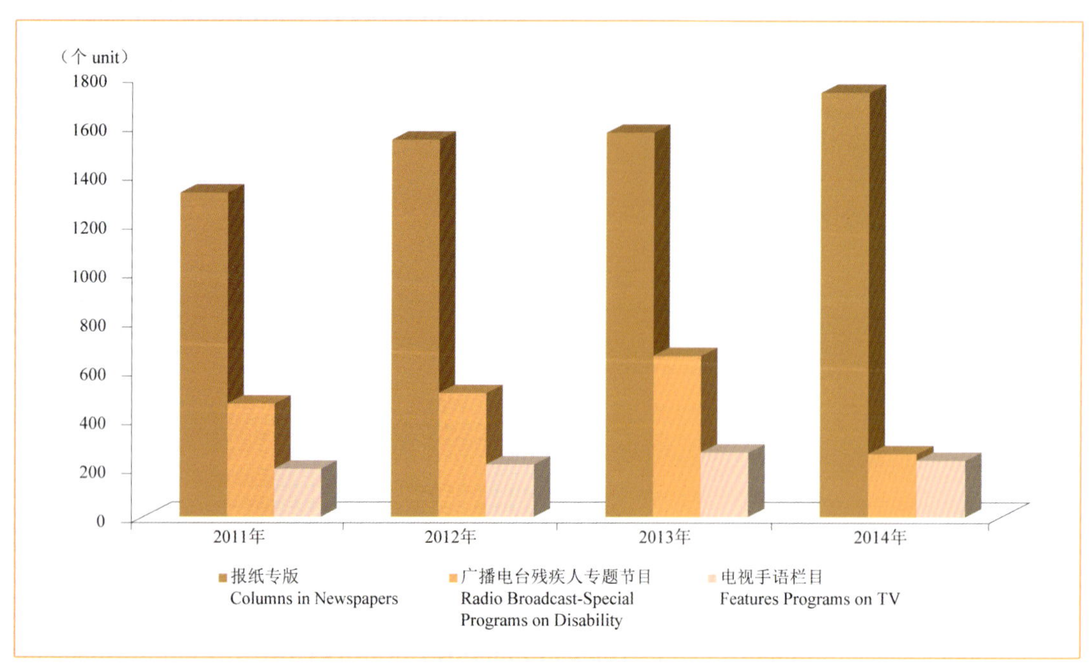

图-13 2011-2014省、地市两级残疾人参加群众体育健身活动情况

Chart13 PWDs Participating Mass Sports or Fitness Activities during 2011-2014

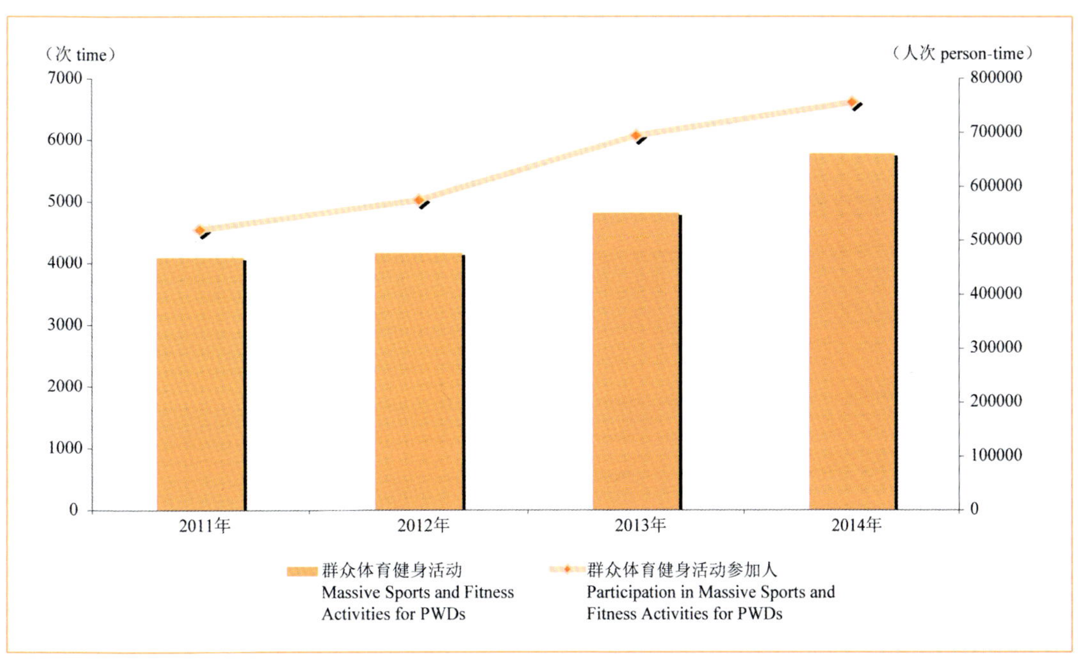

图-14 2011-2014年残疾人法律救助机构及服务情况

Chart 14 Legal Aid Centers (Stations) for PWDS and Their Service during 2011-2014

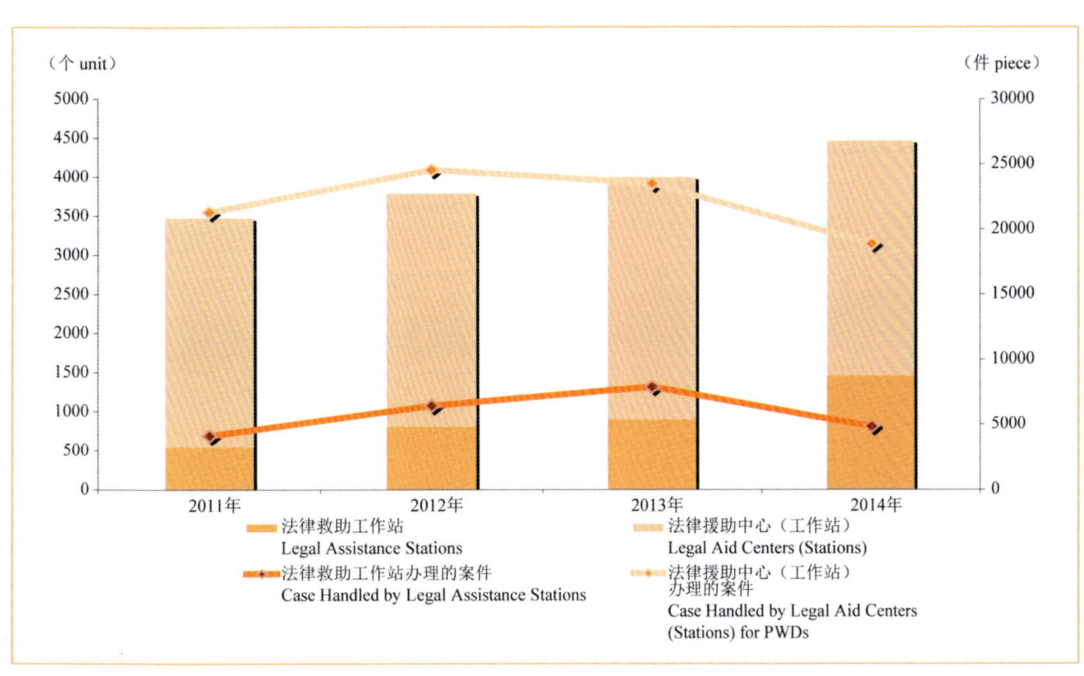

图-15 2011-2014年残疾人专职委员选聘情况

Chart15 Full-time Workers on Disability at Grass-roots during 2011-2014

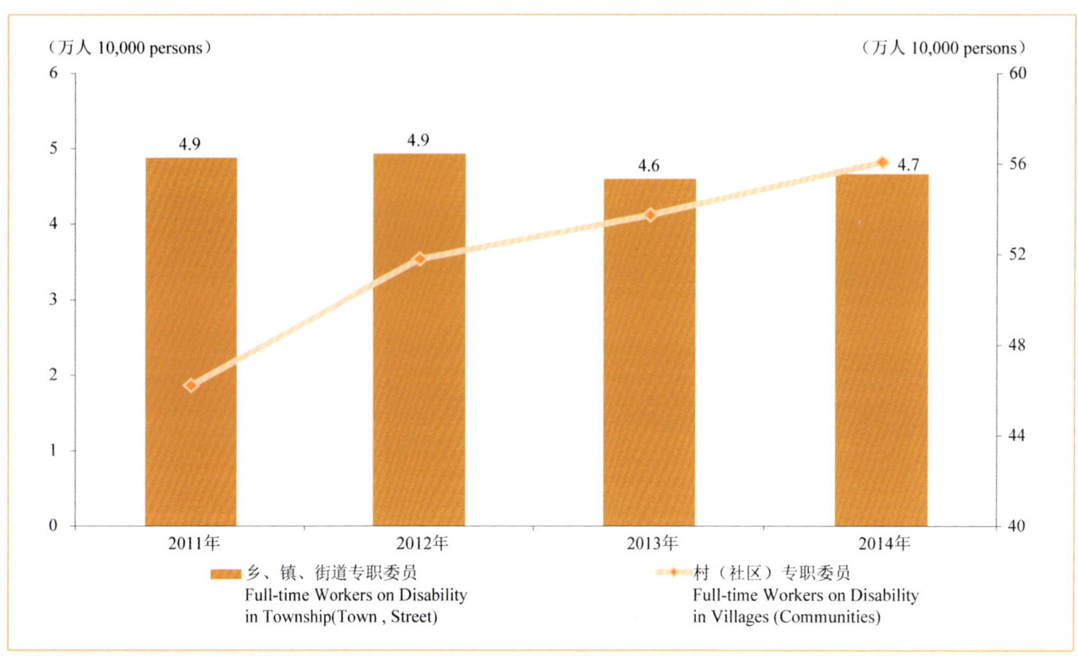

图-16 2014年残疾人服务设施建设情况

Chart16 The Construction of Service Facilities for PWDs in 2014

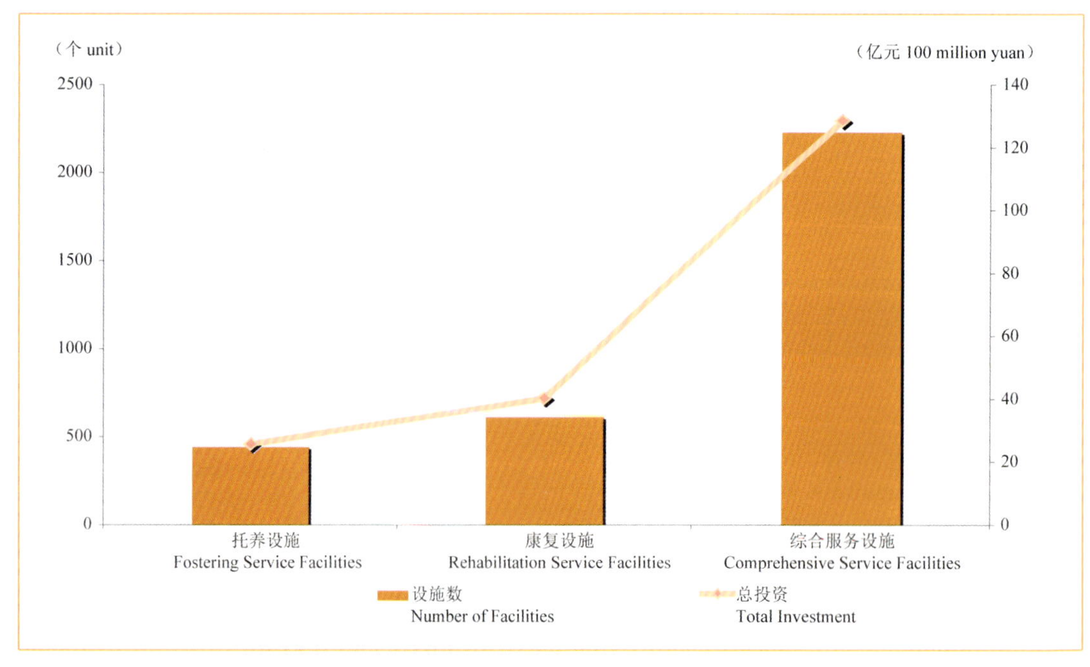

统计公报与专文

Communiqué and Reports

2014年中国残疾人事业发展统计公报

2014年是全国残联系统认真学习党的十八届三中、四中全会精神，深入贯彻中央关于残疾人事业的新部署新要求，全面落实中国残联“六代会”任务的开局之年。一年来，在党中央、国务院领导下，各级残联主动作为，广大残疾人和残疾人工作者共同努力，各项事业在新起点上取得了重要进展。

一、康复

2014年，通过实施一批重点康复工程，使751.5万残疾人得到不同程度的康复服务。

截至2014年底，全国共有康复机构6914个，其中，残联系统康复机构2622个，康复机构在岗人员总数达到23.36万人，其中业务人员16.0万人，管理人员3.05万人，其他人员4.31万人。

在914个市辖区和2023个县（市）开展了社区康复服务工作，累计已建社区康复站的社区总数21.9万个，配备39.2万名社区康复协调员。

1662个县的1958个医疗卫生机构陆续开展残疾儿童筛查工作，年度新诊断0-6岁残疾儿童4.8万人。依托各级各类残疾儿童康复机构建立儿童家长学校1547个，开展家长学校活动3625次，参与残疾儿童家长达94170人次。

开展视力残疾康复机构总数达到891个，完成白内障复明手术74.8万例；为30.0万名贫困白内障患者免费施行复明手术；为14.2万名低视力患者配用助视器，培训低视力儿童家长3.6万名，有效开展家庭康复训练。对12.3万名盲人进行定向行走训练。

推进听力语言康复机构规范化管理，完善基层服务网络。已建设省级听力语言康复机构31个，基层听力语言康复机构1025个。年度新收训聋儿1.9万名，在训聋儿3.2万名；规范聋儿家长学校，开展家庭训练，共培训聋儿家长3.9万名；开展各级各类听力语言康复专业技术人员培训，共培训专业人员5772人；实施贫困聋儿人工耳蜗、助听器抢救性康复项目，资助11200名聋儿免费植入人工耳蜗，资助19600名聋儿免费配戴助听器；开展彩票公益金成年听力残疾人（助听器）康复项目，为38352名贫困成年听力残疾人免费验配助听器，各级康复机构共为4.0万名成年听力残疾人提供技术服务。

开展肢体残疾康复训练服务机构达2181个，其中，省级康复机构42个，地市级、县级康复机构2139个；培训各级各类肢体残疾康复人员3.5万人次；全国共对36.7万肢体残疾者实施康复训练；实施救助项目资助4.0万名脑瘫儿童进行机构康复训练，资助8860名贫困肢体残疾儿童实施矫治手术。

为麻风畸残者实施矫治手术224例，开展宣传普及教育，为麻风患者回归社会营造良好社会氛围。

开展智力残疾康复训练服务的机构1730个，其中，省级康复机构45个，地市级、县级康复机构1685个；培训各级各类智力残疾康复人员1.5万人次；全国共对13.9万名智力残疾人进行康复训练；实施救助项目资助3.1万名智力残疾儿童进行机构康复训练，同时培训儿童家长。

大力推广“社会化、综合性、开放式”精神病防治康复工作。在2664个市县开展精神病防治康复工作，对583.7万重性精神病患者进行综合防治康复，监护率达到79.4 %，显好率达到66.2%，社会参与率达到51.7%，肇事率0.12%；解除关锁4123人；对49.2万贫困精神病患者进行医疗救助。

建立了41个省级孤独症儿童康复训练机构；2.0万名孤独症儿童在各级机构进行了康复训练。

加强残疾人辅助器具服务体系建设，构建覆盖全国的服务网络，培育建设6个国家辅助器具区域中心，建设省级辅助器具服务机构29个，地市级服务机构220个，县级服务机构945个。开展多层次、多形式的专业技术人员培训，共组织培训专业人员6261人次。深入开展辅助器具服务，组织实施系列辅助器具项目，全年共为残疾人减免费用供应辅助器具152.4万件，其中装配假肢2.9万件、矫形器6.4万件，验配助视器17.8万件。

二、教育

2014年，启动实施《特殊教育提升计划

（2014-2016 年）》，残疾人受教育权得到了更好保障。

实施残疾人事业专项彩票公益金助学项目，为全国 1.1 万人次家庭经济困难的残疾儿童享受普惠性学前教育提供资助。各地也积极多渠道争取资金支持，对 2908 名残疾儿童给予学前教育资助。

全国共有特殊教育普通高中班（部）187 个，在校生 7227 人；其中盲生 1054 人，聋生 6173 人。残疾人中等职业学校（班）197 个，在校生 11671 人，毕业生 7240 人，其中 5532 人获得职业资格证书。全国有 7864 名残疾人被普通高等院校录取，1678 名残疾人进入特殊教育学院学习。

三、就业

2014 年，残疾人就业规模总体保持稳定。城镇新就业残疾人 27.8 万，其中，集中就业残疾人 7.6 万，按比例安排残疾人就业 7.0 万，公益性岗位就业 1.2 万，个体就业及其它形式灵活就业 10.7 万，辅助性就业 1.3 万。全国城镇就业人数 436.0 万；1723.6 万农村残疾人在业，其中 1360.4 万残疾人从事农业生产劳动。

全国残疾人职业培训基地达到 6154 个，其中残联兴办 2211 个，依托社会机构兴办 3943 个，38.2 万人次城镇残疾人接受了职业培训。

盲人按摩事业稳定发展，按摩机构迅速增长。2014 年度培训盲人保健按摩人员 21296 名、盲人医疗按摩人员 5623 名；保健按摩机构达到 15609 个，医疗按摩机构达到 1018 个；在专业技术职务资格评审中，分别有 494 人和 1229 人通过盲人医疗按摩人员中级和初级职称评审。

四、社会保障

2014 年新型农村和城镇居民社会养老保险统一合并实施，已有 2180.0 万城乡残疾居民参保，参保率 74.2%，在 60 岁以下的参保残疾人中有 405.0 万重度残疾人，其中 379.2 万得到了政府的参保扶助，代缴补贴比例达到 93.6%。有 234.7 万非重度残疾人也享受了全额或部分代缴的优惠政策。领取养老金待遇的人数达到 858.6 万人。

城镇残疾职工参加基本养老和医疗保险人数稳定在 280 万左右，城镇 261.5 万和农村 844.1 万残疾人纳入最低生活保障范围；城镇集中供养残疾人和农村五保供养残疾人分别达到 11.2 万和 66.2 万；455.0 万和 279.0 万符合条件的城乡残疾人分别享受了稳定的生活补贴和护理补贴。257.7 万城乡残疾人得到了其他救助救济。

残疾人托养服务工作规范推进，残疾人托养服务机构达到 5917 个，共为 16.1 万残疾人提供了托养服务。其中寄宿制托养服务机构 1758 个；日间照料机构 2132 个；综合性托养服务机构 2027 个。在以上机构中，共有 15933 名残疾人实现辅助性就业，3503 名残疾人实现了支持性就业。机构之外接受居家托养服务的残疾人达到 77.1 万人。全年共有 4.9 万名托养服务管理和服务人员接受了各级各类专业培训，其中接受国家级培训 882 人。

五、扶贫开发

2014 年，233.2 万贫困残疾人得到扶持，其中 119.9 万人通过扶贫开发实现脱贫；接受实用技术培训的残疾人达到 72.6 万人次。

康复扶贫贴息贷款扶持 6.1 万农村残疾人，残疾人扶贫基地达到 6593 个，安置 12.4 万残疾人就业，扶持带动 25.8 万残疾人户，其中，本年度新安置残疾人 4.3 万人，新增带动 9.1 万残疾人户。

完成 9.0 万户农村贫困残疾人危房改造，各地投入危房资金 8.5 亿元，10.3 万残疾人受益。

基层党组织助残扶贫项目帮扶 95403 名农村贫困残疾人，其中首次接受帮扶 57678 人。“万村千乡市场工程”助残扶贫项目安置 6865 名贫困残疾人就业，帮扶贫困残疾人创办 1990 个村级农村店。

六、宣传文化

中央电视台《新闻联播》播出残疾人题材报道 44 条，《人民日报》刊登消息、侧记和综述等 84 篇。组织开展第十一届各地人民广播电台残疾人专题节目展播活动以及 2012—2013 年度好新闻事业评选，分别有 40 件和 219 件新闻作品获得等级奖。截至 2014 年底，全国共有省级残疾人专题广播节目 17 个、电视手语栏目 30 个，播出公益广告 42 个；地市级残疾人专题广播节目 241 个、电视手语栏目 201

个，播出公益广告 366 个。

推出“百家图书馆”、“百家博物馆”、“百家新闻媒体”三个百家系列公益助残行动活动，开展“残疾人文化周”、残疾人文化进社区、全国残疾人文化体育示范市创建等活动，全国有 500 多万残疾人走出家门参与各种文化活动，陶冶了情操，丰富了生活，提高了综合素质。截至 2014 年底，全国省地县三级公共图书馆共设立盲文及盲人有声读物阅览室 1616 个，共开展残疾人文化周活动 5568 场次，共举办残疾人文化艺术类比赛及展览 2806 次，全国共有各类残疾人艺术团体 775 个。

七、体育

全国累计培养了 719 名国家级残疾人体育健身指导员。在全国 26 个省（区、市）资助了 150 个示范点；为中西部地区配发了 8 套健身器材，并纳入示范点统一管理；累计共资助建设自强健身示范点 397 个。在北京、河北 1000 个残疾人家庭试点康复体育进家庭项目。组织了第八次全国特奥日活动、特奥足球比赛及家庭论坛等 14 项次系列活动，特奥运动员超过 118 万人。

全年举办了 20 项全国残疾人体育赛事，参赛总人数达 6000 多人。组团参加索契冬季残奥会、仁川亚残运会等 19 项国际赛事交流活动，我轮椅冰壶队在索契冬季残奥会上获得第四名，取得历史性突破。仁川亚残运会上，我代表团夺得 174 枚金牌、317 枚奖牌，实现八连冠。指导训练基地成功举办国际乒联残疾人世锦赛、国际残奥会北京田径公开赛、盲人门球亚洲锦标赛等 5 项国际重要赛事，世界各地 58 支代表队 1000 多名运动员参赛。组织了 39 批次 607 人次的运动员集训，残疾人体育人才队伍和组织建设不断加强。注册登记的残疾人运动员达到 9354 人，审批的裁判员 1188 人、分级员 36 人。国家级残疾人体育培训基地达到 34 所。

组织省级残疾人群众体育健身活动 241 次，6.2 万余人次参加；建设省级残疾人群众体育活动示范点达到 839 个；培训省级残疾人体育健身指导员达到 1.1 万人；组织省级残疾人体育比赛 151 次，参赛运动员达 2.3 万人次；省级残疾人体育训练基地已达 234 个。组织地市级残疾人体育活动 5544 次，69.4 万人次参加；设立地市级残疾人群众体育活动示范点 1930 个；培训地市级残疾人体育健身指导员 1.8 万人。

八、维权

全年修订《残疾人保障法》地方实施办法 1 件；制定或修改了关于残疾人的专门法规、规章省级 8 件、地市级 10 件；制定或修改保障残疾人权益的规范性文件省级 22 件、地市级 71 件、县级 334 件。全国县级以上人大进行《残疾人保障法》执法检查和专题调研 649 次；政协进行视察和专题调研 635 次。全国开展普法宣传教育活动 6510 次，93.3 万人参加；举办法律培训班 1511 个，9.2 万人参加。

截至 2014 年底，全国成立残疾人法律救助工作协调机构 1521 个，建立残疾人法律救助工作站 1348 个，办理案件 4666 件，建立残疾人法律援助中心（工作站）3001 个，办理案件 1.8 万件，有力地推动了法律救助和法律援助工作。

残疾人参政议政工作得到加强，各地残联协助人大代表、政协委员提出议案、建议、提案 1538 件，办理议案、建议、提案 1374 件。

无障碍建设法规、标准进一步完善。全国共出台了 451 个省、地市、县级无障碍建设与管理法规、规章和规范性文件；1506 个市、县、区系统开展无障碍建设；全国开展无障碍建设检查 4906 次，无障碍培训 4 万余人次；为 14.9 万户贫困残疾人家庭实施了无障碍改造；为 67.9 万残疾人发放了残疾人机动轮椅车燃油补贴。

全国各级残联共处理残疾人群众来信 4.8 万件，接待残疾人群众来访 28.6 万人次，其中集体访 1194 批次、1.9 万人次。

九、组织建设

截至 2014 年底，32 个省级残联（含新疆兵团）领导班子中配备了残疾人理事长或副理事长；246 个地市级残联在领导班子中配备了残疾人理事长或副理事长；1631 个县级残联机关配备了残疾人干部；已建乡镇（街道）残联 4.0 万个，已建率达到 98.0%，选聘残疾人专职委员 4.7 万名；已建社区（村）残协 59.0 万个，已建率达到 93.8%，选聘残疾人专职委员 56.1 万名。

全国省市县乡残联实有人员已达 11.5 万人。各级残联共举办培训班 3.3 万期，培训机关干部、协会干部及残疾人专职委员 70.3 万人次。

全国共建立省级以下各类残疾人专门协会 15633 个，其中省级专门协会已建比例为 100%，市级专门协会已建比例为 99.1%，县级专门协会已建比例为 92.9%。全国共建立助残社会组织 2972 个，其中在民政部门注册的为 1581 个，以残联为业务主管单位的 1395 个。

十、服务设施建设

残疾人服务设施建设得到全面发展。截至 2014 年底，全国已竣工并投入使用的各级残疾人综合服务设施 2231 个，总建设规模 460.26 万平方米，总投资 128.64 亿元；已竣工并投入使用的各级残疾人康复设施 613 个，总建设规模 130.01 万平方米，总投资 40.38 亿元；已竣工并投入使用的各级残疾人托养服务设施 442 个，总建设规模 101.39 万平方米，总投资 25.71 亿元。

十一、信息化建设

2014 年，中国残联网站对 60 多项惠残服务内容进行分类分项梳理,全年网站浏览量达到 7510 万，浏览人数 660 万。中国残疾人服务网年度浏览量超过 150 万，累计注册用户数量近 4 万人。为盲人提供图形验证码网上识别服务达 126 万人次。截至 2014 年底，累计服务残疾人求职者达 2.2 万人，为残疾人提供涉残岗位超过 3.1 万个，发布招聘需求企业信息 2.2 万个。截至 2014 年底，全国 33 个省级单位（含新疆兵团、黑龙江垦区）、280 个地市、1347 个县级残联开通网站，比上年增加 43 个。继续推动网站无障碍建设，对 38 个省级及计划单列市残联网站开展评测，对 118 家部委和省政府等政府网站开展年度网站无障碍专项评估，评测结果为推进工作提供依据。

截至 2014 年 12 月 31 日，全国残疾人人口基础数据库录入采集持证残疾人数据达到 2947 万人。依托残疾人人口基础数据库，中国残联和 20 多个省（区、市）残联开展重点业务系统建设和个性化服务，为向残疾人提供精准服务和业务政策的有效落实提供支持和保障。

Communiqué on the Development of the Work on Persons with Disabilities in 2014

The year of 2014 is the starting year for the China Disabled Persons' Federation (CDPF) to study systematically the guiding principles of the 3rd and 4th Sessions of the Party's 18th National Congress, to thoroughly implement new tasks and missions related to the work on disability issues required by the central government, and to efficiently carry out plans by the 6th National Congress of Persons with Disabilities. With the past year, under the leadership of CPC and State Council, disabled persons' federation (DPFs) at all levels proactively worked with persons with disabilities (PWDs) and those working in the area of disability affairs and achieved a series of important progresses.

I. Rehabilitation

In 2014, through implementation of some key projects, 7.515 million PWDs received rehabilitation services at different levels.

By the end of 2014, the number of rehabilitation institutions reached 6914 in whole nation. Among them, 2622 are within the CDPF system. The number of employees working in those rehabilitation institutions reached 233,600, including 160,000 professionals, 30,500 in management and 43,100 others.

Community-based rehabilitation (CBR) was implemented in 914 city districts and 2,023 counties. 219,000 CBR centers were established, and 392,000 CBR coordinators were employed.

Screening for early-stage disability in children was initiated in 1,958 healthcare institutions in 1,662 counties. 48,000 children aged between 0-6 were diagnosed as disabled. With support from rehabilitation institutions at multiple levels, 1,547 parent schools were established, organizing 3,625 activities with 94,170 times of participation by parents of disabled children.

The number of rehabilitation institutions providing services for persons with visual impairment reached 891. 748,000 cases of cataract surges were conducted, including 300,000 free ones for those who can't pay for it. 142,000 low-vision patients received visual aids. 36,000 parents of children with low vision received training on more effective family-based rehabilitation practices. 123,000 blind persons received orientation and mobility trainings.

The management of hearing and speech training institutions was more standardized, and the front service network became more comprehensive. 31 provincial-level institutions for hearing and verbal rehabilitation were established, and 1,025 more covering smaller administrative areas. 32,000 deaf children are currently receiving trainings, and 19,000 of them were enrolled last year. Parent schools were further regulated to improve service quality, and 39,000 parents were trained. 5,772 professionals in the field of hearing and speech training were trained. A "rescuing" rehabilitation project was implemented to provide 11,200 deaf children with free cochlear implants, and 19,600 ones with free hearing aids. The rehabilitation project for adults with hearing disabilities was also carried out and supported by the public welfare lottery fund. 38,352 financially struggling adults with hearing disability received free hearing aids, and 40,000 more received technical services from multiple levels of rehabilitation institutions.

The number of institutions providing rehabilitation and training services for persons with physical disability reached 2,181, including 42 provincial-level and another 2,139 at the city or county levels. Training for rehabilitation skills was provided for 35,000 physical rehabilitation professionals. Rehabilitation services were carried out for 367,000 persons with physical disability nationwide. 40,000 children with cerebral palsy received rehabilitation services and 8,860 children with physical disability coming from poor families received corrective surgeries.

224 cases of corrective surgeries were conducted on persons with leprosy-derived disabilities. Advocation campaigns were carried out to build an inclusive society to support the mainstreaming of persons with leprosy-derived.

The number of institutions providing rehabilitation and training services to persons with intellectual disability reached 1,730, including 45 provincial-level rehabilitation institutions and 1,685 ones at the city or county levels. 15,000 mental rehabilitation professionals received rehabilitation skills training. Nationwide, rehabilitation training was conducted for 139,000 persons with intellectual disability. With the support of projects, 31,000 children with intellectual disability received rehabilitation training, so do their parents in how to perform family-based care.

A "socialized, comprehensive and open" model was promoted for the prevention and rehabilitation of psychiatric diseases. The work of prevention and rehabilitation was carried out in 2,664 cities and counties, covering 5.837 million persons with severe mental illness. 79.4% of the patients lived under guardianship, 66.2% showed obvious signs of recovery, 51.7% participated in societal activities, and 0.12% committed incidents with possible criminal charges. 4,123 persons with mental illness were deinstitutionalized, and 492,000 poor patients received medical assistance.

41 provincial-level autism rehabilitation institutions were established, and 20,000 children with autism were served.

The work on building a network for providing assistive devices was further strengthened, aiming at establishing a nationwide network. 6 regional centers were being fostered. 29 provincial-level institutions providing assistive devices were established, along with another 220 at the prefectural level and 945 at the county level. Professional trainings at multiple levels and in multiple forms were provided for 6,261 technical staff. The work of providing assistive devices was strengthened and a series of projects were implemented. A total of 1.524 million assistive devices, including 29,000 artificial limbs, 64,000 pieces of prosthetics and 178,000 visual assistive devices were provided for PDWs for free or on subsidized prices.

II. Education

In 2014, Special Education Advancement Program for 2014-2016 was launched, and the right to education for PWDs is better protected.

The education project funded by dedicated welfare lottery fund provided financial support to more than 11,000 disabled children from poor families for their preschool education. Funds were also raised through multiple channels to support 2,908 disabled children for the same cause.

Nationwide, there are 187 special education classes at senior high schools, with 7,227 students, among whom, 6,173 were blind and 1,054 were deaf. There were 197 medium-level vocational education schools for PWDs, with 11,671 current students, 7,240 graduates, and 5,532 with professional certificates. 7,864 students with disabilities were accepted in mainstream higher education institutions, and 1,678 disabled students entered special higher education institutions.

III. Employment

In 2014, the number of employed PWDs remained stabled. 278,000 PWDs in urban areas were newly employed, including 76,000 by PWD-concentrated institutions, 70,000 through a quota scheme, 12,000 by welfare job posts, 107,000 through self-employment and other forms of employment and 13,000 through employment for the purpose of rehabilitation, which means employment is another form to offer rehabilitation. This year, 4.36 million PWDs remained or were employed in urban areas. In rural areas, 17.236 million PWDs remained or were employed, and 13.604 million of them were in agricultural production businesses.

Nationwide, there were 6,154 vocational training institutions, including 2,211 established by DPFs and 3,943 by social organizations. A total of 382,000 person-time PWDs in the urban areas received vocational training.

Massage business by the blind grew steadily with a significant increase in the number of massage institutions. In 2014, 21,296 blind health masseurs and 5,623 blind medical masseurs were trained. The number of health massage institutions reached 15,609, and the number of medical massage institutions increased to 1018. Respectively, 494 and 1,229 masseurs passed the intermediate and elementary level professional qualification exams.

IV. Social Security

In 2014, the new rural social endowment insurance and urban social endowment insurance were combined. 21.8 million or 74.2% of PWDs in rural and urban areas participated in the endowment insurance. There are 4.05 million persons with severe disabilities are under the age of 60, including 3.792million receiving government's subsidies for the participation, covering 93.6% of them. Another 2.347 million persons whose disabilities were not that severe also enjoyed full-amount or partial subsidies for the endowment insurance participation. 8.586 million PWDs received pension benefits.

The number of urban workers with disabilities covered by both social endowment insurance and medical insurance maintained at around 2.8 million. 2.615 million urban PWDs and 8.441 million rural PWDs were covered by minimum living standard allowance. The number of urban PWDs served by concentrated foster care institutions and rural full-guaranteed PWDs reached 112,000 and 66,200 respectively. After passing the assessment of conditions, 4.55 million PWDs received regular living allowances and 2.79 million received nursing subsidies. Another 2.577 million urban and rural PWDs received other forms of assistance or economic aid.

Foster service for PWDs made steady progresses. The number of foster care institutions for PWDs increased to 5,917, which have together served 161,000 PWDs. Among the foster care institutions, 1,758 are boarding institutions, 2,132 are day-care institutions and 2,027 include both boarding and day-care services. Through these institutions, 15,933 PWDs obtained employment required to perform simpler tasks, and 3,503 PWDs obtained employment by having supporting staff helping them at the initial phase of their working. Another 771,000 PWDs received their foster care services at home. Throughout the year, 49,000 foster service managements and professionals received various levels and categories of training, and 882 of them received national-level training.

V. Poverty Alleviation

In 2014, 2.332 million PWDs in poverty were financially supported, including 1.199 million lifted themselves out of poverty through a series of poverty alleviation projects. Training on the application of technologies was provided for 726,000 person-time PWDs.

61,000 rural PWDs were granted subsidies on loan interest through rehabilitation projects. The number of poverty alleviation centers increased to 6,593, with a total of 124,000 PWDs under its employment, supporting 258,000 PWDs and their families. Among them, 43,000 were newly hired and 91,000 families were newly supported in the year.

850 million RMB were invested to benefit 103,000 PWDs of 90,000 poor rural households to have their houses renovated.

Through primary-level poverty alleviation projects, 95,403 PWDs living in rural areas received financial support, and 57,678 of them were first-time receivers. Another project called "Market Building in Ten Thousand Villages" helped 6,865 PWDs find their employment, which opened 1,990 village shops.

VI. Publicity and Cultural Activities

This year, 44 news reports on disability-related issues were aired on CCTV's Evening News, and 84 editorials, reports and reviews were published on People's Daily. The 11th National Exhibition of Disability-related Programs by Local Broadcasting Stations and the Contest of News on Disability-related Issues for the 2012-2013 Period were organized, during which 40 programs and 219 news reports were awarded. By the end of 2014, at the provincial level, there were 17 radio programs on disability issues, 30 TV news programs displaying sign language, and 42 public educational advertisements were aired. At the district/city level, there were 241 radio programs broadcasting on disability issues, and 201 TV news programs with sign language and 366 public educational advertisements were aired.

Three "One Hundred" public interest events aiming for enriching the cultural lives of PWDs, "One Hundred Libraries," "One Hundred Museums" and "One Hundred Medias" were held. Other events like "Culture Week for Persons with Disabilities," "Integration into Communities: Culture of Persons with Disabilities" and "Construction of National Pilot Cities of Persons with Disabilities Cultural and Sports Activities" were also held. In the past year, five million PWDs went out of their homes to participate in various cultural activities, which enriched their lives and enhanced capacities. By the end of 2014, 1,616 reading rooms with Braille and audible reading materials were established nationwide in provincial, city and county levels. During the year, 5,568 sub-events of "Persons with Disabilities Cultural Week" were held, and 2,806 cultural and art competitions and exhibitions were organized. There are 775 disabled persons' art organizations in the whole country.

VII. Sports

In the whole country, 719 national-level sports and fitness coaches were trained. 26 provinces (municipalities or autonomous regions) provided financial support to 150 demonstration sites of self-improvement fitness for PWDs. Eight sets of fitness devices were donated to middle and western China and were managed by the demonstration sites. Cumulatively, 397 self-improvement fitness demonstration sites were set up. In Beijing and Hebei Province, 1,000 households had joined the pilot Rehabilitation Sports Home Integration Project. A series of 14 events, including China's 8th "Day of Special Olympics," Special Olympic Competition of Football Matches, and Forum of Parents were organized. The number of athletes for Special Olympics has reached 1.18 million.

At the national level, 20 sports matches were organized, participated by more than 6,000 PWDs. China participated 19 international sports games, including the Sochi Winter Paralympics, and the Incheon Asian Para Games. In the Sochi Winter Paralympics Games, China's wheelchair curling team won the 4th, which was a historical breakthrough. At the Incheon Asian Para Games, Chinese delegation won 317 medals, and 174 of them are gold, ranking 1st for the 8th consecutive time. Five major international sports games were held, including the 8th ITTF Wheelchair Table Tennis World Champaign, IPC Beijing Athletics Open, and the Asian Goalball Tournament were held in training bases of PWDs. The games were participated by 58 foreign teams and more than 1,000 athletes. 39 training sessions for PWDs were organized for a total of 607 person-time athletes in the whole country. The number of registered athletes reached 9,354, with 1,188 qualified judges and 36 classifiers. The number of country-level bases of sports for PWDs reached 34.

The promotion of PWDs' sports and fitness activities was also extensively carried out at the provincial levels. 241 fitness events were organized for PWDs, with 62,000 persons participating. 839 sports activity demonstration sties of PWDs were established, training 11,000 fitness coaches for PWDs. 151 sports competitions of PWDs were organized, with 23,000 persons participating. The number of provincial sports training bases of PWDs amounted to 234. At the city level, 5,544 sports events of PWDs were organized, with 694,000 persons participating. 1,930 sports activity of PWDs demonstration sites at the city level were established, training 18,000 fitness coaches for PWDs.

VIII. Rights Protection

One local implementation guidelines for the Protection of Persons with Disabilities Law was amended. Eight provincial and ten city-level disability-specific regulations were established or amended. 22 provincial, 71 city-level and 334 county-level regulations on the protection of PWDs' rights were established or amended. People's Congress at and above the county level carried out inspections on the enforcement of the Protection of Persons with

Disabilities Law for 649 times. The Political Consultative Conferences at all levels carried out inspections and studies for 635 times. 6,510 times of promotion and education events for the law were held, with 933,000 participating. 1,511 education sessions for legal professionals were organized for 92,000 participants.

By the end of 2014, 1,521 coordination organizations of legal assistance for PWDs were established, with 1,348 of them legal assistance stations, handed 4,666 cases of rights violations against PWDs last year. 3001 legal aid stations were established, handing 18,000 cases of rights violations against PWDs last year. The work of legal assistance services for PWDs was greatly promoted.

PWDs took more active parts in political affairs. In 2014, 1,538 bills and proposals were raised by the People's Congress deputies and members of political consultative conferences from DPF systems. 1,374 pieces of bills and proposals were brought up.

Legislation and standards of accessibility were further improved. 451 regulations, rules and guidelines on accessibility were issued. 1,506 cities, counties and districts initiated the construction of accessibility facilities. 4,906 inspections on accessibility were carried out. More than 40,000 persons received relevant trainings. Renovation of houses to increase accessibility was made for 149,000 poor families with PWDs. 679,000 PWDs received subsidies on gasoline used by motorized wheelchairs.

The DPFs at all levels received and handled 48,000 compliant letters, and reception for 286,000 visitors were made. Among the complaint visits, 1,194 are group visits and 19,000 by individuals.

IX. Organizational Development

By the end of 2014, 32 provincial-level DPFs (inducing the DPF of Xinjiang Production and Construction Corps) had disabled persons as presidents or vice presidents. 246 city-level federations had disabled presidents or vice presidents in their offices. 1,631 county-level federations had disabled staffs in their offices. 40,000 towns (streets) had DPFs, accounting for 98% of the total ought-to-be established offices, recruiting 47,000 disability commissioners. 590,000 communities (villages) had disabled persons' associations, accounting for 93.8% of the ought-to-be established associations, recruiting 561,000 disability commissioners.

The number of workers in the city, county and township level DPFs increased to 115,000 persons. 33,000 training sessions were organized for 703,000 persons.

Nationwide, there are 15,633 special associations of PWDs of different disabilities. 100% provinces, 99.1% cities, and 92.9% counties had established their special associations of PWDs. 2,972 civil organizations as siting PWDs were established nationwide, among them, 1,581 are registered with the Ministry of Civil Affairs, and 1395 are under the management of respective levels of DPFs.

X. Service Facilities for PWDs

The construction of service facilities was developed in a comprehensive way. By the end of 2014, 2,231 full-service facilities at multiple levels were completed and out into use, totaling 4.6026 million square meters of servicing area. The total investment amounted to 12.864 billion RMB. 613 rehabilitation facilities were completed, totaling 1.3001 million square meters of servicing area. The total investment amounted to 4.038 billion RMB. 442 nursing institutions are currently in use, totaling 1.0139 million square meters, and 2.571 billion RMB were invested.

XI. Informationization

In 2014, the official website of CDPF made the information about more than 60 preferential treatments for PWDs easily accessible online. The website recorded 75.1 million visits by 6.6 unique visitors. The China Disabled Persons' Service Network recorded 1.5 million visits, with nearly 40,000 registered users. We have provided 1.26 million services to help visually impaired persons to pass the verification process while they were surfing the Internet. By the end of 2014, we provided support for 22,000 PWDs applying for jobs, providing information on more than 31,000 openings that are PWD-related, and 22,000 openings in private companies.

By the end of 2014, 33 DPFs at the provincial level (including the DPFs of Xinjiang Production and Construction Corps and Heilongjiang Agricultural Reclamation Department), 280 DPFs at the city level and 1,347 DPFs at the county level have their own websites, which is 43 more compared with last year. The websites of 38 DPFs of provinces and cities with independent budgetary status were tested and evaluated. Annual accessibility evaluation was conducted for 118 websites of ministries and of provincial governments. Results of the evaluation provided the ground to improve our future work.

By December 31st, 2014, the National Basic Database of Disabled Population recorded 29.47 million PWDs holding certificates for disability. Based on data from the Basic Database of Disabled Population, CDPF and more than 20 provincial-level DPFs are constructing the information systems for key services to guard the efficient implementation of PWD-related policies and services.

综合统计资料

Comprehensive Statistical Data

中国残疾人事业“十二五”发展纲要执行简要情况
(2011－2014)

指 标 名 称		Item	
康 复		**Rehabilitation**	
得到不同程度康复残疾人	**(万人)**	**PWDs Received Rehabilitation Services of Different Degrees**	**(10,000 persons)**
1. 社区康复		**Community-based Rehabilitation (CBR)**	
开展社区康复服务的县、区	(个)	Counties and Districts Where CBR Has Been Conducted	(unit)
接受社区康复服务的残疾人	(万人)	Disabled Persons Who Began to Get CBR Service	(10,000 persons)
社区康复协调员	(万人)	CBR Coordinators at Communities	(10,000 persons)
2. 视力残疾康复		**Rehabilitation of Persons with Visual Disability**	
白内障复明手术	(万例)	Sight-restoring Surgeries for Cataract Patients	(10,000 cases)
其中：贫困患者免费手术	(万例)	Free Surgeries for Poor Catarant Patients	(10,000 cases)
低视力配用助视器	(万人)	Persons with Low Vision Fitted with Vision-aids	(10,000 persons)
培训低视力儿童家长	(万人)	Trained Parents of Children with Low Vision	(10,000 persons)
盲人定向行走训练	(万人)	Blind Persons Receiving Orientation Skills Training	(10,000 persons)
3. 听力语言残疾康复		**Rehabilitation of Persons with Hearing/Speech Disabilities**	
聋儿康复训练	(万人)	Deaf Children Trained	(10,000 persons)
聋儿家长培训	(万人)	Parents Trained	(10,000 persons)
4. 肢体残疾康复		**Rehabilitation of Persons with Physical Disability**	
肢体残疾(脑瘫)儿童机构康复训练	(万人)	Children with Physical Disability Receiving Rehabilitation Training in Institutions	(10000 persons)
肢体残疾人社区、家庭康复训练	(万人)	Persons with Physical Disability Receiving Rehabilitation Training in Communities and Families	(10000 persons)
贫困肢体残疾儿童矫治手术	(例)	Orthopedic Surgeries Conducted for Poor Children with Physical Disability	(case)
麻风畸残矫治手术	(例)	Orthopedic Surgeries Conducted for Persons with Leprosy- induced Disability	(case)
5. 智力残疾康复		**Rehabilitation of Persons with Intellectual Disability**	
智力残疾儿童康复训练	(万人)	Children with Intellectual Disability Receiving Rehabilitation Training	(10000 persons)
成年智力残疾人社区、家庭康复训练	(万人)	Adults with Physical Disability Receiving Rehabilitation Training in Communities and Families	(10000 persons)
6. 精神病防治康复		**Prevention and Rehabilitation of Mental Illness (PRMI)**	
监护精神病人	(万人)	People with Mental Illness under Guardianship	(10000 persons)
接受医疗救助的贫困精神病患者	(万人)	People with Mental Illness in Poverty Who Have Gotten Medical Assistance	(10000 persons)
孤独症儿童康复训练机构	(个)	Rehabilitation Institutions for Children with Autism	(unit)
孤独症儿童康复训练	(人)	Children with Autism Trained in Institutions	(person)

Brief Summary on Development of the Work for Persons with Disabilities during the 12th Five-year Plan Period (2011 – 2014)

"十一五"完成/达到 the 11th Five-year Accomplishment	"十二五"任务 the 12th Five-year Plan	"十二五"完成情况 the 12th Five-year Accomplishment (2011 – 2014)				
		累计完成/达到 Total	2011	2012	2013	2014
1037.9	**1300**	**1185.4**	**631.8**	**760.2**	**746.8**	**751.5**
2507	2860	2937	2697	2794	2915	2937
1036	—	976.5	303.5	328.8	169.0	175.2
32.9	30	39.2	31.4	35.3	37.9	39.2
423.6	328	304.7	75.8	79.6	74.6	74.8
127.6	—	123.5	31.0	33.4	29.1	30.0
17.3	50	42.4	3.6	11.7	12.9	14.2
6.5	20	11.7	0.7	3.7	3.8	3.6
6.3	50	38.7	2.5	12.0	12.0	12.3
9.8	10	7.7	1.8	2.0	2.0	1.9
12.2	10	14.6	2.9	3.9	3.9	3.9
7.8	3	12.3	1.8	3.0	3.5	4.0
41.6	85	112.2	14.9	32.8	31.8	32.6
10535	12000	23113	1311	6221	6721	8860
8524	1000	1259	159	458	418	224
13.2	41.0	34.8	2.8	11.5	10.1	10.4
—	—	9.1	—	2.5	3.1	3.5
416.2	780	463.5	421.2	449.0	461.9	463.5
36.6	20	176.0	35.6	44.4	46.9	49.2
426	—	1345	839	929	1108	1345
13743	50000	54412	6910	11119	16656	19727

续表 1

指 标 名 称		Item	
7. 残疾人辅助器具供应服务		**Provision of Assistive Devices**	
辅助器具供应	(万件)	Assistive Devices Provided	(10,000 pieces)
其中：贫困残疾人免费发放	(万件)	Assistive Devices Provided to Disabled Persons Free of Charge	(10,000 pieces)
残疾人普及型假肢装配	(万例)	Low-cost Artificial Limbs Fitted	(10,000 case)
残疾人矫形器装配	(万例)	Orthotic Devices Fitted	(10,000 case)
教 育		**Education**	
1. 学前教育		**Pre-school Rehabilitation and Education**	
残疾人事业专项彩票公益金助学项目资助	(人)	Support of Educational Project Funded by Dedicated Welfare Lottery Fund	(person)
其他残疾儿童学前教育助学项目资助	(人)	Support of Other Pre-School Educational Project for Disabled Children	(person)
2. 残疾人高级中等教育		**Senior Secondary Education for PWDs**	
特教普通高中	(个)	Special Education Senior High Schools	(unit)
特教普通高中在校学生	(人)	Students at Special Education Senior High Schools	(person)
中等职业教育机构	(个)	Secondary Vocational Schools	(unit)
中等职业教育在校学生	(人)	Students at Secondary Vocational Schools	(person)
3. 残疾人高等教育		**Higher Education for PWDs**	
高等特殊教育院校	(个)	Higher Special Education Institutions	(unit)
高等特殊教育院校录取残疾考生	(人)	Disable Students Enrolled by Higher Special Education Institutions	(person)
普通高等院校录取残疾考生	(人)	Disable Students Enrolled by Ordinary Higher Education Institutions	(person)
就 业		**Employment**	
1. 城镇残疾人就业状况		**Employment of PWDs in Urban Areas**	
在业	(万人)	Employed Disabled Persons	(10,000 persons)
新增安排就业	(万人)	Newly Employed	(10,000 persons)
其中：集中就业	(万人)	Employed by Collective Form	(10,000 persons)
按比例就业	(万人)	Employed in Quoto Scheme	(10,000 persons)
公益性岗位就业	(万人)	Employed though Welfare Post	(10,000 persons)
个体及其他形式就业	(万人)	Self-Employed or Employed in Other Forms	(10,000 persons)
辅助性就业	(万人)	Assistive Employment	(10,000 persons)
2. 农村残疾人就业状况		**Employment of PWDs in Rural Areas**	
已就业	(万人)	Employed Disabled Persons	(10,000 persons)
3. 残疾人职业培训		**Vocational Education and Training for PWDs**	
残疾人职业培训基地	(个)	Vocational Training Bases for PWDs	(unit)
城镇残疾人职业培训	(万人次)	Vocational Training for Urban PWDs	(10,000 person-time)
4. 盲人按摩		**Blind Massage**	
按摩人员培训		**Massage Training**	
保健按摩人员	(人)	Training for Health-care Masseurs	(person)
医疗按摩人员	(人)	Training for Blind Therapeutical Masseurs	(person)
按摩机构		**Institutions of Blind Massage**	
医疗按摩机构	(个)	Therapeutical Blind Massage Clinics	(unit)
保健按摩机构	(个)	Health-care Blind Massage Houses	(unit)

Continued 1

"十一五"完成/达到 the 11th Five-year Accomplishment	"十二五"任务 the 12th Five-year Plan	"十二五"完成情况 the 12th Five-year Accomplishment (2011－2014)				
		累计完成/达到 Total	2011	2012	2013	2014
514.7	500	469.5	74.3	114.5	128.3	152.4
242.3	50	150.5	41.2	33.8	36.2	39.3
12.1	7	12.8	3.1	3.9	2.9	2.9
7.7	5	16.7	1.5	4.0	4.7	6.4
—	51400	42556	10280	10280	10468	11528
—		17453	6627	4429	3489	2908
99	—	187	179	186	194	187
6067	—	7227	7207	7043	7313	7227
147	—	197	131	152	198	197
11506	—	11671	11572	10442	11350	11671
—	—	18	18	20	15	18
5357	—	5077	877	1134	1388	1678
29915	—	29781	7150	7229	7538	7864
	—					
	—					
441.2	—	436.0	440.5	444.8	445.6	436.0
179.7	100	129.4	31.8	32.9	36.9	27.8
53.4	—	38.2	9.7	10.2	10.7	7.6
49.6	—	31.2	7.5	8.0	8.7	7.0
—	—	6.6	2.1	1.8	1.5	1.2
76.8	—	50.1	12.5	12.3	14.6	10.7
—	—	3.3	—	0.7	1.3	1.3
1749.7	1800	1723.6	1748.8	1770.3	1757.2	1723.6
—	—	6154	5254	5271	5357	6154
137.9	180	135.8	29.9	29.9	37.8	38.2
61147	30000	71988	14067	16514	20111	21296
28357	20000	19978	3736	4925	5694	5623
1152	—	1018	1031	848	936	1018
11616	—	15609	12170	12887	14704	15609

续表 2

指 标 名 称		Item	
社会保障		**Social Security**	
1. 社会保险		**Social Insurance**	
残疾职工参加社会保险		Urban Workers with Disabilities Covered by Social Insurance	
参加养老保险	(万人)	Covered by Pension Insurance	(10,000 persons)
参加医疗保险	(万人)	Covered by Medical Care Insurance	(10,000 persons)
残疾居民参加城乡社会养老保险	(万人)	Residents with Disabilities Covered by Pension Insurance	(10,000 persons)
2. 社会救助		**Social Relief**	
城镇		Urban	
纳入最低生活保障	(万人)	Covered by the Basic Living Allowance System	(10,000 persons)
集中供养	(万人次)	Linving in Institutions	(10,000 person-time)
其他救助救济	(万人次)	Provided with Other Assistance and Relief	(10,000 person-time)
农村		Rural	
纳入最低生活保障	(万人)	Covered by the Basic Living Allowance System	(10,000 persons)
五保供养及其他救助救济	(万人次)	Supported with Five Guarantees	(10,000 person-time)
其他救助救济	(万人次)	Provided with Other Assistance and Relief	(10,000 person-time)
3. 社会福利		**Social Welfare**	
贫困残疾人享受生活补贴	(万人次)	Poor PWDs with Living Subsidy	(10,000 person-time)
重度残疾人享受护理补贴	(万人次)	PWDs with Severe Disability with Nursing Subsidy	(10,000 person-time)
4. 托养服务		**Fostering Service**	
托养服务机构	(个)	Fostering Services Facilities	(unit)
机构内托养残疾人	(万人次)	PWDs in Boarding and Day-Care Fostering Institutions	(10,000 person-time)
享受居家托养服务	(万人次)	PWDs Receiving Fostering Service an Home	(10,000 person-time)
扶贫		**Poverty Alleviation**	
1. 扶贫效果		**Outcome of Poverty Alleviation**	
扶持贫困残疾人	(万人次)	Impoverished PWDs Assisted	(10,000 person-time)
实际脱贫	(万人次)	Out of Poverty	(10,000 person-time)
实用技术培训	(万人次)	Training on Applied Technologies for PWDs	(10,000 person-time)
2. 残疾人扶贫资金落实情况		**Poverty Alleviation Fund for PWDs**	
中央安排康复扶贫贴息贷款	(亿元)	Interest-subsidized Loans for Rehabilitation from the Central Fiscal Budget	(100 million yuan)
项目贷款扶持贫困残疾人	(万人)	Poor Disabled Persons Supported by Loans for Project	(10,000 persons)
到户贷款扶持贫困残疾人	(万人)	Poor Disabled Persons Supported by Loans to Households	(10,000 persons)

Continued 2

"十一五"完成/达到 the 11th Five-year Accomplishment	"十二五"任务 the 12th Five-year Plan	"十二五"完成情况 the 12th Five-year Accomplishment (2011 - 2014)				
		累计完成/达到 Total	2011	2012	2013	2014
198.5	—	282.8	156.8	173.4	186.9	282.8
155.5	—	282.8	142.2	164.9	182.4	282.8
—	—	2180.0	1659.1	1492.5	2039.8	2180.0
246.3	—	261.5	257.8	266.5	264.8	261.5
48.6	—	47.1	12.0	12.2	11.7	11.2
508.7	—	266.2	59.7	68.1	69.7	68.7
680.8	—	844.1	773.6	804.0	828.2	844.1
277.8	—	268.4	68.5	68.5	65.2	66.2
1426.9	—	751.0	172.5	193.2	196.3	189.0
—		1196.5	136.2	239.1	366.2	455.0
—		421.3	14.0	36.3	92.0	279.0
4029	—	5917	6289	7275	5677	5917
33.2	—	67.3	16.5	18.7	16.0	16.1
43.5	—	255.7	44.2	56.0	78.4	77.1
932.2	1000	913.7	211.8	229.9	238.7	233.2
618.4	—	470.1	92.3	137.3	120.6	119.9
414.3	100	336.6	92.3	86.1	85.6	72.6
40.0	—	40.8	11.0	10.3	10.1	9.4
12.0	—	11.6	4.2	2.4	2.6	2.4
7.3	—	14.9	2.9	3.1	5.3	3.7

续表 3

指 标 名 称		Item	
3. 残疾人扶贫基地建设		**Poverty Alleviation Bases for PWDs in Rural Areas**	
残疾人扶贫基地	(个)	Poverty Alleviation Bases for PWDs	(unit)
安置残疾人就业	(万人)	Providing Employment for PWDs	(10,000 persons)
扶持带动贫困残疾人	(万户)	Supporting and Leading Households with PWDs	(10,000 households)
4. 农村贫困残疾人危房改造		**House Renovation for Poor PWDs in Rural Areas**	
危房改造	(万户)	Houses Renovated for PWDs	(10,000 households)
受益残疾人	(万人)	PWDs Who Benefited	(10,000 persons)
宣传文化		**Publicity and Culture**	
1. 宣传		**Publicity at Provincial and Prefectural/City Level**	
省、市级报纸专版	(个)	Features in Newspapers	(unit)
省、市级广播电台残疾人专题节目	(个)	Radio Broadcast-Special Programs on Disability	(unit)
省、市级电视手语栏目	(个)	Programmes with Sign Language on TV	(unit)
2. 文化		**Culture at Provincial and Prefectural/City Level**	
省、市级盲文及盲人有声读物阅览室	(个)	Reading Rooms with Braille and Audio Reading Materials	(unit)
残疾人文化周	(场次)	Culture Week for PWDs	(session)
残疾人文化艺术类比赛及展览	(次)	Culture or Art Competitions and Exhibitions for PWDs	(time)
体 育		**Sports**	
1. 残疾人群众体育健身		**Massive Sports and Fitness for PWDs at Provincial and Prefectural/City Level**	
省、市级残疾人群众体育健身活动	(次)	Massive Sports and Fitness Activities for PWDs	(time)
省、市级残疾人群众体育健身活动参加人	(万人次)	Participations in Massive Sports and Fitness Activities for PWDs	(10,000 person-time)
省、市级残疾人群众体育活动示范点	(个)	Sports Activity Demonstration Sites for PWDs	(unit)
省、市级残疾人体育健身指导员	(人)	Coaches for Fitness Activity for PWDs	(person)
2. 残疾人体育比赛		**Sports Events for PWDs at Provincial Level**	
省级残疾人体育比赛	(次)	Sports Events for PWDs	(time)
参加省级残疾人体育比赛运动员	(人次)	Disabled Athletes Who Participated in Sports Events for PWDs	(person-time)
省级残疾人体育训练基地	(个)	Sports Training Bases for PWDs	(unit)
维 权		**Safeguarding the Rights of PWDs**	
1. 法规体系和政策文件		**Legal System**	
制定或修改关于残疾人的专门法规、规章	(个)	Regulations Enacted or Reviewed for Assisting PWDs	(unit)
制定或修改保障残疾人权益的规范性文件	(个)	Policies Enacted for Protecting the Rights of PWDs	(unit)
2. 执法检查		**Inspections on Law Performance**	
人大执法检查	(次)	Inspections by Officials of People's Congresses	(time)
政协视察或专题调研	(次)	Inspections and Investigations by Officials of People's Political Consultative Conferences	(time)

Continued 3

"十一五"完成/达到 the 11th Five-year Accomplishment	"十二五"任务 the 12th Five-year Plan	"十二五"完成情况 the 12th Five-year Accomplishment (2011 - 2014)				
		累计完成/达到 Total	2011	2012	2013	2014
—	—	6593	3985	5226	6201	6593
—	—	47.7	8.7	10.2	16.4	12.4
—	—	91.8	15.6	25.8	24.6	25.8
49.4		43.8	9.4	13.2	12.2	9.0
68.1	—	52.0	11.5	15.7	14.4	10.3
418	—	1736	1325	1543	1572	1736
400	—	258	463	506	659	258
523	—	231	196	214	263	231
441	—	462	438	479	596	462
—	—	6776	1426	1782	2212	1356
3164	—	4568	1085	1125	1399	959
—	—	18871	4093	4171	4822	5785
—	—	254.5	52.0	57.5	69.4	75.6
—	1200	2769	799	1391	2187	2769
—	30000	28716	4150	9452	16926	28716
519	—	445	100	80	114	151
74962	—	60743	12155	12574	13139	22875
221	—	234	220	200	207	234
36	—	18	40	30	31	18
849	—	2547	871	706	543	427
5375	—	3195	824	923	799	649
5243	—	3036	845	810	746	635

续表 4

指 标 名 称		Item	
3. **法律救助**		**Legal Aid**	
残疾人法律救助工作站	(个)	Legal Assistance Stations for PWDs	(unit)
残疾人法律救助工作站办理的案件	(件)	Cases Handled by Legal Assistance Stations for PWDs	(case)
残疾人法律援助中心(工作站)	(个)	Legal Aid Centers (Stations) for PWDs	(unit)
残疾人法律援助中心(工作站)办理的案件	(件)	Cases Handled by Legal Aid Centers (Stations) for PWDs	(case)
4. **参政议政**		**PWDs Participating in the Administration and Discussion of State Affairs**	
协助人大、政协代表提出议案、建议、提案	(件)	Proposals Put forward at People's Congresses with Assistance of PWDs	(case)
办理人大政协交办的议案、建议、提案	(件)	Handling Proposals of Peoples'Congresses and Motions of People's Political Consultative Conferences	(case)
5. **无障碍设施建设**		**Accessible Environment Building**	
无障碍设施建设法规、政府令	(个)	Regulations and Decrees on Accessible Environment Building and Management	(unit)
贫困残疾人家庭无障碍改造	(万户)	Accessibility Renovation for Homes of Poor PWDs	(10,000 households)
6. **残疾人机动轮椅车燃油补贴**	**(万人)**	**Subsidy for Petrol Used by Motorized Wheelchairs of PWDs**	**(10,000 persons)**
7. **残疾人信访**		**Complaint Letter and Visit**	
来信	(万件)	Complaint Letter	(10,000 cases)
来访	(万人次)	Complaint Visit	(10,000 person-time)
组织建设		**Organizational Structure**	
1. **省市县乡残联实有人员**	**(万人)**	**Staff of Disabled Persons'Federations at Provincial, City, County and Township Level**	**(10,000 persons)**
2. **市(地)级残联**		**Disabled Persons'Federations at Cities and Prefectures Level**	
配备残疾人领导干部的残联	(个)	Disabled Persons' Federations Whose Leadership Include PWDs	(unit)
残疾人干部	(人)	Staff with Disability	(person)
3. **县(市、区)级残联**		**Disabled Persons' Federations at County Level**	
配备残疾人干部的残联	(个)	Disabled Persons' Federations Whose Leadership Include PWDs	(unit)
残疾人干部	(人)	Staff with Disability	(person)
4. **乡、镇、街道残联与村(社区)残疾人协会**		**Disabled Persons' Federations in Township(Town, Street) and Villages(Communities)**	
已建乡、镇、街道残联	(万个)	Disabled Persons' Federation Established	(10,000 units)
其中：已配专兼职理事长	(万人)	Full-time(part-time) Presidents	(10,000 persons)
已建村(社区)残疾人协会	(万个)	Associations of Disabled Persons Established in Villages(Communities)	(10,000 units)
已选聘残疾人专职委员	(万人)	Full-time Workers on Disability	(10,000 persons)

Continued 4

"十一五"完成/达到 the 11th Five-year Accomplishment	"十二五"任务 the 12th Five-year Plan	"十二五"完成情况 the 12th Five-year Accomplishment (2011 - 2014)				
		累计完成/达到 Total	2011	2012	2013	2014
—	500	1348	545	811	901	1348
—	—	23177	4153	6453	7905	4666
2934	—	3001	2933	2979	3096	3001
99576	—	87027	21306	24550	23498	17673
10580	—	6925	1873	1771	1743	1538
7548	—	5643	1370	1435	1464	1374
385	—	451	426	438	444	451
—	8	52.8	10.2	14.1	13.6	14.9
—	—	231.0	41.9	55.4	65.7	67.9
30.2	—	21.7	6.0	5.5	5.4	4.8
204.2		130.3	34.9	34.4	32.3	28.6
9.9	—	11.5	10.9	12	11.1	11.5
227	—	246	222	232	251	246
328	—	433	375	376	433	433
1744	—	1631	1599	1624	1625	1631
2133	—	2234	2114	2207	2221	2234
4.0	—	4.0	3.7	3.9	4.0	4.0
3.7	—	2.8	2.3	3.3	3.1	2.8
60.4	—	59.0	61.1	60.7	58.1	59.0
55.9	70	60.7	51.1	56.7	58.4	60.7

续表 5

指标名称		Item	
5. 省级以下各类专门协会		**Special Associations below Provincial Level**	
盲人协会	(个)	Associations of Persons with Visual Disability	(unit)
聋人协会	(个)	Associations of Persons with Hearing Disability	(unit)
肢残人协会	(个)	Associations of Persons with Physical Disability	(unit)
智力残疾人及亲友协会	(个)	Associations of Persons with Intellectual Disability and Their Relatives and Friends	(unit)
精神残疾人及亲友协会	(个)	Associations of Persons with Psychiatric Disability and Their Relatives and Friends	(unit)
智力残疾人及亲友协会和精神残疾人及亲友协会合一的协会	(个)	Joint Associations of people with Mental or Psychiatric Disability and Their Relatives and Friends	(unit)
残疾人服务设施建设		**Service Facilities for PWDs**	
1. 残疾人综合服务设施		**Comprehensive Service Facilities for PWDs**	
建设完成已投入使用项目	(个)	Accumulated Projects in Operation	(unit)
总建设规模	(万平米)	Construction Area	(10,000 sq.m)
2. 残疾人康复设施		**Rehabilitation Service Facilities for PWDs**	
建设完成已投入使用项目	(个)	Accumulated Projects in Operation	(unit)
总建设规模	(万平米)	Construction Area	(10,000 sq.m)
3. 残疾人托养设施		**Fostering Service Facilities for PWDs**	
建设完成已投入使用项目	(个)	Accumulated Projects in Operation	(unit)
总建设规模	(万平米)	Construction Area	(10,000 sq.m)
信息化建设		**Informatization**	
1. 残疾人人口库综合数据	**(万人)**	**Data of the National Basic Database of Persons with Disabilities**	**(10,000 persons)**
2. 信息化专业人才	**(人)**	**IT Professionals**	**(person)**
3. 省、市、县各级残联网站	**(个)**	**Websites at Provincial, City, County Level**	**(unit)**

Continued 5

"十一五"完成/达到 the 11th Five-year Accomplishment	"十二五"任务 the 12th Five-year Plan	"十二五"完成情况 the 12th Five-year Accomplishment (2011 - 2014)				
		累计完成/达到 Total	2011	2012	2013	2014
3132	—	3161	3095	3089	3110	3128
3113	—	3146	3077	3073	3097	3113
3168	—	3172	3127	3113	3117	3139
3011	—	2990	2973	2983	3001	2958
3013	—	2986	2973	2985	3003	2954
63	—	178	90	78	82	177
	—					
2544	—	2231	1935	1971	2094	2231
487.7	—	460.3	334.0	355.8	424.1	460.3
—	—	613	224	231	542	613
—	—	130.0	60.7	67.0	100.7	130.0
—	—	442	130	155	353	442
—	—	101.4	34.2	43.1	78.2	101.4
1793.7	3000	2946.7	2195.1	2527.2	2811.5	2946.7
869	—	4971	4770	4948	5019	4971
1241	—	1660	1411	1540	1617	1660

全国残疾人人口基础数据库主要数据

Brief Data of the National Basic Information Database of Persons with Disabilities

单位：人 (截止时间：2014年12月31日) (person)

地 区	Region	已办理残疾人证 PWDs with Disabled Persons Certificate	0-14岁 Age 0-14	15-59岁 Age 15-59	60岁及以上 Age 60 and above
全 国	**Total**	**29467418**	**834284**	**17353946**	**11279188**
北 京	Beijing	273463	3355	156143	113965
天 津	Tianjin	267815	4074	171549	92192
河 北	Hebei	1563544	43976	918493	601075
山 西	Shanxi	831339	20661	518454	292224
内蒙古	Inner Mongolia	723954	13778	481007	229169
辽 宁	Liaoning	881323	15385	610832	255106
吉 林	Jilin	685186	13804	477180	194202
黑龙江	Heilongjiang	855368	16017	620806	218545
上 海	Shanghai	393990	2728	210143	181119
江 苏	Jiangsu	1480935	30166	873138	577631
浙 江	Zhejiang	1052740	20639	605336	426765
安 徽	Anhui	1465244	39186	809436	616622
福 建	Fujian	950732	24683	449006	477043
江 西	Jiangxi	926953	34427	586443	306083
山 东	Shandong	1884307	54729	1089652	739926
河 南	Henan	1831672	69174	1109552	652946
湖 北	Hubei	1180384	26267	754303	399814
湖 南	Hunan	1337723	41855	814445	481423
广 东	Guangdong	1196786	53330	720985	422471
广 西	Guangxi	1415636	41437	575164	799035
海 南	Hainan	144544	6239	91125	47180
重 庆	Chongqing	781803	23327	462993	295483
四 川	Sichuan	2265867	62745	1232085	971037
贵 州	Guizhou	972310	39094	568964	364252
云 南	Yunnan	1133686	41397	705866	386423
西 藏	Tibet	75658	6371	50189	19098
陕 西	Shaanxi	1315507	20032	671923	623552
甘 肃	Gansu	666853	22009	407674	237170
青 海	Qinghai	143295	7863	96642	38790
宁 夏	Ningxia	218391	8026	125283	85082
新 疆	Xinjiang	454250	25668	315674	112908
新疆兵团	Xinjiang Corps	63991	1345	48678	13968
黑龙江垦区	Heilongjiang Land Reclamation	32169	497	24783	6889

续表 1　Continued 1

单位：人　　(person)

地区	Region	已办理证件残疾人 PWDs with Disabled Persons Certificate					
		性别 Gender		残疾等级 Disability Grading			
		男性 Male	女性 Female	残疾一级 Grade-1	残疾二级 Grade-2	残疾三级 Grade-3	残疾四级 Grade-4
全国	**Total**	**17648238**	**11819180**	**4002097**	**7533206**	**8046536**	**9885579**
北京	Beijing	152397	121066	32562	62066	72209	106626
天津	Tianjin	155916	111899	30847	73346	88389	75233
河北	Hebei	941035	622509	194848	340829	372612	655255
山西	Shanxi	524213	307126	102198	196085	215377	317679
内蒙古	Inner Mongolia	440319	283635	81733	177051	216679	248491
辽宁	Liaoning	554596	326727	109039	211446	274706	286132
吉林	Jilin	426481	258705	89812	171580	216724	207070
黑龙江	Heilongjiang	540138	315230	101864	208619	268056	276829
上海	Shanghai	214084	179906	51227	70211	103516	169036
江苏	Jiangsu	826943	653992	223941	456611	450301	350082
浙江	Zhejiang	634103	418637	150239	203738	322442	376321
安徽	Anhui	847707	617537	221265	663873	324872	255234
福建	Fujian	536020	414712	110153	272182	234443	333954
江西	Jiangxi	570924	356029	109147	228977	258735	330094
山东	Shandong	1162323	721984	278322	493997	521189	590799
河南	Henan	1112074	719598	280041	527364	476284	547983
湖北	Hubei	718815	461569	191838	333392	299832	355322
湖南	Hunan	844263	493160	202716	374628	324528	435851
广东	Guangdong	722508	474278	219478	333055	335316	308937
广西	Guangxi	792357	623279	133328	273535	342260	666513
海南	Hainan	85367	59177	54687	26223	33231	30403
重庆	Chongqing	477233	304570	95392	200061	208450	277900
四川	Sichuan	1354849	911018	311739	538494	599085	816549
贵州	Guizhou	608449	363861	96791	159896	258654	456969
云南	Yunnan	685564	448122	138697	220966	272924	501099
西藏	Tibet	39894	35764	11453	15417	18530	30258
陕西	Shaanxi	746247	569260	145789	258571	494793	416354
甘肃	Gansu	394831	272022	111434	166389	184315	204715
青海	Qinghai	83678	59617	24694	54423	33341	30837
宁夏	Ningxia	121429	96962	28110	72593	56565	61123
新疆	Xinjiang	274631	179619	58570	122591	139036	134053
新疆兵团	Xinjiang Corps	38613	25378	6342	18885	19118	19646
黑龙江垦区	Heilongjiang Land Reclamation	20237	11932	3801	6112	10024	12232

续表 2 Continued 2

单位：人 (person)

地 区	Region	已办理证件残疾人 PWDs with Disabled Persons Certificate				
		残疾类别 Disability Category				
		视力残疾人 Persons with Visual Disability	听力残疾人 Persons with Hearing Disability	言语残疾人 Persons with Speech Disability	肢体残疾人 Persons with Physical Disability	智力残疾人 Persons with Intellectual Disability
全 国	**Total**	**3512185**	**2300864**	**547914**	**17183466**	**2429466**
北 京	Beijing	28669	19123	1630	152708	29197
天 津	Tianjin	23593	17152	3671	169035	27640
河 北	Hebei	145483	109061	38169	1015857	122648
山 西	Shanxi	87338	66225	18687	517193	74564
内蒙古	Inner Mongolia	75316	66994	16076	437956	58708
辽 宁	Liaoning	93144	68104	9050	489357	105978
吉 林	Jilin	76111	56156	12241	399034	62862
黑龙江	Heilongjiang	90594	67820	11553	531930	70033
上 海	Shanghai	72894	38631	4078	173441	55640
江 苏	Jiangsu	182740	95632	9751	817851	187348
浙 江	Zhejiang	113592	140083	17627	542764	105738
安 徽	Anhui	167332	94987	28982	785557	133080
福 建	Fujian	143075	119342	12214	477117	80819
江 西	Jiangxi	102073	69432	14306	534935	75504
山 东	Shandong	154873	118502	24113	1186497	170775
河 南	Henan	173251	137067	52499	1182206	155578
湖 北	Hubei	157285	74048	32766	640124	96023
湖 南	Hunan	175359	68954	26888	782807	99429
广 东	Guangdong	116868	88727	22046	625999	118565
广 西	Guangxi	193691	134176	22299	849393	68799
海 南	Hainan	15797	4984	2688	82964	12349
重 庆	Chongqing	125934	45431	13093	434717	64294
四 川	Sichuan	346344	176729	38911	1332670	148911
贵 州	Guizhou	123261	57481	20165	641112	43553
云 南	Yunnan	151544	81882	28096	691682	62608
西 藏	Tibet	12883	7828	3817	37370	2332
陕 西	Shaanxi	165499	139371	29881	760457	71088
甘 肃	Gansu	75026	52580	11497	388966	51915
青 海	Qinghai	18422	16979	3272	78761	11478
宁 夏	Ningxia	28060	21629	4238	123603	17888
新 疆	Xinjiang	64467	39105	12227	247827	34524
新疆兵团	Xinjiang Corps	8147	4349	821	34016	6296
黑龙江垦区	Heilongjiang Land Reclamation	3520	2300	562	17560	3302

续表 3 Continued 3

单位：人 (person)

地 区	Region	已办理证件残疾人 PWDs with Disabled Persons Certificate			
		残疾类别 Disability Category		户口性质 Household Register Type	
		精神残疾人 Persons with Psychiatric Disability	多重残疾人 Persons with Multiple Disabilities	农业 Rural	非农业 Non-Rural
全 国	**Total**	**2185208**	**1308315**	**22288307**	**7179111**
北 京	Beijing	27366	14770	112936	160527
天 津	Tianjin	23262	3462	106897	160918
河 北	Hebei	71147	61179	1334191	229353
山 西	Shanxi	39680	27652	672453	158886
内蒙古	Inner Mongolia	39690	29214	484569	239385
辽 宁	Liaoning	85616	30074	482636	398687
吉 林	Jilin	56445	22337	392188	292998
黑龙江	Heilongjiang	55753	27685	421950	433418
上 海	Shanghai	44960	4346	75637	318353
江 苏	Jiangsu	141827	45786	267697	1213238
浙 江	Zhejiang	105008	27928	849617	203123
安 徽	Anhui	158349	96957	1221691	243553
福 建	Fujian	72370	45795	793815	156917
江 西	Jiangxi	81525	49178	743399	183554
山 东	Shandong	143802	85745	1645610	238697
河 南	Henan	78195	52876	1597306	234366
湖 北	Hubei	117715	62423	935236	245148
湖 南	Hunan	105549	78737	1131514	206209
广 东	Guangdong	153746	70835	898769	298017
广 西	Guangxi	73319	73959	1274821	140815
海 南	Hainan	18755	7007	107697	36847
重 庆	Chongqing	69369	28965	611175	170628
四 川	Sichuan	150858	71444	1915918	349949
贵 州	Guizhou	30648	56090	862438	109872
云 南	Yunnan	68131	49743	997756	135930
西 藏	Tibet	4428	7000	69466	6192
陕 西	Shaanxi	73210	76001	1139879	175628
甘 肃	Gansu	33743	53126	559279	107574
青 海	Qinghai	3847	10536	112442	30853
宁 夏	Ningxia	13091	9882	158653	59738
新 疆	Xinjiang	31397	24703	308680	145570
新疆兵团	Xinjiang Corps	8308	2054	1430	62561
黑龙江垦区	Heilongjiang Land Reclamation	4099	826	562	31607

续表 4 Continued 4

单位：人 (person)

地区	Region	已办理证件残疾人 PWDs with Disabled Persons Certificate					
		15岁及以上受教育程度 Education of Age 15 and above					
		文盲 Illiterate	小学 Primary School	初中 Junior High School	高中及中专 Senior High School	大学专科及以上 Junior College and above	其他 Other
总计	**Total**	**5620389**	**11884917**	**8863145**	**2423279**	**423437**	**252251**
北京	Beijing	41761	50418	103275	53654	22005	2350
天津	Tianjin	32136	65131	104120	50094	13596	2738
河北	Hebei	189485	648517	553282	129635	20366	22259
山西	Shanxi	110591	292048	332909	74579	13335	7877
内蒙古	Inner Mongolia	126734	247034	254700	78189	13575	3722
辽宁	Liaoning	100171	274209	392306	93389	16602	4646
吉林	Jilin	77476	219623	275822	99457	10324	2484
黑龙江	Heilongjiang	71681	276640	369647	112303	17564	7533
上海	Shanghai	35559	83237	169528	82079	23587	
江苏	Jiangsu	505537	463811	383281	104193	23714	399
浙江	Zhejiang	236578	466228	275407	54749	14239	5539
安徽	Anhui	383142	643895	353423	69039	12876	2869
福建	Fujian	186414	474103	209101	54959	8722	17433
江西	Jiangxi	133703	403565	295966	69737	8710	15272
山东	Shandong	343012	692585	634474	175185	23098	15953
河南	Henan	442866	577447	601509	162580	22117	25153
湖北	Hubei	246269	383609	395002	132617	17805	5082
湖南	Hunan	194284	564423	415939	141177	12991	8909
广东	Guangdong	200760	500305	345530	97896	16488	35807
广西	Guangxi	191503	771273	350398	72840	9251	20371
海南	Hainan	31932	45993	50247	13886	1837	649
重庆	Chongqing	91409	411306	214104	45540	7198	12246
四川	Sichuan	369529	1225084	540678	108551	17613	4412
贵州	Guizhou	287510	421736	212291	37146	9423	4204
云南	Yunnan	309625	536624	216953	51732	13843	4909
西藏	Tibet	42839	27996	3198	923	376	326
陕西	Shaanxi	265094	502597	416045	110267	16339	5165
甘肃	Gansu	211229	247168	145591	51767	8737	2361
青海	Qinghai	33791	74167	22772	9323	2547	695
宁夏	Ningxia	61496	81361	53000	16161	4764	1609
新疆	Xinjiang	59331	188285	131621	51163	15383	8467
新疆兵团	Xinjiang Corps	5110	17672	25508	11676	3464	561
黑龙江垦区	Heilongjiang Land Reclamation	1832	6827	15518	6793	948	251

分省统计资料

Statistical Data of Provinces

1-1　社区康复

Community-Based Rehabilitation(CBR)

地　区	Region	开展社区康复服务的市辖区 Districts Where CBR Has Been Conducted	本年度新开展 Counties and Cities where CBR was Introduced in 2014	开展社区康复服务的县(市) Counties and Cities Where CBR Has Been Conducted	本年度新开展 Counties and Cities Where CBR Was Introduced in 2014
		个 unit	个 unit	个 unit	个 unit
全　国	**Total**	**914**	**9**	**2023**	**22**
北　京	Beijing	14		2	
天　津	Tianjin	13		3	
河　北	Hebei	36		138	
山　西	Shanxi	23		90	
内蒙古	Inner Mongolia	22		82	1
辽　宁	Liaoning	62		44	
吉　林	Jilin	30		41	1
黑龙江	Heilongjiang	57		62	
上　海	Shanghai	16		1	
江　苏	Jiangsu	59		44	
浙　江	Zhejiang	33	1	57	2
安　徽	Anhui	44		57	1
福　建	Fujian	26		56	
江　西	Jiangxi	23		79	
山　东	Shandong	58	3	88	
河　南	Henan	60	1	104	
湖　北	Hubei	39		59	
湖　南	Hunan	37		88	
广　东	Guangdong	63		62	
广　西	Guangxi	39	4	75	
海　南	Hainan	3		10	
重　庆	Chongqing	23		17	
四　川	Sichuan	31		103	3
贵　州	Guizhou	10		75	1
云　南	Yunnan	11		109	1
西　藏	Tibet	1		20	5
陕　西	Shaanxi	28		83	
甘　肃	Gansu	18		69	
青　海	Qinghai	4		42	
宁　夏	Ningxia	9		13	
新　疆	Xinjiang	11		80	
新疆兵团	Xinjiang Corps	11		132	7
黑龙江垦区	Heilongjiang Land Reclamation			38	

1-1 续表 1 Continued 1

地 区	Region	开展社区康复服务的社区(村) Communities (villages) Where CBR Has Been Conducted	社区康复协调员累计 Accumulative CBR Coordinators at Communities	本年度新增社区康复协调员 CBR Coordinators Who Were Engaged in 2014
		个 unit	人 person	人 person
全 国	**Total**	**330200**	**391678**	**42332**
北 京	Beijing	6416	5968	683
天 津	Tianjin	4613	3909	116
河 北	Hebei	29889	39750	2217
山 西	Shanxi	10343	18742	1782
内蒙古	Inner Mongolia	4956	11182	760
辽 宁	Liaoning	11951	13345	1417
吉 林	Jilin	6689	9122	696
黑龙江	Heilongjiang	3080	3873	1071
上 海	Shanghai	456	5547	236
江 苏	Jiangsu	16843	18199	843
浙 江	Zhejiang	17065	11345	2165
安 徽	Anhui	7247	12864	3443
福 建	Fujian	9740	10504	1464
江 西	Jiangxi	8968	13130	1603
山 东	Shandong	51950	49205	2508
河 南	Henan	39680	36632	4392
湖 北	Hubei	9323	7750	488
湖 南	Hunan	13347	15664	1428
广 东	Guangdong	15903	19241	1289
广 西	Guangxi	6456	11710	1938
海 南	Hainan	575	1490	129
重 庆	Chongqing	7662	11073	3356
四 川	Sichuan	16668	15908	957
贵 州	Guizhou	4335	8903	2459
云 南	Yunnan	7763	11923	605
西 藏	Tibet	12	58	30
陕 西	Shaanxi	5426	8833	2695
甘 肃	Gansu	5653	8366	718
青 海	Qinghai	2163	2249	250
宁 夏	Ningxia	843	1282	273
新 疆	Xinjiang	3951	3472	251
新疆兵团	Xinjiang Corps	189	308	30
黑龙江垦区	Heilongjiang Land Reclamation	45	131	40

1-1 续表 2 Continued 2

地 区	Region	接受过培训的社区康复协调员 Trained CBR Coordinators	已建社区康复站的社区累计 Accumulative Communities Where CBR Stations Have Been Established	本年度新建社区康复站的社区 Communities Where CBR Stations Were Established in 2014	已建社区康复服务档案的残疾人 PWDs who have been Established Files of CBR Service	本年度新增接受社区康复服务残疾人 PWDs Who Began to Get CBR Service in 2014
		人 person	个 unit	个 unit	万人 10,000 persons	万人 10,000 persons
全 国	**Total**	**374145**	**219104**	**6099**	**2223.4**	**175.2**
北 京	Beijing	5950	3909	283	43.8	3.9
天 津	Tianjin	3391	1701	43	30.5	3.4
河 北	Hebei	35668	17331	801	191.6	3.7
山 西	Shanxi	17710	5080	49	70.0	3.1
内蒙古	Inner Mongolia	10921	2103	40	32.0	1.8
辽 宁	Liaoning	13094	10382	102	118.2	3.0
吉 林	Jilin	9002	2875	26	110.2	43.6
黑龙江	Heilongjiang	3582	1397	40	31.2	1.2
上 海	Shanghai	5544	218		36.6	1.7
江 苏	Jiangsu	18159	14937	260	189.2	8.2
浙 江	Zhejiang	11140	10082	337	76.0	5.2
安 徽	Anhui	12701	4604	421	66.4	2.0
福 建	Fujian	9792	3877	77	75.0	6.4
江 西	Jiangxi	12743	3951	184	74.6	8.1
山 东	Shandong	47806	42162	282	172.7	4.7
河 南	Henan	34619	54128	2076	184.3	12.9
湖 北	Hubei	7436	4760	77	90.5	2.2
湖 南	Hunan	14955	5442	74	79.4	2.4
广 东	Guangdong	18408	8154	290	122.9	7.2
广 西	Guangxi	11167	2371	5	36.5	2.0
海 南	Hainan	1158	628	5	3.2	0.0
重 庆	Chongqing	11069	3313	141	82.3	20.5
四 川	Sichuan	15623	7048	124	104.3	8.2
贵 州	Guizhou	7271	709	26	22.4	0.5
云 南	Yunnan	11026	2481	60	47.5	5.4
西 藏	Tibet	58	11	4	0.2	0.0
陕 西	Shaanxi	8765	1350	68	38.3	4.7
甘 肃	Gansu	8131	1275	26	47.0	2.1
青 海	Qinghai	2207	485	1	4.6	0.4
宁 夏	Ningxia	1276	554	30	5.4	0.3
新 疆	Xinjiang	3340	1624	131	29.9	6.1
新疆兵团	Xinjiang Corps	302	144	16	2.9	0.2
黑龙江垦区	Heilongjiang Land Reclamation	131	18		3.8	0.0

1-1 续表 3 Continued 3

地 区	Region	开展家长学校工作的残疾人康复机构 Rehabilitation Institutions for Parents Training of PWDs	省级 at Provincial Level	地市级 at Prefectural/ City Level	县级 at County Level	参加培训的家长 Parents Trained	省级 at Provincial Level	地市级 at Prefectural/ City Level	县级 at County Level
		个 unit	个 unit	个 unit	个 unit	人次 person-time	人次 person-time	人次 person-time	人次 person-time
全 国	**Total**	**1379**	**29**	**231**	**1119**	**139083**	**17068**	**25496**	**96519**
北 京	Beijing	100	1		99	35288	4235		31053
天 津	Tianjin	4			4	178			178
河 北	Hebei	60	1	10	49	3471	750	1630	1091
山 西	Shanxi	45	3	14	28	2511	900	948	663
内蒙古	Inner Mongolia	38	1	25	12	1319	372	452	495
辽 宁	Liaoning	18		3	15	525		369	156
吉 林	Jilin	61	2	35	24	5761	1150	2206	2405
黑龙江	Heilongjiang	3			3	19			19
上 海	Shanghai	330	3		327	20869	605		20264
江 苏	Jiangsu	75	1	8	66	8060	662	1142	6256
浙 江	Zhejiang	48	2	7	39	11047	1451	1227	8369
安 徽	Anhui	66	1	26	39	9570	2000	4066	3504
福 建	Fujian	10			10	337	12		325
江 西	Jiangxi	27			27	1326		36	1290
山 东	Shandong	122		8	114	4529		223	4306
河 南	Henan	74		30	44	4062	10	2564	1488
湖 北	Hubei	5			5	567		23	544
湖 南	Hunan	69	1	24	44	9216	2305	4918	1993
广 东	Guangdong	41		12	29	7144	10	1905	5229
广 西	Guangxi	11	2	3	6	2603	632	1790	181
海 南	Hainan								
重 庆	Chongqing	54	6		48	2108	500		1608
四 川	Sichuan	23		6	17	1645		601	1044
贵 州	Guizhou	7		1	6	243		22	221
云 南	Yunnan	6	1	1	4	402	60	150	192
西 藏	Tibet								
陕 西	Shaanxi	3		2	1	745		670	75
甘 肃	Gansu	2			2	8			8
青 海	Qinghai	9			9	100			100
宁 夏	Ningxia	14	3	4	7	1913	1251	256	406
新 疆	Xinjiang	54	1	12	41	3517	163	298	3056
新疆兵团	Xinjiang Corps								
黑龙江垦区	Heilongjiang Land Reclamation								

1-2 视力残疾康复

Rehabilitation of Persons with Visual Disability

地 区	Region	白内障复明 Sight-restoring of Persons with Cataract-induced Blindness		低视力康复 Rehabilitation of Persons with Low Vision		盲人定向行走训练 Skills Training for Blind Persons	
		白内障复明手术 Sight-restoring Surgeries for Cataract Victims	贫困白内障患者免费手术 Free Surgeries for Poor Cataract Victims	低视力者配用助视器 Persons Fitted with Vision-aids	培训低视力儿童家长 Trained Parents of Children with Low Vision	盲人定向行走训练 Blind Persons Who Have Gotten Orientation Skills Training	盲人定向行走训练指导师 Orientation Skills Trainers for Blind Persons
		例 case	例 case	人 person	人 person	人 person	人 person
全 国	**Total**	**748089**	**300117**	**141625**	**35761**	**122724**	**5744**
北 京	Beijing	12577	1731	837	22	1289	244
天 津	Tianjin	6416	773	2081	498	1312	20
河 北	Hebei	26136	1014	9336	1783	5992	253
山 西	Shanxi	20017	4960	3669	1414	5851	182
内蒙古	Inner Mongolia	9825	6063	2669	578	2474	65
辽 宁	Liaoning	17929	5287	7136	1467	4853	380
吉 林	Jilin	15467	3326	3038	1400	4254	279
黑龙江	Heilongjiang	10673	4280	11756	1434	4578	78
上 海	Shanghai	62433	4439	7262	1078	2065	453
江 苏	Jiangsu	60404	16840	6408	1153	7706	181
浙 江	Zhejiang	34103	18960	1481	391	2541	226
安 徽	Anhui	36657	14653	5552	2048	11622	911
福 建	Fujian	15819	11818	827	359	3515	66
江 西	Jiangxi	18977	1418	2917	680	4700	29
山 东	Shandong	50717	20556	5041	567	6451	312
河 南	Henan	8204	3190	6564	3697	8721	291
湖 北	Hubei	30337	10161	5420	10015	6000	189
湖 南	Hunan	25919	12482	5746	1963	5410	176
广 东	Guangdong	103241	37006	4511	273	6311	158
广 西	Guangxi	23289	13241	6008	531	2468	101
海 南	Hainan	2628	2463	937	200	1519	17
重 庆	Chongqing	18947	7676	2193	546	1177	96
四 川	Sichuan	42302	26841	5368	920	6910	269
贵 州	Guizhou	13385	9292	2745	297	2300	85
云 南	Yunnan	33816	30352	9841	1172	2688	230
西 藏	Tibet	1396	1235	18		281	
陕 西	Shaanxi	11613	8631	9294	40	3700	228
甘 肃	Gansu	13330	8338	3574	338	2199	49
青 海	Qinghai	3735	3723	2438	191	1137	30
宁 夏	Ningxia	2789	2406	1685	358	1205	7
新 疆	Xinjiang	12793	6010	4446	161	1221	135
新疆兵团	Xinjiang Corps	1751	909	687	126	134	4
黑龙江垦区	Heilongjiang Land Reclamation	464	43	140	61	140	

1-3 视力残疾康复机构

Rehabilitation Institutions for Persons with Visual Disability

地 区	Region	开展视力残疾康复训练服务机构 Rehabilitation Institutions for Persons with Visual Disability	省级 at Provincial Level	地市级 at Prefectural/ City Level	县级 at County Level	本年度新建机构 Established in 2014	本年度注销机构 Cancelled Registration in 2014
		个 unit	个 unit	个 unit	个 unit	个 unit	个 unit
全 国	**Total**	**891**	**24**	**187**	**680**	**149**	**23**
北 京	Beijing	13			13	2	
天 津	Tianjin	5	1		4		
河 北	Hebei	19		6	13	1	
山 西	Shanxi	40	1	16	23	3	5
内蒙古	Inner Mongolia	21		6	15	6	
辽 宁	Liaoning	31	1	9	21	3	
吉 林	Jilin	50	1	18	31	2	5
黑龙江	Heilongjiang	24		7	17	4	
上 海	Shanghai	42	1		41	7	
江 苏	Jiangsu	64	1	9	54	10	6
浙 江	Zhejiang	21	1	2	18	3	1
安 徽	Anhui	11	1	3	7		
福 建	Fujian	30		4	26	8	
江 西	Jiangxi	10		4	6		
山 东	Shandong	101		14	87	16	
河 南	Henan	28	1	11	16	2	
湖 北	Hubei	20		5	15	6	
湖 南	Hunan	35		11	24	4	3
广 东	Guangdong	78	1	27	50	7	1
广 西	Guangxi	7	1	1	5		
海 南	Hainan	5	5			5	
重 庆	Chongqing	41			41	6	
四 川	Sichuan	24	1	2	21	6	
贵 州	Guizhou	12		5	7	5	1
云 南	Yunnan	28	1	8	19	14	
西 藏	Tibet	1	1				
陕 西	Shaanxi	65	2	4	59	16	1
甘 肃	Gansu	21	1	5	15	1	
青 海	Qinghai	5	1		4	2	
宁 夏	Ningxia	4	1	1	2	1	
新 疆	Xinjiang	35		9	26	9	
新疆兵团	Xinjiang Corps						
黑龙江垦区	Heilongjiang Land Reclamation						

1-3　续表　Continued

地　区	Region	视力残疾康复机构在岗人员 Staff of Rehabilitation Institutions for Persons with Visual Disability			
		在岗人员总数 Total Staff	专业技术人员 Technicians and Professionals	管理人员 Managerial Personnels	其他 Other Staff Members
		人 person	人 person	人 person	人 person
全　国	**Total**	**15292**	**10170**	**2588**	**2534**
北　京	Beijing	318	259	47	12
天　津	Tianjin	26	17	8	1
河　北	Hebei	134	85	34	15
山　西	Shanxi	3428	2705	380	343
内蒙古	Inner Mongolia	424	312	67	45
辽　宁	Liaoning	206	105	54	47
吉　林	Jilin	686	463	168	55
黑龙江	Heilongjiang	257	184	37	36
上　海	Shanghai	368	197	47	124
江　苏	Jiangsu	665	411	119	135
浙　江	Zhejiang	841	492	224	125
安　徽	Anhui	190	130	29	31
福　建	Fujian	535	348	94	93
江　西	Jiangxi	122	53	39	30
山　东	Shandong	2201	1438	347	416
河　南	Henan	314	212	62	40
湖　北	Hubei	183	86	36	61
湖　南	Hunan	830	491	177	162
广　东	Guangdong	1037	628	130	279
广　西	Guangxi	24	7	8	9
海　南	Hainan	156	133	14	9
重　庆	Chongqing	674	382	113	179
四　川	Sichuan	124	68	34	22
贵　州	Guizhou	227	147	42	38
云　南	Yunnan	356	193	70	93
西　藏	Tibet	3	1	2	
陕　西	Shaanxi	480	283	110	87
甘　肃	Gansu	273	217	41	15
青　海	Qinghai	25	12	6	7
宁　夏	Ningxia	15	9	3	3
新　疆	Xinjiang	170	102	46	22
新疆兵团	Xinjiang Corps				
黑龙江垦区	Heilongjiang Land Reclamation				

1-4 听力语言残疾康复

Rehabilitation of Persons with Hearing and Speech Disabilities

地区	Region	新收训聋儿 Newly Trained Deaf Children	机构训练 Deaf Children Trained in Institutions	家庭训练 Deaf Children Trained in Families	在训聋儿 Deaf Children Being Trained	培训家长 Parents Trained
		人 person	人 person	人 person	人 person	人 person
全 国	**Total**	**19401**	**16429**	**2972**	**31701**	**38970**
北 京	Beijing	168	168		378	414
天 津	Tianjin	51	51		100	132
河 北	Hebei	2063	1115	948	2704	2925
山 西	Shanxi	404	404		659	1714
内蒙古	Inner Mongolia	369	307	62	536	825
辽 宁	Liaoning	507	444	63	1000	1209
吉 林	Jilin	362	279	83	457	1100
黑龙江	Heilongjiang	309	267	42	525	651
上 海	Shanghai	136	80	56	374	370
江 苏	Jiangsu	985	947	38	2706	2756
浙 江	Zhejiang	581	575	6	1050	1194
安 徽	Anhui	1802	1788	14	2697	3719
福 建	Fujian	552	522	30	935	1172
江 西	Jiangxi	556	392	164	837	835
山 东	Shandong	1078	1024	54	1999	2415
河 南	Henan	2466	1992	474	3411	3298
湖 北	Hubei	829	815	14	1023	1128
湖 南	Hunan	721	663	58	1482	1936
广 东	Guangdong	1222	1149	73	2496	3208
广 西	Guangxi	560	455	105	916	1153
海 南	Hainan	60	60		108	108
重 庆	Chongqing	349	293	56	498	1079
四 川	Sichuan	855	726	129	1224	1260
贵 州	Guizhou	383	322	61	540	690
云 南	Yunnan	520	284	236	699	1047
西 藏	Tibet	23	23		23	60
陕 西	Shaanxi	564	504	60	876	1197
甘 肃	Gansu	478	387	91	569	518
青 海	Qinghai	69	51	18	154	217
宁 夏	Ningxia	45	41	4	123	114
新 疆	Xinjiang	147	146	1	314	408
新疆兵团	Xinjiang Corps	27	5	22	63	82
黑龙江垦区	Heilongjiang Land Reclamation	17	7	10	17	36

1-4　续表 1　Continued 1

地　区	Region	本年度接受国家项目救助 Subsidized by State Projects in 2014		本年度接受地方项目救助 Subsidized by Local Projects in 2014	专业人员培训 Professionals Trained		
		接受人工耳蜗救助 Poor Deaf Children Subsidized by CDPF Rescuing Project through Cochlear Implantation	接受助听器救助 Poor Deaf Children Subsidized by CDPF Hearing Aids Rescuing Project			培训省级机构专业人员 Professionals of Institutions at Provincial Level	培训地市级机构专业人员 Professionals of Institutions at Prefectual/ City Level
		人 person	人 person	人 person	人 person	人 person	人 person
全　国	**Total**	**3374**	**16351**	**6613**	**5772**	**2402**	**1508**
北　京	Beijing	2	103	95	174	30	
天　津	Tianjin	5	96	157	33	31	
河　北	Hebei	211	1000	146	134	13	92
山　西	Shanxi	116	368	20	339	274	54
内蒙古	Inner Mongolia	25	325	117	59	31	26
辽　宁	Liaoning	95	652	39	343	187	156
吉　林	Jilin	106	425	57	271	86	133
黑龙江	Heilongjiang	110	590	1	195	116	41
上　海	Shanghai			113	173	86	
江　苏	Jiangsu	110	794	862	343	64	46
浙　江	Zhejiang	65	439	260	160	27	86
安　徽	Anhui	140	760	423	323	194	45
福　建	Fujian	72	463	400	129	34	41
江　西	Jiangxi	181	507	210	103	46	21
山　东	Shandong	270	1290	592	231	9	50
河　南	Henan	368	1156	155	257	38	39
湖　北	Hubei	233	462	597	52	21	16
湖　南	Hunan	212	766	241	321	88	187
广　东	Guangdong	163	445	1072	1170	655	364
广　西	Guangxi	170	589	46	222	97	48
海　南	Hainan	8	95	48	2		1
重　庆	Chongqing	106	393	141	265	96	
四　川	Sichuan	178	1149	167	170	19	30
贵　州	Guizhou	122	589	135			
云　南	Yunnan	42	825	239	50	5	
西　藏	Tibet	6	19		1	1	
陕　西	Shaanxi	106	463	152	130	101	25
甘　肃	Gansu	80	860	59	7	1	1
青　海	Qinghai	12	133	21	60	3	1
宁　夏	Ningxia	10	130	6	40	40	
新　疆	Xinjiang	50	350	30	15	9	5
新疆兵团	Xinjiang Corps		25	12			
黑龙江垦区	Heilongjiang Land Reclamation		90				

1-4 续表 2 Continued 2

地 区	Region	培训县级机构专业人员 Professionals of Institutions at County Level	成年听力语言康复技术服务 Adults Received Hearing and Speech Rehabilitation Services	训练后走向 Directions in which Children have gone After Rehabilitation			
				普小 Ordinary Primary Schools	普幼 Ordinary Kindergartens	特殊教育学校(聋校) Special Education Schools (Schools for Deaf Students)	其他 Other Directions
		人 person	人次 person-time	人 person	人 person	人 person	人 person
全 国	**Total**	**1862**	**40148**	**1200**	**1482**	**1915**	**1978**
北 京	Beijing	144	467	10	23	16	75
天 津	Tianjin	2	569	12	15	3	
河 北	Hebei	29	1204	33	45	118	213
山 西	Shanxi	11	2367	31	53	30	25
内蒙古	Inner Mongolia	2	187	7	11	19	11
辽 宁	Liaoning		702	44	100	25	20
吉 林	Jilin	52	394	2	33	8	12
黑龙江	Heilongjiang	38	111	12	10	22	24
上 海	Shanghai	87	10366	35	31	10	18
江 苏	Jiangsu	233	2125	85	85	118	167
浙 江	Zhejiang	47	3222	54	53	37	94
安 徽	Anhui	84	1620	196	82	184	123
福 建	Fujian	54	962	46	78	98	58
江 西	Jiangxi	36	444	11	10	7	9
山 东	Shandong	172	784	63	53	103	58
河 南	Henan	180	1360	88	173	110	117
湖 北	Hubei	15	592	29	35	37	51
湖 南	Hunan	46	912	143	126	274	191
广 东	Guangdong	151	1485	73	127	90	159
广 西	Guangxi	77	1003	33	66	73	128
海 南	Hainan	1					
重 庆	Chongqing	169	1961	9	45	25	65
四 川	Sichuan	121	608	51	69	157	55
贵 州	Guizhou		413	20	18	39	12
云 南	Yunnan	45	3457	38	48	154	211
西 藏	Tibet		188	3	1	5	2
陕 西	Shaanxi	4	91	13	51	99	25
甘 肃	Gansu	5	56	16	8	11	24
青 海	Qinghai	56	100	6		10	7
宁 夏	Ningxia			2	14		
新 疆	Xinjiang	1	1988	31	17	23	17
新疆兵团	Xinjiang Corps		380	4	2	10	7
黑龙江垦区	Heilongjiang Land Reclamation		30				

1-5　听力语言康复机构
Rehabilitation Institutions of Hearing and Speech

地　区	Region	机构概况 Rehabilitation Institutions			
		累计建设 Rehab-institutions Established	省级 at Provincial Level	地市级 at Prefectural/City Level	县级 at County Level
		个 unit	个 unit	个 unit	个 unit
全　国	**Total**	**1056**	**31**	**351**	**674**
北　京	Beijing	25	1		24
天　津	Tianjin	8	1		7
河　北	Hebei	96	1	14	81
山　西	Shanxi	44	1	14	29
内蒙古	Inner Mongolia	24	1	17	6
辽　宁	Liaoning	46	1	22	23
吉　林	Jilin	20	1	9	10
黑龙江	Heilongjiang	29	1	13	15
上　海	Shanghai	20	1		19
江　苏	Jiangsu	65	1	10	54
浙　江	Zhejiang	28	1	12	15
安　徽	Anhui	65	1	33	31
福　建	Fujian	30	1	8	21
江　西	Jiangxi	25	1	8	16
山　东	Shandong	83	1	22	60
河　南	Henan	80	1	27	52
湖　北	Hubei	39	1	16	22
湖　南	Hunan	58	1	15	42
广　东	Guangdong	68	1	27	40
广　西	Guangxi	36	1	12	23
海　南	Hainan	4	1		3
重　庆	Chongqing	14	1		13
四　川	Sichuan	32	1	16	15
贵　州	Guizhou	17	1	6	10
云　南	Yunnan	18	1	14	3
西　藏	Tibet	1	1		
陕　西	Shaanxi	36	1	11	24
甘　肃	Gansu	17	1	10	6
青　海	Qinghai	6	1	4	1
宁　夏	Ningxia	6	1	3	2
新　疆	Xinjiang	16	1	8	7
新疆兵团	Xinjiang Corps				
黑龙江垦区	Heilongjiang Land Reclamation				

1-5 续表 Continued

地 区	Region	在岗专业人员 On-the-job Professionals				
		教师 Teachers	个别化教师 Individualized Teachers	医技 Doctors and Technicians	助听器验配师 Technicians That Check and Fit Hearing Aids	管理者 Managerial Personnels
		人 person	人 person	人 person	人 person	人 person
全 国	**Total**	**10064**	**3919**	**1836**	**754**	**2288**
北 京	Beijing	254	108	43	13	75
天 津	Tianjin	57	12	7	5	15
河 北	Hebei	834	264	140	53	249
山 西	Shanxi	396	122	32	16	100
内蒙古	Inner Mongolia	306	72	42	14	65
辽 宁	Liaoning	447	101	53	24	104
吉 林	Jilin	229	86	39	21	39
黑龙江	Heilongjiang	345	88	43	17	74
上 海	Shanghai	112	58	12	5	23
江 苏	Jiangsu	723	266	115	49	144
浙 江	Zhejiang	233	125	47	20	51
安 徽	Anhui	558	262	61	27	107
福 建	Fujian	245	129	61	24	66
江 西	Jiangxi	166	60	54	21	42
山 东	Shandong	940	392	254	93	188
河 南	Henan	898	344	204	72	184
湖 北	Hubei	295	102	82	42	84
湖 南	Hunan	575	227	78	25	141
广 东	Guangdong	735	363	93	54	111
广 西	Guangxi	316	158	70	29	65
海 南	Hainan	53	19	11	6	11
重 庆	Chongqing	135	63	30	10	43
四 川	Sichuan	271	116	40	18	71
贵 州	Guizhou	139	59	53	20	52
云 南	Yunnan	130	47	27	15	26
西 藏	Tibet	5	1	2	2	2
陕 西	Shaanxi	417	152	47	20	84
甘 肃	Gansu	93	58	70	23	32
青 海	Qinghai	20	6	12	5	7
宁 夏	Ningxia	46	16	1	1	8
新 疆	Xinjiang	91	43	13	10	25
新疆兵团	Xinjiang Corps					
黑龙江垦区	Heilongjiang Land Reclamation					

1-6 肢体残疾康复
Rehabilitation of Persons with Physical Disability

地 区	Region	肢体残疾康复 Rehabilitation of Persons with Physical Disability					
		肢体残疾康复训练 Persons with Physical Disability Receiving Rehabilitation Training	脑瘫儿童机构康复训练 Systematic Rehabilitation Training in Institutions for Children with Cerebral Palsy	肢体残疾儿童社区、家庭康复训练 Children with Physical Disability Receiving Rehabilitation Training in Communities and Families	肢体残疾人社区、家庭康复训练 Persons with Physical Disability Receiving Rehabilitation Training in Communities and Families	贫困肢体残疾儿童矫治手术 Orthopedic Surgeries Conducted for Poor Children with Physical Disability	麻风畸残矫治手术 Orthopedic Surgeries Conducted for Persons with Leprosy-induced Disability
		人 person	人 person	人 person	人 person	例 case	例 case
全 国	**Total**	**366589**	**40099**	**32215**	**294275**	**8860**	**224**
北 京	Beijing	5601	248	93	5260		
天 津	Tianjin	3547	127	134	3286	43	
河 北	Hebei	10683	727	1217	8739	523	
山 西	Shanxi	5259	380	351	4528	245	
内蒙古	Inner Mongolia	6636	444	600	5592	158	
辽 宁	Liaoning	15778	763	878	14137	371	
吉 林	Jilin	5320	489	80	4751	162	
黑龙江	Heilongjiang	6194	554	303	5337	162	
上 海	Shanghai	5431	1019	632	3780	10	
江 苏	Jiangsu	36256	5845	2055	28356	220	
浙 江	Zhejiang	6449	601	522	5326	130	
安 徽	Anhui	26722	2093	1737	22892	491	
福 建	Fujian	9113	1542	1174	6397	135	
江 西	Jiangxi	10273	875	647	8751	170	
山 东	Shandong	50633	3721	1668	45244	842	
河 南	Henan	15660	2634	4612	8414	535	
湖 北	Hubei	12542	2651	1039	8852	333	
湖 南	Hunan	13485	1873	1055	10557	395	
广 东	Guangdong	37893	3464	3128	31301	58	20
广 西	Guangxi	7007	529	1622	4856	240	
海 南	Hainan	2151	105	676	1370	38	
重 庆	Chongqing	5987	374	746	4867	325	
四 川	Sichuan	24731	5365	2932	16434	931	1
贵 州	Guizhou	1793	374	347	1072	252	89
云 南	Yunnan	9858	472	1526	7860	509	114
西 藏	Tibet	533	122	125	286	84	
陕 西	Shaanxi	9828	858	737	8233	637	
甘 肃	Gansu	5090	515	670	3905	509	
青 海	Qinghai	1400	177	173	1050	111	
宁 夏	Ningxia	5240	204	135	4901	95	
新 疆	Xinjiang	6608	909	385	5314	80	
新疆兵团	Xinjiang Corps	2612	20	215	2377	38	
黑龙江垦区	Heilongjiang Land Reclamation	276	25	1	250	28	

1–6 续表 Continued

地 区	Region	肢体残疾康复、管理技术人员培训 Training for Managerial and Technical Personnel on Physical Disability Rehabilitation	国家级 at State Level	省级 at Provincial Level	地市级 at Prefectural/city Level	县级 at County Level
		人次 person-time	人次 person-time	人次 person-time	人次 person-time	人次 person-time
全 国	**Total**	**35030**	**80**	**1237**	**8696**	**25017**
北 京	Beijing	4462		114		4348
天 津	Tianjin	377	2	10		365
河 北	Hebei	450	4	1	5	440
山 西	Shanxi	351	2	80	41	228
内蒙古	Inner Mongolia	126	2		3	121
辽 宁	Liaoning	3542	2		1225	2315
吉 林	Jilin	825	2		250	573
黑龙江	Heilongjiang	226	2			224
上 海	Shanghai	2348		500		1848
江 苏	Jiangsu	3641	4		190	3447
浙 江	Zhejiang	6296	4		5624	668
安 徽	Anhui	63	4		18	41
福 建	Fujian	182	2	80	6	94
江 西	Jiangxi	205	3		18	184
山 东	Shandong	4098	4		249	3845
河 南	Henan	71	4			67
湖 北	Hubei	228	3		4	221
湖 南	Hunan	337	4		105	228
广 东	Guangdong	1622	4	100	566	952
广 西	Guangxi	108	3			105
海 南	Hainan	5	1			4
重 庆	Chongqing	898	2	72		824
四 川	Sichuan	1469	4		173	1292
贵 州	Guizhou	213	3		2	208
云 南	Yunnan	1856	3	220		1633
西 藏	Tibet	1				1
陕 西	Shaanxi	162	3		120	39
甘 肃	Gansu	59	3			56
青 海	Qinghai	227	2		1	224
宁 夏	Ningxia	156	3			153
新 疆	Xinjiang	425		60	96	269
新疆兵团	Xinjiang Corps					
黑龙江垦区	Heilongjiang Land Reclamation	1	1			

1-7　肢体残疾康复训练服务机构
Rehabilitation Institutions for Persons with Physical Disability

地　区	Region	机构合计 Rehabilitation Institutions	省级 at Provincial Level	残联办 Run by Disabled Persons' Federations	其他办 Run by Others
		个 unit	个 unit	个 unit	个 unit
全　国	**Total**	**2181**	**42**	**29**	**13**
北　京	Beijing	26	1	1	
天　津	Tianjin	10	2	1	1
河　北	Hebei	126	1	1	
山　西	Shanxi	39	2	2	
内蒙古	Inner Mongolia	35			
辽　宁	Liaoning	71	3	1	2
吉　林	Jilin	119	1	1	
黑龙江	Heilongjiang	48	1	1	
上　海	Shanghai	116	2	2	
江　苏	Jiangsu	123			
浙　江	Zhejiang	51	1	1	
安　徽	Anhui	79	1	1	
福　建	Fujian	78	1	1	
江　西	Jiangxi	25	1	1	
山　东	Shandong	282	1		1
河　南	Henan	77	1	1	
湖　北	Hubei	54	1	1	
湖　南	Hunan	51	1	1	
广　东	Guangdong	257	1	1	
广　西	Guangxi	25	1	1	
海　南	Hainan	6	4		4
重　庆	Chongqing	37	1	1	
四　川	Sichuan	72	1	1	
贵　州	Guizhou	14	1	1	
云　南	Yunnan	31	2	2	
西　藏	Tibet	2	1	1	
陕　西	Shaanxi	157	4	1	3
甘　肃	Gansu	28	1	1	
青　海	Qinghai	14	1	1	
宁　夏	Ningxia	19	1	1	
新　疆	Xinjiang	87			
新疆兵团	Xinjiang Corps	3	1		1
黑龙江垦区	Heilongjiang Land Reclamation	19	1		1

1-7 续表 1 Continued 1

地区	Region	开展肢体残疾康复训练机构 Rehabilitation Institutions					
		地市级 at Prefectural/ City Level	残联办 Run by Disabled Persons' Federations	其他办 Run by Others	县级 at County Level	残联办 Run by Disabled Persons' Federations	其他办 Run by Others
		个 unit	个 unit	个 unit	个 unit	个 unit	个 unit
全国	**Total**	**357**	**152**	**205**	**1782**	**745**	**1037**
北京	Beijing				25	1	24
天津	Tianjin				8	3	5
河北	Hebei	18	4	14	107	28	79
山西	Shanxi	11	7	4	26	15	11
内蒙古	Inner Mongolia	7	1	6	28	15	13
辽宁	Liaoning	19	11	8	49	21	28
吉林	Jilin	12	7	5	106	24	82
黑龙江	Heilongjiang	22	3	19	25	8	17
上海	Shanghai				114	8	106
江苏	Jiangsu	24	11	13	99	36	63
浙江	Zhejiang	7	7		43	28	15
安徽	Anhui	18	6	12	60	12	48
福建	Fujian	10	4	6	67	17	50
江西	Jiangxi	5	2	3	19	5	14
山东	Shandong	34	9	25	247	70	177
河南	Henan	26	8	18	50	18	32
湖北	Hubei	17	6	11	36	26	10
湖南	Hunan	15	4	11	35	18	17
广东	Guangdong	40	24	16	216	164	52
广西	Guangxi	6	2	4	18	13	5
海南	Hainan	2		2			
重庆	Chongqing				36	5	31
四川	Sichuan	13	10	3	58	42	16
贵州	Guizhou	4		4	9	2	7
云南	Yunnan	9	4	5	20	15	5
西藏	Tibet	1	1				
陕西	Shaanxi	8	3	5	145	73	72
甘肃	Gansu	8	5	3	19	14	5
青海	Qinghai	3	3		10	8	2
宁夏	Ningxia	5	5		13	11	2
新疆	Xinjiang	10	3	7	77	29	48
新疆兵团	Xinjiang Corps	1	1		1	1	
黑龙江垦区	Heilongjiang Land Reclamation	2	1	1	16	15	1

1-7 续表 2 Continued 2

地 区	Region	残联办机构在岗人员 Staff of Rehabilitation Institutions Owned by PWDs' Federations	省级 at Provincial Level	医技 Doctors and Technicians	教师 Teachers	管理 Managerial Personnels	其他 Other Staff Members
		人 person	人 person	人 person	人 person	人 person	人 person
全 国	**Total**	**9351**	**1112**	**800**	**66**	**147**	**99**
北 京	Beijing	17	15	10	3	2	
天 津	Tianjin	40	30	27		1	2
河 北	Hebei	283	4	2	1	1	
山 西	Shanxi	261	48	40	4	4	
内蒙古	Inner Mongolia	84					
辽 宁	Liaoning	194	30	15	2	2	11
吉 林	Jilin	370	40	18	2	1	19
黑龙江	Heilongjiang	113	63	63			
上 海	Shanghai	474	381	257	4	91	29
江 苏	Jiangsu	814					
浙 江	Zhejiang	754	2	2			
安 徽	Anhui	146	26	25		1	
福 建	Fujian	163	28	20	4	1	3
江 西	Jiangxi	52	24	12	8	2	2
山 东	Shandong	710					
河 南	Henan	496	27	21	3	2	1
湖 北	Hubei	372	13		12	1	
湖 南	Hunan	251	77	54	5	11	7
广 东	Guangdong	1723	13	7	5	1	
广 西	Guangxi	111	22	16		2	4
海 南	Hainan						
重 庆	Chongqing	41	9	6		1	2
四 川	Sichuan	418	12	10		2	
贵 州	Guizhou	293	7	6		1	
云 南	Yunnan	146	40	30		10	
西 藏	Tibet	31	27	15		2	10
陕 西	Shaanxi	483	117	93	12	4	8
甘 肃	Gansu	214	33	29		3	1
青 海	Qinghai	42	10	9		1	
宁 夏	Ningxia	113	14	13	1		
新 疆	Xinjiang	111					
新疆兵团	Xinjiang Corps	6					
黑龙江垦区	Heilongjiang Land Reclamation	25					

1-7 续表 3 Continued 3

地 区	Region	残联办机构在岗人员 Staff of Institutions Run by PWDs' Federations				
		地市级 at Prefectural/ City Level	医技 Doctors and Technicians	教师 Teachers	管理 Managerial Personnels	其他 Other Staff Members
		人 person	人 person	人 person	人 person	人 person
全 国	**Total**	**2829**	**1337**	**415**	**354**	**723**
北 京	Beijing					
天 津	Tianjin					
河 北	Hebei	166	99	4	13	50
山 西	Shanxi	113	54	19	13	27
内蒙古	Inner Mongolia	19	7	7	4	1
辽 宁	Liaoning	67	10	27	15	15
吉 林	Jilin	49	16	18	11	4
黑龙江	Heilongjiang	25	11	5	6	3
上 海	Shanghai					
江 苏	Jiangsu	177	59	44	27	47
浙 江	Zhejiang	367	267	5	21	74
安 徽	Anhui	85	27	23	7	28
福 建	Fujian	71	57	3	9	2
江 西	Jiangxi	7	3	1	2	1
山 东	Shandong	123	75	11	12	25
河 南	Henan	232	166	23	25	18
湖 北	Hubei	108	57	14	17	20
湖 南	Hunan	55	19	27	6	3
广 东	Guangdong	819	246	136	107	330
广 西	Guangxi	12	8		2	2
海 南	Hainan					
重 庆	Chongqing					
四 川	Sichuan	105	34	29	17	25
贵 州	Guizhou					
云 南	Yunnan	20	8	1	4	7
西 藏	Tibet	4				4
陕 西	Shaanxi	42	23		7	12
甘 肃	Gansu	104	78	1	14	11
青 海	Qinghai	9	5	1	2	1
宁 夏	Ningxia	29	5	16	6	2
新 疆	Xinjiang	12	3		4	5
新疆兵团	Xinjiang Corps	2			1	1
黑龙江垦区	Heilongjiang Land Reclamation	7			2	5

1-7 续表 4 Continued 4

地 区	Region	残联办机构在岗人员 Staff of Institutions Run by PWDs' Federations				
		县级 at County Level	医技 Doctors and Technicians	教师 Teachers	管理 Managerial Personnels	其他 Other Staff Members
		人 person	人 person	人 person	人 person	人 person
全 国	**Total**	**5410**	**2111**	**838**	**1175**	**1286**
北 京	Beijing	2	2			
天 津	Tianjin	10		2	5	3
河 北	Hebei	113	27	19	38	29
山 西	Shanxi	100	43	11	21	25
内蒙古	Inner Mongolia	65	24	12	14	15
辽 宁	Liaoning	97	9	3	51	34
吉 林	Jilin	281	71	17	48	145
黑龙江	Heilongjiang	25	4	4	11	6
上 海	Shanghai	93	59		12	22
江 苏	Jiangsu	637	317	172	73	75
浙 江	Zhejiang	385	177	28	59	121
安 徽	Anhui	35	9	8	8	10
福 建	Fujian	64	16	5	18	25
江 西	Jiangxi	21	6	5	6	4
山 东	Shandong	587	278	73	137	99
河 南	Henan	237	107	49	48	33
湖 北	Hubei	251	99	44	49	59
湖 南	Hunan	119	29	44	24	22
广 东	Guangdong	891	214	178	208	291
广 西	Guangxi	77	17	24	16	20
海 南	Hainan					
重 庆	Chongqing	32	3	16	9	4
四 川	Sichuan	301	109	45	74	73
贵 州	Guizhou	286	239		27	20
云 南	Yunnan	86	10	18	42	16
西 藏	Tibet					
陕 西	Shaanxi	324	154	21	76	73
甘 肃	Gansu	77	38	10	16	13
青 海	Qinghai	23	5	1	9	8
宁 夏	Ningxia	70	13	22	22	13
新 疆	Xinjiang	99	30	6	38	25
新疆兵团	Xinjiang Corps	4	1	1	1	1
黑龙江垦区	Heilongjiang Land Reclamation	18	1		15	2

1-8 智力残疾康复

Rehabilitation of Persons with Intellectual Disability

地 区	Region	智力残疾儿童康复训练 Children with Intellectual Disability Receiving Rehabilitation Training	机构康复训练 Trained in Institutions	社区、家庭康复训练 Trained in Communities and Families	成年智力残疾人社区、家庭康复训练 Adults with Intellectual Disability Trained in Communities and Families
		人 person	人 person	人 person	人 person
全 国	**Total**	**104275**	**30910**	**73365**	**34815**
北 京	Beijing	709	589	120	4009
天 津	Tianjin	952	198	754	119
河 北	Hebei	4726	584	4142	748
山 西	Shanxi	1972		1972	61
内蒙古	Inner Mongolia	1993	487	1506	315
辽 宁	Liaoning	3474	640	2834	1081
吉 林	Jilin	1912	362	1550	65
黑龙江	Heilongjiang	2943	838	2105	456
上 海	Shanghai	3026	1574	1452	7616
江 苏	Jiangsu	7551	3011	4540	4443
浙 江	Zhejiang	2197	838	1359	614
安 徽	Anhui	6419	1937	4482	1008
福 建	Fujian	2314	900	1414	562
江 西	Jiangxi	3030	470	2560	324
山 东	Shandong	7492	2580	4912	2417
河 南	Henan	6860	1281	5579	287
湖 北	Hubei	4588	1379	3209	893
湖 南	Hunan	6829	2759	4070	2205
广 东	Guangdong	8849	3421	5428	3444
广 西	Guangxi	3112	525	2587	304
海 南	Hainan	823	135	688	509
重 庆	Chongqing	2300	301	1999	621
四 川	Sichuan	6206	1311	4895	266
贵 州	Guizhou	931	562	369	161
云 南	Yunnan	3296	576	2720	814
西 藏	Tibet	187	10	177	18
陕 西	Shaanxi	4003	1902	2101	255
甘 肃	Gansu	2140	665	1475	85
青 海	Qinghai	471	184	287	175
宁 夏	Ningxia	805	396	409	40
新 疆	Xinjiang	1752	430	1322	335
新疆兵团	Xinjiang Corps	246	15	231	564
黑龙江垦区	Heilongjiang Land Reclamation	167	50	117	1

1-8 续表 Continued

地 区	Region	智力残疾康复、管理技术人员培训 Training for Managerial and Technical Personnel on Intellectual Disabilities Rehabilitation	国家级 at State Level	省级 at Provincial Level	地市级 at Prefectural/City Level	县级 at County Level
		人次 person-time	人次 person-time	人次 person-time	人次 person-time	人次 person-time
全 国	**Total**	**15468**	**110**	**633**	**3314**	**11411**
北 京	Beijing	1800	5	172		1623
天 津	Tianjin	97	3	8		86
河 北	Hebei	380	4	2	26	348
山 西	Shanxi	157	4	6	47	100
内蒙古	Inner Mongolia	194	3		3	188
辽 宁	Liaoning	1176	3	1	199	973
吉 林	Jilin	196	3			193
黑龙江	Heilongjiang	118	3		3	112
上 海	Shanghai	1379	3			1376
江 苏	Jiangsu	1668	4	5	364	1295
浙 江	Zhejiang	2249	3		1897	349
安 徽	Anhui	144	4	120	5	15
福 建	Fujian	311	4	200	20	87
江 西	Jiangxi	120	6		13	101
山 东	Shandong	573	3		75	495
河 南	Henan	64	4	1	22	37
湖 北	Hubei	248	4		32	212
湖 南	Hunan	243	5		105	133
广 东	Guangdong	710	4	80	166	460
广 西	Guangxi	80	4		40	36
海 南	Hainan	4	3			1
重 庆	Chongqing	471	3	33		435
四 川	Sichuan	807	4			803
贵 州	Guizhou	152	2		1	149
云 南	Yunnan	1596	3	5		1588
西 藏	Tibet	2	2			
陕 西	Shaanxi	298	4		289	5
甘 肃	Gansu	25	3			22
青 海	Qinghai	158	3		1	154
宁 夏	Ningxia	5	4			1
新 疆	Xinjiang	43	3		6	34
新疆兵团	Xinjiang Corps					
黑龙江垦区	Heilongjiang Land Reclamation					

1-9 智力残疾康复训练服务机构
Rehabilitation Institutions for Persons with Intellectual Disability

地 区	Region	机构合计 Rehabilitation Institutions for Persons with Intellectual Disability	省级 at Provincial Level	残联办 Run by Disabled Persons' Federations	其他办 Run by Others
		个 unit	个 unit	个 unit	个 unit
全 国	**Total**	**1730**	**45**	**32**	**13**
北 京	Beijing	43	1	1	
天 津	Tianjin	13	1	1	
河 北	Hebei	61	1	1	
山 西	Shanxi	38	2	2	
内蒙古	Inner Mongolia	33	1	1	
辽 宁	Liaoning	62	3	1	2
吉 林	Jilin	36	1	1	
黑龙江	Heilongjiang	47	1	1	
上 海	Shanghai	219	2	2	
江 苏	Jiangsu	96	1	1	
浙 江	Zhejiang	47	1	1	
安 徽	Anhui	75	1	1	
福 建	Fujian	61	1	1	
江 西	Jiangxi	20	1	1	
山 东	Shandong	132	1		1
河 南	Henan	57	1	1	
湖 北	Hubei	56	1	1	
湖 南	Hunan	73	1	1	
广 东	Guangdong	261	1	1	
广 西	Guangxi	24	1	1	
海 南	Hainan	9	7		7
重 庆	Chongqing	41	1	1	
四 川	Sichuan	64	1	1	
贵 州	Guizhou	17	1	1	
云 南	Yunnan	21	2	2	
西 藏	Tibet	2	1	1	
陕 西	Shaanxi	36	2	1	1
甘 肃	Gansu	28	1	1	
青 海	Qinghai	11	1	1	
宁 夏	Ningxia	19	1	1	
新 疆	Xinjiang	26	1	1	
新疆兵团	Xinjiang Corps	1	1		1
黑龙江垦区	Heilongjiang Land Reclamation	1	1		1

1-9　续表 1　Continued 1

地区	Region	机构 Intellectual Disability Rehabilitation Institutions					
		地市级 at Prefectural/ City Level	残联办 Run by PWDs' Federations	其他办 Run by Others	县级 at County Level	残联办 Run by PWDs' Federations	其他办 Run by Others
		个 unit	个 unit	个 unit	个 unit	个 unit	个 unit
全　国	**Total**	**334**	**128**	**206**	**1351**	**648**	**703**
北　京	Beijing				42	1	41
天　津	Tianjin				12	3	9
河　北	Hebei	16	5	11	44	11	33
山　西	Shanxi	10	8	2	26	9	17
内蒙古	Inner Mongolia	9	1	8	23	11	12
辽　宁	Liaoning	16	10	6	43	17	26
吉　林	Jilin	14	6	8	21	10	11
黑龙江	Heilongjiang	20	4	16	26	8	18
					217	158	59
上　海	Shanghai	11	8	3	84	25	59
江　苏	Jiangsu	7	7		39	16	23
浙　江	Zhejiang	34	5	29	40	7	33
安　徽	Anhui	7	5	2	53	11	42
福　建	Fujian	9	1	8	10	3	7
江　西	Jiangxi	21	6	15	110	24	86
山　东	Shandong	20	7	13	36	13	23
河　南	Henan	13	2	11	42	26	16
湖　北	Hubei	16	3	13	56	21	35
湖　南	Hunan	44	17	27	216	165	51
广　东	Guangdong	9	6	3	14	6	8
广　西	Guangxi	2		2			
海　南	Hainan				40	6	34
重　庆	Chongqing	10	9	1	53	35	18
四　川	Sichuan	5		5	11	1	10
贵　州	Guizhou	7	2	5	12	6	6
云　南	Yunnan	1	1				
西　藏	Tibet	5	1	4	29	15	14
陕　西	Shaanxi	12	3	9	15	8	7
甘　肃	Gansu	2	2		8	8	
青　海	Qinghai	5	5		13	11	2
宁　夏	Ningxia	9	4	5	16	13	3
新　疆	Xinjiang						
新疆兵团	Xinjiang Corps						
黑龙江垦区	Heilongjiang Land Reclamation						

1-9 续表 2 Continued 2

地 区	Region	残联办机构在岗人员 Staff of Rehabilitation Institutions Owned by PWDs' Federations	省级 at Provincial Level	医技 Doctors and Technicians	教师 Teachers	管理 Managerial Personnels	其他 Other Staff Members
		人 person	人 person	人 person	人 person	人 person	人 person
全 国	**Total**	**7323**	**517**	**179**	**229**	**55**	**54**
北 京	Beijing	15	11	5	4	2	
天 津	Tianjin	29	11		7	1	3
河 北	Hebei	196	4	1	2	1	
山 西	Shanxi	172	34	14	15	4	1
内蒙古	Inner Mongolia	70	10		9	1	
辽 宁	Liaoning	166	15	2	12	1	
吉 林	Jilin	108	14		7	1	6
黑龙江	Heilongjiang	100	11	1	8	1	1
上 海	Shanghai	678	21	15		3	3
江 苏	Jiangsu	338	15	1	12	1	1
浙 江	Zhejiang	184	2	2			
安 徽	Anhui	100	8		5	1	2
福 建	Fujian	151	2		2		
江 西	Jiangxi	85	32	12	6	2	12
山 东	Shandong	657					
河 南	Henan	526	20	4	12	1	3
湖 北	Hubei	301	18		17	1	
湖 南	Hunan	252	23	2	10	9	2
广 东	Guangdong	1618	12	3	8	1	
广 西	Guangxi	174	42	18	15	5	4
海 南	Hainan						
重 庆	Chongqing	69	6	2	3	1	
四 川	Sichuan	349	12	10		2	
贵 州	Guizhou	384	45		39	3	3
云 南	Yunnan	75	6	1	4	1	
西 藏	Tibet	6	4	1	2	1	
陕 西	Shaanxi	206	97	77	8	4	8
甘 肃	Gansu	98	28	8	11	5	4
青 海	Qinghai	35	5		3	1	1
宁 夏	Ningxia	110	2		2		
新 疆	Xinjiang	71	7		6	1	
新疆兵团	Xinjiang Corps						
黑龙江垦区	Heilongjiang Land Reclamation						

1-9　续表 3　Continued 3

地　区	Region	残联办机构在岗人员 Staff of Rehabilitation Institutions Run by PWDs' Federations				
		地市级 at Prefectural/ City Level	医技 Doctors and Technicians	教师 Teachers	管理 Managerial Personnels	其他 Other Staff Members
		人 person	人 person	人 person	人 person	人 person
全　国	**Total**	**2066**	**615**	**729**	**299**	**423**
北　京	Beijing					
天　津	Tianjin					
河　北	Hebei	114	15	43	29	27
山　西	Shanxi	83	34	24	13	12
内蒙古	Inner Mongolia	15	7	3	4	1
辽　宁	Liaoning	73	3	41	16	13
吉　林	Jilin	47	8	27	8	4
黑龙江	Heilongjiang	60	5	32	10	13
上　海	Shanghai					
江　苏	Jiangsu	135	16	67	27	25
浙　江	Zhejiang	64	5	42	5	12
安　徽	Anhui	38	6	16	5	11
福　建	Fujian	48	4	25	8	11
江　西	Jiangxi	12	2	5	2	3
山　东	Shandong	74	31	21	11	11
河　南	Henan	270	164	40	25	41
湖　北	Hubei	19	11	1	3	4
湖　南	Hunan	30	16	10	3	1
广　东	Guangdong	682	240	194	80	168
广　西	Guangxi	90	9	45	11	25
海　南	Hainan					
重　庆	Chongqing					
四　川	Sichuan	124	23	68	16	17
贵　州	Guizhou					
云　南	Yunnan	9	1	1	3	4
西　藏	Tibet	2				2
陕　西	Shaanxi	7	1		1	5
甘　肃	Gansu	21	9	2	4	6
青　海	Qinghai	4	1	1	1	1
宁　夏	Ningxia	26	1	17	6	2
新　疆	Xinjiang	19	3	4	8	4
新疆兵团	Xinjiang Corps					
黑龙江垦区	Heilongjiang Land Reclamation					

1-9 续表 4 Continued 4

地区	Region	残联办机构在岗人员 Staff of Rehabilitation Agencies Run by Disabled Persons' Federations				
		县级 at County Level	医技 Doctors and Technicians	教师 Teachers	管理 Managerial Personnels	其他 Other Staff Members
		人 person	人 person	人 person	人 person	人 person
全国	**Total**	**4740**	**1072**	**1462**	**979**	**1227**
北京	Beijing	4		3	1	
天津	Tianjin	18		9	5	4
河北	Hebei	78	13	26	18	21
山西	Shanxi	55	23	12	11	9
内蒙古	Inner Mongolia	45	14	9	12	10
辽宁	Liaoning	78	4	18	26	30
吉林	Jilin	47	7	16	15	9
黑龙江	Heilongjiang	29	3	10	7	9
上海	Shanghai	657		109	172	376
江苏	Jiangsu	188	39	84	32	33
浙江	Zhejiang	118	25	37	21	35
安徽	Anhui	54	7	31	7	9
福建	Fujian	101	26	34	28	13
江西	Jiangxi	41	10	19	5	7
山东	Shandong	583	72	355	72	84
河南	Henan	236	107	57	43	29
湖北	Hubei	264	66	69	64	65
湖南	Hunan	199	48	86	27	38
广东	Guangdong	924	185	245	200	294
广西	Guangxi	42	8	24	6	4
海南	Hainan					
重庆	Chongqing	63	1	43	14	5
四川	Sichuan	213	46	72	59	36
贵州	Guizhou	339	283		26	30
云南	Yunnan	60	1	19	31	9
西藏	Tibet					
陕西	Shaanxi	102	43	11	21	27
甘肃	Gansu	49	17	13	10	9
青海	Qinghai	26	3	7	9	7
宁夏	Ningxia	82	10	31	22	19
新疆	Xinjiang	45	11	13	15	6
新疆兵团	Xinjiang Corps					
黑龙江垦区	Heilongjiang Land Reclamation					

1-10 精神病防治康复

Prevention and Rehabilitation of Mental Illness

地 区	Region	开展精防康复工作县(市、区) Counties/Cities/Districts where Prevention and Rehabilitation of Mental Illness have been Conducted	精神病人 People with Mental Illness	监护病人 People with Mental Illness under Guardianship	监护率 Guardian-ship Rate
		个 unit	万人 10,000 persons	万人 10,000 persons	%
全 国	**Total**	**2664**	**583.7**	**463.5**	**79.4**
北 京	Beijing	16	7.3	6.5	88.7
天 津	Tianjin	16	7.3	6.8	94.4
河 北	Hebei	169	24.9	21.6	86.9
山 西	Shanxi	65	9.9	8.2	82.6
内蒙古	Inner Mongolia	98	6.8	5.4	80.5
辽 宁	Liaoning	107	27.0	24.1	89.2
吉 林	Jilin	69	16.2	15.7	96.8
黑龙江	Heilongjiang	125	18.2	14.7	80.7
上 海	Shanghai	17	11.4	11.2	98.9
江 苏	Jiangsu	103	52.0	41.4	79.7
浙 江	Zhejiang	77	18.7	17.2	91.8
安 徽	Anhui	94	28.1	23.5	83.7
福 建	Fujian	84	12.1	10.4	86.0
江 西	Jiangxi	101	18.4	14.7	80.3
山 东	Shandong	134	37.4	31.4	83.9
河 南	Henan	156	43.7	21.4	49.1
湖 北	Hubei	93	34.7	22.8	65.5
湖 南	Hunan	120	34.1	32.3	94.5
广 东	Guangdong	130	37.9	31.0	81.6
广 西	Guangxi	94	12.6	10.0	79.5
海 南	Hainan	18	1.8	1.2	65.4
重 庆	Chongqing	40	18.1	14.6	80.7
四 川	Sichuan	145	40.8	31.8	78.1
贵 州	Guizhou	85	7.9	6.7	85.3
云 南	Yunnan	123	15.3	10.3	67.1
西 藏	Tibet	1	0.0	0.0	77.0
陕 西	Shaanxi	110	20.5	11.7	57.4
甘 肃	Gansu	62	12.1	10.4	85.7
青 海	Qinghai	34	0.4	0.3	65.2
宁 夏	Ningxia	21	3.4	3.1	91.0
新 疆	Xinjiang	69	2.3	1.6	68.7
新疆兵团	Xinjiang Corps	6	1.0	0.7	73.3
黑龙江垦区	Heilongjiang Land Reclamation	82	1.5	0.7	45.3

1-10 续表 1 Continued 1

地 区	Region	显好病人 People with Mental Illness who have gotten Effective Treatment	显好率 Significant Improvement Rate	参与社会总人数 People with Mental Illness who have Participated into Social Life after Rehabilitation	参与率 Social Involvement Rate	肇事人次 People with Mental Illness who Caused Serious Troubles	肇事率 Violent Events Rate
		万人 10,000 persons	%	万人 10,000 persons	%	人次 person-time	%
全 国	**Total**	**307.1**	**66.2**	**239.8**	**51.7**	**7250**	**0.16**
北 京	Beijing	4.6	70.7	3.4	52.8	8	0.01
天 津	Tianjin	5.2	76.2	4.6	67.5	36	0.05
河 北	Hebei	14.3	66.0	11.3	52.3	95	0.04
山 西	Shanxi	5.7	70.3	4.2	51.9	29	0.04
内蒙古	Inner Mongolia	3.3	61.0	2.8	51.5	130	0.24
辽 宁	Liaoning	16.0	66.1	12.4	51.3	17	0.01
吉 林	Jilin	11.0	69.7	9.1	57.6	43	0.03
黑龙江	Heilongjiang	9.4	63.9	5.8	39.8	52	0.04
上 海	Shanghai	11.1	98.7	9.7	86.6	3	0.00
江 苏	Jiangsu	31.2	75.3	26.5	63.8	36	0.01
浙 江	Zhejiang	12.7	73.9	10.6	61.6	628	0.37
安 徽	Anhui	13.8	58.6	11.1	47.3	58	0.02
福 建	Fujian	7.6	72.8	5.6	53.7	93	0.09
江 西	Jiangxi	8.4	57.0	6.2	42.3	1949	1.32
山 东	Shandong	23.6	75.0	19.7	62.8	105	0.03
河 南	Henan	10.7	49.8	7.9	36.7	458	0.21
湖 北	Hubei	14.2	62.2	10.9	47.8	386	0.17
湖 南	Hunan	15.9	49.2	11.8	36.7	181	0.06
广 东	Guangdong	20.4	66.0	16.0	51.7	219	0.07
广 西	Guangxi	6.4	63.5	5.2	52.1	462	0.46
海 南	Hainan	0.2	18.4	0.2	13.3	5	0.04
重 庆	Chongqing	11.9	81.5	9.4	64.8	218	0.15
四 川	Sichuan	19.8	62.3	11.3	35.6	1319	0.41
贵 州	Guizhou	4.6	67.9	3.8	56.4	193	0.29
云 南	Yunnan	6.4	61.9	5.1	49.8	200	0.19
西 藏	Tibet	0.0	93.5				
陕 西	Shaanxi	7.9	67.1	6.6	56.2	136	0.12
甘 肃	Gansu	7.3	69.9	5.6	54.3	59	0.06
青 海	Qinghai	0.1	45.9	0.1	28.4	5	0.20
宁 夏	Ningxia	2.2	70.6	1.8	58.5	113	0.37
新 疆	Xinjiang	0.8	47.5	0.5	29.0	5	0.03
新疆兵团	Xinjiang Corps	0.5	67.2	0.4	52.2	9	0.13
黑龙江垦区	Heilongjiang Land Reclamation	0.2	36.1	0.1	11.9		

1-10　续表 2　Continued 2

地　区	Region	接受治疗的精神病患者 People with Mental Illness who have gotten Medical Treatment	接受康复训练 People with Mental Illness who have gotten Rehabilitation Training	精神康复机构 Rehabilitation Institutions for People with Mental Illness	精神病人 People with Mental Illness who have gotten Rehabilitation Training in Those Institutions
		人 person	人 person	个 unit	人 person
全　国	**Total**	**1855943**	**1023270**	**2178**	**524573**
北　京	Beijing	30903	14497	18	4640
天　津	Tianjin	12360	8721	13	2876
河　北	Hebei	89453	56300	83	7958
山　西	Shanxi	27053	13137	58	16953
内蒙古	Inner Mongolia	18110	7477	27	1668
辽　宁	Liaoning	58600	35806	151	20367
吉　林	Jilin	35222	41232	56	12429
黑龙江	Heilongjiang	22567	7246	39	5067
上　海	Shanghai	65484	21599	193	5245
江　苏	Jiangsu	174491	132568	108	40851
浙　江	Zhejiang	103088	71929	42	11219
安　徽	Anhui	93594	32740	45	7237
福　建	Fujian	55200	38899	55	14248
江　西	Jiangxi	67091	32372	81	29540
山　东	Shandong	197593	108178	234	46563
河　南	Henan	87582	63424	95	32585
湖　北	Hubei	112584	52168	93	49930
湖　南	Hunan	108375	52140	92	19517
广　东	Guangdong	126641	71020	299	56382
广　西	Guangxi	69914	19888	30	17695
海　南	Hainan	3449	667	2	250
重　庆	Chongqing	99539	52006	41	18947
四　川	Sichuan	78258	36510	108	41009
贵　州	Guizhou	14262	12944	32	5857
云　南	Yunnan	31184	8977	44	20345
西　藏	Tibet			1	5
陕　西	Shaanxi	41588	20723	62	24638
甘　肃	Gansu	14343	3394	31	2045
青　海	Qinghai	649	71	4	58
宁　夏	Ningxia	6364	2616	6	1517
新　疆	Xinjiang	4794	2308	27	4260
新疆兵团	Xinjiang Corps	3070	1713	6	2149
黑龙江垦区	Heilongjiang Land Reclamation	2538		2	523

1-10 续表 3 Continued 3

地 区	Region	贫困患者 People with Mental Illness Living in Poverty	接受医疗救助的贫困患者 Those who have gotten Medical Assistance	接受国家专项彩金免费服药项目医疗救助的贫困患者 Poor Patients who Received Free Medicines Funded by National Lottery Medical Assistance Project	接受国家专项彩金免费住院项目医疗救助的贫困患者 Poor Patients who Received Free Treatment in Hospital Funded by National Lottery Medical Assistance Project	接受其他项目医疗救助的贫困患者 Poor Patients who Received Medical Assistance Funded by Other Projects
		人 person	人 person	人 person	人 person	人 person
全 国	**Total**	**1406729**	**491919**	**149063**	**25589**	**317267**
北 京	Beijing	11234	7684			7684
天 津	Tianjin	7802	4324			4324
河 北	Hebei	24644	9246	5074	1008	3164
山 西	Shanxi	17733	6623	4922	603	1098
内蒙古	Inner Mongolia	21890	3231	2380	409	442
辽 宁	Liaoning	73414	23787	5086	837	17864
吉 林	Jilin	53871	17812	6160	1520	10132
黑龙江	Heilongjiang	25744	5687	4438	727	522
上 海	Shanghai	13915	13063	46		13017
江 苏	Jiangsu	90450	42089	5000	1060	36029
浙 江	Zhejiang	31291	20608	1888	240	18480
安 徽	Anhui	103674	73549	10453	1148	61948
福 建	Fujian	40810	11847	5310	652	5885
江 西	Jiangxi	77124	20737	6761	527	13449
山 东	Shandong	88968	28504	9773	1786	16945
河 南	Henan	51333	16830	6480	1500	8850
湖 北	Hubei	83983	17758	11712	1284	4762
湖 南	Hunan	73275	11892	4800	1000	6092
广 东	Guangdong	112400	49469	5878	903	42688
广 西	Guangxi	62295	11642	8068	1315	2259
海 南	Hainan	5953	3035	2318	463	254
重 庆	Chongqing	68766	14446	4540	604	9302
四 川	Sichuan	103661	21983	8335	1447	12201
贵 州	Guizhou	19325	5774	2814	1169	1791
云 南	Yunnan	45300	15204	6093	1876	7235
西 藏	Tibet	30				
陕 西	Shaanxi	47876	16763	8343	1542	6878
甘 肃	Gansu	21925	3263	2484	519	260
青 海	Qinghai	1914	1635	1034	306	295
宁 夏	Ningxia	11456	5397	4832	560	5
新 疆	Xinjiang	7477	5436	2726	419	2291
新疆兵团	Xinjiang Corps	3027	2139	853	165	1121
黑龙江垦区	Heilongjiang Land Reclamation	4169	462	462		

1-10 续表 4 Continued 4

地 区	Region	发现关锁病人 People with Mental Illness who were Found being Locked-up	解除关锁病人 Freed from Locked-up	培训精防康复管理、技术人员 Trained Managerial Personnels and Technicians of Prevention and Rehabilitation
		人 person	人 person	人 person
全 国	**Total**	**5860**	**4123**	**41862**
北 京	Beijing			1181
天 津	Tianjin			1133
河 北	Hebei	212	86	1997
山 西	Shanxi	402	206	235
内蒙古	Inner Mongolia	91	54	108
辽 宁	Liaoning	79	65	1229
吉 林	Jilin	8	4	1108
黑龙江	Heilongjiang	19	6	55
上 海	Shanghai	44	44	9010
江 苏	Jiangsu	36	35	3523
浙 江	Zhejiang	55	42	6441
安 徽	Anhui	31	26	350
福 建	Fujian	147	64	671
江 西	Jiangxi	306	226	287
山 东	Shandong	118	51	4645
河 南	Henan	834	612	234
湖 北	Hubei	359	222	587
湖 南	Hunan	331	269	612
广 东	Guangdong	878	722	4320
广 西	Guangxi	92	29	239
海 南	Hainan	175	25	
重 庆	Chongqing	68	52	1749
四 川	Sichuan	946	862	981
贵 州	Guizhou	258	234	174
云 南	Yunnan	79	43	643
西 藏	Tibet			
陕 西	Shaanxi	131	86	212
甘 肃	Gansu	92	21	10
青 海	Qinghai	2	2	33
宁 夏	Ningxia	19	17	24
新 疆	Xinjiang	48	18	24
新疆兵团	Xinjiang Corps			47
黑龙江垦区	Heilongjiang Land Reclamation			

1-11 孤独症儿童康复训练

Rehabilitation Training for Children with Autism

地区	Region	孤独症儿童康复训练机构 Rehabilitation Institutions for Children with Autism	省级机构 at Provincial Level	地市级及以下其他机构 at Prefectural/City Level and Lower	机构内教师 Teachers Working in Those Institutions	省级机构内教师 at Provincial Level	地市级及以下其他机构内教师 at Prefectural/City Level and Lower
		个 unit	个 unit	个 unit	人 person	人 person	人 person
全国	**Total**	**1345**	**41**	**1304**	**9534**	**467**	**9067**
北京	Beijing	26	1	25	306	27	279
天津	Tianjin	21	2	19	353	16	337
河北	Hebei	40	1	39	167	1	166
山西	Shanxi	16	2	14	99	16	83
内蒙古	Inner Mongolia	42	1	41	214	9	205
辽宁	Liaoning	49	1	48	270	35	235
吉林	Jilin	45	1	44	440	23	417
黑龙江	Heilongjiang	45	1	44	318	15	303
上海	Shanghai	33	1	32	195	7	188
江苏	Jiangsu	94	1	93	617	5	612
浙江	Zhejiang	67	1	66	372	10	362
安徽	Anhui	78	1	77	542	7	535
福建	Fujian	63	1	62	472	24	448
江西	Jiangxi	28	1	27	116	6	110
山东	Shandong	126	1	125	1235	10	1225
河南	Henan	108	1	107	472	12	460
湖北	Hubei	37	1	36	352	17	335
湖南	Hunan	57	1	56	338	12	326
广东	Guangdong	123	1	122	1280	7	1273
广西	Guangxi	19	1	18	197	13	184
海南	Hainan	7	6	1	100	92	8
重庆	Chongqing	20	1	19	197	3	194
四川	Sichuan	60	1	59	206	5	201
贵州	Guizhou	26	1	25	180	39	141
云南	Yunnan	31	1	30	166	8	158
西藏	Tibet	1	1		2	2	
陕西	Shaanxi	24	2	22	133	14	119
甘肃	Gansu	23	1	22	25	10	15
青海	Qinghai	11	1	10	20	3	17
宁夏	Ningxia	18	1	17	70	12	58
新疆	Xinjiang	4	1	3	76	5	71
新疆兵团	Xinjiang Corps	1	1		1	1	
黑龙江垦区	Heilongjiang Land Reclamation	2	1	1	3	1	2

1-11 续表 1 Continued 1

地 区	Region	机构内在训儿童 Children with Autism Trained in Those Institutions	省级机构在训儿童 at Provincial Level	地市级及以下其他机构在训儿童 at City Level and Lower	贫困孤独症儿童救助 Poor Children with Autism Supported
		人 person	人 person	人 person	人 person
全 国	**Total**	**19727**	**2105**	**17622**	**9413**
北 京	Beijing	426	128	298	107
天 津	Tianjin	386	79	307	253
河 北	Hebei	495	10	485	197
山 西	Shanxi	311	58	253	299
内蒙古	Inner Mongolia	516	25	491	436
辽 宁	Liaoning	580	125	455	368
吉 林	Jilin	567	82	485	537
黑龙江	Heilongjiang	516	63	453	255
上 海	Shanghai	445	8	437	340
江 苏	Jiangsu	1323	20	1303	605
浙 江	Zhejiang	471		471	233
安 徽	Anhui	1070	42	1028	535
福 建	Fujian	1164	36	1128	407
江 西	Jiangxi	395	65	330	81
山 东	Shandong	1678	35	1643	611
河 南	Henan	1193	120	1073	407
湖 北	Hubei	820	156	664	290
湖 南	Hunan	563	58	505	528
广 东	Guangdong	3559	43	3516	1904
广 西	Guangxi	289	30	259	107
海 南	Hainan	172	160	12	22
重 庆	Chongqing	392	55	337	360
四 川	Sichuan	557	171	386	101
贵 州	Guizhou	308	52	256	146
云 南	Yunnan	87	1	86	135
西 藏	Tibet				
陕 西	Shaanxi	459	265	194	18
甘 肃	Gansu	194	69	125	64
青 海	Qinghai	161	52	109	8
宁 夏	Ningxia	160	50	110	56
新 疆	Xinjiang	465	45	420	3
新疆兵团	Xinjiang Corps				
黑龙江垦区	Heilongjiang Land Reclamation	5	2	3	

1-11 续表 2 Continued 2

地 区	Region	儿童训练后走向 Directions in which Children have gone After Rehabilitation					
		省级 at Provincial Level			地市级及以下 at Prefectural/ City Level and Lower		
		普幼及普小 Ordinary Kindergartens or Primary Schools	特殊教育学校 Special Education Schools	其他 Other Directions	普幼及普小 Ordinary Kindergartens or Primary Schools	特殊教育学校 Special Education Schools	其他 Other Directions
		人 person	人 person	人 person	人 person	人 person	人 person
全 国	**Total**	**172**	**30**	**155**	**1124**	**666**	**1587**
北 京	Beijing	14		26	46	19	13
天 津	Tianjin				32	7	10
河 北	Hebei	1			20	1	21
山 西	Shanxi	1		15	8	2	36
内蒙古	Inner Mongolia	25			46	14	82
辽 宁	Liaoning				8	32	19
吉 林	Jilin				62	18	28
黑龙江	Heilongjiang	3		7	32	2	6
上 海	Shanghai	8			30	101	78
江 苏	Jiangsu	1	3	1	77	54	23
浙 江	Zhejiang				16	26	25
安 徽	Anhui	2			72	34	23
福 建	Fujian				50	4	159
江 西	Jiangxi		20		25	5	27
山 东	Shandong	7	2	1	60	172	119
河 南	Henan	13		16	153	37	323
湖 北	Hubei				17	3	94
湖 南	Hunan	4		2	44	23	56
广 东	Guangdong	5	1	8	238	35	173
广 西	Guangxi	6		2		9	48
海 南	Hainan	1		6			
重 庆	Chongqing	27		2	20	1	11
四 川	Sichuan	53			19	26	42
贵 州	Guizhou				24	5	106
云 南	Yunnan			1		10	22
西 藏	Tibet						
陕 西	Shaanxi	1	2		5	1	9
甘 肃	Gansu			16	5	4	10
青 海	Qinghai			52	4	1	22
宁 夏	Ningxia				11	19	
新 疆	Xinjiang						1
新疆兵团	Xinjiang Corps						
黑龙江垦区	Heilongjiang Land Reclamation		2			1	1

1-12　辅助器具供应服务

Provision of Assistive Devices

地　区	Region	辅助器具供应 Assistive Devices Provided	辅助器具供应品种 Categories of Assistive Devices Provided	矫形器装配 Orthotic Devices Fitted	国家彩金项目装配 Fitted for PWDs by the National	上肢矫形器 Orthoses for Upper Limbs	脊柱矫形器 Orthoses for Spinal Cord	下肢矫形器 Orthoses for Lower Limbs
		件 piece	种 category	例 case	例 case	例 case	例 case	例 case
全　国	**Total**	**1524223**	**1116**	**64226**	**12442**	**527**	**342**	**11573**
北　京	Beijing	18406	42	89				
天　津	Tianjin	33827	116	167	143	6	1	136
河　北	Hebei	38115	60	917	843	13	2	828
山　西	Shanxi	22875	220	280	176	1	66	109
内蒙古	Inner Mongolia	18325	31	173	153	9	1	143
辽　宁	Liaoning	87128	414	730	498	4		494
吉　林	Jilin	102515	40	223	198	8	6	184
黑龙江	Heilongjiang	27125	228	317	307	9	19	279
上　海	Shanghai	231799	500	45926				
江　苏	Jiangsu	114792	250	1917	1076	20	5	1051
浙　江	Zhejiang	28003	326	123	11			11
安　徽	Anhui	28797	48	1039	794	35	8	751
福　建	Fujian	21006	54	301	236	11	7	218
江　西	Jiangxi	17874	240	146	99	15	7	77
山　东	Shandong	87171	697	589	425	4	7	414
河　南	Henan	108598	140	739	696		2	694
湖　北	Hubei	32002	248	735	564	16	53	495
湖　南	Hunan	64414	280	1097	865	87	51	727
广　东	Guangdong	71637	720	4094	2019	15		2004
广　西	Guangxi	20458	90	205	171	5	5	161
海　南	Hainan	9014	36	233	233	42	12	179
重　庆	Chongqing	16675	1116	378	173	3	2	168
四　川	Sichuan	92843	500	571	290	98	30	162
贵　州	Guizhou	19118	155	439	368	8	3	357
云　南	Yunnan	50938	170	871	660	22	9	629
西　藏	Tibet	1727	30	96	43		5	38
陕　西	Shaanxi	60073	202	177	157			157
甘　肃	Gansu	26311	52	282	237	30	20	187
青　海	Qinghai	23505	78	587	507	18	12	477
宁　夏	Ningxia	10815	52	297	190		1	189
新　疆	Xinjiang	32772	131	337	242	47	8	187
新疆兵团	Xinjiang Corps	3384	27	50	50			50
黑龙江垦区	Heilongjiang Land Reclamation	2181	15	101	18	1		17

1－12　续表 1　Continued 1

地 区	Region	假肢装配 Artificial Limbs Fitted	国家彩金项目装配 Fitted for PWDs by the National Lottery Project	大腿 Upper-knee Artificial Limbs Fitted	小腿 Lower-knee Artificial Limbs Fitted
		例 case	例 case	例 case	例 case
全　国	**Total**	**28644**	**15203**	**5724**	**6773**
北　京	Beijing	245	87	29	34
天　津	Tianjin	325	95	22	20
河　北	Hebei	1106	898	319	409
山　西	Shanxi	436	259	59	68
内蒙古	Inner Mongolia	709	276	96	130
辽　宁	Liaoning	2514	715	247	246
吉　林	Jilin	397	380	100	100
黑龙江	Heilongjiang	458	216	82	102
上　海	Shanghai	875			
江　苏	Jiangsu	1475	838	324	393
浙　江	Zhejiang	1206	180	79	92
安　徽	Anhui	742	665	219	208
福　建	Fujian	436	289	117	90
江　西	Jiangxi	926	256	128	117
山　东	Shandong	1057	578	223	308
河　南	Henan	1888	1624	724	659
湖　北	Hubei	1597	926	374	521
湖　南	Hunan	1767	691	232	253
广　东	Guangdong	1600	878	302	440
广　西	Guangxi	941	656	327	293
海　南	Hainan	62	29	15	7
重　庆	Chongqing	240	179	66	49
四　川	Sichuan	1513	497	219	222
贵　州	Guizhou	654	528	206	260
云　南	Yunnan	1443	1047	396	590
西　藏	Tibet	56	30	8	18
陕　西	Shaanxi	1276	902	331	404
甘　肃	Gansu	1059	344	128	152
青　海	Qinghai	448	361	76	190
宁　夏	Ningxia	298	275	100	158
新　疆	Xinjiang	607	362	125	156
新疆兵团	Xinjiang Corps	127	127	49	73
黑龙江垦区	Heilongjiang Land Reclamation	161	15	2	11

1-12 续表 2 Continued 2

地 区	Region	膝离断 Knee From off	髋离断 Hip From off	功能性上肢 Functional Upper Limbs	装饰假手 Artificial Hands for Decoration Purpose
		例 case	例 case	例 case	例 case
全 国	**Total**	**703**	**414**	**473**	**1116**
北 京	Beijing			24	
天 津	Tianjin	16	16		21
河 北	Hebei	32	19	36	83
山 西	Shanxi	35	26	40	31
内蒙古	Inner Mongolia	16	17	16	1
辽 宁	Liaoning	11	8	72	131
吉 林	Jilin	42	37	54	47
黑龙江	Heilongjiang	13	3	4	12
上 海	Shanghai				
江 苏	Jiangsu	16	11	14	80
浙 江	Zhejiang	4	5		
安 徽	Anhui	77	30	36	95
福 建	Fujian	8	10	3	61
江 西	Jiangxi	1	1	3	6
山 东	Shandong	21	24	2	
河 南	Henan	64	43	73	61
湖 北	Hubei	7	5	4	15
湖 南	Hunan	64	43	31	68
广 东	Guangdong	7	11	1	117
广 西	Guangxi	7	6	6	17
海 南	Hainan	6	1		
重 庆	Chongqing	47	13		4
四 川	Sichuan	29	24	1	2
贵 州	Guizhou	43	12	7	
云 南	Yunnan	23	2	5	31
西 藏	Tibet		2		2
陕 西	Shaanxi	48	15	6	98
甘 肃	Gansu	16	6	21	21
青 海	Qinghai	38	6	6	45
宁 夏	Ningxia	8	9		
新 疆	Xinjiang	3	5	8	65
新疆兵团	Xinjiang Corps	1	4		
黑龙江垦区	Heilongjiang Land Reclamation				2

1-12 续表 3 Continued 3

地 区	Region	其他辅助器具供应 Other Assistive Devices Provided	国家彩金项目免费发放 Assistive Devices Provided to PWDs by the National Lottery Project	助视器 Vision-Aids	免费发放 Free of Charge	重度残疾人适配 Fitted for PWDs with Severe Disabilities	就学、就业适配 Fitted for PWDs of Schooling and Employment
		件 piece	件 piece	件 piece	件 piece	件 piece	件 piece
全 国	**Total**	**1431353**	**365136**	**177779**	**126375**	**56478**	**4504**
北 京	Beijing	18072	4900	1637		2990	273
天 津	Tianjin	33335	6465	3993	704	1638	130
河 北	Hebei	36092	25726	11906	10843	1837	1140
山 西	Shanxi	22159	8327	4881	1997	1400	49
内蒙古	Inner Mongolia	17443	6275	3086	2871	314	4
辽 宁	Liaoning	83884	28773	7879	3926	16759	209
吉 林	Jilin	101895	7483	4572	1105	1642	164
黑龙江	Heilongjiang	26350	21123	16292	4421	404	6
上 海	Shanghai	184998					
江 苏	Jiangsu	111400	16031	8134	6140	1672	85
浙 江	Zhejiang	26674	3352	973	2164	201	14
安 徽	Anhui	27016	17724	11700	3896	1937	191
福 建	Fujian	20269	3480	831	1785	854	10
江 西	Jiangxi	16802	7497	3666	3188	535	108
山 东	Shandong	85525	17043	9151	6945	901	46
河 南	Henan	105971	16617	8935	6931		751
湖 北	Hubei	29670	15129	5651	8108	1103	267
湖 南	Hunan	61550	16818	6230	8268	2155	165
广 东	Guangdong	65943	9624	5040	2337	2215	32
广 西	Guangxi	19312	14747	8748	2632	3273	94
海 南	Hainan	8719	2762	1053	1150	404	155
重 庆	Chongqing	16057	5196	2720	2476		
四 川	Sichuan	90759	12634	4765	6777	1053	39
贵 州	Guizhou	18025	6751	3671	2624	406	50
云 南	Yunnan	48624	22199	12998	7610	1478	113
西 藏	Tibet	1575	1380	18	756	606	
陕 西	Shaanxi	58620	25662	11021	6757	7797	87
甘 肃	Gansu	24970	7483	3838	2727	733	185
青 海	Qinghai	22470	6610	2155	3758	693	4
宁 夏	Ningxia	10220	4485	3026	1395	64	
新 疆	Xinjiang	31828	20015	8101	10566	1222	126
新疆兵团	Xinjiang Corps	3207	1334	858	284	185	7
黑龙江垦区	Heilongjiang Land Reclamation	1919	1491	250	1234	7	

1-13 辅助器具供应服务机构
Assistive Devices Provision and Service Centers

地 区	Region	地市级机构 Assistive Devices Provision and Service Centers at Prefectural/city Level	本年度新建 Established in 2014	县级机构 Assistive Devices Provision and Service Centers at County Level	本年度新建 Established in 2014
		个 unit	个 unit	个 unit	个 unit
全 国	**Total**	**220**	**19**	**945**	**129**
北 京	Beijing			10	3
天 津	Tianjin			12	1
河 北	Hebei	11		52	
山 西	Shanxi	7	1	34	
内蒙古	Inner Mongolia	7	1	25	5
辽 宁	Liaoning	14		94	5
吉 林	Jilin	8		33	
黑龙江	Heilongjiang	5		11	2
上 海	Shanghai			17	1
江 苏	Jiangsu	11	1	49	5
浙 江	Zhejiang	7		37	9
安 徽	Anhui	6	1	7	3
福 建	Fujian	9	1	33	4
江 西	Jiangxi	5		16	
山 东	Shandong	15		66	10
河 南	Henan	14	2	38	9
湖 北	Hubei	9	2	32	11
湖 南	Hunan	14	1	84	7
广 东	Guangdong	19		61	4
广 西	Guangxi	7	1	12	2
海 南	Hainan			1	
重 庆	Chongqing			30	4
四 川	Sichuan	8	1	25	5
贵 州	Guizhou	2	1	10	2
云 南	Yunnan	11	1	39	9
西 藏	Tibet	1			
陕 西	Shaanxi	9	2	24	10
甘 肃	Gansu	7		56	6
青 海	Qinghai	3		9	5
宁 夏	Ningxia	2	1	3	1
新 疆	Xinjiang	6	2	22	6
新疆兵团	Xinjiang Corps	2			
黑龙江垦区	Heilongjiang Land Reclamation	1		3	

1-14 儿童残疾预防
Disability Prevention for Children

地 区	Region	残疾儿童筛查 Screening for Children with Disabilities						
		开展残疾儿童筛查工作县 Counties Which has Developed the Screening for Children with Disabilities	开展残疾儿童筛查工作的医疗卫生机构 Medical Care Institutions Which has Developed the Screening for Children with	省级 at Provincial Level	地市级 at Prefectural/ City Level	县级 at County Level	本年度新诊断0-6岁残疾儿童 Children with Disabilities Newly Diagnosed from 0-6 Years Old in 2014	视力残疾儿童 Children with Visual Disability
		个 unit	个 unit	个 unit	个 unit	个 unit	人 person	人 person
全 国	**Total**	**1662**	**1958**	**16**	**144**	**1798**	**48397**	**4982**
北 京	Beijing	16	27			27	418	12
天 津	Tianjin	16	22	1		21	675	59
河 北	Hebei	38	39		2	37	858	64
山 西	Shanxi	88	107	8	15	84	935	84
内蒙古	Inner Mongolia	102	37			37	760	64
辽 宁	Liaoning	52	26		11	15	1140	51
吉 林	Jilin	26	26		7	19	644	116
黑龙江	Heilongjiang	56	31	1	2	28	654	44
上 海	Shanghai	17	247	2		245	1327	464
江 苏	Jiangsu	103	129		3	126	4598	990
浙 江	Zhejiang	50	120		3	117	990	18
安 徽	Anhui	73	40		4	36	3524	207
福 建	Fujian	19	17		2	15	1262	23
江 西	Jiangxi	28	41			41	2653	920
山 东	Shandong	111	139		1	138	4028	175
河 南	Henan	13	5			5	477	25
湖 北	Hubei	53	74		10	64	1986	64
湖 南	Hunan	66	60		9	51	3689	508
广 东	Guangdong	56	163		41	122	3786	130
广 西	Guangxi	53	138		7	131	1951	63
海 南	Hainan	3	4	4			333	32
重 庆	Chongqing	40	123			123	2086	65
四 川	Sichuan	78	90		1	89	4587	409
贵 州	Guizhou	22	8		2	6	580	48
云 南	Yunnan	81	56		1	55	1561	121
西 藏	Tibet	3	14			14	116	8
陕 西	Shaanxi	27	25		3	22	979	103
甘 肃	Gansu	76	43			43	657	56
青 海	Qinghai	21	30		1	29	421	29
宁 夏	Ningxia	11	10		1	9	400	10
新 疆	Xinjiang	17	11			11	277	18
新疆兵团	Xinjiang Corps	144	49		11	38	44	2
黑龙江垦区	Heilongjiang Land Reclamation	103	7		7		1	

1-14 续表 1 Continued 1

地 区	Region	本年度新诊断0-6岁残疾儿童 Children with Disabilities Newly Diagnosed from 0-6 Years Old in 2014					
		听力残疾儿童 Children with Hearing Disability	言语残疾儿童 Children with Speech Disability	肢体残疾儿童 Children with Physical Disability	智力残疾儿童 Children with Intellectual Disability	精神残疾儿童 Children with Psychiatric Disability	多重残疾儿童 Children with Multiple Disability
		人 person	人 person	人 person	人 person	人 person	人 person
全 国	**Total**	**6797**	**3225**	**14601**	**9738**	**3893**	**5161**
北 京	Beijing	89	7	86	133	62	29
天 津	Tianjin	264	11	201	101	33	6
河 北	Hebei	138	59	317	148	32	100
山 西	Shanxi	149	93	313	152	30	114
内蒙古	Inner Mongolia	98	64	166	173	104	91
辽 宁	Liaoning	262	28	311	217	231	40
吉 林	Jilin	135	61	196	77	33	26
黑龙江	Heilongjiang	86	35	201	151	92	45
上 海	Shanghai	76	12	548	86	128	13
江 苏	Jiangsu	598	152	890	451	402	1115
浙 江	Zhejiang	210	43	262	280	88	89
安 徽	Anhui	615	349	1128	628	284	313
福 建	Fujian	165	48	386	446	83	111
江 西	Jiangxi	280	298	419	408	99	229
山 东	Shandong	536	187	1354	966	357	453
河 南	Henan	61	27	169	121	10	64
湖 北	Hubei	291	134	864	296	166	171
湖 南	Hunan	491	314	950	806	238	382
广 东	Guangdong	407	199	1282	771	566	431
广 西	Guangxi	383	97	587	452	111	258
海 南	Hainan	50	29	86	69	36	31
重 庆	Chongqing	214	116	850	525	151	165
四 川	Sichuan	553	408	1432	1101	345	339
贵 州	Guizhou	63	42	174	158	29	66
云 南	Yunnan	201	147	606	243	32	211
西 藏	Tibet	2	8	77	13	2	6
陕 西	Shaanxi	187	126	207	218	51	87
甘 肃	Gansu	82	57	184	135	29	114
青 海	Qinghai	52	38	189	88	10	15
宁 夏	Ningxia	35	24	56	190	49	36
新 疆	Xinjiang	19	12	96	114	7	11
新疆兵团	Xinjiang Corps	5		13	21	3	
黑龙江垦区	Heilongjiang Land Reclamation			1			

1-14 续表 2 Continued 2

地 区	Region	儿童残疾预防宣传 Prevention of Children with Disability		残疾儿童家长学校 Schools for Training Parents of Children with Disabilities			
		发放儿童残疾预防宣传材料 Distributed Advocacy Materials	举办儿童残疾预防宣传活动 Advocacy Activities Holded	残疾儿童家长学校累计数 Total	省级 at Provincial Level	地市级 at Prefectural/ City Level	县级 at County Level
		份 piece	次 time	个 unit	个 unit	个 unit	个 unit
全 国	**Total**	**2782197**	**4890**	**1547**	**30**	**182**	**1335**
北 京	Beijing	46786	61	56	1		55
天 津	Tianjin	20082	38	7	4		3
河 北	Hebei	118061	155	53	1	10	42
山 西	Shanxi	63215	73	61	3	16	42
内蒙古	Inner Mongolia	12124	44	41	1	26	14
辽 宁	Liaoning	39037	63	33	2	16	15
吉 林	Jilin	12825	36	26	2	8	16
黑龙江	Heilongjiang	33285	60	10		1	9
上 海	Shanghai	172539	335	103	3		100
江 苏	Jiangsu	204938	291	62	1	3	58
浙 江	Zhejiang	84407	157	84	2	6	76
安 徽	Anhui	149513	193	92	1	31	60
福 建	Fujian	55920	98	15			15
江 西	Jiangxi	61627	29	6			6
山 东	Shandong	264571	177	98		13	85
河 南	Henan	8600	9	3		1	2
湖 北	Hubei	92586	77	9			9
湖 南	Hunan	98286	109	61		13	48
广 东	Guangdong	81887	178	56	1	28	27
广 西	Guangxi	120173	70	6		1	5
海 南	Hainan	3000	4	1	1		
重 庆	Chongqing	211511	151	55	6		49
四 川	Sichuan	209388	1290	577		1	576
贵 州	Guizhou	57732	588	3		1	2
云 南	Yunnan	212354	157	7		1	6
西 藏	Tibet	1030	9				
陕 西	Shaanxi	117175	88	3		2	1
甘 肃	Gansu	158254	105				
青 海	Qinghai	10426	41	7			7
宁 夏	Ningxia	31012	28	11	1	4	6
新 疆	Xinjiang	7866	30	1			1
新疆兵团	Xinjiang Corps	20552	130				
黑龙江垦区	Heilongjiang Land Reclamation	1435	16				

1-14 续表 3 Continued 3

地 区	Region	残疾儿童家长学校 Schools for Training Parents of Children with Disabilities							
		本年度开展家长学校活动 Activities Holded for Parents of Children with Disabilities in 2014	省级 at Provincial Level	地市级 at Prefectural/ City Level	县级 at County Level	本年度残疾儿童家长参与人数 Parents of Children with Disabilities Participating in 2014	省级 at Provincial Level	地市级 at Prefectural/ City Level	县级 at County Level
		次 time	次 time	次 time	次 time	人次 person time	人次 person time	人次 person time	人次 person time
全 国	**Total**	**3625**	**489**	**728**	**2408**	**94170**	**21643**	**16740**	**55787**
北 京	Beijing	415	64		351	16193	4235		11958
天 津	Tianjin	35	30		5	1090	1000		90
河 北	Hebei	153	60	20	73	4273	800	1695	1778
山 西	Shanxi	201	80	57	64	2958	1200	749	1009
内蒙古	Inner Mongolia	46	1	35	10	736	373	141	222
辽 宁	Liaoning	65	2	43	20	1501	402	805	294
吉 林	Jilin	63	10	14	39	4003	830	1539	1634
黑龙江	Heilongjiang	10		1	9	91		40	51
上 海	Shanghai	312	23		289	9974	605		9369
江 苏	Jiangsu	174	4	21	149	7469	81	802	6586
浙 江	Zhejiang	533	11	39	483	5115	1450	1190	2475
安 徽	Anhui	691	120	325	246	10413	4000	4056	2357
福 建	Fujian	33			33	696			696
江 西	Jiangxi	11			11	215			215
山 东	Shandong	182		12	170	4932		275	4657
河 南	Henan	3			3	135			135
湖 北	Hubei	25			25	1090			1090
湖 南	Hunan	163		89	74	5226		3056	2170
广 东	Guangdong	240	62	31	147	7831	4751	1018	2062
广 西	Guangxi	22		15	7	553		190	363
海 南	Hainan	3	3			165	165		
重 庆	Chongqing	135	18		117	2734	500		2234
四 川	Sichuan	49		1	48	3432		120	3312
贵 州	Guizhou	4		2	2	35		17	18
云 南	Yunnan	12		3	9	422		150	272
西 藏	Tibet					1			1
陕 西	Shaanxi	9		8	1	691		670	21
甘 肃	Gansu								
青 海	Qinghai	4			4	241			241
宁 夏	Ningxia	31	1	12	18	1954	1251	227	476
新 疆	Xinjiang	1			1	1			1
新疆兵团	Xinjiang Corps								
黑龙江垦区	Heilongjiang Land Reclamation								

1–15 康复人才
Rehabilitation Professionals

地区	Region	康复机构在岗人员 Staff of Rehabilitation Institutions	省级 Staff of Rehabilitation Institutions at Provincial Level	业务人员 Professionals	管理人员 Managerial Personnels	其他人员 Other Staff Members
		人 person	人 person	人 person	人 person	人 person
全　国	**Total**	**233631**	**10735**	**8088**	**1529**	**1118**
北　京	Beijing	3599	86	61	18	7
天　津	Tianjin	3235	198	159	25	14
河　北	Hebei	7155	75	30	25	20
山　西	Shanxi	9513	247	169	56	22
内蒙古	Inner Mongolia	4537	58	44	13	1
辽　宁	Liaoning	12038	2912	2315	538	59
吉　林	Jilin	8304	249	192	17	40
黑龙江	Heilongjiang	7628	532	481	23	28
上　海	Shanghai	4330	538	372	125	41
江　苏	Jiangsu	11210	71	48	18	5
浙　江	Zhejiang	5493	160	80	15	65
安　徽	Anhui	5010	131	79	21	31
福　建	Fujian	6021	108	69	11	28
江　西	Jiangxi	4638	124	30	26	68
山　东	Shandong	27261	83	47	5	31
河　南	Henan	18238	102	40	28	34
湖　北	Hubei	9228	39	30	5	4
湖　南	Hunan	12314	352	297	14	41
广　东	Guangdong	21088	136	90	29	17
广　西	Guangxi	5044	112	70	25	17
海　南	Hainan	675	453	363	56	34
重　庆	Chongqing	5987	61	22	31	8
四　川	Sichuan	10129	593	477	116	
贵　州	Guizhou	5357	57	35	14	8
云　南	Yunnan	4770	123	93	22	8
西　藏	Tibet	62	54	44	10	
陕　西	Shaanxi	11390	2044	1531	139	374
甘　肃	Gansu	3061	653	539	38	76
青　海	Qinghai	272	38	23	9	6
宁　夏	Ningxia	409	76	56	10	10
新　疆	Xinjiang	4565	73	45	23	5
新疆兵团	Xinjiang Corps	715	34	12	6	16
黑龙江垦区	Heilongjiang Land Reclamation	355	163	145	18	

1-15 续表 1 Continued 1

地 区	Region	康复机构在岗人员 Staff of Rehabilitation Institutions			
		地市级康复机构在岗人员 Staff of Rehabilitation Institutions at Prefectural/City Level	业务人员 Professionals	管理人员 Managerial Personnels	其他人员 Other Staff Members
		人 person	人 person	人 person	人 person
全 国	**Total**	**63533**	**46365**	**7453**	**9715**
北 京	Beijing				
天 津	Tianjin				
河 北	Hebei	3180	2284	467	429
山 西	Shanxi	3967	3030	437	500
内蒙古	Inner Mongolia	1172	825	205	142
辽 宁	Liaoning	3306	2285	449	572
吉 林	Jilin	3771	2433	741	597
黑龙江	Heilongjiang	4226	3082	637	507
上 海	Shanghai				
江 苏	Jiangsu	1557	943	289	325
浙 江	Zhejiang	664	403	71	190
安 徽	Anhui	1594	1100	175	319
福 建	Fujian	1356	1162	99	95
江 西	Jiangxi	389	187	56	146
山 东	Shandong	5520	4135	656	729
河 南	Henan	8901	6947	585	1369
湖 北	Hubei	2757	2056	366	335
湖 南	Hunan	4035	2760	387	888
广 东	Guangdong	4227	2985	535	707
广 西	Guangxi	645	475	84	86
海 南	Hainan	177	143	29	5
重 庆	Chongqing				
四 川	Sichuan	766	578	85	103
贵 州	Guizhou	2128	1574	298	256
云 南	Yunnan	1742	1194	128	420
西 藏	Tibet	8	6	1	1
陕 西	Shaanxi	2835	2025	343	467
甘 肃	Gansu	1381	1099	159	123
青 海	Qinghai	128	84	18	26
宁 夏	Ningxia	126	92	11	23
新 疆	Xinjiang	2616	2236	108	272
新疆兵团	Xinjiang Corps	259	201	11	47
黑龙江垦区	Heilongjiang Land Reclamation	100	41	23	36

1-15 续表 2 Continued 2

地 区	Region	康复机构在岗人员 Staff of Rehabilitation Institutions			
		县级康复机构在岗人员 Staff of Rehabilitation Institutions at County Level	业务人员 Professionals	管理人员 Managerial Personnels	其他人员 Other Staff Members
		人 person	人 person	人 person	人 person
全 国	**Total**	**159363**	**105528**	**21535**	**32300**
北 京	Beijing	3513	2534	569	410
天 津	Tianjin	3037	1856	269	912
河 北	Hebei	3900	2449	748	703
山 西	Shanxi	5299	3568	578	1153
内蒙古	Inner Mongolia	3307	2096	566	645
辽 宁	Liaoning	5820	3259	748	1813
吉 林	Jilin	4284	2404	777	1103
黑龙江	Heilongjiang	2870	1930	367	573
上 海	Shanghai	3792	2305	709	778
江 苏	Jiangsu	9582	6351	1281	1950
浙 江	Zhejiang	4669	2897	756	1016
安 徽	Anhui	3285	1944	548	793
福 建	Fujian	4557	2775	661	1121
江 西	Jiangxi	4125	2471	532	1122
山 东	Shandong	21658	16295	2286	3077
河 南	Henan	9235	6559	1212	1464
湖 北	Hubei	6432	4532	768	1132
湖 南	Hunan	7927	5289	1173	1465
广 东	Guangdong	16725	11538	2140	3047
广 西	Guangxi	4287	3046	398	843
海 南	Hainan	45	32	7	6
重 庆	Chongqing	5926	4020	934	972
四 川	Sichuan	8770	5120	1025	2625
贵 州	Guizhou	3172	2036	489	647
云 南	Yunnan	2905	1679	416	810
西 藏	Tibet				
陕 西	Shaanxi	6511	4363	953	1195
甘 肃	Gansu	1027	562	166	299
青 海	Qinghai	106	50	27	29
宁 夏	Ningxia	207	122	38	47
新 疆	Xinjiang	1876	1165	261	450
新疆兵团	Xinjiang Corps	422	244	101	77
黑龙江垦区	Heilongjiang Land Reclamation	92	37	32	23

1-15 续表 3 Continued 3

地 区	Region	康复人才培训情况 Training for Staff of Rehabilitation Institutions					
		本年度举办康复管理人员培训班 Training Courses for Rehabilitation Managerial Staff in 2014	培训康复管理人员 Rehabilitation Managerial Staff Trained	本年度举办康复业务人员培训班 Training Courses for Rehabilitation Professionals in 2014	培训康复业务人员 Rehabilitation Professionals Trained	本年度举办社区康复协调员培训班 Training Courses for Community-Based Rehabilitation Coordinators in 2014	培训社区康复协调员 Community-Based Rehabilitation Coordinators Trained
		期 course	人 person	期 course	人 person	期 course	人 person
全 国	**Total**	**1742**	**25790**	**2224**	**55903**	**3140**	**169802**
北 京	Beijing	38	2342	47	2202	81	5625
天 津	Tianjin	12	247	10	411	13	1222
河 北	Hebei	104	864	103	1671	129	5647
山 西	Shanxi	42	692	46	1327	115	4485
内蒙古	Inner Mongolia	28	383	33	436	61	5472
辽 宁	Liaoning	97	1908	108	2631	172	8178
吉 林	Jilin	74	776	83	1399	81	5635
黑龙江	Heilongjiang	32	260	38	446	95	1945
上 海	Shanghai	88	806	193	1966	73	9702
江 苏	Jiangsu	90	1591	113	3979	148	12041
浙 江	Zhejiang	47	719	75	2569	66	7223
安 徽	Anhui	52	2369	61	4228	170	6368
福 建	Fujian	34	486	47	975	65	3518
江 西	Jiangxi	48	479	77	591	145	2332
山 东	Shandong	261	3269	266	6659	227	19328
河 南	Henan	28	175	36	1145	111	5328
湖 北	Hubei	36	942	38	1124	235	3553
湖 南	Hunan	45	780	52	1378	117	5647
广 东	Guangdong	151	2404	263	7021	145	13546
广 西	Guangxi	20	347	30	805	52	3842
海 南	Hainan	6	54	5	31	10	785
重 庆	Chongqing	58	724	71	2013	89	10684
四 川	Sichuan	78	821	117	1391	144	8134
贵 州	Guizhou	19	206	18	430	35	1488
云 南	Yunnan	80	1031	82	2930	116	7493
西 藏	Tibet	6	42	3	89	8	74
陕 西	Shaanxi	39	340	32	1570	70	3779
甘 肃	Gansu	31	209	62	2909	145	2585
青 海	Qinghai	47	158	38	420	57	664
宁 夏	Ningxia	6	86	5	65	17	579
新 疆	Xinjiang	31	239	58	1048	110	2772
新疆兵团	Xinjiang Corps					7	35
黑龙江垦区	Heilongjiang Land Reclamation	14	41	14	44	31	93

2-1 学前教育阶段
Pre-school Rehabilitation and Education

地 区	Region	残疾人事业专项彩票公益金助学项目资助 Support of Educational Project Funded by Dedicated Welfare Lottery Fund in 2014	视力残疾 Children with Visual Disability	听力残疾 Children with Hearing Disability	言语残疾 Children with Speech Disability	肢体残疾 Children with Physical Disability
		人 person	人 person	人 person	人 person	人 person
全 国	**Total**	**11528**	**410**	**2758**	**581**	**1828**
北 京	Beijing	276	1	44	4	27
天 津	Tianjin	100		5	3	8
河 北	Hebei	613	1	143	21	60
山 西	Shanxi	260	8	66	35	15
内蒙古	Inner Mongolia	356	23	43	18	117
辽 宁	Liaoning	960	15	189	14	164
吉 林	Jilin	260	12	17	6	45
黑龙江	Heilongjiang	300	2	34	9	44
上 海	Shanghai					
江 苏	Jiangsu	720	9	266	17	43
浙 江	Zhejiang	570	18	232	7	97
安 徽	Anhui	300		82	12	47
福 建	Fujian	330	6	56	8	83
江 西	Jiangxi	300	12	121	2	23
山 东	Shandong	745	14	154	21	165
河 南	Henan	780	84	222	115	44
湖 北	Hubei	500	23	112	22	130
湖 南	Hunan	400	9	128	30	29
广 东	Guangdong	550	16	75	22	163
广 西	Guangxi	466	7	117	36	29
海 南	Hainan	111	2	15		18
重 庆	Chongqing	200	3	44	12	13
四 川	Sichuan	901	84	186	62	141
贵 州	Guizhou	290	19	52	31	80
云 南	Yunnan	260	4	59	20	25
西 藏	Tibet	30	12	2	11	2
陕 西	Shaanxi	200	7	113	12	2
甘 肃	Gansu	272	3	50	6	82
青 海	Qinghai	70	1	12	3	25
宁 夏	Ningxia	158	9	18	12	53
新 疆	Xinjiang	200	1	93	9	28
新疆兵团	Xinjiang Corps	30	4	7		12
黑龙江垦区	Heilongjiang Land Reclamation	20	1	1	1	14

2-1 续表 Continued

地 区	Region				其他残疾儿童学前教育助学项目资助 Support of Other Pre-School Educational Project for Disabled Children in 2013
		智力残疾 Chidren with Intellectual Disability	精神残疾 Children with Psychiatric Disability	多重残疾 Children with Multi-disabilities	
		人 person	人 person	人 person	人 person
全 国	**Total**	**2989**	**1136**	**1826**	**2908**
北 京	Beijing	76	74	50	
天 津	Tianjin	82		2	60
河 北	Hebei	247	42	99	3
山 西	Shanxi	64	33	39	
内蒙古	Inner Mongolia	74	29	52	3
辽 宁	Liaoning	286	190	102	
吉 林	Jilin	82	80	18	
黑龙江	Heilongjiang	102	90	19	
上 海	Shanghai				186
江 苏	Jiangsu	162	78	145	93
浙 江	Zhejiang	107	71	38	354
安 徽	Anhui	72	13	74	108
福 建	Fujian	112	26	39	41
江 西	Jiangxi	33	37	72	2
山 东	Shandong	219	49	123	134
河 南	Henan	177	27	111	
湖 北	Hubei	140	8	65	24
湖 南	Hunan	90	17	97	205
广 东	Guangdong	94	81	99	397
广 西	Guangxi	144	29	104	135
海 南	Hainan	20	53	3	
重 庆	Chongqing	78	11	39	77
四 川	Sichuan	258	45	125	441
贵 州	Guizhou	23	31	54	45
云 南	Yunnan	69	4	79	11
西 藏	Tibet			3	
陕 西	Shaanxi	4	1	61	25
甘 肃	Gansu	86	7	38	173
青 海	Qinghai	18		11	311
宁 夏	Ningxia	41	3	22	63
新 疆	Xinjiang	22	5	42	
新疆兵团	Xinjiang Corps	5	1	1	17
黑龙江垦区	Heilongjiang Land Reclamation	2	1		

2-2 义务教育阶段未入学学龄残疾儿童少年
School-age Children with Disabilities Unable to Enter Schools

地 区	Region	未入学学龄残疾儿童少年 School-age Children with Disabilities Unable to Enter Schools	视力残疾 Children with Visual Disability	听力残疾 Children with Hearing Disability	言语残疾 Children with Speech Disability
		人 person	人 person	人 person	人 person
全 国	**Total**	**85107**	**3996**	**4619**	**4693**
北 京	Beijing	76			
天 津	Tianjin	186	2	4	5
河 北	Hebei	1065	38	51	50
山 西	Shanxi	3715	155	268	238
内蒙古	Inner Mongolia	1433	37	44	83
辽 宁	Liaoning	2494	73	118	70
吉 林	Jilin	2498	64	110	124
黑龙江	Heilongjiang	1073	39	52	33
上 海	Shanghai	18	1		
江 苏	Jiangsu	1300	46	152	13
浙 江	Zhejiang	463	13	40	9
安 徽	Anhui	4148	133	231	162
福 建	Fujian	1581	34	87	35
江 西	Jiangxi	6175	289	431	233
山 东	Shandong	5942	191	238	191
河 南	Henan	7496	338	519	489
湖 北	Hubei	2017	106	108	106
湖 南	Hunan	5012	205	186	307
广 东	Guangdong	3693	113	122	149
广 西	Guangxi	4910	205	241	388
海 南	Hainan	659	25	22	28
重 庆	Chongqing	1671	73	37	75
四 川	Sichuan	4240	301	225	309
贵 州	Guizhou	4635	511	288	384
云 南	Yunnan	4690	268	287	392
西 藏	Tibet	252	21	23	39
陕 西	Shaanxi	4246	186	252	239
甘 肃	Gansu	3618	192	206	177
青 海	Qinghai	754	53	54	43
宁 夏	Ningxia	1003	62	49	58
新 疆	Xinjiang	3877	216	167	258
新疆兵团	Xinjiang Corps	40	4	1	1
黑龙江垦区	Heilongjiang Land Reclamation	127	2	6	5

2-2 续表 Continued

地 区	Region	肢体残疾 Children with Physical Disability	智力残疾 Children with Intellectual Disability	精神残疾 Children with Psychiatric Disability	多重残疾 Children with Multi-disabilities
		人 person	人 person	人 person	人 person
全 国	**Total**	**26322**	**28269**	**3607**	**13601**
北 京	Beijing	19	28	12	17
天 津	Tianjin	58	102	1	14
河 北	Hebei	395	364	25	142
山 西	Shanxi	1120	1328	112	494
内蒙古	Inner Mongolia	438	459	69	303
辽 宁	Liaoning	906	944	155	228
吉 林	Jilin	785	917	236	262
黑龙江	Heilongjiang	320	408	92	129
上 海	Shanghai	8	6		3
江 苏	Jiangsu	362	612	37	78
浙 江	Zhejiang	132	180	23	66
安 徽	Anhui	1140	1416	237	829
福 建	Fujian	441	708	103	173
江 西	Jiangxi	1537	2430	233	1022
山 东	Shandong	1915	2210	332	865
河 南	Henan	2838	2539	75	698
湖 北	Hubei	693	598	73	333
湖 南	Hunan	1766	1509	170	869
广 东	Guangdong	987	1251	377	694
广 西	Guangxi	1404	1347	123	1202
海 南	Hainan	182	235	52	115
重 庆	Chongqing	463	837	58	128
四 川	Sichuan	1412	1337	120	536
贵 州	Guizhou	1232	1167	196	857
云 南	Yunnan	1509	1164	90	980
西 藏	Tibet	98	20	12	39
陕 西	Shaanxi	1351	1187	186	845
甘 肃	Gansu	1194	1026	136	687
青 海	Qinghai	233	265	13	93
宁 夏	Ningxia	261	372	38	163
新 疆	Xinjiang	1065	1238	208	725
新疆兵团	Xinjiang Corps	16	11	3	4
黑龙江垦区	Heilongjiang Land Reclamation	42	54	10	8

2−3 高中教育阶段
Senior High Education

地 区	Region	特殊教育普通高中学校(班) Special Education Senior High Schools/classes	盲普通高中 Senior High Schools for Blind Students	聋普通高中 Senior High Schools for Deaf Students	其他 Others	学生 Students 招生 Newly Enrolled Students with Disabilities	盲 Students with Visual Disability	聋 Students with Hearing Disability
		个 unit	个 unit	个 unit	个 unit	人 person	人 person	人 person
全 国	**Total**	**187**	**27**	**122**	**38**	**2322**	**353**	**1969**
北 京	Beijing	2	1	1		4	4	
天 津	Tianjin	2	1	1		34	9	25
河 北	Hebei	13	2	11		227	68	159
山 西	Shanxi	5	1	4		166	29	137
内蒙古	Inner Mongolia	7		3	4	63	5	58
辽 宁	Liaoning	10	2	7	1	13		13
吉 林	Jilin	4		4		8		8
黑龙江	Heilongjiang	1		1				
上 海	Shanghai	1	1			5	5	
江 苏	Jiangsu	4		4		148		148
浙 江	Zhejiang	4		4		41		41
安 徽	Anhui	3		3		173	10	163
福 建	Fujian	26	6	13	7	219	23	196
江 西	Jiangxi	4		4		56		56
山 东	Shandong	23	2	15	6	180	17	163
河 南	Henan	5	1	3	1	71	6	65
湖 北	Hubei	8		7	1	137		137
湖 南	Hunan	9	1	7	1	108	4	104
广 东	Guangdong	8		5	3	60	4	56
广 西	Guangxi	10	3	6	1	33	4	29
海 南	Hainan	1			1			
重 庆	Chongqing	2	1	1		89	87	2
四 川	Sichuan	14	1	5	8	76	14	62
贵 州	Guizhou	8		7	1	30		30
云 南	Yunnan							
西 藏	Tibet							
陕 西	Shaanxi	3	1	2		30		30
甘 肃	Gansu	6	2	1	3	282	44	238
青 海	Qinghai	2		2		14	14	
宁 夏	Ningxia	1	1			13	6	7
新 疆	Xinjiang	1		1		42		42
新疆兵团	Xinjiang Corps							
黑龙江垦区	Heilongjiang Land Reclamation							

2-3　续表 1　Continued 1

地　区	Region	学生 Students					
		在校生 Students at Schools	盲 Students with Visual Disability	聋 Students with Hearing Disability	毕业生 Graduates	盲 Students with Visual Disability	聋 Students with Hearing Disability
		人 person	人 person	人 person	人 person	人 person	人 person
全　国	**Total**	**7227**	**1054**	**6173**	**1856**	**212**	**1644**
北　京	Beijing	80	12	68	30	8	22
天　津	Tianjin	114	29	85	38	9	29
河　北	Hebei	434	100	334	174	49	125
山　西	Shanxi	975	159	816	125	7	118
内蒙古	Inner Mongolia	116	7	109	50	7	43
辽　宁	Liaoning	51	3	48	30	8	22
吉　林	Jilin	34		34	13		13
黑龙江	Heilongjiang						
上　海	Shanghai	185	185		7	7	
江　苏	Jiangsu	422		422	107	5	102
浙　江	Zhejiang	191		191	59		59
安　徽	Anhui	503	10	493	93		93
福　建	Fujian	472	53	419	208	10	198
江　西	Jiangxi	129		129	41	6	35
山　东	Shandong	567	49	518	121	12	109
河　南	Henan	220	23	197	110	9	101
湖　北	Hubei	420		420	73		73
湖　南	Hunan	420	5	415	125		125
广　东	Guangdong	151	20	131	76	7	69
广　西	Guangxi	273	45	228	44	3	41
海　南	Hainan	70		70	70		70
重　庆	Chongqing	194	192	2	27	25	2
四　川	Sichuan	256	67	189	63	16	47
贵　州	Guizhou	94		94	48		48
云　南	Yunnan						
西　藏	Tibet						
陕　西	Shaanxi	106	8	98	17		17
甘　肃	Gansu	327	54	273	62	16	46
青　海	Qinghai	51		51	2		2
宁　夏	Ningxia	275	33	242	19	8	11
新　疆	Xinjiang	97		97	24		24
新疆兵团	Xinjiang Corps						
黑龙江垦区	Heilongjiang Land Reclamation						

2-3 续表 2 Continued 2

地 区	Region	残疾人中等职业学校(班) Secondary Vocational Schools/classes for PWDs	教育部门办 Established by Education Administrative Departments	残联部门办 Established by Disabled Persons' Federations	其他 Others
		个 unit	个 unit	个 unit	个 unit
全 国	**Total**	**197**	**150**	**18**	**29**
北 京	Beijing	5	5		
天 津	Tianjin	1		1	
河 北	Hebei	4	3		1
山 西	Shanxi	1			1
内蒙古	Inner Mongolia	8	5	1	2
辽 宁	Liaoning	8	6	1	1
吉 林	Jilin	6	5	1	
黑龙江	Heilongjiang	7	4		3
上 海	Shanghai	2	2		
江 苏	Jiangsu	15	14	1	
浙 江	Zhejiang	8	7	1	
安 徽	Anhui	6	5	1	
福 建	Fujian	15	12	1	2
江 西	Jiangxi	3	3		
山 东	Shandong	17	12	2	3
河 南	Henan	9	9		
湖 北	Hubei	9	2	1	6
湖 南	Hunan	13	10	1	2
广 东	Guangdong	9	8	1	
广 西	Guangxi	11	9		2
海 南	Hainan	2		2	
重 庆	Chongqing	5	3		2
四 川	Sichuan	10	9		1
贵 州	Guizhou	1	1		
云 南	Yunnan	5	4	1	
西 藏	Tibet				
陕 西	Shaanxi	6	3	1	2
甘 肃	Gansu	5	4		1
青 海	Qinghai	2	2		
宁 夏	Ningxia	1	1		
新 疆	Xinjiang	2	1	1	
新疆兵团	Xinjiang Corps	1	1		
黑龙江垦区	Heilongjiang Land Reclamation				

2-3 续表 3 Continued 3

地区	Region	残疾人中等职业学校(班)学生 Students of Secondary Vocational Schools/classes for PWDs			
		招生 Newly Enrolled Students	盲 Students with Visual Disability	聋 Students with Hearing Disability	肢残 Students with Physical Disability
		人 person	人 person	人 person	人 person
全国	**Total**	**5180**	**1329**	**1982**	**1869**
北京	Beijing	71	40	31	
天津	Tianjin				
河北	Hebei	128	67	10	51
山西	Shanxi	115	100		15
内蒙古	Inner Mongolia	32		18	14
辽宁	Liaoning	62	30	32	
吉林	Jilin	223	163	60	
黑龙江	Heilongjiang	52	2	43	7
上海	Shanghai	28		28	
江苏	Jiangsu	458	51	355	52
浙江	Zhejiang	95		77	18
安徽	Anhui	275	62	109	104
福建	Fujian	26	7	11	8
江西	Jiangxi	51	8	16	27
山东	Shandong	627	227	349	51
河南	Henan	184	81	97	6
湖北	Hubei	210	11	40	159
湖南	Hunan	452	111	184	157
广东	Guangdong	303	82	132	89
广西	Guangxi	57	2	17	38
海南	Hainan	88	40		48
重庆	Chongqing	178	56	34	88
四川	Sichuan	54		5	49
贵州	Guizhou				
云南	Yunnan	234	10	117	107
西藏	Tibet				
陕西	Shaanxi	993	135	167	691
甘肃	Gansu	35		30	5
青海	Qinghai				
宁夏	Ningxia				
新疆	Xinjiang	149	44	20	85
新疆兵团	Xinjiang Corps				
黑龙江垦区	Heilongjiang Land Reclamation				

2-3 续表 4 Continued 4

地 区	Region	残疾人中等职业学校(班)学生 Students of Secondary Vocational Schools/classes for PWDs			
		在校学生 Students at Schools	盲 Students with Visual Disability	聋 Students with Hearing Disability	肢残 Students with Physical Disability
		人 person	人 person	人 person	人 person
全 国	**Total**	**11671**	**3274**	**5083**	**3314**
北 京	Beijing	236	91	145	
天 津	Tianjin				
河 北	Hebei	118	65	8	45
山 西	Shanxi	286	256		30
内蒙古	Inner Mongolia	145	33	83	29
辽 宁	Liaoning	279	203	76	
吉 林	Jilin	662	320	321	21
黑龙江	Heilongjiang	76	5	57	14
上 海	Shanghai	143		143	
江 苏	Jiangsu	1023	163	703	157
浙 江	Zhejiang	261		209	52
安 徽	Anhui	562	262	136	164
福 建	Fujian	59	15	28	16
江 西	Jiangxi	91	20	32	39
山 东	Shandong	1719	613	916	190
河 南	Henan	429	153	261	15
湖 北	Hubei	262	11	63	188
湖 南	Hunan	1129	350	417	362
广 东	Guangdong	848	274	345	229
广 西	Guangxi	177	2	82	93
海 南	Hainan	88	40		48
重 庆	Chongqing	261	51	84	126
四 川	Sichuan	272	33	78	161
贵 州	Guizhou	19	6	13	
云 南	Yunnan	625	52	321	252
西 藏	Tibet				
陕 西	Shaanxi	1374	98	470	806
甘 肃	Gansu	49	14	30	5
青 海	Qinghai	21		13	8
宁 夏	Ningxia	15			15
新 疆	Xinjiang	440	144	49	247
新疆兵团	Xinjiang Corps	2			2
黑龙江垦区	Heilongjiang Land Reclamation				

2-3 续表 5 Continued 5

地 区	Region	残疾人中等职业学校(班)学生 Students of Secondary Vocational Schools/classes for PWDs			
		毕业生 Graduates	盲 Students with Visual Disability	聋 Students with Hearing Disability	肢残 Students with Physical Disability
		人 person	人 person	人 person	人 person
全 国	**Total**	**7240**	**2045**	**1559**	**3636**
北 京	Beijing	91	51	40	
天 津	Tianjin				
河 北	Hebei	73	17	16	40
山 西	Shanxi	67	59		8
内蒙古	Inner Mongolia	198	170	14	14
辽 宁	Liaoning	55	40	15	
吉 林	Jilin	153	92	34	27
黑龙江	Heilongjiang	18		18	
上 海	Shanghai	47		47	
江 苏	Jiangsu	280	56	153	71
浙 江	Zhejiang	124		103	21
安 徽	Anhui	196	54	74	68
福 建	Fujian	21	5	9	7
江 西	Jiangxi	39	6	12	21
山 东	Shandong	438	148	237	53
河 南	Henan	132	31	101	
湖 北	Hubei	109	12	23	74
湖 南	Hunan	411	141	146	124
广 东	Guangdong	296	65	119	112
广 西	Guangxi	26		7	19
海 南	Hainan	72			72
重 庆	Chongqing	3144	947	27	2170
四 川	Sichuan	74	9	32	33
贵 州	Guizhou				
云 南	Yunnan	155	13	92	50
西 藏	Tibet				
陕 西	Shaanxi	722	51	191	480
甘 肃	Gansu	102	16	25	61
青 海	Qinghai				
宁 夏	Ningxia				
新 疆	Xinjiang	197	62	24	111
新疆兵团	Xinjiang Corps				
黑龙江垦区	Heilongjiang Land Reclamation				

2-3 续表 6 Continued 6

地区	Region	残疾人中等职业学校(班)学生 Students of Secondary Vocational Schools/classes for PWDs			
		毕业生获得职业资格证书 Graduates Who were Issued Professional Qualification Certificates	盲 Students with Visual Disability	聋 Students with Hearing Disability	肢残 Students with Physical Disability
		人 person	人 person	人 person	人 person
全国	**Total**	**5532**	**1714**	**726**	**3092**
北京	Beijing	72	51	21	
天津	Tianjin				
河北	Hebei	12	2	1	9
山西	Shanxi	67	59		8
内蒙古	Inner Mongolia	143	141	1	1
辽宁	Liaoning	43	40	3	
吉林	Jilin	119	92		27
黑龙江	Heilongjiang				
上海	Shanghai	25		25	
江苏	Jiangsu	231	48	118	65
浙江	Zhejiang	43		38	5
安徽	Anhui	120	51	44	25
福建	Fujian	11	3	7	1
江西	Jiangxi	36	6	12	18
山东	Shandong	402	148	214	40
河南	Henan				
湖北	Hubei	79		23	56
湖南	Hunan	182	51	73	58
广东	Guangdong	176	30	71	75
广西	Guangxi	26		7	19
海南	Hainan	72			72
重庆	Chongqing	3065	910	27	2128
四川	Sichuan	10			10
贵州	Guizhou				
云南	Yunnan	39		10	29
西藏	Tibet				
陕西	Shaanxi	383	22	11	350
甘肃	Gansu	4			4
青海	Qinghai				
宁夏	Ningxia				
新疆	Xinjiang	172	60	20	92
新疆兵团	Xinjiang Corps				
黑龙江垦区	Heilongjiang Land Reclamation				

2-4 高等教育
Higher Education

地 区	Region	高等特殊教育学院 Higher Special Education Institutions							
		机构 Institutions	录取残疾考生 Newly Enrolled Students	本科 Under-graduates	盲 Students with Visual Disability	聋 Students with Hearing Disability	专科(高职) Postsecondary Specialised College Students (Vocational College Students)	盲 Students with Visual Disability	聋 Students with Hearing Disability
		个 unit	人 person	人 person	人 person	人 person	人 person	人 person	人 person
全 国	**Total**	**18**	**1678**	**705**	**196**	**509**	**973**	**139**	**834**
北 京	Beijing	1	165	100	33	67	65		65
天 津	Tianjin	2	135	108		108	27		27
河 北	Hebei								
山 西	Shanxi								
内蒙古	Inner Mongolia								
辽 宁	Liaoning	1	95				95	41	54
吉 林	Jilin	1	205	205	77	128			
黑龙江	Heilongjiang								
上 海	Shanghai								
江 苏	Jiangsu	3	242	24		24	218	18	200
浙 江	Zhejiang	1	139	15	15		124	15	109
安 徽	Anhui								
福 建	Fujian	1	30				30		30
江 西	Jiangxi								
山 东	Shandong	1	71	71	71				
河 南	Henan	3	333	100		100	233	65	168
湖 北	Hubei								
湖 南	Hunan	1	147	62		62	85		85
广 东	Guangdong	1	66				66		66
广 西	Guangxi								
海 南	Hainan								
重 庆	Chongqing	1	20	20		20			
四 川	Sichuan								
贵 州	Guizhou								
云 南	Yunnan								
西 藏	Tibet								
陕 西	Shaanxi	1	30				30		30
甘 肃	Gansu								
青 海	Qinghai								
宁 夏	Ningxia								
新 疆	Xinjiang								
新疆兵团	Xinjiang Corps								
黑龙江垦区	Heilongjiang Land Reclamation								

2-4 续表 1 Continued 1

地 区	Region	普通高等院校 Ordinary Higher Education Institutions					
		残疾考生达到录取分数线 Students who Passed the Admission Line	录取人数 Students Enrolled	本科 Undergraduates	盲 Students with Visual Disability	聋 Students with Hearing Disability	肢残 Students with Physical Disability
		人 person	人 person	人 person	人 person	人 person	人 person
全 国	**Total**	**8183**	**7864**	**3889**	**354**	**506**	**2848**
北 京	Beijing	75	75	43	6	9	28
天 津	Tianjin	116	116	57	3	7	45
河 北	Hebei	412	406	242	35	48	152
山 西	Shanxi	246	246	101	2	1	98
内蒙古	Inner Mongolia	239	239	125	10	14	95
辽 宁	Liaoning	241	241	116	11	19	86
吉 林	Jilin	163	162	109	14	19	71
黑龙江	Heilongjiang	155	155	93	10	18	60
上 海	Shanghai	66	64	45	10	11	17
江 苏	Jiangsu	363	363	204			204
浙 江	Zhejiang	279	257	133	10	30	89
安 徽	Anhui	479	446	224	20	36	150
福 建	Fujian	295	277	150	20	18	104
江 西	Jiangxi	242	242	98	7	8	80
山 东	Shandong	347	322	183	18	33	124
河 南	Henan	426	426	211	21	21	169
湖 北	Hubei	381	369	167	15	53	98
湖 南	Hunan	358	318	176	12	9	123
广 东	Guangdong	352	327	72	7	13	50
广 西	Guangxi	294	279	114	3	7	91
海 南	Hainan	69	69	30			30
重 庆	Chongqing	168	166	94	8	11	64
四 川	Sichuan	435	415	186	24	13	138
贵 州	Guizhou	439	417	167	3	11	143
云 南	Yunnan	480	437	230	15	15	195
西 藏	Tibet	10	10				
陕 西	Shaanxi	272	272	178	11	20	138
甘 肃	Gansu	267	243	80	29	30	21
青 海	Qinghai	82	82	51	5	1	41
宁 夏	Ningxia	124	123	52	10	7	34
新 疆	Xinjiang	281	273	144	13	22	102
新疆兵团	Xinjiang Corps	26	26	14	2	2	8
黑龙江垦区	Heilongjiang Land Reclamation	1	1				

2-4　续表 2　Continued 2

地　区	Region	普通高等院校 Ordinary Higher Education Institutions 录取残疾考生 Students Enrolled 专科(高职) Postsecondary Specialised College Students (Vocational College Students) 人 person	盲 Students with Visual Disability 人 person	聋 Students with Hearing Disability 人 person	肢残 Students with Physical Disability 人 person
全　国	**Total**	**3975**	**340**	**460**	**2868**
北　京	Beijing	32	4	3	25
天　津	Tianjin	59	2	16	36
河　北	Hebei	164	21	36	99
山　西	Shanxi	145		2	143
内蒙古	Inner Mongolia	114	7	17	85
辽　宁	Liaoning	125	8	15	100
吉　林	Jilin	53	3	5	37
黑龙江	Heilongjiang	62	8	11	38
上　海	Shanghai	19	2	1	13
江　苏	Jiangsu	159			159
浙　江	Zhejiang	124	8	35	66
安　徽	Anhui	222	20	30	140
福　建	Fujian	127	7	33	75
江　西	Jiangxi	144	8	13	118
山　东	Shandong	139	15	30	83
河　南	Henan	215	27	25	163
湖　北	Hubei	202	53	33	113
湖　南	Hunan	142	6	4	107
广　东	Guangdong	255	32	27	193
广　西	Guangxi	165	11	10	120
海　南	Hainan	39		4	34
重　庆	Chongqing	72	9	13	40
四　川	Sichuan	229	13	5	191
贵　州	Guizhou	250		16	209
云　南	Yunnan	207	15	22	161
西　藏	Tibet	10	4	1	2
陕　西	Shaanxi	94	5	8	76
甘　肃	Gansu	163	25	18	75
青　海	Qinghai	31	2	2	22
宁　夏	Ningxia	71	15	7	39
新　疆	Xinjiang	129	10	18	94
新疆兵团	Xinjiang Corps	12			11
黑龙江垦区	Heilongjiang Land Reclamation	1			1

3-1 城镇残疾人就业状况
Employment of PWDs in Urban Areas

地 区	Region	就业合计 Employed PWDs	集中就业 PWDs Employed in Collective Form	本年度新安排 Newly Employed in Collective Form in 2014	按比例就业 PWDs Employed by quota Scheme	本年度新安排 Newly Employed by Quota Scheme in 2014	公益性岗位就业 PWDs Employed through Welfare Post
		人 person	人 person	人 person	人 person	人 person	人 person
全 国	**Total**	**4359517**	**1124506**	**76053**	**1163029**	**69619**	**98380**
北 京	Beijing	74689	4180	190	43216	1805	1698
天 津	Tianjin	40164	7088	573	26732	3125	1001
河 北	Hebei	195754	51583	4816	80398	3222	5942
山 西	Shanxi	113621	36499	1947	21509	911	1235
内蒙古	Inner Mongolia	112187	14227	1268	16677	1026	3370
辽 宁	Liaoning	315547	100365	2217	80215	2168	2633
吉 林	Jilin	158163	36965	1583	25212	779	3785
黑龙江	Heilongjiang	127348	34202	2608	21380	1611	8090
上 海	Shanghai	66575	14532	556	37017	1333	4979
江 苏	Jiangsu	284337	95158	5797	79964	7071	4979
浙 江	Zhejiang	205933	83308	1839	73895	3811	5558
安 徽	Anhui	153006	23738	1604	26208	1752	2115
福 建	Fujian	89439	21043	1647	18516	1353	2195
江 西	Jiangxi	152615	32560	3132	16123	950	5945
山 东	Shandong	240028	71655	5119	76562	6337	2296
河 南	Henan	315512	109066	11635	53645	5734	7517
湖 北	Hubei	220649	51181	3558	56502	2753	4095
湖 南	Hunan	279949	59987	3478	64359	2232	4723
广 东	Guangdong	204020	21710	2615	83376	6216	4379
广 西	Guangxi	77938	16935	1162	23882	1624	2150
海 南	Hainan	11601	1006	88	4610	389	278
重 庆	Chongqing	140316	51971	1327	30728	1151	1339
四 川	Sichuan	269086	60844	9574	50173	3983	4893
贵 州	Guizhou	75959	26235	1384	10948	1572	555
云 南	Yunnan	77133	27096	1478	24221	1247	595
西 藏	Tibet	1784	998	136	387	25	85
陕 西	Shaanxi	106043	23130	1454	34754	1783	3167
甘 肃	Gansu	107070	24137	1273	19836	1097	5894
青 海	Qinghai	6766	2229	546	1380	159	550
宁 夏	Ningxia	26133	4003	214	9755	151	653
新 疆	Xinjiang	76146	14993	1008	33958	1694	1198
新疆兵团	Xinjiang Corps	18170	1840	226	11397	520	213
黑龙江垦区	Heilongjiang Land Reclamation	15836	42	1	5494	35	275

3-1　续表　Continued

地区	Region	本年度新安排 Newly Employed in 2014	个体及其他形式就业 PWDs Self-employed or Employed in Other Forms	本年度新安排 Newly Employed in 2014	辅助性就业 PWDs of Assistive Employment	本年度新安排 Newly Employed in 2014
		人 person	人 person	人 person	人 person	人 person
全　国	**Total**	**12158**	**1922550**	**107221**	**51052**	**12571**
北　京	Beijing	97	20952	1918	4643	275
天　津	Tianjin	93	4494	287	849	135
河　北	Hebei	269	57468	2872	363	201
山　西	Shanxi	290	53536	3090	842	578
内蒙古	Inner Mongolia	335	76995	3353	918	313
辽　宁	Liaoning	497	132142	3845	192	73
吉　林	Jilin	635	91550	5178	651	495
黑龙江	Heilongjiang	582	63436	4337	240	187
上　海	Shanghai	152	6631	294	3416	923
江　苏	Jiangsu	250	101538	4616	2698	1286
浙　江	Zhejiang	937	38904	3311	4268	956
安　徽	Anhui	226	97496	4558	3449	224
福　建	Fujian	218	45937	3367	1748	653
江　西	Jiangxi	699	96136	5174	1851	214
山　东	Shandong	254	87780	5166	1735	593
河　南	Henan	808	142571	11261	2713	234
湖　北	Hubei	439	107828	3584	1043	531
湖　南	Hunan	834	150113	4110	767	299
广　东	Guangdong	580	91305	3542	3250	647
广　西	Guangxi	176	33893	2863	1078	105
海　南	Hainan	15	5525	356	182	30
重　庆	Chongqing	95	52465	2004	3813	291
四　川	Sichuan	885	147428	12541	5748	768
贵　州	Guizhou	143	38067	3566	154	109
云　南	Yunnan	145	24820	1827	401	241
西　藏	Tibet	10	314	5		
陕　西	Shaanxi	494	44313	2192	679	194
甘　肃	Gansu	1505	55652	3737	1551	911
青　海	Qinghai	121	2571	531	36	10
宁　夏	Ningxia	130	11685	557	37	7
新　疆	Xinjiang	203	25284	2919	713	306
新疆兵团	Xinjiang Corps	40	3762	179	958	767
黑龙江垦区	Heilongjiang Land Reclamation	1	9959	81	66	15

3−2 农村残疾人就业状况
Employment of PWDs in Rural Areas

地 区	Region	实际就业 Employed PWDs	从事农业生产劳动 PWDs Engaged in Farming	从事其他形式就业 PWDs Employed in Other Forms
		万人 10,000 persons	万人 10,000 persons	万人 10,000 persons
全 国	**Total**	**1723.6**	**1360.4**	**363.2**
北 京	Beijing	6.2	4.0	2.2
天 津	Tianjin	6.8	4.6	2.1
河 北	Hebei	88.0	69.5	18.5
山 西	Shanxi	37.3	26.8	10.5
内蒙古	Inner Mongolia	26.6	21.6	5.0
辽 宁	Liaoning	39.9	29.1	10.9
吉 林	Jilin	30.6	25.4	5.2
黑龙江	Heilongjiang	24.2	19.7	4.5
上 海	Shanghai	2.6	0.5	2.0
江 苏	Jiangsu	67.8	50.5	17.4
浙 江	Zhejiang	32.4	21.5	10.9
安 徽	Anhui	76.4	62.8	13.6
福 建	Fujian	31.9	24.5	7.4
江 西	Jiangxi	55.9	42.0	14.0
山 东	Shandong	138.7	109.9	28.8
河 南	Henan	190.4	152.9	37.5
湖 北	Hubei	87.4	66.8	20.5
湖 南	Hunan	93.9	69.0	24.9
广 东	Guangdong	60.8	49.7	11.1
广 西	Guangxi	65.1	52.0	13.1
海 南	Hainan	6.9	5.9	1.0
重 庆	Chongqing	46.3	36.9	9.4
四 川	Sichuan	175.5	141.9	33.6
贵 州	Guizhou	74.8	59.5	15.2
云 南	Yunnan	98.6	85.4	13.2
西 藏	Tibet	1.3	1.2	0.1
陕 西	Shaanxi	65.3	49.0	16.2
甘 肃	Gansu	53.3	44.2	9.1
青 海	Qinghai	5.2	4.5	0.7
宁 夏	Ningxia	10.9	9.4	1.5
新 疆	Xinjiang	22.7	19.7	3.0
新疆兵团	Xinjiang Corps			
黑龙江垦区	Heilongjiang Land Reclamation			

3-3　城镇残疾人登记失业与职业培训

Unemployment Registration of PWDs in Urban Areas and Vocational Training

地区	Region	本年度城镇残疾人新登记失业 PWDs in Urban Areas who Registered as being Unemployed Newly Added in 2014	残疾人职业培训 Vocational Training for PWDs			
			职业培训基地 Vocational Training Base	残联兴办 Established by Disabled Persons' Federations	依托社会机构兴办 Established by Social Organizations	本年度城镇职业培训 PWDs in Urban Areas Receiving Vocational Training in 2014
		人 person	个 unit	个 unit	个 unit	人 person
全　国	**Total**	**48925**	**6154**	**2211**	**3943**	**382490**
北　京	Beijing	777	64	7	57	9260
天　津	Tianjin		30	6	24	2272
河　北	Hebei	2056	203	46	157	24912
山　西	Shanxi	437	588	326	262	7497
内蒙古	Inner Mongolia	1148	68	21	47	10881
辽　宁	Liaoning	761	163	62	101	16217
吉　林	Jilin	6613	199	54	145	12412
黑龙江	Heilongjiang	1020	102	32	70	11835
上　海	Shanghai	1021	30	13	17	16589
江　苏	Jiangsu	2637	234	80	154	21102
浙　江	Zhejiang	1290	333	114	219	14931
安　徽	Anhui	525	82	23	59	11697
福　建	Fujian	840	323	200	123	9421
江　西	Jiangxi	1553	229	46	183	4788
山　东	Shandong	2272	845	107	738	20627
河　南	Henan	1375	251	53	198	41816
湖　北	Hubei	2411	277	205	72	11820
湖　南	Hunan	1318	243	97	146	6164
广　东	Guangdong	9574	272	190	82	10919
广　西	Guangxi	644	70	26	44	10055
海　南	Hainan	21	10	3	7	1969
重　庆	Chongqing	915	34	5	29	5092
四　川	Sichuan	2702	424	144	280	34104
贵　州	Guizhou	2900	40	17	23	5142
云　南	Yunnan	612	126	39	87	8843
西　藏	Tibet	36	5	3	2	207
陕　西	Shaanxi	2070	372	134	238	12637
甘　肃	Gansu	377	50	25	25	21659
青　海	Qinghai	72	31	16	15	1762
宁　夏	Ningxia	288	37	6	31	2232
新　疆	Xinjiang	526	417	110	307	12714
新疆兵团	Xinjiang Corps	134	2	1	1	914
黑龙江垦区	Heilongjiang Land Reclamation					

4-1 残疾人参加社会保险情况

PWDs Covered by Social Insurance

地 区	Region	残疾职工参加社会保险 Workers with Disabilities Covered by Social Insurance		残疾居民参加城乡社会养老保险 Residents with Disabilities Covered by Pension Insurance		
		参加养老保险 Covered by Pension Insurance	参加医疗保险 Covered by Medical Insurance		享受养老保金 PWDs Covered by the Insurance Pension	重度残疾人 Persons with Severe Disability
		万人 10,000 persons	万人 10,000 persons	万人 10,001 persons	万人 10,000 persons	万人 10,000 persons
全 国	**Total**	**282.8**	**282.8**	**2180.0**	**858.6**	**233.4**
北 京	Beijing	7.4	7.2	9.7	1.2	0.6
天 津	Tianjin	4.3	4.3	5.8	3.5	1.2
河 北	Hebei	15.9	16.6	122.0	37.2	9.5
山 西	Shanxi	8.2	8.2	95.6	48.5	6.2
内蒙古	Inner Mongolia	4.4	5.2	28.6	12.3	4.7
辽 宁	Liaoning	23.7	22.9	52.0	14.8	3.9
吉 林	Jilin	6.5	5.9	25.3	6.9	2.1
黑龙江	Heilongjiang	7.8	6.5	25.1	12.1	2.0
上 海	Shanghai	7.3	7.3	5.9	2.0	0.5
江 苏	Jiangsu	23.3	23.0	130.4	67.0	12.4
浙 江	Zhejiang	17.2	17.2	44.1	19.2	6.2
安 徽	Anhui	7.3	7.2	101.3	40.2	16.4
福 建	Fujian	4.1	4.6	55.1	27.2	11.4
江 西	Jiangxi	4.9	4.9	58.2	30.6	4.6
山 东	Shandong	18.0	17.1	134.9	51.5	16.8
河 南	Henan	17.6	17.5	296.4	123.7	20.9
湖 北	Hubei	14.0	15.1	104.6	42.6	10.3
湖 南	Hunan	15.5	14.6	162.1	62.4	23.4
广 东	Guangdong	10.8	10.9	61.5	22.5	10.3
广 西	Guangxi	4.0	4.7	97.4	49.5	13.8
海 南	Hainan	0.6	0.5	17.0	6.5	1.9
重 庆	Chongqing	8.3	8.6	45.1	17.0	6.7
四 川	Sichuan	18.7	17.4	178.3	45.5	14.8
贵 州	Guizhou	4.5	4.6	54.2	28.2	6.0
云 南	Yunnan	5.2	5.2	79.0	22.6	7.4
西 藏	Tibet	1.2	1.4	1.8	0.9	0.2
陕 西	Shaanxi	7.5	7.4	43.9	13.6	3.9
甘 肃	Gansu	4.8	5.0	92.7	29.9	7.6
青 海	Qinghai	0.6	0.6	4.0	2.7	0.5
宁 夏	Ningxia	1.5	1.5	18.7	8.2	4.3
新 疆	Xinjiang	5.3	6.3	28.2	8.5	2.5
新疆兵团	Xinjiang Corps	1.7	1.7	1.0	0.3	0.3
黑龙江垦区	Heilongjiang Land Reclamation	1.0	1.5			

4-1 续表 Continued

地 区	Region	60周岁以下参保残疾人 PWDs under Age 60	重度残疾人 Persons with Severe Disability	全部或部分代缴 Paid by Subsidy Totally or Partially	其他残疾人 Other PWDs	全部或部分代缴 Paid by Subsidy Totally or Partially
		万人 10,000 persons	万人 10,000 persons	万人 10,000 persons	万人 10,000 persons	万人 10,000 persons
全 国	**Total**	**1321.3**	**405.0**	**379.2**	**916.4**	**234.7**
北 京	Beijing	8.5	4.4	4.4	4.2	3.6
天 津	Tianjin	2.4	1.8	1.8	0.6	0.6
河 北	Hebei	84.8	16.8	16.1	67.9	16.3
山 西	Shanxi	47.1	13.7	13.2	33.4	6.3
内蒙古	Inner Mongolia	16.3	5.6	5.1	10.7	3.3
辽 宁	Liaoning	37.2	9.6	9.0	27.6	19.1
吉 林	Jilin	18.4	7.3	6.7	11.1	5.4
黑龙江	Heilongjiang	13.0	3.2	2.7	9.7	2.3
上 海	Shanghai	3.9	3.4	3.4	0.5	0.5
江 苏	Jiangsu	63.3	18.8	17.2	44.5	14.1
浙 江	Zhejiang	24.9	10.5	9.6	14.4	7.0
安 徽	Anhui	61.1	22.3	20.8	38.8	3.5
福 建	Fujian	27.9	12.0	11.2	15.9	11.5
江 西	Jiangxi	27.5	7.4	7.4	20.1	5.9
山 东	Shandong	83.3	26.9	23.7	56.4	16.3
河 南	Henan	172.7	59.4	53.7	113.3	2.2
湖 北	Hubei	62.0	16.4	15.3	45.6	19.2
湖 南	Hunan	99.7	28.9	28.4	70.8	6.1
广 东	Guangdong	38.9	16.2	15.0	22.8	7.8
广 西	Guangxi	48.0	12.7	11.9	35.3	8.1
海 南	Hainan	10.6	3.6	3.6	6.9	0.1
重 庆	Chongqing	28.1	10.1	10.0	18.0	10.6
四 川	Sichuan	132.8	29.7	29.4	103.1	14.3
贵 州	Guizhou	26.1	7.9	7.7	18.2	2.5
云 南	Yunnan	56.3	14.8	14.1	41.6	15.9
西 藏	Tibet	0.9	0.2	0.2	0.7	0.5
陕 西	Shaanxi	30.3	8.3	8.0	22.0	12.8
甘 肃	Gansu	62.8	21.5	19.0	41.4	6.3
青 海	Qinghai	1.4	1.0	0.9	0.4	0.2
宁 夏	Ningxia	10.5	4.9	4.8	5.6	3.4
新 疆	Xinjiang	19.8	5.1	4.7	14.7	8.8
新疆兵团	Xinjiang Corps	0.7	0.4	0.3	0.4	0.2
黑龙江垦区	Heilongjiang Land Reclamation					

4-2 社会救助与社会福利

Social Relief and Welfare

地 区	Region	社会救助 Social Relief			
		城镇 in Urban Areas			农村 in Rural Areas
		已纳入最低生活保障范围 PWDs Covered by Basic Living Allowance System	集中供养 PWDs Living in Welfare Institutions	其他救助救济 Other Assistance and Relief	已纳入最低生活保障范围 PWDs Covered by Basic Living Allowance System
		万人 10,000 persons	万人 10,000 persons	万人 10,000 persons	万人 10,000 persons
全 国	**Total**	**261.46**	**11.18**	**68.68**	**844.06**
北 京	Beijing	2.09	0.01	1.45	2.04
天 津	Tianjin	3.59	0.00	1.24	2.57
河 北	Hebei	6.77	0.32	0.97	34.44
山 西	Shanxi	6.78	0.13	1.62	24.35
内蒙古	Inner Mongolia	9.43	0.26	4.90	21.26
辽 宁	Liaoning	16.13	0.52	2.05	18.35
吉 林	Jilin	12.70	0.44	1.52	16.01
黑龙江	Heilongjiang	16.23	0.37	1.69	14.07
上 海	Shanghai	1.50	0.01	4.29	0.27
江 苏	Jiangsu	8.15	0.65	4.47	22.50
浙 江	Zhejiang	2.79	0.21	1.07	15.31
安 徽	Anhui	12.66	0.58	0.95	43.24
福 建	Fujian	3.54	0.10	0.91	22.38
江 西	Jiangxi	10.75	1.08	1.52	25.85
山 东	Shandong	7.71	0.73	2.32	37.72
河 南	Henan	20.09	0.80	4.13	67.36
湖 北	Hubei	17.66	1.19	2.16	52.65
湖 南	Hunan	20.53	0.79	4.97	65.88
广 东	Guangdong	8.45	0.40	3.01	27.59
广 西	Guangxi	6.79	0.22	0.77	39.90
海 南	Hainan	1.53	0.03	0.53	4.59
重 庆	Chongqing	6.71	0.36	2.70	12.81
四 川	Sichuan	17.44	0.85	6.56	78.59
贵 州	Guizhou	5.22	0.18	1.13	43.34
云 南	Yunnan	8.00	0.26	1.84	57.97
西 藏	Tibet	0.12		0.07	1.36
陕 西	Shaanxi	7.73	0.32	5.72	30.50
甘 肃	Gansu	6.79	0.10	1.30	35.47
青 海	Qinghai	0.58	0.09	0.24	2.25
宁 夏	Ningxia	1.52	0.04	0.57	7.78
新 疆	Xinjiang	6.42	0.09	0.78	15.68
新疆兵团	Xinjiang Corps	2.02	0.02	0.80	
黑龙江垦区	Heilongjiang Land Reclamation	3.05	0.01	0.41	

4-2 续表 Continued

地 区	Region	社会救助 Social Relief		社会福利 Social Welfare	
		农村 in Rural Areas			
		五保供养 PWDs Living in Welfare Institutions	其他救助救济 Other Assistance and Relief	享受生活补贴 PWDs with Living Subsidy	享受护理补贴 PWDs with Nursing Subsidy
		万人 10,000 persons	万人 10,000 persons	万人 10,000 persons	万人 10,000 persons
全 国	**Total**	**66.20**	**189.03**	**454.96**	**278.99**
北 京	Beijing	0.04	1.42	12.08	
天 津	Tianjin	0.29	0.98	6.35	1.22
河 北	Hebei	2.38	3.70	14.21	0.90
山 西	Shanxi	2.54	5.00	4.64	5.29
内蒙古	Inner Mongolia	1.81	8.24	21.28	23.37
辽 宁	Liaoning	2.45	3.15	0.14	0.17
吉 林	Jilin	1.28	1.47	0.03	0.18
黑龙江	Heilongjiang	1.06	3.00	0.81	3.16
上 海	Shanghai	0.03	1.10	4.35	3.40
江 苏	Jiangsu	2.29	8.72	32.10	11.61
浙 江	Zhejiang	0.75	8.26	22.40	8.51
安 徽	Anhui	3.92	4.61	54.58	0.75
福 建	Fujian	1.10	5.39	30.86	1.73
江 西	Jiangxi	2.60	3.87		14.61
山 东	Shandong	3.09	7.30	26.70	8.14
河 南	Henan	5.50	13.29	31.39	0.26
湖 北	Hubei	4.03	6.10	24.06	2.55
湖 南	Hunan	6.94	11.97	18.02	45.41
广 东	Guangdong	1.74	3.51	40.57	41.68
广 西	Guangxi	4.43	5.75	0.98	31.69
海 南	Hainan	0.25	1.19	0.26	3.93
重 庆	Chongqing	2.08	5.78	1.22	1.88
四 川	Sichuan	5.63	15.71	9.45	60.88
贵 州	Guizhou	1.12	5.71		
云 南	Yunnan	4.39	10.38	2.13	0.06
西 藏	Tibet	0.07	0.17	0.38	0.01
陕 西	Shaanxi	2.02	31.82	74.79	0.06
甘 肃	Gansu	1.82	8.85	8.56	6.61
青 海	Qinghai	0.08	0.51	4.76	0.13
宁 夏	Ningxia	0.17	1.09	6.90	
新 疆	Xinjiang	0.29	0.99	0.90	0.80
新疆兵团	Xinjiang Corps			0.03	
黑龙江垦区	Heilongjiang Land Reclamation				

4-3 托养服务

Fostering Service

地区	Region	托养服务机构合计 Fostering Institutions	寄宿制托养服务 Boarding Fostering Services	日间照料托养服务机构 Day-Care Fostering Service	综合托养服务机构 Combined Fostering Services Facilities	托养残疾人 PWDs in the Institutions	寄宿制机构中托养残疾人 PWDs Fostered in the Form of Boarding
		个 unit	个 unit	个 unit	个 unit	人 person	人 person
全国	**Total**	**5917**	**1758**	**2132**	**2027**	**931825**	**46872**
北京	Beijing	98	77		21	107792	660
天津	Tianjin	88	17	68	3	25329	348
河北	Hebei	192	70	34	88	23017	2490
山西	Shanxi	64	22	9	33	14801	239
内蒙古	Inner Mongolia	111	74	7	30	19099	1929
辽宁	Liaoning	203	72	101	30	35840	3746
吉林	Jilin	18	8	2	8	16771	412
黑龙江	Heilongjiang	93	33	5	55	19516	2016
上海	Shanghai	754	364	381	9	28692	5357
江苏	Jiangsu	1123	36	312	775	61312	1039
浙江	Zhejiang	841	388	174	279	96574	7013
安徽	Anhui	84	15	13	56	17945	440
福建	Fujian	125	26	49	50	27849	597
江西	Jiangxi	21	10	3	8	15655	1055
山东	Shandong	499	192	84	223	45200	5684
河南	Henan	42	7	1	34	20244	438
湖北	Hubei	219	58	114	47	23589	1028
湖南	Hunan	109	19	51	39	21935	493
广东	Guangdong	462	21	400	41	31206	802
广西	Guangxi	32	3	27	2	34304	138
海南	Hainan	6	6			14963	582
重庆	Chongqing	87	22	40	25	21316	559
四川	Sichuan	153	37	77	39	44391	1544
贵州	Guizhou	11	3	3	5	14480	268
云南	Yunnan	44	16	8	20	22709	768
西藏	Tibet					3168	
陕西	Shaanxi	132	67	16	49	27552	4415
甘肃	Gansu	50	23	7	20	20479	918
青海	Qinghai	39	13	8	18	18034	135
宁夏	Ningxia	55	10	38	7	16249	328
新疆	Xinjiang	126	19	97	10	32498	593
新疆兵团	Xinjiang Corps	29	24	2	3	7809	473
黑龙江垦区	Heilongjiang Land Reclamation	7	6	1		1507	365

4-3　续表 1　continued 1

地　区	Region								
		智力残疾人 Persons with Intellectual Disability	精神残疾人 Persons with Psychiatric Disability	重度肢体残疾人 Persons with Severe Physical Disability	日间照料机构中托养残疾人 PWDs Fostered in the Form of Day Care	智力残疾人 Persons with Intellectual Disability	精神残疾人 Persons with Psychiatric Disability	重度肢体残疾人 Persons with Severe Physical Disability	综合托养服务机构中托养残疾人 PWDs in Combined Fostering Services Facilities
		人 person	人 person	人 person	人 person	人 person	人 person	人 person	人 person
全　国	**Total**	**11942**	**17851**	**11198**	**53781**	**24523**	**16635**	**6966**	**60500**
北　京	Beijing	282	76	157					637
天　津	Tianjin	180	53	115	1032	542	274	189	58
河　北	Hebei	577	1219	545	726	145	122	269	3956
山　西	Shanxi	53	149	16	403	142	111	133	358
内蒙古	Inner Mongolia	318	184	468	98	24	12	16	767
辽　宁	Liaoning	1269	1215	536	1783	1466	151	103	1578
吉　林	Jilin	26	356	25	43	18	23	2	371
黑龙江	Heilongjiang	267	1085	394	130	93	35		1756
上　海	Shanghai	2205	1941	1019	10144	6184	3270	360	172
江　苏	Jiangsu	326	104	518	5146	2120	1309	942	15833
浙　江	Zhejiang	1413	2050	2585	4396	2330	1636	205	10696
安　徽	Anhui	72	223	115	121	78	36	7	1833
福　建	Fujian	117	284	126	878	484	136	20	1364
江　西	Jiangxi	635	315	68	71	33	28	5	328
山　东	Shandong	1718	1841	1643	5296	1923	2059	855	5828
河　南	Henan	42	189	128	30	6	9	15	1066
湖　北	Hubei	348	353	163	5668	1874	2335	663	2003
湖　南	Hunan	180	151	121	1446	553	406	247	1417
广　东	Guangdong	263	292	204	9874	3972	3030	1377	2859
广　西	Guangxi	4	134		923	535	164	163	21
海　南	Hainan	51	516	1					
重　庆	Chongqing	94	292	133	467	184	83	160	548
四　川	Sichuan	198	1039	166	1376	816	265	170	1233
贵　州	Guizhou	5	251	11	8	5	1	2	267
云　南	Yunnan	61	599	41	235	67	51	68	427
西　藏	Tibet								
陕　西	Shaanxi	671	1947	1148	230	88	61	20	2371
甘　肃	Gansu	187	97	332	234	75	59	64	1925
青　海	Qinghai	18	4	47	85	18	11	39	326
宁　夏	Ningxia	132	119	51	1342	175	664	368	284
新　疆	Xinjiang	186	97	215	1511	555	240	491	183
新疆兵团	Xinjiang Corps	17	384	61	75	18	54	3	35
黑龙江垦区	Heilongjiang Land Reclamation	27	292	46	10			10	

4-3 续表 2 continued 2

地 区	Region	以寄宿制方式托养的残疾人 PWDs Fostered in the Form of Boarding	智力残疾人 Persons with Intellectual Disability	精神残疾人 Persons with Psychiatric Disability	重度肢体残疾人 Persons with Severe Physical Disability	以日间照料方式托养的残疾人 PWDs Fostered in the Form of Day Care	智力残疾人 Persons with Intellectual Disability	精神残疾人 Persons with Psychiatric Disability	重度肢体残疾人 Persons with Severe Physical Disability	享受居家托养服务残疾人 PWDs Recieving Fostering Service at Home
		人 person	人 person	人 person	人 person	人 person	人 person	人 person	人 person	人 person
全 国	**Total**	**37791**	**10622**	**9838**	**9494**	**22709**	**9050**	**5131**	**4614**	**770672**
北 京	Beijing	419	63	209	65	218	57	21	59	106495
天 津	Tianjin	41	20	4	8	17	11	2	4	23891
河 北	Hebei	1456	293	703	319	2500	230	422	1327	15845
山 西	Shanxi	273	51	82	64	85	24	15	21	13801
内蒙古	Inner Mongolia	614	171	38	216	153	13	13	97	16305
辽 宁	Liaoning	1229	422	352	306	349	171	40	106	28733
吉 林	Jilin	363	175	111	45	8	6	2		15945
黑龙江	Heilongjiang	1550	363	253	495	206	102	32	42	15614
上 海	Shanghai	89	1	87		83		83		13019
江 苏	Jiangsu	10601	3873	1601	2786	5232	1800	813	1209	39294
浙 江	Zhejiang	4220	715	1432	1330	6476	4192	1615	266	74469
安 徽	Anhui	1677	271	107	531	156	65	38	28	15551
福 建	Fujian	832	192	409	108	532	166	248	34	25010
江 西	Jiangxi	278	130	105	33	50	37	3	5	14201
山 东	Shandong	4628	1317	1294	1468	1200	411	277	333	28392
河 南	Henan	917	233	189	334	149	38	12	62	18710
湖 北	Hubei	1133	152	317	44	870	291	218	140	14890
湖 南	Hunan	894	205	477	152	523	177	173	128	18579
广 东	Guangdong	1981	766	631	231	878	241	140	188	17671
广 西	Guangxi	21	12	9						33222
海 南	Hainan									14381
重 庆	Chongqing	417	79	251	7	131	88	23		19742
四 川	Sichuan	874	185	405	177	359	119	50	89	40238
贵 州	Guizhou	243	45	69	34	24	12	2	10	13937
云 南	Yunnan	332	57	178	49	95	34	43	4	21279
西 藏	Tibet									3168
陕 西	Shaanxi	1541	527	240	405	830	242	204	270	20536
甘 肃	Gansu	653	194	233	93	1272	446	597	109	17402
青 海	Qinghai	234	31	6	100	92	8	2	12	17488
宁 夏	Ningxia	120	56	15	30	164	48	28	57	14295
新 疆	Xinjiang	126	18	7	61	57	21	15	14	30211
新疆兵团	Xinjiang Corps	35	5	24	3					7226
黑龙江垦区	Heilongjiang Land Reclamation									1132

5-1　农村贫困残疾人扶持效果
Poverty Alleviation for PWDs in Rural Areas

地　区	Region	贫困残疾人扶持效果 Results of Assisting PWDs to Get Rid of Poverty				残疾人实用技术培训 Training on Applied Technologies for PWDs	
		本年扶持贫困残疾人户 Poor Households with Disabled Member Assisted in 2014	本年扶持贫困残疾人 PWDs Assisted in 2014	本年实际脱贫 Rural PWDs who Got Rid of Poverty in 2014	本年返贫 Reimpoverished PWDs in 2014	本年度培训残疾人 Training on Applied Technologies for PWDs in 2014	本年度培训投入经费 Fund for Training on Applied Technologies for PWDs in 2014
		万户 10,000 households	万人次 10,000 person-times	万人 10,000 persons	万人 10,000 persons	万人次 10,000 person-times	万元 10,000 yuan
全　国	**Total**	**158.41**	**233.23**	**119.91**	**18.48**	**72.62**	**25017.33**
北　京	Beijing					0.29	31.50
天　津	Tianjin	2.16	2.48			0.27	89.57
河　北	Hebei	16.27	21.59	13.84	1.09	4.97	1439.82
山　西	Shanxi	5.64	8.10	3.85	1.14	1.36	453.06
内蒙古	Inner Mongolia	2.30	4.13	4.23	0.64	1.69	465.12
辽　宁	Liaoning	5.06	6.36	3.37	0.42	1.57	382.83
吉　林	Jilin	1.82	2.85	2.18	0.12	2.57	380.88
黑龙江	Heilongjiang	1.73	1.83	1.36	0.13	1.61	115.80
上　海	Shanghai	0.31	0.46			0.63	265.09
江　苏	Jiangsu	2.24	3.04	2.21	0.10	1.84	1126.80
浙　江	Zhejiang	7.45	10.42	2.98	0.45	1.97	1413.36
安　徽	Anhui	10.90	15.22	3.18	0.67	2.27	764.07
福　建	Fujian	2.53	3.07	1.70	0.11	1.57	769.65
江　西	Jiangxi	2.57	4.06	4.75	0.38	0.76	400.00
山　东	Shandong	8.69	13.73	6.30	0.43	4.44	1405.39
河　南	Henan	6.22	16.90	7.91	0.59	4.74	2094.35
湖　北	Hubei	5.79	12.91	4.86	0.41	2.99	608.17
湖　南	Hunan	5.41	8.85	4.14	0.66	1.45	1192.33
广　东	Guangdong	2.74	5.09	2.19	0.06	1.38	636.08
广　西	Guangxi	3.43	5.98	3.84	0.65	3.15	820.59
海　南	Hainan	0.34	0.65	0.22	0.06	0.74	423.85
重　庆	Chongqing	4.25	4.94	2.33	0.46	2.14	955.34
四　川	Sichuan	19.60	21.24	14.06	3.31	11.35	3143.79
贵　州	Guizhou	5.69	9.15	5.95	1.04	1.70	560.36
云　南	Yunnan	5.45	7.45	3.09	1.46	4.37	1807.81
西　藏	Tibet	0.04	0.07	0.01		0.02	295.00
陕　西	Shaanxi	14.60	21.53	8.27	1.34	1.55	969.43
甘　肃	Gansu	8.56	12.68	9.69	2.31	4.43	1008.64
青　海	Qinghai	1.12	1.43	0.81	0.06	0.60	124.54
宁　夏	Ningxia	1.47	1.62	1.28	0.19	0.72	154.19
新　疆	Xinjiang	2.73	3.30	0.97	0.16	1.96	317.12
新疆兵团	Xinjiang Corps	0.87	1.56	0.19	0.05	1.20	329.55
黑龙江垦区	Heilongjiang Land Reclamation	0.43	0.54	0.15		0.30	73.28

5-2 扶贫资金与残疾人扶贫贷款
Poverty Alleviation Fund and Loans

地 区	Region	扶贫资金 Poverty Alleviation Fund		残疾人扶贫贷款 Poverty Alleviation Fund and Loans		
				康复扶贫贴息贷款 Interest-subsidized Loans for Rehabilitation		
		省级财政投入 Poverty Alleviation Fund from the Provincial Budget	社会募集 Fund Raised From Society	本年度贷款实际落实 Actually Allocated Loans in 2014	本年度项目贷款扶持贫困残疾人 Poor PWDs Supported by Loans for Project in 2014	本年度到户贷款扶持贫困残疾人 Poor PWDs Supported by Loans to the Households in 2014
		万元 10,000 yuan	万元 10,000 yuan	万元 10,000 yuan	人 person	人 person
全 国	**Total**	**34932.7**	**2791.1**	**94135.8**	**24104**	**36522**
北 京	Beijing	3458.6				
天 津	Tianjin	1505.7				
河 北	Hebei			5498.5	924	1695
山 西	Shanxi	250.0	5.5	4742.9	746	1715
内蒙古	Inner Mongolia		7.0	4282.8	417	3132
辽 宁	Liaoning	560.0		4640.0	1349	599
吉 林	Jilin			4056.0	336	1573
黑龙江	Heilongjiang	715.7	31.3	1543.7	181	336
上 海	Shanghai					
江 苏	Jiangsu	530.0	14.5	1800.0	431	737
浙 江	Zhejiang	10214.5	862.1	1380.6	289	605
安 徽	Anhui	542.8	0.2	4192.9	1084	202
福 建	Fujian	629.5	64.0	1151.2	618	337
江 西	Jiangxi	107.9	30.0	5074.0	2531	986
山 东	Shandong	815.3	279.3	4000.0	1460	360
河 南	Henan	1000.0	0.5	5503.0	1118	811
湖 北	Hubei	302.0	24.0	4800.0	2027	1762
湖 南	Hunan	320.0	747.9	4586.0		1415
广 东	Guangdong	63.4	59.5	1800.0	900	300
广 西	Guangxi	5281.8	264.2	2891.0	612	897
海 南	Hainan	146.9		686.0	142	14
重 庆	Chongqing	3000.0	251.2	2075.0	661	109
四 川	Sichuan	1471.8	3.5	5504.0	1241	1218
贵 州	Guizhou	67.4		2314.4	103	316
云 南	Yunnan	463.9	33.0	3389.0	1249	881
西 藏	Tibet					
陕 西	Shaanxi	2298.4	40.0	5503.0	2101	12461
甘 肃	Gansu	363.0	24.0	3857.0	1007	1163
青 海	Qinghai	106.4	19.7	1813.0	181	469
宁 夏	Ningxia	35.0		1890.8	1160	386
新 疆	Xinjiang	86.7	1.0	3771.0	907	1807
新疆兵团	Xinjiang Corps	596.0		1303.0	300	236
黑龙江垦区	Heilongjiang Land Reclamation		28.8	87.0	29	

5-3 社会帮扶与残疾人扶贫基地建设

Social Assistance and Construction of Poverty Alleviation Bases

地 区	Region	社会帮扶 Social Assistance for Needy PWDs		残疾人扶贫基地建设 Poverty Alleviation bases for PWDs		
		结对帮扶单位 Companies or Units who Assisted PWDs in One-to-one way	结对帮扶个人 Individuals who Assisted PWDs in One-to-one way	残疾人扶贫基地 Poverty Alleviation Bases for PWDs	安置残疾人就业 Providing Employment for Disabled Persons	扶持带动贫困残疾人 Supporting and Leading Disabled Persons
		个 unit	人 person	个 unit	人 person	户 household
全 国	**Total**	**74058**	**456131**	**6593**	**124031**	**257987**
北 京	Beijing			121	3814	3824
天 津	Tianjin	167	255	176	1904	3640
河 北	Hebei	1221	6392	216	4897	11543
山 西	Shanxi	989	2592	216	3640	5092
内蒙古	Inner Mongolia	2392	6132	108	2101	3286
辽 宁	Liaoning	3476	20152	42	1400	1878
吉 林	Jilin	1649	4218	259	3861	8520
黑龙江	Heilongjiang	2629	3800	156	5033	7415
上 海	Shanghai	451	1161	66	1617	1825
江 苏	Jiangsu	1870	10716	457	11622	16254
浙 江	Zhejiang	10405	101462	1242	8981	23378
安 徽	Anhui	1125	9203	122	1998	2569
福 建	Fujian	1235	3484	199	4413	4605
江 西	Jiangxi	2601	12288	167	2269	2927
山 东	Shandong	10427	20711	782	15783	37320
河 南	Henan	1975	52475	341	11175	15490
湖 北	Hubei	1525	6124	102	2797	10475
湖 南	Hunan	2183	10855	196	4834	11337
广 东	Guangdong	1501	8242	94	3666	5614
广 西	Guangxi	7151	18149	128	2427	14050
海 南	Hainan	275	341	6	101	258
重 庆	Chongqing	991	8698	91	1130	1611
四 川	Sichuan	4478	27710	378	9834	19821
贵 州	Guizhou	550	4843	174	1179	15133
云 南	Yunnan	2339	24035	175	1943	7847
西 藏	Tibet	32	143			
陕 西	Shaanxi	1698	9119	226	4404	10314
甘 肃	Gansu	5141	71109	99	2398	3540
青 海	Qinghai	346	867	37	457	444
宁 夏	Ningxia	377	1413	32	632	2169
新 疆	Xinjiang	1643	6017	160	3342	4891
新疆兵团	Xinjiang Corps	1117	2779	22	351	881
黑龙江垦区	Heilongjiang Land Reclamation	99	646	3	28	36

5-4 农村贫困残疾人危房改造

House Renovation for Poor PWDs in Rural Areas

地区	Region	本年度危房改造实际完成 Houses Renovated for PWDs in 2014	本年度危房改造项目受益贫困残疾人 Poor PWDs who Benefited by House Renovation Project in 2014	本年度投入资金 Fund Input in Houses Renovation in 2014	省级投入资金 Fund from the Provincial Budgets	地市级投入资金 Fund from the Prefectural/ City Level Budgets	县级投入资金 Fund from the County Level Budgets
		户 household	人 person	万元 10,000 yuan	万元 10,000 yuan	万元 10,000 yuan	万元 10,000 yuan
全国	**Total**	**89566**	**103272**	**84725.9**	**35641.2**	**13147.4**	**35937.2**
北京	Beijing	657	677	553.2	41.1	242.3	269.8
天津	Tianjin	1433	1470	5019.0	1353.0		3666.0
河北	Hebei	2651	3491	813.4	64.6	37.0	711.8
山西	Shanxi	9	13	10.0		6.0	4.0
内蒙古	Inner Mongolia	7033	8005	5455.2	1263.3	1512.1	2679.8
辽宁	Liaoning	3074	3341	3810.9		1154.5	2656.4
吉林	Jilin	143	153	152.1	41.8		110.3
黑龙江	Heilongjiang	1290	1327	1236.0	600.0	358.0	278.0
上海	Shanghai	301	316	1007.4	326.7	469.6	211.0
江苏	Jiangsu	682	785	239.2		2.5	236.7
浙江	Zhejiang	3802	4347	4631.9	242.7	732.3	3656.9
安徽	Anhui	6644	8104	3712.7	2662.3	479.8	570.6
福建	Fujian	4269	5476	6078.2	2488.6	1629.9	1959.8
江西	Jiangxi	2413	2498	1225.4	836.5	170.0	218.9
山东	Shandong	1986	2271	2761.8	581.9	1149.8	1030.2
河南	Henan	1636	1820	364.4			364.4
湖北	Hubei	513	582	138.6	82.0		56.6
湖南	Hunan	6997	8285	5680.0	2735.2	827.8	2117.0
广东	Guangdong	1324	1377	1464.6	59.5	904.0	501.1
广西	Guangxi	5848	6109	5639.3	3307.0	1046.7	1285.5
海南	Hainan	318	624	430.0	50.0		380.0
重庆	Chongqing	3607	3681	6454.2	2400.0		4054.2
四川	Sichuan	2889	3198	1763.3	402.9	69.1	1291.3
贵州	Guizhou	986	1426	947.6	413.2	22.2	512.2
云南	Yunnan	2395	3063	1693.3	441.9	364.8	886.6
西藏	Tibet	28	36	5.0			5.0
陕西	Shaanxi	3168	3588	4419.9	2140.0	697.5	1582.4
甘肃	Gansu	15020	18618	9085.9	6002.3	654.3	2429.3
青海	Qinghai	2031	2100	2532.2	1603.9	9.2	919.0
宁夏	Ningxia	75	81	49.1	49.1		
新疆	Xinjiang	5140	5188	1954.8	633.4	519.0	802.4
新疆兵团	Xinjiang Corps	854	858	5307.6	4818.3	89.0	400.3
黑龙江垦区	Heilongjiang Land Reclamation	350	364	90.0			90.0

6-1 省(自治区、直辖市)专门协会建立情况
Establishment of Special Associations in Prefectures

地 区	Region	盲人协会 Associations of Persons with Visual Disability Established	聋人协会 Associations of Persons with Hearing Disability Established	肢残人协会 Associations of Persons with Physical Disability Established	智力残疾人及亲友协会 Associations of Persons with Intellectual Disability and Their Relatives and Friends Established	精神残疾人及亲友协会 Associations of Persons with Psychiatric Disability and Their Relatives and Friends Established	备注 Remarks
		个 unit	个 unit	个 unit	个 unit	个 unit	个 unit
全 国	**Total**	**33**	**33**	**33**	**32**	**32**	**1**
北 京	Beijing	1	1	1	1	1	
天 津	Tianjin	1	1	1	1	1	
河 北	Hebei	1	1	1	1	1	
山 西	Shanxi	1	1	1	1	1	
内蒙古	Inner Mongolia	1	1	1	1	1	
辽 宁	Liaoning	1	1	1	1	1	
吉 林	Jilin	1	1	1	1	1	
黑龙江	Heilongjiang	1	1	1	1	1	
上 海	Shanghai	1	1	1	1	1	
江 苏	Jiangsu	1	1	1	1	1	
浙 江	Zhejiang	1	1	1	1	1	
安 徽	Anhui	1	1	1	1	1	
福 建	Fujian	1	1	1	1	1	
江 西	Jiangxi	1	1	1	1	1	
山 东	Shandong	1	1	1	1	1	
河 南	Henan	1	1	1	1	1	
湖 北	Hubei	1	1	1	1	1	
湖 南	Hunan	1	1	1	1	1	
广 东	Guangdong	1	1	1	1	1	
广 西	Guangxi	1	1	1	1	1	
海 南	Hainan	1	1	1	1	1	
重 庆	Chongqing	1	1	1	1	1	
四 川	Sichuan	1	1	1	1	1	
贵 州	Guizhou	1	1	1	1	1	
云 南	Yunnan	1	1	1	1	1	
西 藏	Tibet	1	1	1			
陕 西	Shaanxi	1	1	1	1	1	
甘 肃	Gansu	1	1	1	1	1	1
青 海	Qinghai	1	1	1	1	1	
宁 夏	Ningxia	1	1	1	1	1	
新 疆	Xinjiang	1	1	1	1	1	
新疆兵团	Xinjiang Corps	1	1	1	1	1	
黑龙江垦区	Heilongjiang Land Reclamation	1	1	1	1	1	

备注：指智力残疾人及亲友协会和精神残疾人及亲友协会合一的协会。

6－2 市(地、州、盟)专门协会建立情况
Establishment of Special Associations in Cities

地 区	Region	盲人协会 Associations of Persons with Visual Disability Established	聋人协会 Associations of Persons with Hearing Disability Established	肢残人协会 Associations of Persons with Physical Disability Established	智力残疾人及亲友协会 Associations of Persons with Intellectual Disability and Their Relatives and Friends Established	精神残疾人及亲友协会 Associations of Persons with Psychiatric Disability and Their Relatives and Friends Established	备注 Remarks
		个 unit	个 unit	个 unit	个 unit	个 unit	个 unit
全 国	**Total**	**340**	**341**	**342**	**331**	**330**	**12**
北 京	Beijing						
天 津	Tianjin						
河 北	Hebei	11	11	11	11	11	
山 西	Shanxi	11	11	11	11	11	
内蒙古	Inner Mongolia	12	12	12	11	11	2
辽 宁	Liaoning	14	14	14	14	14	
吉 林	Jilin	10	10	10	10	10	
黑龙江	Heilongjiang	13	13	13	13	13	
上 海	Shanghai						
江 苏	Jiangsu	13	13	13	13	13	
浙 江	Zhejiang	10	10	10	7	7	3
安 徽	Anhui	15	15	15	15	15	
福 建	Fujian	9	9	9	9	9	
江 西	Jiangxi	11	11	11	11	11	
山 东	Shandong	17	17	17	15	15	1
河 南	Henan	18	18	18	18	18	
湖 北	Hubei	13	13	13	13	13	
湖 南	Hunan	14	14	14	14	14	
广 东	Guangdong	21	21	21	21	21	
广 西	Guangxi	14	14	14	14	14	
海 南	Hainan	2	2	2	2	2	
重 庆	Chongqing						
四 川	Sichuan	21	21	21	21	21	
贵 州	Guizhou	7	7	7	7	7	
云 南	Yunnan	16	16	16	16	15	
西 藏	Tibet						
陕 西	Shaanxi	10	10	10	10	10	
甘 肃	Gansu	14	14	14	14	14	
青 海	Qinghai	8	8	8	8	8	
宁 夏	Ningxia	4	4	4	4	4	
新 疆	Xinjiang	13	14	13	13	13	3
新疆兵团	Xinjiang Corps	10	10	12	7	7	3
黑龙江垦区	Heilongjiang Land Reclamation	9	9	9	9	9	

备注：指智力残疾人及亲友协会和精神残疾人及亲友协会合一的协会。

6-3 县(县级市、市辖区)专门协会建立情况

Establishment of Special Associations in Districts under Cities

地 区	Region	盲人协会 Associations of Persons with Visual Disability Established	聋人协会 Associations of Persons with Hearing Disability Established	肢残人协会 Associations of Persons with Physical Disability Established	智力残疾人及亲友协会 Associations of Persons with Intellectual Disability and Their Relatives and Friends Established	精神残疾人及亲友协会 Associations of Persons with Psychiatric Disability and Their Relatives and Friends Established	备注 Remarks
		个 unit	个 unit	个 unit	个 unit	个 unit	个 unit
全 国	**Total**	**2788**	**2772**	**2797**	**2627**	**2624**	**165**
北 京	Beijing	16	16	16	16	16	
天 津	Tianjin	16	16	16	16	16	
河 北	Hebei	172	172	172	168	168	4
山 西	Shanxi	116	116	116	109	109	8
内蒙古	Inner Mongolia	101	101	102	86	86	20
辽 宁	Liaoning	103	103	104	102	102	1
吉 林	Jilin	63	62	63	62	62	
黑龙江	Heilongjiang	132	132	132	132	132	1
上 海	Shanghai	17	17	17	17	17	
江 苏	Jiangsu	102	102	102	92	92	10
浙 江	Zhejiang	89	87	90	53	52	31
安 徽	Anhui	95	94	97	87	84	9
福 建	Fujian	83	82	83	73	73	10
江 西	Jiangxi	77	77	77	76	76	2
山 东	Shandong	133	128	131	124	124	7
河 南	Henan	159	158	159	158	158	2
湖 北	Hubei	96	94	97	83	84	10
湖 南	Hunan	122	121	124	111	115	3
广 东	Guangdong	120	120	120	114	114	6
广 西	Guangxi	111	111	111	111	111	1
海 南	Hainan	15	15	15	14	13	2
重 庆	Chongqing	39	38	39	36	36	4
四 川	Sichuan	166	164	167	162	162	4
贵 州	Guizhou	69	69	70	68	68	6
云 南	Yunnan	126	126	126	120	119	8
西 藏	Tibet						
陕 西	Shaanxi	108	108	108	107	108	1
甘 肃	Gansu	82	82	82	81	81	3
青 海	Qinghai	46	45	45	45	45	
宁 夏	Ningxia	20	20	20	18	18	2
新 疆	Xinjiang	91	93	93	83	80	10
新疆兵团	Xinjiang Corps						
黑龙江垦区	Heilongjiang Land Reclamation	103	103	103	103	103	

备注：指智力残疾人及亲友协会和精神残疾人及亲友协会合一的协会。

7-1 盲人按摩

Blind Massage

地 区	Region	保健按摩人员本年度培训 Blind Health-care Masseurs Trained in 2014	医疗按摩人员本年度培训 Blind Therapeutical Masseurs Trained in 2014	按摩机构 Institutions of Blind Massage	
				医疗按摩机构 Therapeutical Blind Massage Clinics	保健按摩机构 Health-care Blind Massage Houses
		人 person	人 person	人 person	人 person
全 国	**Total**	**21296**	**5623**	**1018**	**15609**
北 京	Beijing	1491	279	4	396
天 津	Tianjin	21	18	4	167
河 北	Hebei	711	804	57	441
山 西	Shanxi	729	326	53	442
内蒙古	Inner Mongolia	237	125	51	287
辽 宁	Liaoning	550	168	28	875
吉 林	Jilin	1080	265	34	442
黑龙江	Heilongjiang	435	186	58	247
上 海	Shanghai	335	46		100
江 苏	Jiangsu	891	216	19	995
浙 江	Zhejiang	659	207	35	874
安 徽	Anhui	1214	119	126	411
福 建	Fujian	542	105	10	329
江 西	Jiangxi	747	291	72	542
山 东	Shandong	755	310	79	1266
河 南	Henan	1798	511	95	707
湖 北	Hubei	1137	219	51	822
湖 南	Hunan	1472	225	24	597
广 东	Guangdong	745	462	7	848
广 西	Guangxi	662	30	1	181
海 南	Hainan	387	30	3	166
重 庆	Chongqing	798	85	12	735
四 川	Sichuan	1160	105	48	1491
贵 州	Guizhou	496	48	10	433
云 南	Yunnan	595	49	11	714
西 藏	Tibet	17	10		17
陕 西	Shaanxi	752	54	65	351
甘 肃	Gansu	339	116	29	230
青 海	Qinghai	276	83	4	216
宁 夏	Ningxia	121	16	2	136
新 疆	Xinjiang	139	114	18	120
新疆兵团	Xinjiang Corps	5	1	7	29
黑龙江垦区	Heilongjiang Land Reclamation			1	2

7-1 续表 Continued

地 区	Region	盲人医疗按摩人员专业技术职务任职资格评审 Vocational Qualification Appraisal for the Blind Therapeutical Masseurs		盲人保健按摩人员就业 Employed Blind Health-care Masseurs	盲人医疗按摩人员就业 Employed Blind Therapeutical Masseurs	扶持特困盲人按摩师就业 Employed Blind Masseurs in Poverty Assisted in 2014
		中级 Middle Level Blind Therapeutical Masseurs	初级 Junior Level Blind Therapeutical Masseurs			
		人 person	人 person	人 person	人 person	人 person
全 国	**Total**	**494**	**1229**	**26515**	**2581**	**6920**
北 京	Beijing			688	32	5
天 津	Tianjin			487	21	33
河 北	Hebei	16	89	930	135	265
山 西	Shanxi	17	72	465	68	135
内蒙古	Inner Mongolia	13	24	464	75	247
辽 宁	Liaoning	12	8	418	60	82
吉 林	Jilin	14	36	835	143	254
黑龙江	Heilongjiang	56	64	385	69	95
上 海	Shanghai	15	37	362	6	
江 苏	Jiangsu	56	108	1087	65	275
浙 江	Zhejiang	5	121	1689	203	286
安 徽	Anhui	38	63	1387	131	239
福 建	Fujian	53	74	1215	138	262
江 西	Jiangxi	43	78	882	107	167
山 东	Shandong	9	35	1142	303	301
河 南	Henan	12	7	1230	192	656
湖 北	Hubei	23	99	1237	185	650
湖 南	Hunan	19	108	1607	222	447
广 东	Guangdong			1752	71	246
广 西	Guangxi		2	753	3	264
海 南	Hainan	9	27	555	20	209
重 庆	Chongqing	4	2	401	85	182
四 川	Sichuan	5	3	3532	79	596
贵 州	Guizhou	17	69	1087	28	173
云 南	Yunnan		8	410		303
西 藏	Tibet	9	6	6	2	1
陕 西	Shaanxi	26	20	742	51	148
甘 肃	Gansu	8	13	255	43	129
青 海	Qinghai	4	15	206	30	198
宁 夏	Ningxia	1	8	154	1	18
新 疆	Xinjiang		25	141	13	50
新疆兵团	Xinjiang Corps	6	3	6		4
黑龙江垦区	Heilongjiang Land Reclamation	4	5	5		

8-1 宣传文化
Publicity and Culture

地区	Region	宣传 Publicity					
		省级 at Provincial Level					
		中央级媒体采用稿件 Articles Used by Central Media	主要新闻媒体刊播稿件 Articles Used by Major Media	报纸专版 Features in Newspapers	广播电台残疾人专题栏目 Radio Broadcast Special Programs on Disability	电视手语栏目 Sign Language TV Programmes	电视公益广告片 Advertisement for Public Interest on TV
		件 piece	件 piece	个 unit	个 unit	个 unit	个 unit
全国	**Total**	**1145**	**13096**	**260**	**17**	**30**	**23**
北京	Beijing	346	986	51		1	3
天津	Tianjin	3	2150	6	1	2	1
河北	Hebei	25	810	5	1	1	2
山西	Shanxi		350	6	1	1	
内蒙古	Inner Mongolia		25			1	1
辽宁	Liaoning	28	420	18	1	1	
吉林	Jilin	31	515	6		1	1
黑龙江	Heilongjiang	20	80	10	1	1	1
上海	Shanghai	10	85	30	1	1	1
江苏	Jiangsu	12	307	3	1	2	3
浙江	Zhejiang	18	89	4		1	4
安徽	Anhui	35	534	3		1	
福建	Fujian	4	200	1		1	
江西	Jiangxi	89	106	5	2	1	
山东	Shandong	5	400	1			
河南	Henan	5	260	4		1	
湖北	Hubei	28	1500	22	1	1	1
湖南	Hunan	14	25	2		1	
广东	Guangdong	4	90	4	1	1	
广西	Guangxi		115	2	1	1	
海南	Hainan		185	4		1	
重庆	Chongqing	50	650	24	1	1	2
四川	Sichuan	10	100	15			
贵州	Guizhou						
云南	Yunnan		241	15		1	
西藏	Tibet	7	76	1			
陕西	Shaanxi	227	419			1	
甘肃	Gansu	69	680	7	1	2	2
青海	Qinghai	16	812		1	1	
宁夏	Ningxia		523	3	1	1	
新疆	Xinjiang	89	357	8	1	1	1
新疆兵团	Xinjiang Corps						
黑龙江垦区	Heilongjiang Land Reclamation		6				

8-1　续表 1　Continued 1

地　区　Region	宣传 Publicity					
	省级 at Provincial Level		地市级 at Prefectural/City Level			
	报纸公益广告 Advertisement for Public Interest on Newspaper	新促会 Societies for Promoting News Relating to PWDs	主要新闻媒体刊播稿件 Articles Used by Major Media	报纸专版 Features in Newspapers	广播电台残疾人专题栏目 Radio Broadcast Special Programs on Disability	电视手语栏目 Sign Language TV Programmes
	个 unit	个 unit	件 piece	个 unit	个 unit	个 unit
全　国　Total	**19**	**27**	**55701**	**1476**	**241**	**201**
北　京　Beijing		1	1023	72		3
天　津　Tianjin	1	1	228	8	1	3
河　北　Hebei			3190	65	10	10
山　西　Shanxi			1697	24	3	1
内蒙古　Inner Mongolia		1	1768	4	10	7
辽　宁　Liaoning		1	6316	44	6	10
吉　林　Jilin		1	1741	30	6	9
黑龙江　Heilongjiang	1	1	625	62	8	7
上　海　Shanghai		1	583	68	1	15
江　苏　Jiangsu	12	1	2765	137	15	14
浙　江　Zhejiang		1	4178	36	10	10
安　徽　Anhui			4865	131	9	10
福　建　Fujian		1	885	15	5	8
江　西　Jiangxi		1	645	9	3	5
山　东　Shandong		1	3658	58	12	9
河　南　Henan		1	750	32	9	4
湖　北　Hubei	1	1	2097	117	16	5
湖　南　Hunan		2	3036	122	7	1
广　东　Guangdong		1	2913	57	10	9
广　西　Guangxi		1	534	12	3	4
海　南　Hainan		1			1	
重　庆　Chongqing	1	1	1076	76	7	14
四　川　Sichuan		1	2461	67	25	4
贵　州　Guizhou			282	30	4	4
云　南　Yunnan		1	1533	67	5	7
西　藏　Tibet			2			
陕　西　Shaanxi		1	800	6	2	9
甘　肃　Gansu	2	1	3483	37	46	12
青　海　Qinghai		1	136	48		
宁　夏　Ningxia		1	347	12	2	4
新　疆　Xinjiang	1	1	617	25	5	3
新疆兵团　Xinjiang Corps			1274	5		
黑龙江垦区　Heilongjiang Land Reclamation			193			

8-1 续表 2 Continued 2

地 区	Region	宣传 Publicity			文化 Culture		
		地市级 at Prefectural/City Level			省级 at Provincial Level		
		电视公益广告片 Advertisement for Public Interest on TV	报纸公益广告 Advertisement for Public Interest on Newspaper	新促会 Societies for Promoting News Relating to PWDs	公共图书馆盲文及盲人有声读物图书室 Reading Rooms with Braille and Audio Reading Materials in Public Library	残疾人文化周 Culture Week for PWDs	残疾人文化艺术类比赛及展览 Cultural or Art Competitions and Exhibitions of PWDs
		个 unit	个 unit	个 unit	个 unit	场次 time	次 time
全 国	**Total**	**160**	**206**	**131**	**68**	**140**	**178**
北 京	Beijing	3	1	1	6	20	46
天 津	Tianjin	1	1	2	2	5	5
河 北	Hebei	14	12	6	1	3	5
山 西	Shanxi			3	2	1	1
内蒙古	Inner Mongolia	4		3	1	1	
辽 宁	Liaoning	1	3	3	1	3	2
吉 林	Jilin	7	4	6	2	5	2
黑龙江	Heilongjiang	2	2	4	1	1	2
上 海	Shanghai			2	1	16	4
江 苏	Jiangsu	23	79	9	1	5	7
浙 江	Zhejiang	8	4	8	1	1	5
安 徽	Anhui	2	8	4	1	2	1
福 建	Fujian	1		5	2	1	1
江 西	Jiangxi	6	3		1	2	3
山 东	Shandong	6	4	9	1	1	3
河 南	Henan	2	11	13	3	1	
湖 北	Hubei	12	28		20	17	18
湖 南	Hunan	4	10	6	8	1	3
广 东	Guangdong	19	1	22	2	4	4
广 西	Guangxi	3			1	1	
海 南	Hainan				1	3	1
重 庆	Chongqing	11	3	1	1	5	1
四 川	Sichuan	17	21			27	52
贵 州	Guizhou		2	3			
云 南	Yunnan	1	1	9	1		
西 藏	Tibet						
陕 西	Shaanxi	1	1	3	1	4	1
甘 肃	Gansu	10	6	6	1	1	2
青 海	Qinghai				1	5	5
宁 夏	Ningxia				1	1	
新 疆	Xinjiang	2	1	3	3	2	4
新疆兵团	Xinjiang Corps						
黑龙江垦区	Heilongjiang Land Reclamation					1	

8-1　续表 3　Continued 3

地　区	Region	文化 Culture 省级 at Provincial Level 残疾人艺术团 PWDs' Performing Art Troupes	地市级 at Prefectural/City Level 公共图书馆盲文及盲人有声读物图书室 Reading Rooms with Braille and Audio Reading Materials in Public Library	残疾人文化周 Culture Week for PWDs	残疾人文化艺术类比赛及展览 Cultural or Art Competitions and Exhibitions of PWDs	残疾人艺术团 PWDs' Performing Art Troupes
		个 unit	个 unit	场次 time	次 time	个 unit
全　国	**Total**	**56**	**394**	**1216**	**781**	**208**
北　京	Beijing	1				
天　津	Tianjin	4				
河　北	Hebei		22	115	46	7
山　西	Shanxi		14	21	18	6
内蒙古	Inner Mongolia		19	19	17	7
辽　宁	Liaoning	1	22	93	54	9
吉　林	Jilin		9	22	18	6
黑龙江	Heilongjiang	1	16	30	40	13
上　海	Shanghai	1				
江　苏	Jiangsu	1	17	81	73	16
浙　江	Zhejiang	2	9	18	16	14
安　徽	Anhui		25	121	31	12
福　建	Fujian	1	9	5	13	4
江　西	Jiangxi	1	9	13	10	6
山　东	Shandong	1	30	105	53	21
河　南	Henan	1	18	66	38	3
湖　北	Hubei	19	10	43	22	7
湖　南	Hunan		28	108	92	29
广　东	Guangdong	1	40	79	31	12
广　西	Guangxi	1	8	19	2	5
海　南	Hainan	1	1	5	3	
重　庆	Chongqing					
四　川	Sichuan	1	23	32	77	3
贵　州	Guizhou		9	18	9	1
云　南	Yunnan	14	13	55	29	12
西　藏	Tibet				1	
陕　西	Shaanxi	1	17	20	13	4
甘　肃	Gansu	1	13	37	35	2
青　海	Qinghai	1	4	8	5	1
宁　夏	Ningxia		5	12	15	2
新　疆	Xinjiang	1	3	35	5	6
新疆兵团	Xinjiang Corps		1	17	4	
黑龙江垦区	Heilongjiang Land Reclamation			19	11	

9-1 体　育
Sports

地　区	Region	省级 at Provincial Level					
		残疾人群众体育健身活动 Massive Sports and Fitness Activities for PWDs	残疾人群众体育健身活动参加人数 Participation in Massive Sports and Fitness Activities for PWDs	残疾人群众体育活动示范点 Sports Activity Demonstration Sites for PWDs	残疾人体育健身指导员 Coaches for Fitness Activity for PWDs	残疾人体育比赛 Sports Events for PWDs	参赛残疾人运动员 Disabled Athletes who Participated in the Sports Events
		次 time	人次 person-time	个 unit	人 person	次 time	人次 person-time
全　国	**Total**	**241**	**61797**	**839**	**11045**	**151**	**22875**
北　京	Beijing	30	15500	69	1500	30	532
天　津	Tianjin	11	7085	34	255	9	3000
河　北	Hebei	20	1556	58	210	25	1000
山　西	Shanxi	2	360	30	549	1	405
内蒙古	Inner Mongolia	3	150	6	14	7	25
辽　宁	Liaoning				137	1	556
吉　林	Jilin	3	2300	50	264	1	378
黑龙江	Heilongjiang	3	270	43	420	5	340
上　海	Shanghai	14	2455	273	351	22	4600
江　苏	Jiangsu	6	2980	16	224	3	278
浙　江	Zhejiang	4	1230	7	240	3	705
安　徽	Anhui				558	1	686
福　建	Fujian	30	3000	30	212	1	150
江　西	Jiangxi	3	621	35	936	1	210
山　东	Shandong	4	2000	20	2100	1	2000
河　南	Henan	1	1700		50	1	800
湖　北	Hubei	17	2500	25	1003	1	400
湖　南	Hunan	8	663	8	110	4	1382
广　东	Guangdong	7	920	25	218	4	250
广　西	Guangxi	1	100	3	284	1	546
海　南	Hainan	4	250		115	1	350
重　庆	Chongqing	5	1600	13	120	2	968
四　川	Sichuan	5	3000	5	35	1	90
贵　州	Guizhou			15	50		
云　南	Yunnan	2	57	8	12	1	887
西　藏	Tibet				1		
陕　西	Shaanxi	41	4000	30	390	15	220
甘　肃	Gansu	2	1200	18	507	2	697
青　海	Qinghai	12	2600	5	70	6	850
宁　夏	Ningxia	2	2200	13	107		
新　疆	Xinjiang	1	1500			1	570
新疆兵团	Xinjiang Corps				3		
黑龙江垦区	Heilongjiang Land Reclamation						

9-1　续表　Continued

地　区	Region	省级 at Provincial Level			地市级 at Prefectural/City Level			
		残疾人体育训练基地 Sports Training Bases for PWDs	残疾人体育训练基地在编人员 Full-time Staff at Sports Training Bases for PWDs	聘任教练员 Stable Coaches	残疾人体育活动 Sports Activity of PWDs	残疾人体育活动参加残疾人 Participants with Disabilities in Sports Activity of PWDs	残疾人群众体育活动示范点 Sports Activity Demonstration Sites for PWDs	残疾人体育健身指导员 Coaches for Fitness Activity for PWDs
		个 unit	人 person	人 person	次 time	人次 person-time	个 unit	人 person
全　国	**Total**	**234**	**598**	**785**	**5544**	**693930**	**1930**	**17671**
北　京	Beijing	10	65	32	1538	97750	87	761
天　津	Tianjin	6	42	13	142	6124	51	527
河　北	Hebei	16	50	53	126	10662	165	1826
山　西	Shanxi			18	54	1982	40	282
内蒙古	Inner Mongolia	2			19	1171	24	148
辽　宁	Liaoning	28	50	25	98	53570	57	629
吉　林	Jilin	16	46	15	80	6447	193	853
黑龙江	Heilongjiang	5	5	8	19	3890	11	279
上　海	Shanghai	5	17	160	1078	266852	206	629
江　苏	Jiangsu	2	20	32	96	9081	98	93
浙　江	Zhejiang	7	72	35	26	6179	183	1000
安　徽	Anhui	1	7	15	937	34729	58	494
福　建	Fujian	15	38	58	55	2719	43	1397
江　西	Jiangxi	2	8	13	15	1045	4	13
山　东	Shandong	4	36	20	81	3149	61	288
河　南	Henan	6	6	10	63	7912	19	2400
湖　北	Hubei	10	10	24	126	17177	80	237
湖　南	Hunan	8	8	18	138	8858	66	1003
广　东	Guangdong	12	15	30	141	17009	46	879
广　西	Guangxi	1		40	26	3449	16	421
海　南	Hainan	10	15	20	2	80	3	4
重　庆	Chongqing	5	10	15	300	24807	129	486
四　川	Sichuan	13	13	45	178	13403	177	1686
贵　州	Guizhou	4	8	11	10	1912	16	130
云　南	Yunnan	1	10	20	65	7916	21	495
西　藏	Tibet							1
陕　西	Shaanxi	28	30	16	51	4181	32	186
甘　肃	Gansu	9	9	22	30	77729	18	221
青　海	Qinghai	1	1	8	5	353	1	4
宁　夏	Ningxia	2	2	3	8	232	19	52
新　疆	Xinjiang	5	5	6	22	2177	4	160
新疆兵团	Xinjiang Corps				15	1385	2	87
黑龙江垦区	Heilongjiang Land Reclamation							

10-1 法规体系
Legal System

地 区	Region	省级修订《残疾人保障法实施办法》 Revision of the Implementation Method of the Law on the Protection of PWDs	制定或修改关于残疾人的专门法规、规章 Laws and Regulations Enacted or Reviewed Specially for PWDs	省级 at Provincial Level	地市级 at Prefectural/ City Level	制定或修改保障残疾人权益的规范性文件 Regulations Enacted Or Reviewed Directly Related to PWDs	省级 at Provincial Level	地市级 at Prefectural/ City Level	县级 at County Level
		个 unit	个 unit	个 unit	个 unit	个 unit	个 unit	个 unit	个 unit
全 国	**Total**	**1**	**18**	**8**	**10**	**427**	**22**	**71**	**334**
北 京	Beijing								
天 津	Tianjin					11	10		1
河 北	Hebei					32	1	6	25
山 西	Shanxi					9		1	8
内蒙古	Inner Mongolia					3		1	2
辽 宁	Liaoning					4		1	3
吉 林	Jilin					11		2	9
黑龙江	Heilongjiang		2		2	3	1	1	1
上 海	Shanghai					5			5
江 苏	Jiangsu					27		1	26
浙 江	Zhejiang		2	1	1	44	1	8	35
安 徽	Anhui					5		2	3
福 建	Fujian					9		2	7
江 西	Jiangxi		2		2	16		5	11
山 东	Shandong		2	1	1	67		14	53
河 南	Henan					20	1	5	14
湖 北	Hubei					5			5
湖 南	Hunan					14		1	13
广 东	Guangdong					13		5	8
广 西	Guangxi					10		2	8
海 南	Hainan								
重 庆	Chongqing					16			16
四 川	Sichuan		2		2	38	1	5	32
贵 州	Guizhou	1	1		1	7	1	1	5
云 南	Yunnan					7		2	5
西 藏	Tibet					1			1
陕 西	Shaanxi					3	2		1
甘 肃	Gansu		6	6		38	2	5	31
青 海	Qinghai					3	1		2
宁 夏	Ningxia		1		1	2		1	1
新 疆	Xinjiang					3			3
新疆兵团	Xinjiang Corps								
黑龙江垦区	Heilongjiang Land Reclamation					1	1		

10-2 执法检查
Inspections on Law Enforcement

地 区	Region	人大执法检查或专题调研 Inspections and Investigations by Officials of People's Congresses	省级 at Provincial Level	地市级 at Prefectural/City Level	县级 at County Level
		次 time	次 time	次 time	次 time
全 国	**Total**	**649**	**12**	**100**	**537**
北 京	Beijing	2			2
天 津	Tianjin	7			7
河 北	Hebei	51		6	45
山 西	Shanxi	29		4	25
内蒙古	Inner Mongolia	16		2	14
辽 宁	Liaoning	15		4	11
吉 林	Jilin	6			6
黑龙江	Heilongjiang	15		2	13
上 海	Shanghai	3	1		2
江 苏	Jiangsu	34		5	29
浙 江	Zhejiang	52	1	6	45
安 徽	Anhui	36	1	7	28
福 建	Fujian	18	1	3	14
江 西	Jiangxi	30	1	3	26
山 东	Shandong	58	1	7	50
河 南	Henan	42	1	17	24
湖 北	Hubei	32	1	8	23
湖 南	Hunan	25		3	22
广 东	Guangdong	11	1	5	5
广 西	Guangxi	6			6
海 南	Hainan	1			1
重 庆	Chongqing	16			16
四 川	Sichuan	41	1	4	36
贵 州	Guizhou	15	1	3	11
云 南	Yunnan	18		3	15
西 藏	Tibet	2			2
陕 西	Shaanxi	10			10
甘 肃	Gansu	39		6	33
青 海	Qinghai	5		1	4
宁 夏	Ningxia	3			3
新 疆	Xinjiang	11	1	1	9
新疆兵团	Xinjiang Corps				
黑龙江垦区	Heilongjiang Land Reclamation				

10-2 续表 Continued

地 区	Region	政协视察或专题调研 Inspections and Investigations by Officials of People's Political Consultative Conferences	省级 at Provincial Level	地市级 at Prefectural/City Level	县级 at County Level
		次 time	次 time	次 time	次 time
全 国	**Total**	**635**	**12**	**98**	**525**
北 京	Beijing	2			2
天 津	Tianjin	3			3
河 北	Hebei	51	1	4	46
山 西	Shanxi	22		2	20
内蒙古	Inner Mongolia	9		1	8
辽 宁	Liaoning	14		5	9
吉 林	Jilin	7			7
黑龙江	Heilongjiang	17		4	13
上 海	Shanghai	1			1
江 苏	Jiangsu	37		6	31
浙 江	Zhejiang	70	1	7	62
安 徽	Anhui	36	1	4	31
福 建	Fujian	21	1	1	19
江 西	Jiangxi	25	3	4	18
山 东	Shandong	35		3	32
河 南	Henan	27		7	20
湖 北	Hubei	31		6	25
湖 南	Hunan	33		3	30
广 东	Guangdong	11		7	4
广 西	Guangxi	4		1	3
海 南	Hainan	1			1
重 庆	Chongqing	23			23
四 川	Sichuan	58	1	18	39
贵 州	Guizhou	10		2	8
云 南	Yunnan	14		1	13
西 藏	Tibet				
陕 西	Shaanxi	11	1	1	9
甘 肃	Gansu	37	2	7	28
青 海	Qinghai	12	1	2	9
宁 夏	Ningxia	5		1	4
新 疆	Xinjiang	8		1	7
新疆兵团	Xinjiang Corps				
黑龙江垦区	Heilongjiang Land Reclamation				

10-3 法制宣传
Publicity on Laws

地 区	Region	普法宣传教育活动 Activities for Laws Publicity and Education	省级 at Provincial Level	地市级 at Prefectural/ City Level	县级 at County Level	普法宣传教育活动参加人数 Participants of Activities for Laws Publicity and Education	省级 at Provincial Level	地市级 at Prefectural/ City Level	县级 at County Level
		次 time	次 time	次 time	次 time	人 person	人 person	人 person	人 person
全 国	**Total**	**6510**	**62**	**757**	**5691**	**933256**	**12119**	**107561**	**813576**
北 京	Beijing	143	4		139	12658	800		11858
天 津	Tianjin	37	2		35	1990	200		1790
河 北	Hebei	243	2	30	211	33065	5000	7008	21057
山 西	Shanxi	173	2	26	145	36203	290	18538	17375
内蒙古	Inner Mongolia	205		23	182	17662		2018	15644
辽 宁	Liaoning	194	2	22	170	21035	120	4253	16662
吉 林	Jilin	160	1	19	140	14819	80	1363	13376
黑龙江	Heilongjiang	136	2	24	110	13093	166	3610	9317
上 海	Shanghai	107	6		101	12123	300		11823
江 苏	Jiangsu	406		30	376	40912		4080	36832
浙 江	Zhejiang	248	3	22	223	42312	155	3227	38930
安 徽	Anhui	324	2	44	278	20906	300	3331	17275
福 建	Fujian	195		14	181	12675		1636	11039
江 西	Jiangxi	136	1	21	114	10329	75	806	9448
山 东	Shandong	248	1	34	213	19175	157	4866	14152
河 南	Henan	249		39	210	45624		5782	39842
湖 北	Hubei	169	2	24	143	39165	300	5871	32994
湖 南	Hunan	236		26	210	14502		1784	12718
广 东	Guangdong	248	2	99	147	25517	1000	11269	13248
广 西	Guangxi	211	8	12	191	57087	400	4218	52469
海 南	Hainan	19	2	3	14	2269	226	120	1923
重 庆	Chongqing	192	2		190	67841	212		67629
四 川	Sichuan	683	3	79	601	127740	330	3753	123657
贵 州	Guizhou	269	2	21	246	38342	200	1604	36538
云 南	Yunnan	296		17	279	30455		1480	28975
西 藏	Tibet	96	3	4	89	6718	450	1800	4468
陕 西	Shaanxi	143	1	27	115	16397	50	4568	11779
甘 肃	Gansu	164	1	31	132	60888	50	3783	57055
青 海	Qinghai	79	2	10	67	6589	240	306	6043
宁 夏	Ningxia	44	3	10	31	2595	120	320	2155
新 疆	Xinjiang	215	1	22	192	59551	48	3206	56297
新疆兵团	Xinjiang Corps	178		9	169	19916		1913	18003
黑龙江垦区	Heilongjiang Land Reclamation	64	2	15	47	3103	850	1048	1205

10-3 续表 Continued

地 区	Region	残疾人工作者法律培训班 Training Courses for Laws	省级 at Provincial Level	地市级 at Prefectural/ City Level	县级 at County Level	法律培训班参加人数 Trainees of Laws Courses	省级 at Provincial Level	地市级 at Prefectural/ City Level	县级 at County Level
		次 time	次 time	次 time	次 time	人 person	人 person	人 person	人 person
全 国	**Total**	**1511**	**32**	**170**	**1309**	**91702**	**2581**	**15045**	**74076**
北 京	Beijing	21	1		20	2601	300		2301
天 津	Tianjin	13	1		12	869	125		744
河 北	Hebei	66	1	5	60	2703	120	279	2304
山 西	Shanxi	51		10	41	3224		825	2399
内蒙古	Inner Mongolia	53		2	51	2313		44	2269
辽 宁	Liaoning	53	3	13	37	5768	220	2532	3016
吉 林	Jilin	62	2	5	55	3491	160	339	2992
黑龙江	Heilongjiang	31		9	22	1110		256	854
上 海	Shanghai	28	2		26	1669	65		1604
江 苏	Jiangsu	79	1	10	68	5347	60	651	4636
浙 江	Zhejiang	73	1	9	63	4716	30	960	3726
安 徽	Anhui	65	1	9	55	2860	60	599	2201
福 建	Fujian	39		5	34	5243		410	4833
江 西	Jiangxi	42	1	4	37	2083	60	94	1929
山 东	Shandong	124	3	11	110	5743	400	841	4502
河 南	Henan	76		8	68	4991		1680	3311
湖 北	Hubei	62	2	6	54	2659	100	737	1822
湖 南	Hunan	70	1	7	62	3214	50	398	2766
广 东	Guangdong	49	2	18	29	3979	180	1397	2402
广 西	Guangxi	43	2	2	39	2950	130	101	2719
海 南	Hainan	2		1	1	120		30	90
重 庆	Chongqing	60	2		58	3709	160		3549
四 川	Sichuan	119	2	15	102	7883	5	1140	6738
贵 州	Guizhou	31		4	27	3012		426	2586
云 南	Yunnan	42		1	41	1879		22	1857
西 藏	Tibet								
陕 西	Shaanxi	28	1	5	22	1579	50	710	819
甘 肃	Gansu	50	1	6	43	2651	140	368	2143
青 海	Qinghai	25	1	1	23	910	76	38	796
宁 夏	Ningxia	21		3	18	687		138	549
新 疆	Xinjiang	30		1	29	1589		30	1559
新疆兵团	Xinjiang Corps								
黑龙江垦区	Heilongjiang Land Reclamation	3	1		2	150	90		60

10-4 法律救助
Legal Aid

地 区	Region	建立残疾人法律救助协调组织 Legal Assistance and Coordination Organization for PWDs			
		建立残疾人法律救助工作协调机构 Legal Assistance and Coordination Organization for PWDs	省级 at Provincial Level	地市级 at Prefectural/City Level	县级 at County Level
		个 unit	个 unit	个 unit	个 unit
全 国	**Total**	**1521**	**26**	**207**	**1288**
北 京	Beijing	13	1		12
天 津	Tianjin	17	1		16
河 北	Hebei	145	1	11	133
山 西	Shanxi	17	1	5	11
内蒙古	Inner Mongolia	54		3	51
辽 宁	Liaoning	66	1	13	52
吉 林	Jilin	41	1	9	31
黑龙江	Heilongjiang	3	1	1	1
上 海	Shanghai	5	1		4
江 苏	Jiangsu	79	1	10	68
浙 江	Zhejiang	81	1	11	69
安 徽	Anhui	19	1	5	13
福 建	Fujian	46	1	6	39
江 西	Jiangxi	34	1	4	29
山 东	Shandong	71		8	63
河 南	Henan	110	1	17	92
湖 北	Hubei	98	1	11	86
湖 南	Hunan	76	1	14	61
广 东	Guangdong	44	1	10	33
广 西	Guangxi	39	1	7	31
海 南	Hainan	5			5
重 庆	Chongqing	27			27
四 川	Sichuan	80	1	11	68
贵 州	Guizhou	38	1	4	33
云 南	Yunnan	9	1	4	4
西 藏	Tibet				
陕 西	Shaanxi	77	1	9	67
甘 肃	Gansu	102	1	15	86
青 海	Qinghai	32		4	28
宁 夏	Ningxia	10		1	9
新 疆	Xinjiang	72	1	5	66
新疆兵团	Xinjiang Corps	5	1	4	
黑龙江垦区	Heilongjiang Land Reclamation	6	1	5	

10-4 续表 1 Continued 1

地区	Region	残疾人法律救助工作站 Legal Assistance Station for PWDs			
		残疾人法律救助工作站 Legal Assistance Station for PWDs	省级 at Provincial Level	地市级 at Prefectural/ City Level	县级 at County Level
		个 unit	个 unit	个 unit	个 unit
全　国	**Total**	**1348**	**18**	**188**	**1142**
北　京	Beijing	9			9
天　津	Tianjin	17	1		16
河　北	Hebei	144	1	11	132
山　西	Shanxi	8		4	4
内蒙古	Inner Mongolia	38		3	35
辽　宁	Liaoning	68	1	13	54
吉　林	Jilin	35		9	26
黑龙江	Heilongjiang	2		1	1
上　海	Shanghai	6	1		5
江　苏	Jiangsu	77	1	10	66
浙　江	Zhejiang	82	1	11	70
安　徽	Anhui	6		2	4
福　建	Fujian	45	1	6	38
江　西	Jiangxi	33	1	3	29
山　东	Shandong	69		8	61
河　南	Henan	96	1	14	81
湖　北	Hubei	60	1	11	48
湖　南	Hunan	75	1	13	61
广　东	Guangdong	37	1	10	26
广　西	Guangxi	42	1	7	34
海　南	Hainan	5			5
重　庆	Chongqing	27			27
四　川	Sichuan	67	1	11	55
贵　州	Guizhou	27		2	25
云　南	Yunnan	9	1	4	4
西　藏	Tibet				
陕　西	Shaanxi	64	1	7	56
甘　肃	Gansu	102	1	15	86
青　海	Qinghai	25		4	21
宁　夏	Ningxia	8		1	7
新　疆	Xinjiang	62	1	5	56
新疆兵团	Xinjiang Corps	3		3	
黑龙江垦区	Heilongjiang Land Reclamation				

10-4 续表 2 Continued 2

地 区	Region	残疾人法律救助工作站 Legal Assistance Station for PWDs			
		残疾人法律救助工作站办理的案件 Cases Handled by the Legal Assistance Stations for PWDs	省级 at Provincial Level	地市级 at Prefectural/City Level	县级 at County Level
		件 case	件 case	件 case	件 case
全 国	**Total**	**4666**	**167**	**496**	**4003**
北 京	Beijing	79			79
天 津	Tianjin	289	59		230
河 北	Hebei	245		28	217
山 西	Shanxi	96		14	82
内蒙古	Inner Mongolia	79		1	78
辽 宁	Liaoning	375	8	102	265
吉 林	Jilin	62		7	55
黑龙江	Heilongjiang	4			4
上 海	Shanghai	73	8		65
江 苏	Jiangsu	136	6	10	120
浙 江	Zhejiang	390		88	302
安 徽	Anhui	16		7	9
福 建	Fujian	157	25	5	127
江 西	Jiangxi	110	13	9	88
山 东	Shandong	171		25	146
河 南	Henan	204	2	39	163
湖 北	Hubei	204	1	19	184
湖 南	Hunan	220	7	25	188
广 东	Guangdong	112	3	20	89
广 西	Guangxi	99	2	13	84
海 南	Hainan	3			3
重 庆	Chongqing	238			238
四 川	Sichuan	200	3	21	176
贵 州	Guizhou	71		3	68
云 南	Yunnan	10	1	3	6
西 藏	Tibet				
陕 西	Shaanxi	107	28	6	73
甘 肃	Gansu	310	1	20	289
青 海	Qinghai	446		4	442
宁 夏	Ningxia	27		7	20
新 疆	Xinjiang	116		3	113
新疆兵团	Xinjiang Corps	17		17	
黑龙江垦区	Heilongjiang Land Reclamation				

10-4 续表 3 Continued 3

地区	Region	残疾人法律援助中心(工作站) Legal Aid Centers (Station) for PWDs			
		残疾人法律援助中心(工作站) Legal Aid Centers (Station) for PWDs	省级 at Provincial Level	地市级 at Prefectural/ City Level	县级 at County Level
		个 unit	个 unit	个 unit	个 unit
全国	**Total**	**3001**	**28**	**315**	**2658**
北京	Beijing	16	1		15
天津	Tianjin				
河北	Hebei	184	1	11	172
山西	Shanxi	83		5	78
内蒙古	Inner Mongolia	100	1	11	88
辽宁	Liaoning	115	1	14	100
吉林	Jilin	66	1	8	57
黑龙江	Heilongjiang	117	1	13	103
上海	Shanghai	18	1		17
江苏	Jiangsu	110	1	13	96
浙江	Zhejiang	95	1	11	83
安徽	Anhui	119	1	15	103
福建	Fujian	85	1	8	76
江西	Jiangxi	97	1	10	86
山东	Shandong	143	1	15	127
河南	Henan	168	1	17	150
湖北	Hubei	96	1	13	82
湖南	Hunan	119	1	13	105
广东	Guangdong	123	1	19	103
广西	Guangxi	118	1	14	103
海南	Hainan	15		2	13
重庆	Chongqing	41	1		40
四川	Sichuan	140	1	14	125
贵州	Guizhou	74	1	7	66
云南	Yunnan	134	1	14	119
西藏	Tibet	7	1	6	
陕西	Shaanxi	107	1	9	97
甘肃	Gansu	95	1	15	79
青海	Qinghai	51	1	5	45
宁夏	Ningxia	25		5	20
新疆	Xinjiang	88	1	8	79
新疆兵团	Xinjiang Corps	142	1	12	129
黑龙江垦区	Heilongjiang Land Reclamation	110		8	102

10-4　续表 4　Continued 4

地　区	Region	残疾人法律法律援助中心(工作站) Legal Aid Center(Station) for PWDs			
		残疾人法律援助中心(工作站)办理的案件 Cases Handled by Legal Aid Centers(Stations)	省级 at Provincial Level	地市级 at Prefectural/City Level	县级 at County Level
		件 case	件 case	件 case	件 case
全　国	**Total**	**17673**	**727**	**3372**	**13574**
北　京	Beijing	286	5		281
天　津	Tianjin				
河　北	Hebei	829	170	255	404
山　西	Shanxi	255		81	174
内蒙古	Inner Mongolia	348	2	117	229
辽　宁	Liaoning	787	1	149	637
吉　林	Jilin	320	15	21	284
黑龙江	Heilongjiang	586	24	159	403
上　海	Shanghai	221	5		216
江　苏	Jiangsu	799	6	87	706
浙　江	Zhejiang	858		145	713
安　徽	Anhui	1743	20	414	1309
福　建	Fujian	578	5	55	518
江　西	Jiangxi	723	12	164	547
山　东	Shandong	921	8	196	717
河　南	Henan	585	2	174	409
湖　北	Hubei	1011	133	185	693
湖　南	Hunan	655	9	69	577
广　东	Guangdong	362	3	132	227
广　西	Guangxi	438	1	58	379
海　南	Hainan	43		9	34
重　庆	Chongqing	875			875
四　川	Sichuan	911	3	66	842
贵　州	Guizhou	194	1	14	179
云　南	Yunnan	715	9	118	588
西　藏	Tibet	3		3	
陕　西	Shaanxi	428	28	182	218
甘　肃	Gansu	566	3	58	505
青　海	Qinghai	418	262	7	149
宁　夏	Ningxia	96		37	59
新　疆	Xinjiang	554		177	377
新疆兵团	Xinjiang Corps	437		231	206
黑龙江垦区	Heilongjiang Land Reclamation	128		9	119

10-5 参政议政

PWDs Participating in the Administration and Discussion of State Affairs

地 区	Region	人大代表和政协委员 Disabled deputies of People's Congresses and Committee Members of People's Political Consultative Conferences			
		人大代表 Disabled Deputies of the People's Congresses	省级 at Provincial Level	地市级 at Prefectural/City Level	县级 at County Level
		人 person	人 person	人 person	人 person
全 国	**Total**	**1973**	**38**	**266**	**1669**
北 京	Beijing	29	1		28
天 津	Tianjin	7	1		6
河 北	Hebei	112	4	14	94
山 西	Shanxi	85	2	13	70
内蒙古	Inner Mongolia	88		6	82
辽 宁	Liaoning	83	2	11	70
吉 林	Jilin	59	1	7	51
黑龙江	Heilongjiang	55	3	5	47
上 海	Shanghai	9	1		8
江 苏	Jiangsu	101	1	13	87
浙 江	Zhejiang	144	5	20	119
安 徽	Anhui	78	2	7	69
福 建	Fujian	27		7	20
江 西	Jiangxi	36	1	3	32
山 东	Shandong	86	1	7	78
河 南	Henan	62	1	9	52
湖 北	Hubei	127	1	38	88
湖 南	Hunan	131	1	13	117
广 东	Guangdong	53	1	16	36
广 西	Guangxi	31	1	5	25
海 南	Hainan	5	1		4
重 庆	Chongqing	60			60
四 川	Sichuan	161	2	25	134
贵 州	Guizhou	61	2	6	53
云 南	Yunnan	78		7	71
西 藏	Tibet	6		3	3
陕 西	Shaanxi	54		12	42
甘 肃	Gansu	45	1	12	32
青 海	Qinghai	46	1	2	43
宁 夏	Ningxia	9		1	8
新 疆	Xinjiang	44	1	3	40
新疆兵团	Xinjiang Corps	1		1	
黑龙江垦区	Heilongjiang Land Reclamation				

10-5 续表 1 Continued 1

地 区	Region	人大代表和政协委员 Disabled Deputies of People's Congresses and Committee Members of People's Political Consultative Conferences			
		政协委员 Disabled Committee Members of People's Political Consultative Conferences	省级 at Provincial Level	地市级 at Prefectural/City Level	县级 at County Level
		人 person	人 person	人 person	人 person
全 国	**Total**	**3775**	**85**	**501**	**3189**
北 京	Beijing	22	1		21
天 津	Tianjin	18	1		17
河 北	Hebei	266	8	23	235
山 西	Shanxi	171	1	26	144
内蒙古	Inner Mongolia	121	2	16	103
辽 宁	Liaoning	186	2	33	151
吉 林	Jilin	98	1	12	85
黑龙江	Heilongjiang	146	3	19	124
上 海	Shanghai	16	2		14
江 苏	Jiangsu	168	1	23	144
浙 江	Zhejiang	224	7	22	195
安 徽	Anhui	146	4	22	120
福 建	Fujian	118	3	10	105
江 西	Jiangxi	137	4	33	100
山 东	Shandong	177	2	16	159
河 南	Henan	182	4	23	155
湖 北	Hubei	172	4	47	121
湖 南	Hunan	181	4	19	158
广 东	Guangdong	135	2	35	98
广 西	Guangxi	75	1	9	65
海 南	Hainan	27			27
重 庆	Chongqing	93	1		92
四 川	Sichuan	228	5	39	184
贵 州	Guizhou	103	5	8	90
云 南	Yunnan	165	1	13	151
西 藏	Tibet	9	3	4	2
陕 西	Shaanxi	113	3	10	100
甘 肃	Gansu	120	5	17	98
青 海	Qinghai	52	2	5	45
宁 夏	Ningxia	26	1	6	19
新 疆	Xinjiang	79	2	10	67
新疆兵团	Xinjiang Corps	1		1	
黑龙江垦区	Heilongjiang Land Reclamation				

10-5 续表 2 Continued 2

地区	Region	协助提出建议、议案和提案 PWDs Assisting to Put Forward Proposals and Motions		办理人大政协建议、提案 Handling Proposals of Peoples' Congresses and Motions of People's Political Consultative Conferences	
		协助人大代表提出议案、建议 Proposals Put Forward at People's Congresses with Assistance of PWDs	协助政协委员提出提案 Motions Put forward at People's Political Consultative Conferences with Participation of PWDs	办理人大建议 Proposals of Peoples' Congresses Handled	办理政协提案 Motions of People's Political Consultative Conferences Handled
		件 case	件 case	件 case	件 case
全 国	**Total**	**474**	**1064**	**464**	**910**
北 京	Beijing		3	3	2
天 津	Tianjin			4	8
河 北	Hebei	25	46	15	22
山 西	Shanxi	25	55	21	30
内蒙古	Inner Mongolia	22	52	6	24
辽 宁	Liaoning	15	31	18	29
吉 林	Jilin	7	25	6	9
黑龙江	Heilongjiang	10	25	14	28
上 海	Shanghai	2	3	2	8
江 苏	Jiangsu	17	44	33	68
浙 江	Zhejiang	63	124	67	120
安 徽	Anhui	14	38	22	35
福 建	Fujian	11	39	16	47
江 西	Jiangxi	25	37	16	24
山 东	Shandong	26	62	39	68
河 南	Henan	11	27	10	26
湖 北	Hubei	45	58	19	37
湖 南	Hunan	19	55	19	32
广 东	Guangdong	13	26	36	53
广 西	Guangxi	1	26	4	16
海 南	Hainan	2	5	3	1
重 庆	Chongqing	19	44	17	32
四 川	Sichuan	37	69	31	57
贵 州	Guizhou	11	22	3	16
云 南	Yunnan	8	34	5	19
西 藏	Tibet	1	2	3	3
陕 西	Shaanxi	11	11	12	24
甘 肃	Gansu	14	43	9	33
青 海	Qinghai	15	14	7	7
宁 夏	Ningxia		18	1	18
新 疆	Xinjiang	5	26	3	14
新疆兵团	Xinjiang Corps				
黑龙江垦区	Heilongjiang Land Reclamation				

10-6 无障碍环境建设

Accessible Environment Building

地 区	Region	无障碍建设与管理法规、政府令 Regulations and Decrees on Accessible Environment Building and Management	无障碍建设领导协调组织 Leading and Coordinating Bodies for Building Accessible Environment	系统开展无障碍建设市、县 Cities and Counties that Systematic Accessibitity Construction has been Carried out	地市级 at Prefectural/City Level	县级 at County Level
		个 unit	个 unit	个 unit	个 unit	个 unit
全 国	**Total**	**451**	**1161**	**1506**	**225**	**1281**
北 京	Beijing	2	17	16		16
天 津	Tianjin	9	17	16	16	
河 北	Hebei	45	131	183	11	172
山 西	Shanxi	9	35	68	11	57
内蒙古	Inner Mongolia	5	22	64	6	58
辽 宁	Liaoning	6	40	5	4	1
吉 林	Jilin	14	25	12	4	8
黑龙江	Heilongjiang	4	11	36	8	28
上 海	Shanghai	5	28	17		17
江 苏	Jiangsu	23	73	57	13	44
浙 江	Zhejiang	23	33	26	2	24
安 徽	Anhui	8	24	77	16	61
福 建	Fujian	24	49	48	9	39
江 西	Jiangxi	7	29	72	11	61
山 东	Shandong	31	55	56	5	51
河 南	Henan	31	38	58	5	53
湖 北	Hubei	7	60	76	17	59
湖 南	Hunan	23	32	6	6	
广 东	Guangdong	30	36	131	21	110
广 西	Guangxi	11	37	125	14	111
海 南	Hainan		4	2	2	
重 庆	Chongqing	6	32	38		38
四 川	Sichuan	25	77	35	7	28
贵 州	Guizhou	15	22	26	2	24
云 南	Yunnan	18	36	74	5	69
西 藏	Tibet		2			
陕 西	Shaanxi	13	33	43	3	40
甘 肃	Gansu	39	62	101	15	86
青 海	Qinghai		34	11	3	8
宁 夏	Ningxia	6	15	23	5	18
新 疆	Xinjiang	10	38	2	2	
新疆兵团	Xinjiang Corps					
黑龙江垦区	Heilongjiang Land Reclamation	2	14	2	2	

10-6 续表 Continued

地 区	Region	贫困残疾人家庭无障碍改造 Accessibility Renovation for Homes of Poor Disabled Persons	省级 at Provincial Level	地市级 at Prefectural/City Level	县级 at County Level	无障碍建设检查 Inspections on Accessibility	无障碍培训 Training on Accessibility
		户 household	户 household	户 household	户 household	次 time	人次 person-time
全 国	**Total**	**148510**	**10403**	**13636**	**124471**	**4906**	**40089**
北 京	Beijing	16457			16457	268	7749
天 津	Tianjin	1772			1772	54	465
河 北	Hebei	1932		335	1597	105	585
山 西	Shanxi	1719		90	1629	46	606
内蒙古	Inner Mongolia	5739			5739	198	162
辽 宁	Liaoning	13767		1284	12483	579	5290
吉 林	Jilin	684		143	541	30	353
黑龙江	Heilongjiang	3125	200	20	2905	25	7
上 海	Shanghai	3583	1063		2520	486	4103
江 苏	Jiangsu	16884		44	16840	159	3661
浙 江	Zhejiang	10079		2360	7719	379	2101
安 徽	Anhui	1574		200	1374	144	548
福 建	Fujian	6196		712	5484	214	1375
江 西	Jiangxi	1006		130	876	33	115
山 东	Shandong	11015	5090	195	5730	113	931
河 南	Henan	2739		279	2460	171	424
湖 北	Hubei	2034	850	280	904	119	268
湖 南	Hunan	2926		100	2826	87	390
广 东	Guangdong	8525	1600	1073	5852	136	1212
广 西	Guangxi	3611		11	3600	403	500
海 南	Hainan	609		53	556	38	7
重 庆	Chongqing	2768			2768	82	2419
四 川	Sichuan	20205		5360	14845	551	5001
贵 州	Guizhou	1108	600	4	504	108	142
云 南	Yunnan	1378		60	1318	161	148
西 藏	Tibet	210		37	173	1	
陕 西	Shaanxi	1509		200	1309	27	129
甘 肃	Gansu	2229	1000	210	1019	49	368
青 海	Qinghai	704			704	28	4
宁 夏	Ningxia	761		300	461	31	189
新 疆	Xinjiang	1336		40	1296	78	610
新疆兵团	Xinjiang Corps	176		76	100		10
黑龙江垦区	Heilongjiang Land Reclamation	150		40	110	3	217

10-7 残疾人机动轮椅车燃油补贴
Subsidy for Petrol Used by Motorized Wheelchairs of Disabled Persons

地区	Region	残疾人机动轮椅车燃油补贴 Subsidy for Petrol Used by Motorized Wheelchairs of Disabled Persons	省级 at Provincial Level	地市级 at Prefectural/City level	县级 at County Level
		人 person	人 person	人 person	人 person
全国	**Total**	**679008**	**27661**	**36302**	**615045**
北京	Beijing	23214			23214
天津	Tianjin	18550			18550
河北	Hebei	17534		48	17486
山西	Shanxi	7253		184	7069
内蒙古	Inner Mongolia	25370			25370
辽宁	Liaoning	15515		6	15509
吉林	Jilin	14859			14859
黑龙江	Heilongjiang	18159		4038	14121
上海	Shanghai	14241			14241
江苏	Jiangsu	33244		407	32837
浙江	Zhejiang	11912		1800	10112
安徽	Anhui	27651		168	27483
福建	Fujian	14509			14509
江西	Jiangxi	20153		1438	18715
山东	Shandong	21680		822	20858
河南	Henan	66435		13995	52440
湖北	Hubei	44000	22724	1441	19835
湖南	Hunan	53771		960	52811
广东	Guangdong	29631		1696	27935
广西	Guangxi	17187		5	17182
海南	Hainan	9382		349	9033
重庆	Chongqing	4264			4264
四川	Sichuan	28526		1197	27329
贵州	Guizhou	18771	4918		13853
云南	Yunnan	19502			19502
西藏	Tibet	2094		478	1616
陕西	Shaanxi	18320		1822	16498
甘肃	Gansu	23922		606	23316
青海	Qinghai	11153			11153
宁夏	Ningxia	19699		4039	15660
新疆	Xinjiang	21560			21560
新疆兵团	Xinjiang Corps	5329		780	4549
黑龙江垦区	Heilongjiang Land Reclamation	1618	19	23	1576

10-8 残疾人信访

Complaints by Letter and Visit

地 区	Region	来信 Complaint Letter					
		总计 Subtotal	涉法涉诉类 Complaints Related with Legal Lawsuit	康复类 Rehabilitation	教育类 Education	就业类 Employment	扶贫类 Poverty Alleviation
		件 case	件 case	件 case	件 case	件 case	件 case
全 国	**Total**	**47686**	**1940**	**8004**	**2687**	**5767**	**8331**
北 京	Beijing	6177	307	341	151	441	1338
天 津	Tianjin	236	22	4	1	15	6
河 北	Hebei	984	78	152	83	228	174
山 西	Shanxi	977	25	174	79	120	190
内蒙古	Inner Mongolia	884	44	78	72	92	107
辽 宁	Liaoning	715	63	97	38	106	115
吉 林	Jilin	401	66	85	23	52	87
黑龙江	Heilongjiang	1416	43	419	114	243	192
上 海	Shanghai	1519	33	138	14	108	128
江 苏	Jiangsu	837	54	57	26	136	89
浙 江	Zhejiang	1399	75	110	42	125	321
安 徽	Anhui	1152	41	183	67	179	242
福 建	Fujian	1095	67	171	94	154	142
江 西	Jiangxi	883	87	133	89	155	108
山 东	Shandong	1083	39	166	93	144	152
河 南	Henan	625	27	99	47	103	92
湖 北	Hubei	2397	134	238	55	447	396
湖 南	Hunan	3847	179	773	284	674	795
广 东	Guangdong	3324	64	665	329	398	650
广 西	Guangxi	1337	23	293	72	137	217
海 南	Hainan	309	1	33	12	20	38
重 庆	Chongqing	568	69	53	42	56	80
四 川	Sichuan	3991	131	410	144	624	793
贵 州	Guizhou	1024	16	260	84	120	207
云 南	Yunnan	3254	28	1064	283	206	683
西 藏	Tibet	253				11	111
陕 西	Shaanxi	968	31	87	53	60	140
甘 肃	Gansu	1742	160	379	120	201	256
青 海	Qinghai	302	7	76	27	29	59
宁 夏	Ningxia	210	13	14	6	31	36
新 疆	Xinjiang	3367	12	1180	118	295	314
新疆兵团	Xinjiang Corps	236	1	52	18	41	29
黑龙江垦区	Heilongjiang Land Reclamation	174		20	7	16	44

10-8 续表 1 Continued 1

地 区	Region	来信 Complaint Letter				
		社会保障类 Social Security	文化体育类 Culture and Sports	机动车轮椅类 Motor Vehicle and Wheelchair	意见建议类 Opinions and Suggestions	其他类 Others
		件 case	件 case	件 case	件 case	件 case
全 国	**Total**	**7822**	**610**	**3402**	**1625**	**7498**
北 京	Beijing	1313	108	388	41	1749
天 津	Tianjin	51		86	6	45
河 北	Hebei	111	17	65	46	30
山 西	Shanxi	117	16	165	36	55
内蒙古	Inner Mongolia	118	1	31	291	50
辽 宁	Liaoning	87		48	64	97
吉 林	Jilin	70	1	11	2	4
黑龙江	Heilongjiang	213	21	108	21	42
上 海	Shanghai	167	23	75	154	679
江 苏	Jiangsu	196	5	43	59	172
浙 江	Zhejiang	300	19	93	93	221
安 徽	Anhui	252	37	67	24	60
福 建	Fujian	326	8	58	19	56
江 西	Jiangxi	121	12	91	55	32
山 东	Shandong	236	11	32	37	173
河 南	Henan	86	3	70	31	67
湖 北	Hubei	331	16	117	78	585
湖 南	Hunan	479	82	308	111	162
广 东	Guangdong	673	40	198	49	258
广 西	Guangxi	203	25	121	149	97
海 南	Hainan	169		18		18
重 庆	Chongqing	88	4	85	7	84
四 川	Sichuan	497	36	560	62	734
贵 州	Guizhou	171	13	49	22	82
云 南	Yunnan	537	14	79	8	352
西 藏	Tibet	44	12	74		1
陕 西	Shaanxi	379	38	31	15	134
甘 肃	Gansu	210	20	245	51	100
青 海	Qinghai	17		3		84
宁 夏	Ningxia	41		11	34	24
新 疆	Xinjiang	108	22	46	42	1230
新疆兵团	Xinjiang Corps	41	6	24	7	17
黑龙江垦区	Heilongjiang Land Reclamation	70		2	11	4

10-8 续表 2 Continued 2

地 区	Region	来访 Complaint Visit					
		总计 Subtotal	涉法涉诉类 Complaints Related with Legal Lawsuit	康复类 Rehabilitation	教育类 Education	就业类 Employment	扶贫类 Poverty Alleviation
		人次 person-time	人次 person-time	人次 person-time	人次 person-time	人次 person-time	人次 person-time
全 国	**Total**	**285708**	**9668**	**49383**	**15802**	**37856**	**46816**
北 京	Beijing	4155	737	259	108	348	527
天 津	Tianjin	5059	359	216	91	244	181
河 北	Hebei	6135	341	1335	389	1203	1096
山 西	Shanxi	13343	306	2836	563	1571	2172
内蒙古	Inner Mongolia	3491	32	577	314	482	909
辽 宁	Liaoning	14309	646	1547	467	1444	3055
吉 林	Jilin	5825	138	590	271	651	723
黑龙江	Heilongjiang	5362	267	968	279	961	641
上 海	Shanghai	2873	172	199	73	312	562
江 苏	Jiangsu	7288	265	691	235	939	781
浙 江	Zhejiang	10484	348	2013	923	1357	1404
安 徽	Anhui	12292	296	1471	612	1833	2507
福 建	Fujian	6431	129	1986	714	947	621
江 西	Jiangxi	5617	142	875	375	1193	932
山 东	Shandong	4735	155	537	245	691	834
河 南	Henan	5259	96	669	282	1037	719
湖 北	Hubei	19435	1326	2030	980	2798	3068
湖 南	Hunan	26003	1249	4351	1691	4182	3808
广 东	Guangdong	13844	399	2036	809	1973	1853
广 西	Guangxi	15130	135	3811	775	1826	2222
海 南	Hainan	2725	27	343	204	306	1111
重 庆	Chongqing	4102	204	496	173	411	397
四 川	Sichuan	33030	927	5576	1774	4140	6757
贵 州	Guizhou	7819	95	2196	229	1161	1457
云 南	Yunnan	18300	124	4074	1295	1911	2734
西 藏	Tibet	120		40	7	15	42
陕 西	Shaanxi	10934	304	3045	485	1538	1274
甘 肃	Gansu	6214	253	1356	466	758	1467
青 海	Qinghai	430	13	104	42	46	144
宁 夏	Ningxia	2085	119	410	138	256	473
新 疆	Xinjiang	9811	56	2036	464	945	1503
新疆兵团	Xinjiang Corps	2247	8	340	183	318	737
黑龙江垦区	Heilongjiang Land Reclamation	821		370	146	59	105

10-8 续表 3 Continued 3

地 区	Region	来访 Complaint Visit				
		社会保障类 Social Security	文化体育类 Culture and Sports	机动车轮椅类 Motor Vehicle and Wheelchair	意见建议类 Opinions and Suggestions	其他类 Others
		人次 person-time	人次 person-time	人次 person-time	人次 person-time	人次 person-time
全 国	**Total**	**53716**	**3451**	**33751**	**3618**	**31647**
北 京	Beijing	614	83	357	42	1080
天 津	Tianjin	770	20	2487	27	664
河 北	Hebei	809	66	644	65	187
山 西	Shanxi	1767	134	2355	119	1520
内蒙古	Inner Mongolia	577	15	223	30	332
辽 宁	Liaoning	2640	136	2522	230	1622
吉 林	Jilin	693	10	1260	30	1459
黑龙江	Heilongjiang	934	59	691	92	470
上 海	Shanghai	417	19	203	102	814
江 苏	Jiangsu	868	73	2660	103	673
浙 江	Zhejiang	1956	100	972	205	1206
安 徽	Anhui	3386	267	902	253	765
福 建	Fujian	896	69	464	149	456
江 西	Jiangxi	1117	85	577	155	166
山 东	Shandong	1099	28	204	69	873
河 南	Henan	1016	124	700	88	528
湖 北	Hubei	4278	372	2098	201	2284
湖 南	Hunan	6458	278	2013	284	1689
广 东	Guangdong	3559	176	1834	132	1073
广 西	Guangxi	2874	166	1916	146	1259
海 南	Hainan	264	12	281	7	170
重 庆	Chongqing	1005	51	529	73	763
四 川	Sichuan	5813	461	2486	362	4734
贵 州	Guizhou	866	112	1217	94	392
云 南	Yunnan	3753	202	2365	149	1693
西 藏	Tibet	11		3		2
陕 西	Shaanxi	2437	110	637	45	1059
甘 肃	Gansu	965	119	434	125	271
青 海	Qinghai	18	2	23	3	35
宁 夏	Ningxia	327	7	160	34	161
新 疆	Xinjiang	961	79	426	158	3183
新疆兵团	Xinjiang Corps	467	9	106	40	39
黑龙江垦区	Heilongjiang Land Reclamation	101	7	2	6	25

11−1 省(自治区、直辖市)级残联
Disabled Persons' Federations in Provinces, Autonomous Regions and Municipalities

地区	Region	省市县乡残联实有人员 Actual Total Staff of Disabled Persons' Federations at Provincial,City, County and Township Level	省级残联机关 Disabled Persons' Federations at Provincial Level		省级残联事业单位 Affiliated Institutions at Provincial Level		
			实有人员 Actual Staff	残疾人干部 Staff with Disability	单位 Institu-tions	实有人员 Actual Total Staff	残疾人 Persons with Disability
		人 person	人 person	人 person	个 unit	人 person	人 person
全　国	**Total**	**114700**	**1648**	**151**	**155**	**6500**	**282**
北　京	Beijing	1214	65	12	11	252	
天　津	Tianjin	962	44	5	9	175	31
河　北	Hebei	5575	50	4	4	144	5
山　西	Shanxi	4686	59	5	8	234	7
内蒙古	Inner Mongolia	3174	32	4	4	99	2
辽　宁	Liaoning	4232	47	5	6	434	17
吉　林	Jilin	2865	49	6	4	212	16
黑龙江	Heilongjiang	2948	55	7	2	105	6
上　海	Shanghai	1194	45	6	7	194	12
江　苏	Jiangsu	4904	53	4	5	142	6
浙　江	Zhejiang	4594	43	5	6	330	1
安　徽	Anhui	3657	51	5	4	159	7
福　建	Fujian	2654	40	4	4	176	14
江　西	Jiangxi	4361	65	2	6	118	
山　东	Shandong	6180	53	1	2	169	6
河　南	Henan	8180	56	6	3	155	5
湖　北	Hubei	4220	67	2	5	54	2
湖　南	Hunan	5543	48	4	6	116	3
广　东	Guangdong	7418	51	6	5	326	40
广　西	Guangxi	3167	62	4	5	121	5
海　南	Hainan	683	46	3	2	81	3
重　庆	Chongqing	1960	37	1	3	150	5
四　川	Sichuan	9116	51	10	2	609	4
贵　州	Guizhou	3237	48	4	1	57	2
云　南	Yunnan	3672	56	9	8	246	27
西　藏	Tibet	427	36	3	2	80	7
陕　西	Shaanxi	4608	68	3	7	720	9
甘　肃	Gansu	4020	103	6	11	563	20
青　海	Qinghai	1239	40	4	2	22	1
宁　夏	Ningxia	776	51	5	2	75	
新　疆	Xinjiang	2885	57	5	5	164	17
新疆兵团	Xinjiang Corps	130	13	1	3	14	1
黑龙江垦区	Heilongjiang Land Reclamation	219	7		1	4	1

11-1　续表　Continued

地　区	Region	干部队伍综合培训情况 Training of Staff						志愿者助残情况 Volunteer	
		省级举办综合培训班 Provincial-level General Training Courses	参加省级综合培训人次 Trainees on Provincial-level Training Courses	省级举办残疾人干部培训班 Provincial-level Training Courses for Staff with Disability	参加省级残疾人干部培训人次 Trainees on Provincial-level Training Courses for Staff with Disability	参加全国培训人次 Trainees on State-level Training Courses	参加全国残疾人干部培训人次 Trainees on Stats-level Training Courses for Staff with Disability	志愿者登记在册 Registered Volunteer	受助残疾人 PWDs Helped by Volunteers
		期 course	人次 person-time	期 course	人次 person-time	人次 person-time	人次 person-time	人 persons	人 persons
全　国	**Total**	**124**	**17731**	**35**	**2498**	**752**	**96**	**37113**	**126730**
北　京	Beijing	5	700	3	150				
天　津	Tianjin	1	275	2	112	7	2		
河　北	Hebei	1	45					780	780
山　西	Shanxi	1	160				2	21	21
内蒙古	Inner Mongolia								
辽　宁	Liaoning	5	555						
吉　林	Jilin	1	48	1	80			315	5050
黑龙江	Heilongjiang								
上　海	Shanghai	45	7445	4	510			259	78254
江　苏	Jiangsu	2	100	1	60		2		
浙　江	Zhejiang	3	300	1	110	25	62		
安　徽	Anhui	4	1430	1	70	532	3		
福　建	Fujian	11	1400						
江　西	Jiangxi	1	200	2	80	65	19		
山　东	Shandong					15			
河　南	Henan	1	80	1	59			108	1245
湖　北	Hubei	2	300	2	300				
湖　南	Hunan	1	186	1	92				
广　东	Guangdong	5	150	1	30	95	2		
广　西	Guangxi	10	600	2	140			30	180
海　南	Hainan	1	160						
重　庆	Chongqing	1	80	1	80				
四　川	Sichuan	10	700	6	500				
贵　州	Guizhou	1	108	5	100				
云　南	Yunnan	1	104						
西　藏	Tibet								
陕　西	Shaanxi	1	130						
甘　肃	Gansu	3	324						
青　海	Qinghai	3	1760						
宁　夏	Ningxia	1	107			3	2	35600	41200
新　疆	Xinjiang	1	50	1	25	10	2		
新疆兵团	Xinjiang Corps								
黑龙江垦区	Heilongjiang Land Reclamation	2	234						

11–2 地市级残联

Disabled Persons' Federations in Cities and Prefectures

地 区	Region	残联 Disabled Persons' Federations	配备了残疾人领导干部的残联 Disabled Persons' Federations whose Leadership Include PWDs	残联机关 Disabled Persons' Federations			建立残疾人人才库的残联 Disabled Persons' Federations that have Established Data base of Talents with Disabilities	残疾人人才库入库 PWDs Enrolled in the Data Base of Talents with Disabilities
				实有人员 Actual Staff	残疾人领导干部 Leaders with Disability	残疾人干部 Ordinary Staff with Disability		
		个 unit	个 unit	人 person	人 person	人 person	个 unit	人 person
全 国	**Total**	**359**	**246**	**5356**	**269**	**433**	**237**	**14706**
北 京	Beijing							
天 津	Tianjin							
河 北	Hebei	11	11	226	11	11	11	550
山 西	Shanxi	11	8	167	8	12	6	580
内蒙古	Inner Mongolia	12	11	219	13	30	11	273
辽 宁	Liaoning	14	14	289	16	26	14	1617
吉 林	Jilin	10	4	158	4	9	9	542
黑龙江	Heilongjiang	13	10	160	10	12	13	611
上 海	Shanghai							
江 苏	Jiangsu	13	8	343	9	23	10	777
浙 江	Zhejiang	11	10	198	13	17	8	790
安 徽	Anhui	16	10	213	10	11	10	671
福 建	Fujian	9	9	132	9	13	6	316
江 西	Jiangxi	11	8	142	9	12	8	808
山 东	Shandong	17	14	362	15	23	12	1421
河 南	Henan	18	11	294	13	16	18	1049
湖 北	Hubei	13	5	170	6	13	4	289
湖 南	Hunan	14	10	240	10	18	8	820
广 东	Guangdong	21	13	331	17	27	10	173
广 西	Guangxi	15	12	165	12	16	9	231
海 南	Hainan	2	1	24	1	2	1	19
重 庆	Chongqing							
四 川	Sichuan	21	10	254	10	27	13	1104
贵 州	Guizhou	9	8	123	8	11	3	104
云 南	Yunnan	16	15	212	17	23	9	157
西 藏	Tibet	7	2	72	3	6		
陕 西	Shaanxi	10	9	188	9	14	3	456
甘 肃	Gansu	15	14	274	15	31	15	457
青 海	Qinghai	8	2	68	2	3	6	169
宁 夏	Ningxia	5	4	54	5	2	2	130
新 疆	Xinjiang	14	12	207	13	23	7	475
新疆兵团	Xinjiang Corps	14	1	49	1	2	5	109
黑龙江垦区	Heilongjiang Land Reclamation	9		22			6	8

11-2 续表 Continued

地区 Region	事业单位 Affiliated Institutions			干部队伍综合培训情况 Training of Cadre				志愿者助残情况 Volunteer	
	单位 Institutions	实有人员 Actual Total of Staff	残疾人 Persons with Disability	地市级举办综合培训班 City-level General Training Courses	参加地市级培训人次 Trainees on City-level General Training Courses	地市级举办残疾人干部培训班 City-level Training Courses for Staff with Disability	参加地市级残疾人干部培训人次 Trainees on City-level Training Courses for Staff with Disability	志愿者登记在册 Registered Volunteer	受助残疾人 PWDs Helped by Volunteers
	个 unit	人 person	人 person	期 course	人次 person-time	期 course	人次 person-time	人 persons	人 persons
全 国 Total	**701**	**9402**	**539**	**909**	**51091**	**399**	**20289**	**60224**	**400872**
北 京 Beijing									
天 津 Tianjin									
河 北 Hebei	23	383	22	31	2245	17	647	2550	5116
山 西 Shanxi	38	460	33	24	971	14	545	59	1230
内蒙古 Inner Mongolia	20	110	8	15	1220	5	251	42	170
辽 宁 Liaoning	37	484	40	92	6868	80	4097	440	1148
吉 林 Jilin	23	300	13	32	1310	15	391	2345	9623
黑龙江 Heilongjiang	24	205	9	24	4045	14	409	15	137
上 海 Shanghai									
江 苏 Jiangsu	33	482	15	20	1373	8	525	3271	38506
浙 江 Zhejiang	24	690	23	12	921	12	722	1517	10326
安 徽 Anhui	28	242	13	58	2878	9	365	307	4431
福 建 Fujian	25	213	11	9	833			22243	3364
江 西 Jiangxi	20	96	7	20	816	11	356	48	4925
山 东 Shandong	41	711	70	39	1438	20	1348	287	705
河 南 Henan	44	749	17	31	1597	19	809	20873	242931
湖 北 Hubei	28	213	16	21	363	6	172	68	1837
湖 南 Hunan	30	167	8	37	1912	16	580	118	3652
广 东 Guangdong	76	2392	98	129	2939	15	589	1677	29051
广 西 Guangxi	29	223	19	21	864	4	175	79	2161
海 南 Hainan	3	31		1	41			445	23000
重 庆 Chongqing									
四 川 Sichuan	34	315	17	130	9671	64	4291	88	2333
贵 州 Guizhou	13	51	3	3	100	6	526	50	650
云 南 Yunnan	24	109	12	32	2011	15	1524	149	933
西 藏 Tibet	4	15	1	2	48				
陕 西 Shaanxi	17	143	10	39	2237	15	593		
甘 肃 Gansu	25	403	54	37	3018	14	771	30	501
青 海 Qinghai	6	36		11	338	6	75	45	84
宁 夏 Ningxia	6	50	5	11	173	3	191	3088	10176
新 疆 Xinjiang	17	102	11	25	735	8	310	10	
新疆兵团 Xinjiang Corps	8	24	4					284	2557
黑龙江垦区 Heilongjiang Land Reclamation	1	3		3	126	3	27	96	1325

11-3 县(县级市、市辖区)级残联

Disabled Persons' Federations in Counties, County-Level Cities and Districts under Cities

地区	Region	残联 Disabled Persons' Federations	配备了残疾人干部的残联 Disabled Persons' Federations with Disabled Staff	残联机关 Disabled Persons' Federations 实有人员 Actual Staff	残疾人干部 Ordinary Staff with Disability	建立残疾人人才库的残联 Disabled Persons' Federations that have Established Data base of Talents with Disabilities	残疾人人才库入库 PWDs Enrolled in the Data Base of Talents with Disabilities
		个 unit	个 unit	人 person	人 person	个 unit	人 person
全国	**Total**	**3092**	**1631**	**27214**	**2234**	**1794**	**84259**
北京	Beijing	16	13	212	26	10	468
天津	Tianjin	16	13	155	22	15	466
河北	Hebei	172	172	1442	190	134	7305
山西	Shanxi	119	90	1428	120	95	3037
内蒙古	Inner Mongolia	108	57	937	90	64	1181
辽宁	Liaoning	103	100	748	113	100	2936
吉林	Jilin	71	28	748	43	49	1355
黑龙江	Heilongjiang	132	35	640	40	129	3945
上海	Shanghai	17	8	159	8	13	474
江苏	Jiangsu	105	56	1243	64	72	6456
浙江	Zhejiang	92	62	1017	74	55	2197
安徽	Anhui	114	32	790	38	58	5873
福建	Fujian	84	33	489	37	50	1329
江西	Jiangxi	108	51	919	90	61	3023
山东	Shandong	153	57	1746	75	99	11647
河南	Henan	167	91	2376	116	126	3026
湖北	Hubei	104	47	998	72	39	1901
湖南	Hunan	125	73	1443	100	47	2360
广东	Guangdong	136	49	1106	61	22	314
广西	Guangxi	114	46	796	67	36	806
海南	Hainan	22	11	150	13	4	10
重庆	Chongqing	40	21	306	25	23	2146
四川	Sichuan	188	95	1446	126	116	4529
贵州	Guizhou	89	68	789	101	48	2085
云南	Yunnan	129	91	1210	153	101	2106
西藏	Tibet	74	7	224	9	2	2
陕西	Shaanxi	112	60	1114	104	39	7546
甘肃	Gansu	86	79	1072	132	50	2477
青海	Qinghai	46	14	285	17	19	135
宁夏	Ningxia	21	11	174	14	10	281
新疆	Xinjiang	96	58	840	91	65	2756
新疆兵团	Xinjiang Corps	30		30			
黑龙江垦区	Heilongjiang Land Reclamation	103	3	182	3	43	87

11-3　续表　Continued

地　区	Region	事业单位 Affiliated Institutions			干部队伍综合培训情况 Training of Cadre		志愿者助残情况 Volunteer	
		单位 Institutions	实有人员 Actual Total of Staff	残疾人 Persons with Disability	县级举办综合培训班累计 County-level General Training Courses	参加县级培训 Trainees on County-level General Training Courses	志愿者登记在册 Registered Volunteer	受助残疾人 PWDs Helped by Volunteers
		个 unit	人 person	人 person	期 course	人次 person-time	人 persons	人 persons
全　国	**Total**	**2407**	**13003**	**977**	**6137**	**224021**	**517561**	**5576938**
北　京	Beijing	36	317	30	68	3332	555	16843
天　津	Tianjin	26	208	22	74	3744	2367	23312
河　北	Hebei	96	695	41	354	10571	36177	225025
山　西	Shanxi	144	672	33	226	7464	2938	41708
内蒙古	Inner Mongolia	51	232	42	171	8145	2643	37235
辽　宁	Liaoning	94	488	35	278	12853	9079	64980
吉　林	Jilin	62	353	13	159	5259	52276	615903
黑龙江	Heilongjiang	72	269	36	154	5202	68928	355758
上　海	Shanghai	22	204	22	61	2980	777	100828
江　苏	Jiangsu	128	877	57	329	11532	15245	132887
浙　江	Zhejiang	134	747	58	318	11022	9762	236468
安　徽	Anhui	48	271	28	232	11948	6179	136425
福　建	Fujian	141	343	38	212	8059	30261	192156
江　西	Jiangxi	66	344	24	178	4683	1009	17546
山　东	Shandong	93	635	37	464	9844	17727	194714
河　南	Henan	174	1297	54	267	10273	71097	786205
湖　北	Hubei	111	543	38	163	5379	7217	64128
湖　南	Hunan	126	731	27	198	5407	5143	63100
广　东	Guangdong	185	1065	58	212	8612	5278	96420
广　西	Guangxi	94	339	58	181	7801	7557	267945
海　南	Hainan	13	88	11	23	644	2769	32980
重　庆	Chongqing	43	204	23	129	7244	24903	288321
四　川	Sichuan	89	458	30	575	21523	38379	916563
贵　州	Guizhou	46	191	18	145	5210	2262	42960
云　南	Yunnan	103	291	37	232	9697	1592	32436
西　藏	Tibet				6	54	20	
陕　西	Shaanxi	78	567	35	293	10756	15624	147532
甘　肃	Gansu	50	145	29	199	8184	68569	352361
青　海	Qinghai	20	96	8	54	1387	883	3056
宁　夏	Ningxia	7	65	5	42	1182	1319	5409
新　疆	Xinjiang	55	268	30	140	4030	6722	40145
新疆兵团	Xinjiang Corps						1227	33927
黑龙江垦区	Heilongjiang Land Reclamation						1077	11662

11-4 乡(镇、街道)残联

Disabled Persons' Federations in Townships (Towns, Streets)

地 区	Region	乡(镇、街道)已建残联 Disabled Persons' Federations Established in Townships (Towns, Streets)	残联机关 Disabled Persons' Federation			
			实有人员 Actual Staff	专职残联理事长 Full-time Presidents	兼职残联理事长 Part-time Presidents	残疾人专职委员 Full-time Workers on Disability
		个 unit	人 person	人 person	人 person	人 person
全 国	**Total**	**40034**	**51577**	**11305**	**17023**	**46673**
北 京	Beijing	323	368	251	62	874
天 津	Tianjin	242	380	242		239
河 北	Hebei	2281	2635	748	1533	2283
山 西	Shanxi	1476	1666	333	714	1393
内蒙古	Inner Mongolia	1145	1545	238	561	1308
辽 宁	Liaoning	1516	1742	438	1026	1612
吉 林	Jilin	908	1045	162	724	973
黑龙江	Heilongjiang	1329	1514	161	596	1876
上 海	Shanghai	217	592	10	101	1558
江 苏	Jiangsu	1342	1764	1158	184	1469
浙 江	Zhejiang	1320	1569	619	305	1498
安 徽	Anhui	1522	1931	301	451	1457
福 建	Fujian	1105	1261	207	493	1197
江 西	Jiangxi	1632	2677	493	913	3387
山 东	Shandong	1824	2504	594	397	2073
河 南	Henan	2379	3253	1040	1064	2553
湖 北	Hubei	1249	2175	114	532	1796
湖 南	Hunan	2420	2798	639	1044	2343
广 东	Guangdong	1616	2147	419	656	1642
广 西	Guangxi	1244	1461	149	610	1397
海 南	Hainan	228	263	40	90	243
重 庆	Chongqing	1018	1263	472	435	1042
四 川	Sichuan	4363	5983	610	2021	4436
贵 州	Guizhou	1423	1978	399	422	1395
云 南	Yunnan	1382	1548	529	553	1355
西 藏	Tibet					
陕 西	Shaanxi	1490	1808	301	357	1653
甘 肃	Gansu	1372	1460	512	472	1438
青 海	Qinghai	404	692	16	112	514
宁 夏	Ningxia	228	307	12	107	258
新 疆	Xinjiang	1035	1247	97	487	1288
新疆兵团	Xinjiang Corps			1	1	20
黑龙江垦区	Heilongjiang Land Reclamation	1	1			103

11-4　续表　Continued

地　区	Region	干部队伍综合培训情况 Training of Staff		志愿者助残情况 Volunteer	
		乡镇级举办综合培训班 Township-level General Training Courses	参加乡镇级培训人次 Trainees on Township-level Training	志愿者登记在册 Registered Volunteer	受助残疾人 PWDs Helped by Volunteers
		期 course	人次 person-time	万人 10,000 persons	万人 10,000 persons
全　国	**Total**	**25134**	**386541**	**141.1**	**867.0**
北　京	Beijing	660	14373	0.4	24.0
天　津	Tianjin	226	4719	7.6	21.6
河　北	Hebei	1084	10391	14.5	62.2
山　西	Shanxi	785	12475	0.5	2.5
内蒙古	Inner Mongolia	389	4748	0.9	5.7
辽　宁	Liaoning	921	12665	1.9	9.7
吉　林	Jilin	374	4861	6.0	36.5
黑龙江	Heilongjiang	363	2254	14.6	22.9
上　海	Shanghai	310	2270	0.3	42.8
江　苏	Jiangsu	1206	18165	5.7	58.0
浙　江	Zhejiang	894	18108	1.1	17.8
安　徽	Anhui	1047	13957	0.8	6.5
福　建	Fujian	447	7133	4.1	15.7
江　西	Jiangxi	926	10711	1.2	6.0
山　东	Shandong	2198	37327	5.9	32.5
河　南	Henan	996	7978	19.7	205.5
湖　北	Hubei	896	11567	0.8	7.8
湖　南	Hunan	359	3748	6.2	20.3
广　东	Guangdong	829	7744	22.2	12.7
广　西	Guangxi	600	5498	0.4	7.6
海　南	Hainan	80	637	0.5	3.3
重　庆	Chongqing	1134	37309	3.4	74.0
四　川	Sichuan	4926	70241	5.9	40.9
贵　州	Guizhou	437	7222	3.1	4.4
云　南	Yunnan	619	8549	0.7	7.9
西　藏	Tibet				
陕　西	Shaanxi	1213	26697	1.6	9.0
甘　肃	Gansu	595	14781	9.1	101.6
青　海	Qinghai	106	2203	0.1	0.8
宁　夏	Ningxia	97	1625	1.2	1.4
新　疆	Xinjiang	417	6585	0.4	5.0
新疆兵团	Xinjiang Corps			0.1	0.3
黑龙江垦区	Heilongjiang Land Reclamation			0.0	0.0

11–5 村(社区)残疾人组织

Disabled Persons' Federations in Villages and Communities

地区	Region	已建残协 Associations of PWDs Established		残协情况 Associations		
		村 in Villages	社区 in Communities	已建残疾人活动室 Entertainment Rooms for PWDs Established	村 in Villages	社区 in Communities
		个 unit	个 unit	个 unit	个 unit	个 unit
全国	**Total**	**522716**	**67781**	**390476**	**332220**	**58256**
北京	Beijing	3696	2122	4096	2365	1731
天津	Tianjin	3372	1273	4794	3538	1256
河北	Hebei	48413	3061	51474	48413	3061
山西	Shanxi	21100	1699	13472	12246	1226
内蒙古	Inner Mongolia	11369	1808	8460	5494	2966
辽宁	Liaoning	11555	3890	15184	11292	3892
吉林	Jilin	9475	1542	7274	6059	1215
黑龙江	Heilongjiang	6983	2156	4654	3020	1634
上海	Shanghai	1283	2822	3878	1321	2557
江苏	Jiangsu	15718	4688	18815	14362	4453
浙江	Zhejiang	20532	2416	15724	13445	2279
安徽	Anhui	13647	2052	7348	6020	1328
福建	Fujian	14115	1932	8082	6921	1161
江西	Jiangxi	15655	2260	10831	9088	1743
山东	Shandong	58814	4457	46575	42792	3783
河南	Henan	43872	3398	29653	26570	3083
湖北	Hubei	20627	2879	11444	9511	1933
湖南	Hunan	36256	3029	22958	20476	2482
广东	Guangdong	18407	4966	8438	4854	3584
广西	Guangxi	14515	1455	6806	5849	957
海南	Hainan	2382	251	632	473	159
重庆	Chongqing	8658	1894	7294	5564	1730
四川	Sichuan	40653	4076	33300	29434	3866
贵州	Guizhou	13167	854	7035	6178	857
云南	Yunnan	12556	1492	6016	5101	915
西藏	Tibet					
陕西	Shaanxi	26621	1816	13840	12457	1383
甘肃	Gansu	16074	1124	14343	13219	1124
青海	Qinghai	4184	336	1567	1374	193
宁夏	Ningxia	1673	343	840	589	251
新疆	Xinjiang	7344	1622	5646	4195	1451
新疆兵团	Xinjiang Corps		3			
黑龙江垦区	Heilongjiang Land Reclamation		65	3		3

11-5 续表 Continued

地 区	Region	残协情况 Associations			志愿者助残情况 Volunteers	
		残疾人专职委员选聘情况 Full-time Workers on Disability			志愿者登记在册 Registered Volunteers	受助残疾人 PWDs Assisted by Volunteers
		残疾人专职委员 Full-time Workers on Disability	村 in Villages	社区 in Communties		
		人 person	人 person	人 person	万人 10,000 person	万人 10,000 person
全 国	**Total**	**560823**	**499735**	**61088**	**129.3**	**720.6**
北 京	Beijing	5339	3654	1685	0.5	15.9
天 津	Tianjin	4526	3357	1169	7.1	15.2
河 北	Hebei	51474	48413	3061	10.6	42.4
山 西	Shanxi	23812	22226	1586	0.5	3.4
内蒙古	Inner Mongolia	13368	11515	1853	0.5	2.6
辽 宁	Liaoning	15425	11672	3753	3.3	21.3
吉 林	Jilin	11068	9586	1482	7.2	31.2
黑龙江	Heilongjiang	5853	2902	2951	9.9	12.8
上 海	Shanghai	4319	1806	2513	0.1	6.7
江 苏	Jiangsu	20260	15657	4603	7.2	56.2
浙 江	Zhejiang	20775	18323	2452	1.6	13.1
安 徽	Anhui	17311	15160	2151	1.9	27.3
福 建	Fujian	16187	14465	1722	3.1	13.4
江 西	Jiangxi	13844	12138	1706	1.0	3.6
山 东	Shandong	63495	59784	3711	5.9	22.2
河 南	Henan	48910	45760	3150	21.6	236.0
湖 北	Hubei	18714	16433	2281	1.6	19.3
湖 南	Hunan	35148	32641	2507	5.8	23.2
广 东	Guangdong	23073	19254	3819	13.0	3.6
广 西	Guangxi	16154	14626	1528	0.5	7.4
海 南	Hainan	2714	2522	192	0.4	1.9
重 庆	Chongqing	10412	8324	2088	2.9	37.0
四 川	Sichuan	35053	32529	2524	7.0	37.6
贵 州	Guizhou	14657	13890	767	1.1	1.8
云 南	Yunnan	13358	11913	1445	0.4	3.5
西 藏	Tibet				0.0	
陕 西	Shaanxi	28844	27042	1802	5.4	11.0
甘 肃	Gansu	17212	16151	1061	7.4	45.9
青 海	Qinghai	3137	2933	204	0.1	0.4
宁 夏	Ningxia	1694	1388	306	1.0	1.2
新 疆	Xinjiang	4684	3671	1013	0.5	3.0
新疆兵团	Xinjiang Corps	3		3	0.1	0.2
黑龙江垦区	Heilongjiang Land Reclamation				0.0	0.5

12–1 残疾人综合服务设施
Comprehensive Service Facilities for PWDs

地 区	Region	已投入使用项目 Projects in Operation		
		本年度新投入使用项目 Projects Getting into Operation in 2014		
		项目个数 Number of Projects	建设规模 Construction Area	总投资 Total Investment
		个 unit	平方米 square meter	万元 10,000 yuan
全 国	**Total**	**117**	**324214**	**109281.9**
北 京	Beijing	2	15150	15644.0
天 津	Tianjin			
河 北	Hebei	3	1914	582.2
山 西	Shanxi			
内蒙古	Inner Mongolia	6	34626	11710.0
辽 宁	Liaoning	5	19735	11167.0
吉 林	Jilin	2	1340	208.0
黑龙江	Heilongjiang	1	260	155.0
上 海	Shanghai	2	5741	4200.0
江 苏	Jiangsu	3	17950	5200.0
浙 江	Zhejiang	13	50517	13762.3
安 徽	Anhui	6	16800	4000.0
福 建	Fujian	3	10957	2365.0
江 西	Jiangxi	16	9106	2234.7
山 东	Shandong	1	16320	3232.0
河 南	Henan	3	9483	1580.0
湖 北	Hubei	9	19770	3700.0
湖 南	Hunan	3	5600	914.0
广 东	Guangdong	9	23855	7435.2
广 西	Guangxi	3	9319	2200.0
海 南	Hainan	1	4000	2100.0
重 庆	Chongqing			
四 川	Sichuan	6	7368	1959.5
贵 州	Guizhou	1		75.0
云 南	Yunnan	2	3943	1100.0
西 藏	Tibet			
陕 西	Shaanxi	4	3000	440.0
甘 肃	Gansu	2	740	328.0
青 海	Qinghai	6	26930	10266.0
宁 夏	Ningxia			
新 疆	Xinjiang	5	9790	2724.0
新疆兵团	Xinjiang Corps			
黑龙江垦区	Heilongjiang Land Reclamation			

12-1 续表 1 Continued 1

地 区	Region	已投入使用项目 Projects in Operation		
		累计已投入使用项目 Accumulated Projects in Operation		
		项目个数 Number of Projects	建设规模 Construction Area	总投资 Total Investment
		个 unit	平方米 square meter	万元 10,000 yuan
全 国	**Total**	**2231**	**4602615**	**1286389.0**
北 京	Beijing	6	70771	45323.5
天 津	Tianjin	24	88572	46817.3
河 北	Hebei	145	144125	27198.2
山 西	Shanxi	51	107119	28589.8
内蒙古	Inner Mongolia	71	89139	20616.8
辽 宁	Liaoning	126	264832	91995.2
吉 林	Jilin	46	76912	19057.9
黑龙江	Heilongjiang	101	114575	37030.9
上 海	Shanghai	16	23078	12103.5
江 苏	Jiangsu	75	440164	147618.0
浙 江	Zhejiang	84	476209	175064.9
安 徽	Anhui	74	152812	30574.4
福 建	Fujian	79	164536	52037.8
江 西	Jiangxi	80	58323	14185.9
山 东	Shandong	137	342846	74382.7
河 南	Henan	137	187723	30214.3
湖 北	Hubei	77	137860	25886.5
湖 南	Hunan	96	127228	23982.9
广 东	Guangdong	92	373113	103114.0
广 西	Guangxi	97	139939	24084.7
海 南	Hainan	8	10306	3831.0
重 庆	Chongqing	28	85418	25116.2
四 川	Sichuan	87	193125	55368.0
贵 州	Guizhou	62	55720	9173.2
云 南	Yunnan	127	158801	27118.2
西 藏	Tibet			
陕 西	Shaanxi	77	147956	31500.3
甘 肃	Gansu	90	96224	29582.2
青 海	Qinghai	32	45830	14779.3
宁 夏	Ningxia	17	29792	6957.1
新 疆	Xinjiang	73	187638	51492.6
新疆兵团	Xinjiang Corps	10	6983	983.0
黑龙江垦区	Heilongjiang Land Reclamation	6	4949	608.6

12-1 续表 2 Continued 2

地 区	Region	在建项目 Projects under Construction		
		项目个数 Number of Projects	建设规模 Construction Area	总投资 Total Investment
		个 unit	平方米 square meter	万元 10,000 yuan
全 国	**Total**	**98**	**573188**	**206475.2**
北 京	Beijing			
天 津	Tianjin	1	13456	4200.0
河 北	Hebei	1	500	300.0
山 西	Shanxi	8	21436	6686.0
内蒙古	Inner Mongolia	2	31000	640.0
辽 宁	Liaoning	2	5000	970.0
吉 林	Jilin			
黑龙江	Heilongjiang	3	1600	383.0
上 海	Shanghai			
江 苏	Jiangsu	1	12000	6000.0
浙 江	Zhejiang	2	44341	29630.0
安 徽	Anhui	3	33847	12260.0
福 建	Fujian	5	33982	9313.0
江 西	Jiangxi			
山 东	Shandong			
河 南	Henan	7	25500	7200.0
湖 北	Hubei	5	29616	7621.8
湖 南	Hunan	6	21000	4780.0
广 东	Guangdong	14	178899	78218.9
广 西	Guangxi			
海 南	Hainan	5	26642	11305.3
重 庆	Chongqing	3	17000	4100.0
四 川	Sichuan	10	25682	7036.0
贵 州	Guizhou	2	7500	2100.0
云 南	Yunnan	4	9827	968.0
西 藏	Tibet	3	2992	990.0
陕 西	Shaanxi	5	22286	9803.2
甘 肃	Gansu	4	4082	976.0
青 海	Qinghai	1	1000	394.0
宁 夏	Ningxia			
新 疆	Xinjiang	1	4000	600.0
新疆兵团	Xinjiang Corps			
黑龙江垦区	Heilongjiang Land Reclamation			

12-1　续表 3　Continued 3

地　区	Region	筹建项目 Projects under Discussion and Preparation		
		项目个数 Number of Projects	建设规模 Construction Area	总投资 Total Investment
		个 unit	平方米 square meter	万元 10,000 yuan
全　国	**Total**	**180**	**1325226**	**416838.1**
北　京	Beijing	2	24945	18556.7
天　津	Tianjin	1	17900	13007.6
河　北	Hebei	5	9409	1840.0
山　西	Shanxi	11	48711	9501.9
内蒙古	Inner Mongolia	2	27560	11627.0
辽　宁	Liaoning	2	16489	6836.0
吉　林	Jilin	2	8792	2463.0
黑龙江	Heilongjiang	4	2942	485.0
上　海	Shanghai			
江　苏	Jiangsu	9	112026	45600.0
浙　江	Zhejiang	14	180431	84806.9
安　徽	Anhui	11	53510	9132.0
福　建	Fujian	10	35039	10662.0
江　西	Jiangxi			
山　东	Shandong	5	30516	10708.4
河　南	Henan	12	173908	43773.0
湖　北	Hubei	9	38925	9748.0
湖　南	Hunan			
广　东	Guangdong	9	258579	52717.2
广　西	Guangxi	7	12910	2155.8
海　南	Hainan	4	6522	2191.0
重　庆	Chongqing	3	27171	11250.0
四　川	Sichuan	24	79358	23439.0
贵　州	Guizhou	5	63735	22400.4
云　南	Yunnan	3	16420	4722.0
西　藏	Tibet	8	14126	4383.4
陕　西	Shaanxi	3	19800	5550.0
甘　肃	Gansu	5	5171	1274.5
青　海	Qinghai			
宁　夏	Ningxia	3	13160	2579.8
新　疆	Xinjiang	7	27170	5427.7
新疆兵团	Xinjiang Corps			
黑龙江垦区	Heilongjiang Land Reclamation			

12-2 残疾人康复设施
Rehabilitation Service Facilities for PWDs

地 区	Region	已投入使用项目 Projects in Operation		
		本年度新投入使用项目 Projects Getting into Operation in 2014		
		项目个数 Number of Projects	建设规模 Construction Area	总投资 Total Investment
		个 unit	平方米 square meter	万元 10,000 yuan
全 国	**Total**	**77**	**269961**	**74302.7**
北 京	Beijing			
天 津	Tianjin			
河 北	Hebei			
山 西	Shanxi			
内蒙古	Inner Mongolia	2	189	80.0
辽 宁	Liaoning	1	3000	893.5
吉 林	Jilin			
黑龙江	Heilongjiang	1	1219	293.8
上 海	Shanghai			
江 苏	Jiangsu	3	3650	1010.0
浙 江	Zhejiang	5	10725	3435.3
安 徽	Anhui	6	1992	11013.4
福 建	Fujian			
江 西	Jiangxi			
山 东	Shandong	18	167360	38574.7
河 南	Henan	3	18837	4800.0
湖 北	Hubei	1	500	100.0
湖 南	Hunan	11	7492	613.0
广 东	Guangdong	5	17347	4836.0
广 西	Guangxi			
海 南	Hainan			
重 庆	Chongqing	1	5710	1160.0
四 川	Sichuan	3	5600	1400.0
贵 州	Guizhou			
云 南	Yunnan			
西 藏	Tibet			
陕 西	Shaanxi	12	18178	2660.0
甘 肃	Gansu			
青 海	Qinghai			
宁 夏	Ningxia			
新 疆	Xinjiang	3	185	41.0
新疆兵团	Xinjiang Corps	2	7979	3392.0
黑龙江垦区	Heilongjiang Land Reclamation			

12-2　续表 1　Continued 1

地　区	Region	已投入使用项目 Projects in Operation 累计已投入使用项目 Accumulated Projects in Operation 项目个数 Number of Projects		
		项目个数 Number of Projects	建设规模 Construction Area	总投资 Total Investment
		个 unit	平方米 square meter	万元 10,000 yuan
全　国	**Total**	**613**	**1300056**	**403787.1**
北　京	Beijing	3	13221	8273.7
天　津	Tianjin	8	9550	1966.0
河　北	Hebei	7	33979	8178.1
山　西	Shanxi	32	74856	18438.4
内蒙古	Inner Mongolia	4	4194	510.0
辽　宁	Liaoning	14	62927	13507.4
吉　林	Jilin	8	27942	10356.0
黑龙江	Heilongjiang	4	5465	600.8
上　海	Shanghai	5	62970	44251.7
江　苏	Jiangsu	50	119626	30901.0
浙　江	Zhejiang	25	145403	43479.7
安　徽	Anhui	10	13924	13331.4
福　建	Fujian	210	19948	4627.5
江　西	Jiangxi	4	31703	6940.0
山　东	Shandong	46	251957	66672.7
河　南	Henan	9	63779	14104.0
湖　北	Hubei	12	23237	4545.0
湖　南	Hunan	29	24137	3858.5
广　东	Guangdong	47	105462	32111.2
广　西	Guangxi	1	660	125.0
海　南	Hainan			
重　庆	Chongqing	5	10343	2360.0
四　川	Sichuan	27	111349	56931.0
贵　州	Guizhou	3	11397	2520.0
云　南	Yunnan			
西　藏	Tibet			
陕　西	Shaanxi	31	47204	7152.7
甘　肃	Gansu	2	1300	347.0
青　海	Qinghai	1	1485	380.0
宁　夏	Ningxia	1	1500	100.0
新　疆	Xinjiang	11	5535	1698.0
新疆兵团	Xinjiang Corps	4	15003	5520.5
黑龙江垦区	Heilongjiang Land Reclamation			

12-2 续表 2 Continued 2

地 区	Region	在建项目 Projects under Construction		
		项目个数 Number of Projects	建设规模 Construction Area	总投资 Total Investment
		个 unit	平方米 square meter	万元 10,000 yuan
全 国	**Total**	**58**	**430870**	**131217.3**
北 京	Beijing			
天 津	Tianjin			
河 北	Hebei	1	63000	39000.0
山 西	Shanxi	4	8440	1858.0
内蒙古	Inner Mongolia	2	20000	5800.0
辽 宁	Liaoning	1	7800	3800.0
吉 林	Jilin			
黑龙江	Heilongjiang	3	36000	10140.0
上 海	Shanghai			
江 苏	Jiangsu	1	3000	300.0
浙 江	Zhejiang	1	3375	1960.0
安 徽	Anhui	2	11000	2200.0
福 建	Fujian			
江 西	Jiangxi			
山 东	Shandong	6	60225	13629.0
河 南	Henan	4	12600	2400.0
湖 北	Hubei	5	30471	5530.3
湖 南	Hunan	2	16000	3600.0
广 东	Guangdong	6	26451	7611.8
广 西	Guangxi	6	46348	8929.0
海 南	Hainan			
重 庆	Chongqing	5	29160	10980.2
四 川	Sichuan	4	22000	6234.0
贵 州	Guizhou			
云 南	Yunnan	1	8000	1600.0
西 藏	Tibet			
陕 西	Shaanxi	3	21000	3865.0
甘 肃	Gansu			
青 海	Qinghai	1	6000	1780.0
宁 夏	Ningxia			
新 疆	Xinjiang			
新疆兵团	Xinjiang Corps			
黑龙江垦区	Heilongjiang Land Reclamation			

12-2 续表 3 Continued 3

地 区	Region	筹建项目 Projects under Discussion and Preparation		
		项目个数 Number of Projects	建设规模 Construction Area	总投资 Total Investment
		个 unit	平方米 square meter	万元 10,000 yuan
全 国	**Total**	**160**	**1326266**	**461894.1**
北 京	Beijing			
天 津	Tianjin	2	9270	9008.0
河 北	Hebei	2	24212	8552.3
山 西	Shanxi	8	30022	6650.0
内蒙古	Inner Mongolia	5	42743	14500.0
辽 宁	Liaoning	3	15059	4551.0
吉 林	Jilin	2	16000	3214.0
黑龙江	Heilongjiang	2	16000	4000.0
上 海	Shanghai			
江 苏	Jiangsu	11	123901	65665.5
浙 江	Zhejiang	4	86646	44733.0
安 徽	Anhui	7	61910	11450.0
福 建	Fujian	4	27040	8102.0
江 西	Jiangxi	5	36760	10610.0
山 东	Shandong	19	143383	60204.7
河 南	Henan	5	31313	6751.0
湖 北	Hubei	7	74039	23559.3
湖 南	Hunan	7	42067	9852.0
广 东	Guangdong	13	101614	45167.2
广 西	Guangxi	4	23061	3951.5
海 南	Hainan	3	3365	860.3
重 庆	Chongqing	4	29764	11268.0
四 川	Sichuan	6	24213	8870.0
贵 州	Guizhou	5	60561	14482.0
云 南	Yunnan	4	32000	8000.0
西 藏	Tibet			
陕 西	Shaanxi	5	47980	16252.0
甘 肃	Gansu	6	43730	12170.0
青 海	Qinghai	3	20714	5222.3
宁 夏	Ningxia	5	60639	25648.0
新 疆	Xinjiang	3	31162	6200.0
新疆兵团	Xinjiang Corps	3	46600	8300.0
黑龙江垦区	Heilongjiang Land Reclamation	3	20500	4100.0

12-3 残疾人托养设施
Fostering Service Facilities for PWDs

地 区	Region	已投入使用项目 Projects in Operation		
		本年度新投入使用项目 Projects Getting into Operation in 2014		
		项目个数 Number of Projects	建设规模 Construction Area	总投资 Total Investment
		个 unit	平方米 square meter	万元 10,000 yuan
全 国	**Total**	**75**	**216149**	**54165.4**
北 京	Beijing			
天 津	Tianjin			
河 北	Hebei	1	19400	5860.4
山 西	Shanxi			
内蒙古	Inner Mongolia	4	6738	1158.6
辽 宁	Liaoning	4	9116	1728.0
吉 林	Jilin	1	3000	600.0
黑龙江	Heilongjiang			
上 海	Shanghai			
江 苏	Jiangsu	10	59598	22653.4
浙 江	Zhejiang	6	14750	3670.0
安 徽	Anhui	4	11140	1635.0
福 建	Fujian	2	4350	700.0
江 西	Jiangxi			
山 东	Shandong	8	35924	7114.0
河 南	Henan	3	10006	1672.0
湖 北	Hubei	2	494	60.0
湖 南	Hunan	6	5800	1023.0
广 东	Guangdong	4	710	311.0
广 西	Guangxi			
海 南	Hainan			
重 庆	Chongqing			
四 川	Sichuan	3	1520	156.0
贵 州	Guizhou			
云 南	Yunnan			
西 藏	Tibet			
陕 西	Shaanxi	10	17999	1552.0
甘 肃	Gansu	1	1200	620.0
青 海	Qinghai	4	7940	2050.0
宁 夏	Ningxia			
新 疆	Xinjiang	2	6464	1602.0
新疆兵团	Xinjiang Corps			
黑龙江垦区	Heilongjiang Land Reclamation			

12-3 续表 1 Continued 1

地 区	Region	已投入使用项目 Projects in Operation 累计已投入使用项目 Accumulated Projects in Operation 项目个数 Number of Projects	建设规模 Construction Area	总投资 Total Investment
		个 unit	平方米 square meter	万元 10,000 yuan
全 国	**Total**	**442**	**1013924**	**257073.2**
北 京	Beijing			
天 津	Tianjin	16	10533	3866.0
河 北	Hebei	9	50619	11410.4
山 西	Shanxi	1	2000	400.0
内蒙古	Inner Mongolia	8	11234	1658.6
辽 宁	Liaoning	20	35774	12632.8
吉 林	Jilin	2	7300	2052.0
黑龙江	Heilongjiang	3	10817	3346.0
上 海	Shanghai	12	7260	1593.0
江 苏	Jiangsu	48	228434	77444.4
浙 江	Zhejiang	18	101854	36977.0
安 徽	Anhui	5	12900	1881.0
福 建	Fujian	40	43540	6125.6
江 西	Jiangxi	1	11000	3500.0
山 东	Shandong	33	107525	28239.0
河 南	Henan	5	15406	3172.0
湖 北	Hubei	30	33432	5139.5
湖 南	Hunan	38	34368	4407.1
广 东	Guangdong	38	57031	10678.1
广 西	Guangxi	2	920	70.2
海 南	Hainan			
重 庆	Chongqing	1	68	197.9
四 川	Sichuan	12	22052	4620.7
贵 州	Guizhou	1	1640	252.0
云 南	Yunnan			
西 藏	Tibet			
陕 西	Shaanxi	47	109383	13461.0
甘 肃	Gansu	5	10975	2974.0
青 海	Qinghai	9	17235	4490.0
宁 夏	Ningxia			
新 疆	Xinjiang	9	16766	3928.0
新疆兵团	Xinjiang Corps	27	45338	7209.9
黑龙江垦区	Heilongjiang Land Reclamation	2	8521	5347.0

12-3 续表 2 Continued 2

地 区	Region	在建项目 Projects under Construction		
		项目个数 Number of Projects	建设规模 Construction Area	总投资 Total Investment
		个 unit	平方米 square meter	万元 10,000 yuan
全 国	**Total**	**72**	**293550**	**71976.1**
北 京	Beijing			
天 津	Tianjin			
河 北	Hebei	5	13700	2215.0
山 西	Shanxi	4	41500	3695.0
内蒙古	Inner Mongolia	2	4000	1200.0
辽 宁	Liaoning	6	11100	2490.0
吉 林	Jilin	4	9000	1448.4
黑龙江	Heilongjiang	3	6000	1380.0
上 海	Shanghai			
江 苏	Jiangsu	1	5000	500.0
浙 江	Zhejiang	3	26960	9767.0
安 徽	Anhui	1	2300	460.0
福 建	Fujian	2	18752	5857.0
江 西	Jiangxi			
山 东	Shandong	2	5240	1252.0
河 南	Henan	7	21000	3000.0
湖 北	Hubei	2	5297	696.9
湖 南	Hunan	1	9888	3540.0
广 东	Guangdong	4	33662	14958.0
广 西	Guangxi	6	20783	2933.1
海 南	Hainan	1	3000	812.6
重 庆	Chongqing	2	5528	4480.2
四 川	Sichuan			
贵 州	Guizhou	6	23740	4901.0
云 南	Yunnan	4	7800	1440.0
西 藏	Tibet			
陕 西	Shaanxi	3	13300	3240.0
甘 肃	Gansu			
青 海	Qinghai	3	6000	1710.0
宁 夏	Ningxia			
新 疆	Xinjiang			
新疆兵团	Xinjiang Corps			
黑龙江垦区	Heilongjiang Land Reclamation			

12-3　续表 3　Continued 3

地　区	Region	筹建项目　Projects under Discussion and Preparation		
		项目个数 Number of Projects	建设规模 Construction Area	总投资 Total Investment
		个 unit	平方米 square meter	万元 10,000 yuan
全　国	**Total**	**145**	**560300**	**168697.3**
北　京	Beijing			
天　津	Tianjin			
河　北	Hebei	2	5500	850.0
山　西	Shanxi	5	11225	2092.7
内蒙古	Inner Mongolia	2	5396	1500.0
辽　宁	Liaoning	5	47006	28555.0
吉　林	Jilin	1	3800	800.0
黑龙江	Heilongjiang	7	22120	4156.0
上　海	Shanghai			
江　苏	Jiangsu	9	98697	27801.2
浙　江	Zhejiang	6	46584	19049.0
安　徽	Anhui	1	2800	800.0
福　建	Fujian	2	4748	1050.0
江　西	Jiangxi	10	28569	9417.0
山　东	Shandong	9	28338	9521.9
河　南	Henan	9	28897	5614.0
湖　北	Hubei	7	24127	4514.8
湖　南	Hunan	4	22081	10143.9
广　东	Guangdong	4	12278	3921.0
广　西	Guangxi	5	9635	1605.0
海　南	Hainan	1	1800	461.5
重　庆	Chongqing	3	11558	3767.0
四　川	Sichuan	2	5500	1300.0
贵　州	Guizhou	20	77257	16966.5
云　南	Yunnan	1	2082	330.0
西　藏	Tibet			
陕　西	Shaanxi			
甘　肃	Gansu	6	14052	2650.0
青　海	Qinghai	16	32449	9477.9
宁　夏	Ningxia	1	2000	440.0
新　疆	Xinjiang	3	9601	1438.0
新疆兵团	Xinjiang Corps	4	2200	475.0
黑龙江垦区	Heilongjiang Land Reclamation			

13-1 残疾人事业信息化建设
Informationzation on the Work for PWDs

地 区	Region	门户网站 Websites	省级 at Provincial Level	地市级 at Prefectural/ City Level	县级 at County Level	省级网站本年度发稿量 Articles Published by Provincial-level Websites of Disabled Persons' Federations	各级信息化专业人才 IT Professionals
		个 unit	个 unit	个 unit	个 unit	篇 sheet	人 person
全 国	**Total**	**1660**	**33**	**280**	**1347**	**70293**	**4971**
北 京	Beijing	17	1		16	2339	44
天 津	Tianjin	14	1		13	400	48
河 北	Hebei	35	1	10	24	4369	283
山 西	Shanxi	86	1	11	74	1649	192
内蒙古	Inner Mongolia	46	1	7	38	1000	151
辽 宁	Liaoning	68	1	14	53	4796	184
吉 林	Jilin	46	1	9	36	1753	132
黑龙江	Heilongjiang	31	1	7	23	818	175
上 海	Shanghai	18	1		17	3997	47
江 苏	Jiangsu	110	1	13	96	2317	213
浙 江	Zhejiang	95	1	11	83	3200	161
安 徽	Anhui	99	1	16	82	12000	184
福 建	Fujian	94	1	9	84	2500	164
江 西	Jiangxi	44	1	6	37	479	163
山 东	Shandong	93	1	17	75	1760	208
河 南	Henan	27	1	10	16	950	232
湖 北	Hubei	56	1	12	43	4587	147
湖 南	Hunan	77	1	13	63	2245	198
广 东	Guangdong	83	1	21	61	3554	287
广 西	Guangxi	117	1	15	101	437	197
海 南	Hainan	3	1	1	1	98	39
重 庆	Chongqing	39	1		38	1350	85
四 川	Sichuan	112	1	18	93	600	267
贵 州	Guizhou	25	1	2	22	829	101
云 南	Yunnan	50	1	12	37	2200	212
西 藏	Tibet	1	1			23	13
陕 西	Shaanxi	63	1	10	52	1420	165
甘 肃	Gansu	47	1	14	32	3500	131
青 海	Qinghai	9	1	4	4	606	67
宁 夏	Ningxia	13	1	4	8	1500	35
新 疆	Xinjiang	39	1	13	25	1610	134
新疆兵团	Xinjiang Corps	2	1	1		507	185
黑龙江垦区	Heilongjiang Land Reclamation	1	1			900	127

13-1　续表　Continued

地区	Region	本年度信息工作培训情况 Training for Web Technology and Management in 2014			
		省级 at Provincial Level		地市级 at Prefectural/City Level	
		举办信息工作培训班 Training Course for Web Technology and Management	参加信息工作培训班 Participants of Training Course	举办信息工作培训班 Training Course for Web Technology and Management	参加信息工作培训班 Participants of Training Course
		期 course	人次 person-time	期 course	人次 person-time
全　国	**Total**	**32**	**2281**	**692**	**9671**
北　京	Beijing	1	30		
天　津	Tianjin				
河　北	Hebei	2	80	16	472
山　西	Shanxi			9	158
内蒙古	Inner Mongolia	1	120	14	210
辽　宁	Liaoning	1	40	20	605
吉　林	Jilin	1	53	12	442
黑龙江	Heilongjiang			4	119
上　海	Shanghai	4	300		
江　苏	Jiangsu	1	70	28	1487
浙　江	Zhejiang	2	320	7	270
安　徽	Anhui	1	150	14	213
福　建	Fujian	1	40	11	291
江　西	Jiangxi	1	36	10	147
山　东	Shandong	1	55	18	634
河　南	Henan			22	440
湖　北	Hubei	1	70	345	797
湖　南	Hunan			9	163
广　东	Guangdong			31	650
广　西	Guangxi			10	136
海　南	Hainan	1	35	1	1
重　庆	Chongqing	1	55		
四　川	Sichuan	1	30	24	835
贵　州	Guizhou	1	12	3	185
云　南	Yunnan	2	70	14	302
西　藏	Tibet	2	240	1	18
陕　西	Shaanxi	3	340	9	134
甘　肃	Gansu			20	228
青　海	Qinghai			10	169
宁　夏	Ningxia	1	60	5	87
新　疆	Xinjiang	1	60	9	243
新疆兵团	Xinjiang Corps			9	197
黑龙江垦区	Heilongjiang Land Reclamation	1	15	7	38

分省统计报告

Statistical Report of Provinces

2014年北京市残疾人事业发展统计公报

2014年，在中国残联的指导和北京市委、市政府的正确领导下，我市残疾人工作紧紧围绕“全面建设残疾人工作首善之区，共创残疾人幸福美好新生活”的目标，积极融入首都社会事业发展与社会治理体制改革大局，不断提高残疾人保障和服务水平，圆满完成了各项目标任务。

一、康复

康复服务覆盖面逐步扩大。儿童残疾早期筛查、转介、诊断、康复的服务网络基本建成，精神残疾人免费服药、中途宿舍等综合服务保障模式稳步推进，辅助器具政策修订取得实质进展，18.5万名残疾人得到个性化康复训练与服务。

全市16个区县大力开展了社区康复工作，已有3909个社区建立了社区康复站，配备5968名社区康复协调员。

16个区县的27个医疗卫生机构陆续开展残疾儿童筛查工作，年度新诊断0-6岁残疾儿童418人。

开展视力残疾康复机构总数达到13个，完成白内障复明手术12577例；为1731名贫困白内障患者免费施行复明手术；为837名低视力患者配用助视器，培训低视力儿童家长22名，有效开展家庭康复训练。对1289名盲人进行定向行走训练。

推进听力语言康复机构规范化管理，完善基层服务网络。已建设市级听力语言康复机构1个，基层听力语言康复机构24个。年度新收训聋儿168名，在训聋儿378名；规范聋儿家长学校，开展家庭训练，共培训聋儿家长414名；开展各级各类听力语言康复专业技术人员培训，共培训专业人员174人。

开展肢体残疾康复训练服务机构达26个，其中，市级康复机构1个，区县级康复机构25个；培训各级各类肢体残疾康复人员4462人次；共对5601名肢体残疾者实施康复训练；实施救助项目资助248名脑瘫儿童进行机构康复训练。

开展智力残疾康复训练服务的机构43个，其中，市级康复机构1个，区县级康复机构42个；培训各级各类智力残疾康复人员1800人次；共对4718名智力残疾人进行康复训练；实施救助项目资助589名智力残疾儿童进行机构康复训练。

大力推广“社会化、综合性、开放式”精神病防治康复工作。在16个区县开展精神病防治康复工作，对73364名重性精神病患者进行综合防治康复，对7684名贫困精神病患者进行医疗救助。

建立了1个市级孤独症儿童康复训练机构；426名孤独症儿童在各级机构进行了康复训练。

加强残疾人辅助器具服务体系建设，深入开展辅助器具供应服务，为残疾人减免费用供应辅助器具18406件，其中装配假肢245例、矫形器89例，验配助视器1637件。

二、教育

融合教育稳步发展，制定首个省级特殊教育学校办学条件标准，残疾学生平均公用经费标准达到普通学生的7倍，5621名残疾儿童少年随班就读，312名重度残疾儿童接受送教上门服务；完成全市有意愿脱盲的残疾人青壮年的扫盲工作，组织70名残疾人参加成人高等学历教育，促进更多的残疾人接受教育。

共有特殊教育普通高中班（部）2个，在校生80人；其中聋生68人；盲生12人。残疾人中等职业学校（班）5个，在校生236人，毕业生91人，其中72人获得职业资格证书。有75名残疾人被普通高等院校录取，165名残疾人进入特殊教育学院学习。

三、就业

市委、市人大、市政府、市政协办公厅及市人力社保局首次面向残疾人定向提供了5个公务员岗位，目前已有3名残疾人进入面试阶段。7名盲人医疗按摩师在医疗机构就业。举办残疾人就业系列招聘会41场，与24所高校合作实施残疾人大学生就业助力计划，成功举办第七届残疾人职业技能竞赛。

2014 年，残疾人就业规模总体保持稳定。城镇新就业残疾人 4285 人，其中，集中就业残疾人 190 人，按比例安排残疾人就业 1805 人，公益性岗位就业 97 人，个体就业及其它形式灵活就业 1918 人，辅助性就业 275 人。城镇就业人数 74689 人；62025 名农村残疾人在业，其中 39903 名残疾人从事农业生产劳动。

残疾人职业培训基地达到 64 个，其中残联兴办 7 个，依托社会机构兴办 57 个，其中 9260 人次城镇残疾人接受了职业培训。

盲人按摩事业稳定发展。2014 年度培训盲人保健按摩人员 1491 名、盲人医疗按摩人员 279 名；保健按摩机构达到 396 个，医疗按摩机构达到 4 个。

四、扶贫

2014 年，我市农村残疾人扶贫开发工作进一步推进，农村低收入残疾人生产、生活状况得到较大改善。全力抓好扶贫助残基地规范化管理，促使基地健康可持续发展，充分发挥其带动农村低收入残疾人增收致富的龙头作用。创新科技服务，组织农业专家与扶贫基地和低收入农户开展“结对子”服务，科技扶贫效能显著。协调人社局等部门，探索将益民书屋残疾人管理岗位纳入社会性公益就业岗位，千方百计促进农村残疾人就业。落实农村残疾人危旧房政策，为符合条件的残疾人翻建维修住房。

接受实用技术培训的残疾人达到 2873 人次。残疾人扶贫基地达到 121 个，安置 3814 名残疾人就业，扶持带动 3824 名残疾人。

完成 657 户农村贫困残疾人危房改造，各地投入危房资金 553.24 万元，677 名残疾人受益。基层党组织助残扶贫项目帮扶 72 名农村贫困残疾人，其中首次接受帮扶 6 人。

五、社会保障

新修订完善 10 余项相关福利保障政策，36.6 万人享受生活补助、社会救助及“养老助残九养”政策，残疾人基本生活得到较大程度满足，体现了北京特色和首善标准。

2014 年新型农村和城镇居民社会养老保险统一合并实施，已有 97441 名城乡残疾居民参保，参保率 96.86%，在 60 岁以下的参保残疾人中有 43515 名重度残疾人，全部得到了政府的参保扶助，代缴补贴比例达到 100%。有 35684 名非重度残疾人也享受了全额或部分代缴的优惠政策。领取养老金待遇的人数达到 12275 人。

城镇残疾职工参加养老保险 74438 人，参加医疗保险 71563 人，城镇 20875 人和农村 20416 名残疾人纳入最低生活保障范围；城镇集中供养残疾人和农村五保供养残疾人分别达到 124 名和 367 名；120762 名符合条件的城乡残疾人享受了稳定的生活补贴。28742 名城乡残疾人得到了其他救助救济。

残疾人托养服务工作规范推进，残疾人托养服务机构 98 个，共为 1297 名残疾人提供了托养服务。其中寄宿制托养服务机构 77 个；综合性托养服务机构 21 个。在以上机构中，共有 100 名残疾人实现辅助性就业，2 名残疾人实现了支持性就业。机构之外接受居家托养服务的残疾人达到 106495 人。全年共有 566 名托养服务管理和服务人员接受了各级各类专业培训，其中接受国家级培训 5 人。

六、宣传文化

2014 年 11 月 10 日，亚太经合组织第二十二次领导人会议周期间残疾人主题活动在北京隆重举行，这是 APEC 会议 22 年来首次同期举办的残疾人主题活动。市残联负责牵头联络协调及才艺展示筹备工作。整个活动衔接顺畅、精彩纷呈，向全世界展示了中国残疾人事业发展成果和首都残疾人事业发展成就，受到了各国参会元首夫人及代表一致好评。

文化活动丰富活跃，“爱助梦想”助残日系列活动得到肯定，“乐动心灵”、“心悦书香”等 12 个温馨助残文化品牌影响力不断扩大；首部原创话剧《假如给我三天光明——借光》演出 70 场次，被中国残联作为唯一戏剧作品上报全国“五个一”工程奖；组建“我梦最美”自强模范暨助残先进事迹宣讲团，在全市“最美北京人”宣讲比赛活动中荣获第一名；制作反映残疾人生活的微电影 6 部，其中《不止天使有翅膀》荣获“第二届亚洲微电影艺术节金海棠奖”最佳作品奖；8 名残疾人先进事迹被北京电视台《365 个故事》栏目收录播放，2 名残疾人入选 2014 年度十大“北京榜样”候选人，14

名残疾人入选周榜样，增进了全社会对残疾人的认识和理解。残疾人艺术团队活跃在基层，演出 300 场次，成为展示“人文北京”的亮丽名片。

截至 2014 年底，共有市级电视手语新闻栏目 1 个，播出公益广告 3 个；区县电视手语新闻栏目 3 个，播出公益广告 4 个。

市区县公共图书馆共设立盲文及盲人有声读物阅览室 26 个，残疾人文化周期间共开展活动 353 场次，举办残疾人文化艺术类比赛及展览 204 次。全市有各类残疾人艺术团体 62 个。

七、体育

市残联全力配合 2022 年冬季残奥会申办工作，组建了冰壶队；组队了参加亚洲残疾人运动会，获得 7 金 3 银 3 铜的良好成绩；组织 18 支队伍参加全国单项锦标赛、九运会提前赛，获得 25 枚金牌、24 枚银牌、40 枚铜牌的佳绩；轮椅篮球队代表中国队参加“第一届东吴杯国际轮椅篮球邀请赛”，获得冠军。残疾人健身周活动、自强健身示范点被确定为全国示范样板和示范项目。

全年组织残疾人体育健身活动 1568 次，参加人数 113250 人次。其中市级活动 30 次，参加人数 1.55 万人；区县活动 1538 次，参加人数 9.775 万；全市残疾人体育示范点 156 个，其中市级 69 个，区县级 87 个。残疾人体育健身指导员 2261 人，其中市级 1500 人，区县 761 人，各区县组织残疾人体育比赛 30 次，参与的残疾人运动员 532 人次；全市有残疾人体育训练基地 10 个，聘任教练员 32 人。

八、维权

残疾人法律维权服务进一步改善。建立了残疾人信访网上办公系统、远程服务平台及重大信访诉求的联动会商机制，残疾人反映强烈的机动轮椅车出行、加油和免费停车等问题逐步得到解决；完善了律师值班制度，建立了由公、检、法、司联合参加的残疾人法律维权工作协调机制，加强“12348”、易行维权助残热线管理。

2014 年，区县人大进行《残疾人保障法》执法检查和专题调研 2 次；政协进行视察和专题调研 2 次。开展普法宣传教育活动 143 次，12658 人参加；举办法律培训班 21 个，2601 人参加。

截至 2014 年年底，成立残疾人法律救助工作协调机构 13 个，建立残疾人法律救助工作站 9 个，办理案件 79 件，建立残疾人法律援助中心（工作站）16 个，办理案件 286 件，有力地推动了法律救助和法律援助工作。

残疾人参政议政工作得到加强，各级残联协助人大代表、政协委员提出议案、建议、提案 3 件，办理议案、建议、提案 5 件。

无障碍建设法规、标准进一步完善。共出台了 2 个无障碍建设与管理法规、规章和规范性文件；16 个区县开展无障碍建设，开展无障碍建设检查 268 次，无障碍培训 7749 人次；为 16457 个贫困残疾人家庭实施了无障碍改造；为 23214 名残疾人发放了残疾人机动轮椅车燃油补贴。

共处理残疾人群众来信 6177 件，接待残疾人群众来访 4155 人次。

九、组织建设

以组织、机构、人员调查为契机，积极探索街道乡镇理事长、专职工作者、专职委员、助残志愿服务“四支队伍”管理工作长效机制。开展残疾人基本服务状况和需求专项调查，为持续推动残疾人服务托住底、补短板、保基本、广覆盖工作奠定了基础。

2014 年，我市有 13 个区县残联机关配备了残疾人干部；已建乡镇（街道）残联 323 个，已建率达到 100%，选聘残疾人专职委员 874 名；已建社区（村）残协 5818 个，已建率达到 93.30%，选聘残疾人专职委员 5339 名。

市区（县）、街（乡镇）残联实有人员已达 1214 人。各级残联共举办培训班 736 期，培训机关干部、协会干部及残疾人专职委员 18555 人次。

省级以下各类残疾人专门协会建立 85 个，区县专门协会已建比例为 100%。

十、服务设施

截至 2014 年年底，已竣工并投入使用的各级残疾人综合服务设施 6 个，总建设规模 70771 平方米；已竣工并投入使用的各级残疾人康复设施 3 个，总建设规模 13221 平方米。

十一、信息化

残疾人服务“一卡通”应用启动，残疾人服务“一卡通”是智能化残疾人证试点卡，统一了身份编号、标识设计、基础信息、服务功能、密钥体系、卡片选型、证卡管理，具有身份识别、业务管理、社会服务、金融业务等四重功能，实现了政府公共服务和个人信息管理的集成应用，是残疾人事业向智能化发展的第一步，更是残疾人全面融入社会、平等有尊严地享受公共服务、共享经济社会发展成果的重要体现。截至目前已有 36 万名残疾人陆续提交了领卡申请，首批卡发放完毕。

市残联网站加大对残疾人各项政策、残疾人事业的宣传，年度访问量达到 5000 万次，完成 3748 条信息更新。

北京市残联系统已全部开通了公众服务网站，共有 1 个市级残联网站和 16 个区县级残联网站。2014 年，市级残联开设网站技术培训班 1 期，培训各级残联信息员 30 人次。

2014 年天津市残疾人事业发展统计公报

2014 年，在市委、市政府领导和中国残联指导下，在各区县、各部门和社会各界的共同支持下，天津市全面完成了残疾人事业各项工作的年度任务，积极推进残疾人社会保障、康复、教育、培训、就业、扶贫、维权、无障碍环境建设、托养、重残护理、文化体育、福利基金、组织建设、服务设施和信息化建设等工作，取得了新的成效和新的突破，残疾人物质和文化生活状况得到进一步改善。现根据 2014 年度残疾人事业统计数据和实际情况，进行分析，并公报如下：

一、残疾人康复工作稳步提高

积极推进残疾人社区康复工作。截至 2014 年底，在 13 个市辖区和 3 个县开展了社区康复工作，有 1701 个社区已建立康复站，比 2013 年增加 43 个。目前，有社区康复协调员 3909 人；为 304739 名生活在社区的残疾人建立了社区康复服务档案，比 2013 年增加 40739 人。到 2014 年底，累计有 264010 人接受了社区康复服务，本年度新增接受社区康复服务有 34354 人。从图 1-1 看，"十二五"以来，社区康复工作水平显著提高。

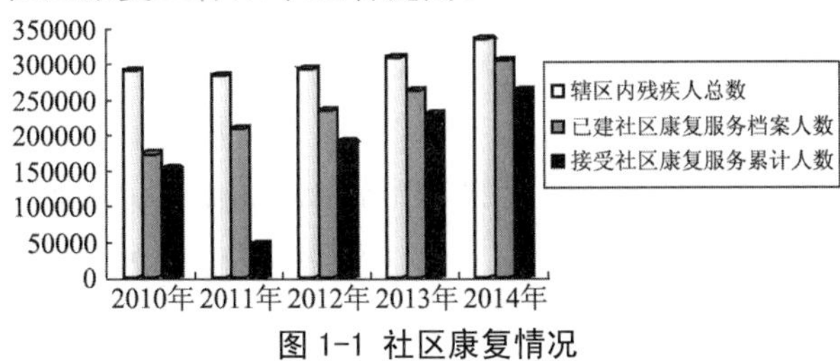

图 1-1 社区康复情况

大力实施重点康复工程和项目。2014 年，通过实施一批重点康复工程，使各类别残疾人得到不同程度的康复。

1. 全年完成白内障复明手术 6416 例，比 2013 年增加 21.1%，其中为贫困白内障患者免费施行复明手术 773 例。全年为 2081 名低视力患者配用助视器，比 2013 年增加 781 人。培训低视力儿童家长 498 名。对 1312 名盲人进行定向行走训练。

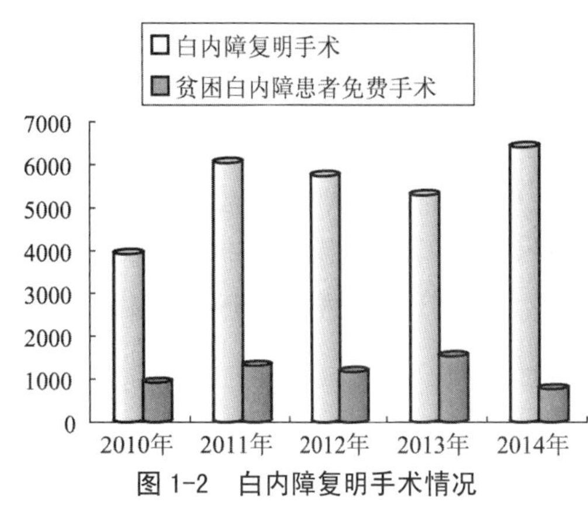

图 1-2　白内障复明手术情况

2. 加强各级聋儿康复机构建设，完善聋儿康复网络。2014 年新收训聋儿 51 名，全年共对 100 名聋儿进行了听力语言康复训练。规范聋儿家长学校，大力开展家庭训练，共培训聋儿家长 132 名，比 2013 年增长了 33.3%；培训各级机构专业人员 33 人。受训聋儿训练后有 12 名进入普通小学，有 15 名进入普通幼儿园，有 3 名进入聋人学校；开展成年听力语言康复技术服务，聋人接受服务 569 人次。

3. 全年开展肢体残疾康复训练服务的机构达到 10 个，完成 43 例贫困肢体残疾儿童矫治手术，装配了矫形器等辅助器具，进行了术后康复训练。对 3547 名肢体残疾人进行了康复训练，比 2013 年增加了 114 人。其中：脑瘫儿童机构康复训练 127 人，肢体残疾儿童社区、家庭康复 134 人，成年肢体残疾人社区、家庭康复 3286 人。

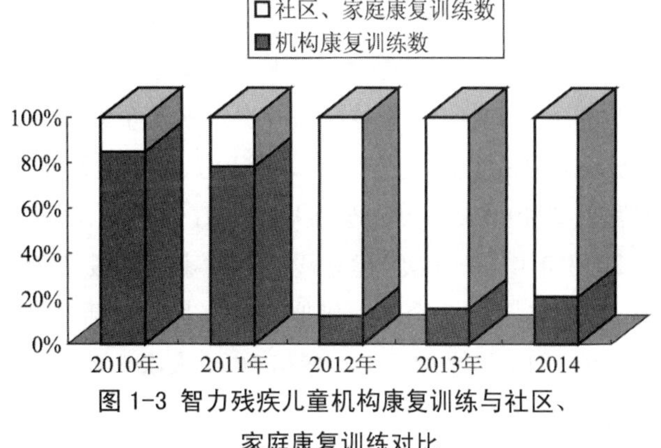

图 1-3　智力残疾儿童机构康复训练与社区、家庭康复训练对比

4. 全年开展智力残疾康复训练服务的机构达到 13 个。智力残疾儿童机构康复训练 198 人，比 2013 年增加了 59 人。智力残疾儿童社区、家庭康复 754

人。不同程度地开展了智力残疾儿童早期康复训练与服务。成年智力残疾人社区、家庭康复 119 人。

5. 大力推广“社会化、综合性、开放式”精神病防治康复工作。2014 年，在 16 个区县开展精神病防治康复工作，覆盖总人口数达到 1138.4 万人。对 72529 名精神病患者进行综合防治康复，监护率达到 94.4%，显好率达到 71.9%，社会参与率达到 63.8%，无关锁病人。接受治疗的精神病患者 12360 人。接受康复训练的精神病人数 8721 人。对 4324 名贫困精神病患者进行医疗救助。建立了 2 个市级孤独症儿童康复训练机构，有 79 名孤独症儿童进行了康复训练。

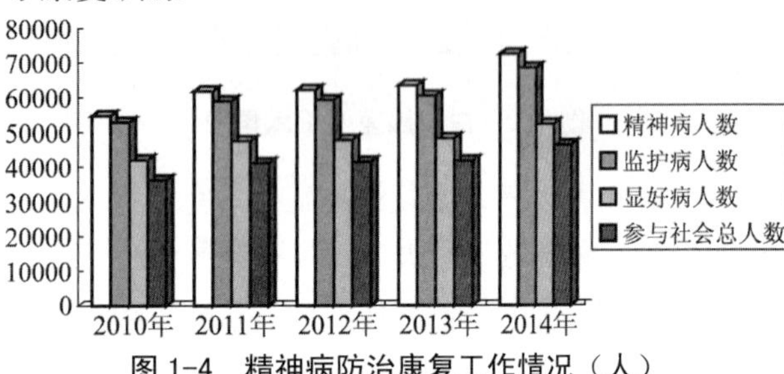

图 1-4　精神病防治康复工作情况（人）

6. 深入开展残疾人辅助器具供应服务，全面推进普及型辅助假肢装配工作，截止 2014 年底，累计建立辅助器具供应服务机构 13 个，全市各类辅助器具供应数达到 33827 件。辅助器具供应品种 116 种。其中为残疾人装配假肢 325 例。装配矫形器 167 例。国家彩票公益金项目为残疾人免费发放 6465 件，比 2013 年增加 857 件。残疾人辅助器具管理水平和供应服务水平日益提高，使更多贫困残疾人得以恢复和改善身体功能，生活自理。从 2014 年与近几年辅助器具各个指标对比上看，辅助器具供应水平呈上升趋势。

7. 大力开展残疾预防工作，与上年相比有较大幅度提高。开展残疾儿童筛查工作区县 16 个。开展残疾儿童筛查工作的医疗卫生机构 22 个，较 2013 年增加 7 个。本年度新诊断 0-6 岁残疾儿童 675 人。发放儿童残疾预防宣传材料 20082 份，比 2013 年增加发放 2949 份。举办儿童残疾预防宣传活动 38 次，较 2013 年增加 15 次；建立残疾儿童家长学校 7 个，较 2013 年增加 2 个；本年度开展家长学校活动 35 次，较 2013 年增加 4 次；参与 1090 人次，比 2013 年增加 65 人次。

二、残疾人教育工作进展良好

2014 年，为接受各阶段教育的残疾学生和贫困残疾人在校健全子女发放助学金，残疾人整体素质有所提高。全市各特教学校义务教育阶段对残疾学生继续实施“三免一补”（免交杂费、教科书费、住宿费，补贴生活费）政策，实现义务教育阶段免费教育。未入学学龄残疾儿童少年总数 186 人，其中视力残疾 2 人，听力残疾 4 人，言语残疾 5 人，肢体残疾 58 人，智力残疾 102 人，精神残疾 1 人，多重残疾 14 人。

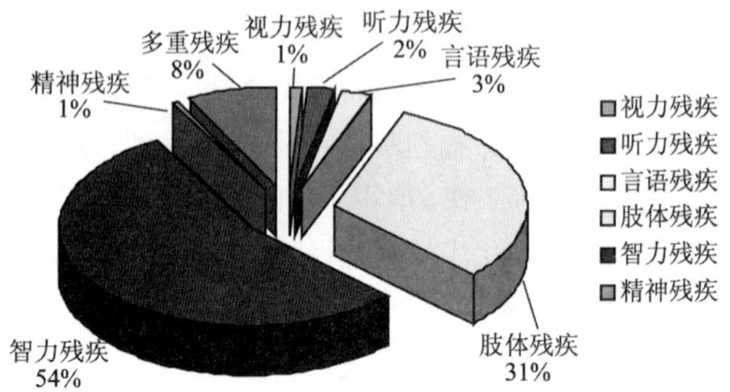

图 2-1　2014 年度未入学学龄残疾儿童少年分类

2014 年，残疾人特殊教育事业发展稳定。开办特殊教育普通高中 2 所，在校生 114 人；其中聋人高中 1 所，在校生 85 人；盲人高中 1 所，在校生 29 人。残疾人中等职业学校 1 所。高等特殊教育机构 2 所，录取残疾考生 135 人。有 116 名残疾考生被普通高等院校录取。

三、残疾人就业工作稳步推进

2014 年，全市城镇新增就业 4213 人，累计安排残疾人就业 40164 人。新就业残疾人中，各区县残疾人城镇集中就业人数本年度新增 573 人；按比例就业人数大幅增加，并且依然是残疾人主要就业形式，本年度新增 3125 人；个体及其他形式就业人数本年度新增 287 人；公益性岗位就业人数本年度新增 93 人；辅助性就业人数本年度新增 135 人。

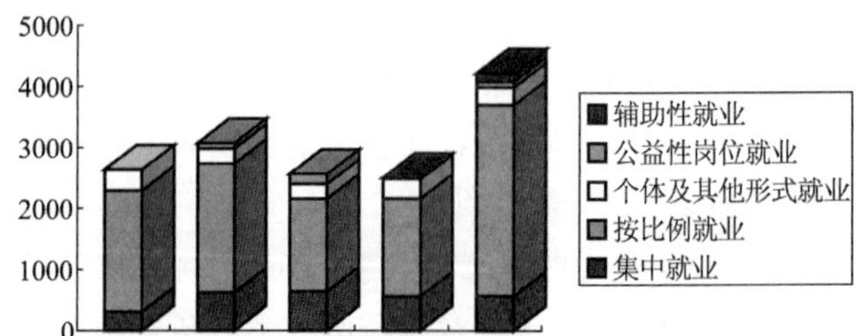

图 3-1　近几年城镇残疾人本年度新增就业状况

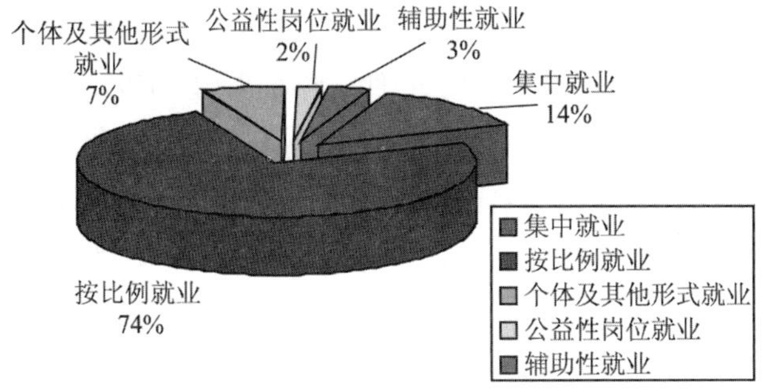

图 3-2 2014 年城镇残疾人五种就业形式本年度新增就业情况

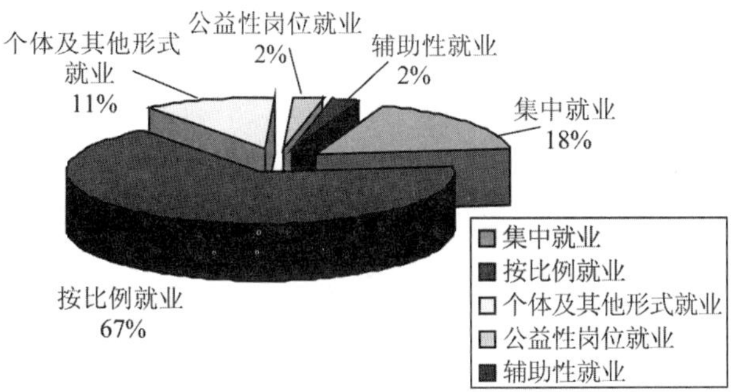

图 3-3 2014 年城镇残疾人五种就业形式累计就业情况

到 2014 年底，农村残疾人实际就业 67714 人，较 2013 年有所增加。农村残疾人从事农业生产劳动 46258 人，占农村残疾人实际就业的 68.3%。

截止 2014 年底，全市城乡残疾人就业合计 107878 人，较 2013 年增加 2017 人。

全市有残疾人职业培训基地 30 个,其中：残联兴办 6 个，依托社会机构兴办 24 个。本年度城镇职业培训 2272 人次。本年培训盲人保健按摩人员 21 人、医疗按摩人员 18 人；保健按摩机构达到 167 个，医疗按摩机构达到 4 个。

四、残疾人社会保障工作切实加强

随着我市残疾人生活保障制度的不断规范和完善，更多的残疾人得到扶助，2014 年，城乡 61643 名残疾人纳入最低生活保障范围，实现了“应保尽保”；城镇已纳入最低生活保障 35913 人，城镇集中供养和其他救助救济 12359 人；农村已纳入最低生活保障 25730 人，农村五保供养和其他救助救济 12682 人。 在城镇，残疾人参加社会保险的人数较 2013 年有所增加，2014 年城镇残疾职工参加养老保险人数 42558 人，参加医疗保险人数 42558 人；在残疾居民参加城乡社会养老保险情况中，实际参保的残疾居民为 58461 人，比 2013 年增加 863 人。

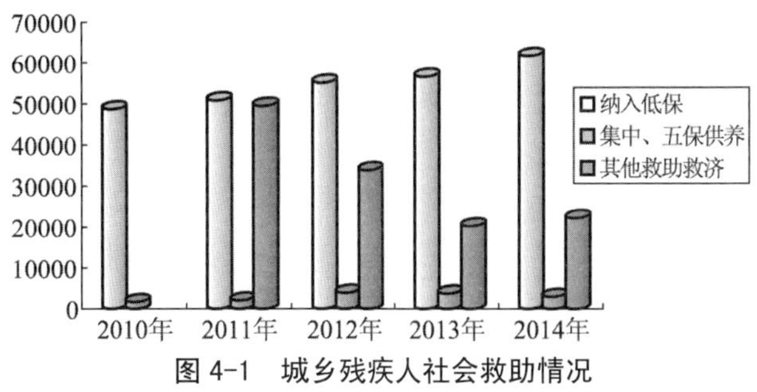

图 4-1 城乡残疾人社会救助情况

截止 2014 年底，全市有符合标准并正常运行的托养服务机构 88 个，比 2013 年增加 4 个；托养残疾人总数 25329 人，比 2013 年增加 8977 人。其中寄宿制托养服务机构 17 个，托养残疾人 348 人；日间照料托养服务机构 68 个，托养残疾人 1032 人；综合托养服务机构 3 个，托养残疾人 58 人；享受居家托养服务残疾人 23891 人。

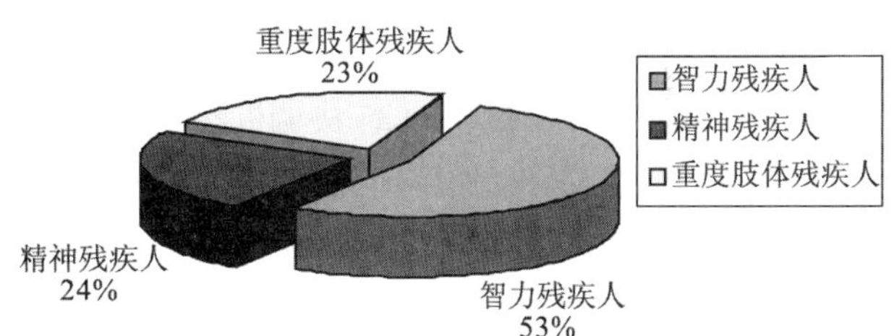

图 4-2 2014 年在托养服务机构中托养的残疾人情况

五、残疾人扶贫工作成效显著

加大农村残疾人扶持力度，加强实用技术培训，扩大扶贫成果，切实改善农村贫困残疾人生活状况。2014 年，扶持贫困残疾人户 21560 户，比 2013 年增加 1429 户，扶持贫困残疾人 24798 人次，无返贫人员。接受实用技术培训的残疾人 2733 人次，投入培训经费 89.6 万元。积极动员机关、企事业单位、志愿者组织及党员、干部、学生、街坊邻里等社会各界，采取多种形式，进行“帮、包、带、扶”，并充分发挥工会、共青团、妇联等团体和组织在残疾人扶贫工作中的作用，结对帮扶单位 167 个，结对帮扶个人 255 人；建立残疾人扶贫基地 176 个，安置残疾人就业 1904 人，扶持带动残疾人户 3640 户。

农村贫困残疾人危房改造成绩显著。2014 年完成 1433 户农村贫困残疾人危房改造，是 2013 年完成户数的 13 倍。投入危房改造资金 5019 万元，是 2013 年投入资金的 28 倍。受益残疾人 1470 人，是 2013 年受益残疾人的 13 倍。

六、残疾人维权工作逐步完善

继续完善残疾人事业法律法规，加大执法检查和监督力度，开展法律服务、法律援助，维护残疾人权益，推动无障碍设施建设。2014年，制定或修改保障残疾人权益的规范性文件 11 个，其中省级10个、县级1个；各级人大、政协的检查或专题调研10次，对残疾人保障法的贯彻实施起到了重要的推动作用。

表1：2014年残疾人执法检查情况表
人大执法检查或

	人大执法检查或专题调研	政协视察或专题调研
省级	0	0
区县级	7	3

已建立残疾人法律救助工作协调机构17个；建立残疾人法律救助工作站 17 个，2014 年办理案件289件，其中，省级59件、区县级230件。2014年残联办理人大建议、政协提案12件，满意率100%；残疾人参政议政工作得到加强。

表2：2014年残疾人法制宣传教育和法律工作者培训班情况表

	法制宣传教育		残疾人工作者法律培训	
	普法宣传教育活动		法律培训班	
	次数	人数	个数	人数
省级	2	200	1	125
县级	35	1790	12	744

截止2014年底，市和区县颁布无障碍建设与管理法规、政府令9个；建立无障碍建设领导协调组织17个；系统开展无障碍建设的区县16个。本年度进行无障碍建设检查54次，有465人次参加了无障碍培训，对1772户贫困残疾人家庭进行了无障碍改造。本年度对18550人发放了残疾人机动轮椅车燃油补贴。全市大多数新建主要城市道路、公共建筑物、居住建筑大都建设了相应的无障碍设施，同时加强了无障碍改造和对已建无障碍设施的管理，我市城市无障碍设施建设得到进一步加强，大大方便了广大残疾人、老年人、妇女、儿童、伤病人和全体社会成员参与社会生活。

2014 年，全市各级残联信访部门共处理来信236件，其中涉法涉诉22件、就业15件、社会保障51件、机动轮椅车86件；接待来访5059人次，其中涉法涉诉359人次、就业244人次、社会保障770人次、机动轮椅车2487人次。整体来看，2014年较前几年来信来访总量有所增加，其中，涉法涉诉、就业、社会保障、机动轮椅车四类分别占总的来信量的 9.3%、6.4%、21.6%、36.4%,占来访量的7.1%、4.8%、15.2%、49.2%；残疾人基本生活、就业、维护权利等问题，尤其是残疾人生活，仍然是我们迫切要解决的重大问题。

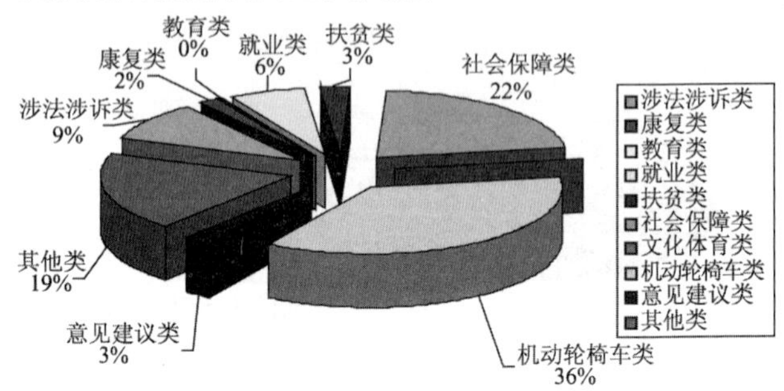

图6-1　2014年残疾人来信（件）情况

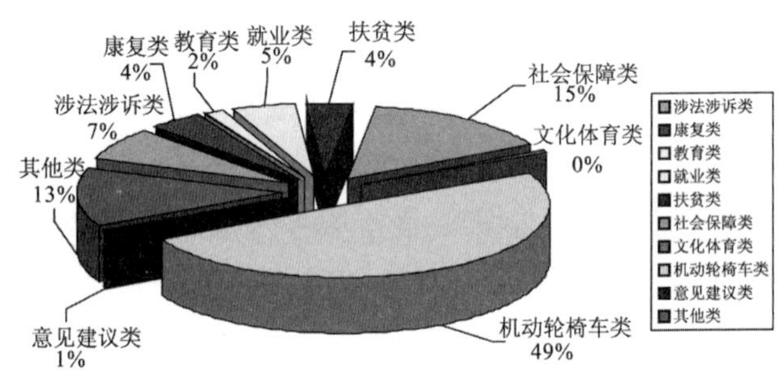

图6-2　2014年残疾人来访（人次）情况

七、宣传文化体育工作广泛深入

2014年，中央级媒体采用稿件3件，省级主要新闻媒体刊播稿件数2150件，省级报纸专版6个，省级广播电台残疾人专题节目 1 个，省级电视手语栏目 2 个，省级电视公益广告片 1 个，省级报纸公益广告1个，省级残疾人事业新闻宣传促进会1个；地市级主要新闻媒体刊播稿件数 228 件，地市级报纸专版8个，地市级广播电台残疾人专题节目1个，地市级电视手语栏目 3 个，地市级电视公益广告片1 个，地市级报纸公益广告 1 个，建立地市级新促会2个。

省级公共图书馆设立盲文及盲人有声读物图书室已达到2个，举办残疾人文化周5场次，9000人次参加了残疾人文化活动，举办残疾人文化艺术类比赛及展览5次，已成立残疾人艺术团队4个。

区县公共图书馆设立盲文及盲人有声读物图书室已达到 19 个，举办残疾人文化周 30 场次，2366 人次参加了残疾人文化活动，举办残疾人文化艺术类比赛及展览 25 次，已成立残疾人艺术团队 15 个。

省级开展残疾人群众体育健身活动 11 次，有 7085 人次参加，建成残疾人群众体育活动示范点 34 个，已培养残疾人体育健身指导员 255 人，举办残疾人体育比赛 9 次，参赛的残疾人运动员 3000 人次，建立残疾人体育训练基地 6 个，聘任教练员 13 人。

地市级开展残疾人体育活动 142 次，有 6124 人次参加，建成残疾人群众体育活动示范点 51 个，已培养残疾人体育健身指导员 527 人。

八、残疾人组织进一步健全

天津市共有各类残疾人 57 万，其中持证残疾人 26 万，占残疾人总数的 46%。截至 2014 年底，全市残联系统实有工作人员共 962 人，其中：市残联机关工作人员 44 名、事业单位工作人员 175 名，区县残联机关工作人员 155 名、事业单位工作人员 208 名，乡镇（街道）残联工作人员 380 名。全市乡（镇、街道）已建残联 242 个，配备残疾人专职委员 239 人，有专职残联理事长 242 名，无兼职残联理事长，基本建立了“一办三站一岗”（残联办公室、残疾人康复站、服务站（社）、志愿者助残联络站、残疾人维权岗），形成了多层次、多项目的残疾人服务载体和服务工作网络，为残疾人服务的能力显著增强。市及区县残联建立了残疾人人才库，有 589 名残疾人入库，其中，市级 123 人，区县级 466 人。目前，村（含农村社区）已建立 3372 个残协，建立了 3538 个残疾人活动室，选聘了 3357 个残疾人专职委员；城市社区已建立 1273 个残协，建立了 1256 个残疾人活动室，选聘了 1169 个残疾人专职委员。随着志愿者队伍的不断壮大，越来越多的残疾人得到不同程度的帮助

。

九、残疾人信息化建设工作力度加大

残疾人信息化建设队伍不断壮大，市及区县残联至少配备了一名统计人员，全系统共有统计人员 24 人，其中 7 人获得了统计从业资格证书；有信息化专业技术人才 48 人，全系统工作人员计算机知识水平较往年有所提高。目前，市残联及 13 个区县残联建立了门户网站。市残联门户网站全年发稿 400 篇。加大信息化基础设施建设、技术保障和安全投入，提高了残疾人信息化工作水平。

2014年河北省残疾人事业发展统计公报

2014年，省残联党组、理事会在省委、省政府坚强领导和中国残联有力指导下，认真学习贯彻党的十八大、十八届三中、四中全会以及习近平总书记系列重要讲话精神，按照省委八届六次、七次全会部署，紧紧围绕“三个河北”建设总目标，大力加强残疾人社会保障和服务体系建设，认真贯彻落实省委各项决策部署，在重点工作上积极探索创新，残疾人事业取得新的进步和发展。

一、康复工作

社区康复服务覆盖面稳步扩大。在36个市辖区、135个县（市）和张家口市的2个管理区、1个高新区的29889个社区（村）开展了社区康复工作，占社区（村）总数的59.1%；累计已建社区康复站的社区总数17331个，配备39750名社区康复协调员。为191.6万名残疾人建立了社区康复服务档案，占辖区残疾人总数的45.7%，截止2014年底，接受过社区康复服务的残疾人累计达39.7万人，比2013年增加了10%。

积极开展视力残疾康复工作。开展视力残疾康复机构总数达到19个，完成白内障复明手术26136例，为1014名贫困白内障患者免费施行复明手术；为9336名低视力患者配用助视器，培训低视力儿童家长1783名，有效开展家庭康复训练。有盲人定向行走训练师253名，对5992名盲人进行定向行走训练。

认真做好听力语言、肢体和智力残疾康复工作。推进听力语言康复机构规范化管理，完善基层服务网络。已建成省级听力语言康复机构1个，基层听力语言康复机构95个。年度新收训聋儿2063名，在训聋儿2704名；规范聋儿家长学校，开展家庭训练，共培训聋儿家长2925名；开展各级各类听力语言康复专业技术人员培训，共培训专业人员134人。

开展肢体残疾康复训练服务机构达126个，其中，省级康复机构1个，地市级、县级康复机构125个；培训各级各类肢体残疾康复人员450人次；全省共对10683名肢体残疾者实施康复训练；实施救助项目资助727名脑瘫儿童进行机构康复训练，资助523名贫困肢体残疾儿童实施矫治手术。

开展智力残疾康复训练服务的机构61个，其中，省级康复机构1个，地市级、县级康复机构60个；培训各级各类智力残疾康复人员380人次；共对5474名智力残疾人进行康复训练；实施救助项目资助584名智力残疾儿童进行机构康复训练，同时培训儿童家长。

大力推广“社会化、综合性、开放式”精神病防治康复工作。在169个县（市、区）开展精神病防治康复工作，对248500名精神病患者进行综合防治康复，监护率达到86.92%，显好率达到66.00%，社会参与率达到52.32%，肇事率0.04%；解除关锁86人；对9246名贫困精神病患者进行医疗救助。

建成省级孤独症儿童康复训练机构1个；495名孤独症儿童在各级机构进行了康复训练。197名贫困孤独症儿童得到康复救助。

加强残疾人辅助器具服务体系建设，深入开展辅助器具供应服务，为残疾人减免费用供应辅助器具38115件，其中装配假肢1106例、矫形器917例，验配助视器11906件。

积极做好残疾预防工作。在石家庄市开展了残疾儿童随报及早期康复工作试点，探索建立早预防、早筛查、早转介、早治疗、早康复的工作机制。全省2个市级、37个县级医疗卫生机构陆续开展残疾儿童筛查工作，年度新诊断0-6岁残疾儿童858人。举办儿童残疾预防宣传活动155次，发放儿童残疾预防宣传材料11.8万份。有残疾儿童家长学校53个，本年度开展家长学校活动153次，本年度参与的残疾儿童家长人数达4273人次。

二、教育工作

积极发展残疾人教育。实施残疾人事业专项彩票公益金助学项目，为613人次家庭经济困难的残疾儿童享受普惠性学前教育提供资助；专项彩票公益金助学项目资助新入园学前残疾儿童265名。

共有特殊教育普通高中班（部）13个，在校生434人；其中聋生334人；盲生100人。残疾人中等职业学校（班）4个，在校生118人，毕业生73人，其中12人获得职业资格证书。有406名残疾人被普通高等院校录取。

三、就业工作

残疾人就业状况稳定。2014年，残疾人就业规模总体保持稳定。城镇新就业残疾人11380人，其中，集中就业残疾人4816人，按比例安排残疾人就业3222人，公益性岗位就业269人，个体就业及其它形式灵活就业2872人，辅助性就业201人。城镇就业人数195754人；879761名农村残疾人在业，其中694549名残疾人从事农业生产劳动。

残疾人职业培训基地达到203个，其中残联兴办46个，依托社会机构兴办157个，其中24912人次城镇残疾人接受了职业培训。

盲人按摩事业稳定发展，按摩机构迅速增长。2014年度培训盲人保健按摩人员711名、盲人医疗按摩人员804名；保健按摩机构达到441个，医疗按摩机构达到57个；在专业技术职务资格评审中，分别有16人和89人通过盲人医疗按摩人员中级和初级职称评审。扶持265名特困盲人按摩师实现就业，1065名盲人按摩人员就业。

四、社会保障工作

2014年新型农村和城镇居民社会养老保险统一合并实施，已有1220090名城乡残疾居民参保，参保率83.65%，在60岁以下的参保残疾人中有168349名重度残疾人，其中160707人得到了政府的参保扶助，代缴补贴比例达到95.46%。有163112名非重度残疾人也享受了全额或部分代缴的优惠政策。领取养老金待遇的人数达到372390人。

城镇残疾职工参加养老保险158616人，参加医疗保险165806人，城镇67743人和农村344355人残疾人纳入最低生活保障范围；城镇集中供养残疾人和农村五保供养残疾人分别达到3216名和23844名；142070名和9040名符合条件的城乡残疾人分别享受了稳定的生活补贴和护理补贴。46679名城乡残疾人得到了其他救助救济。

残疾人托养服务工作规范推进，残疾人托养服务机构达到192个，共为7172名残疾人提供了托养服务。其中寄宿制托养服务机构70个；日间照料机构34个；综合性托养服务机构88个。在以上机构中，共有145名残疾人实现辅助性就业，35名残疾人实现了支持性就业。机构之外接受居家托养服务的残疾人达到15845人。全年共有1735名托养服务管理和服务人员接受了各级各类专业培训，其中接受国家级培训41人。

五、残疾人扶贫工作

2014年，残疾人扶贫开发成效显著，贫困残疾人生产生活状况得到进一步改善。215930名贫困残疾人得到扶持，其中138440人通过扶贫开发实现脱贫；接受实用技术培训的残疾人达到49718人次。

康复扶贫贴息贷款扶持2619名农村残疾人，残疾人扶贫基地达到216个，安置4897名残疾人就业，扶持带动11543名残疾人。

全省共对6343户农村贫困残疾人进行了危房改造。

基层党组织助残扶贫项目帮扶1099名农村贫困残疾人，其中首次接受帮扶598人。“万村千乡市场工程”助残扶贫项目安置193名贫困残疾人就业，帮扶贫困残疾人创办98个村级农村店。

六、残疾人宣传文体工作

截至2014年底，共有省级残疾人专题广播节目1个，播出公益广告2个；地市级残疾人专题广播节目10个，电视手语新闻栏目10个，播出公益广告26个。

截至2014年底，省地县三级公共图书馆共设立盲文及盲人有声读物阅览室64个，共开展残疾人文化周活动225场次，共举办残疾人文化艺术类比赛及展览94次，共有各类残疾人艺术团体14个。

各地深入开展残疾人体育工作。组织省级残疾人群众体育健身活动20次，1556人次参加；建设省级残疾人群众体育活动示范点达到58个；培训省级残疾人体育健身指导员达到210人；组织省级残疾人体育比赛25次，参赛运动员达1000人次；省级残疾人体育训练基地已达16个，组织地市级残疾人体育健身活动126次，10662人次参加；设立地市级残疾人群众体育活动示范点165个；培训地市级残疾人体育健身指导员1826人。

七、残疾人维权工作

继续完善残疾人法规和规章。2014年，制定或修改保障残疾人权益的规范性文件省级1件、地市级6件、县级25件。县级以上人大进行《残疾人保障法》执法检查和专题调研51次；政协进行视察和专题调研51次。开展普法宣传教育活动243次，33065人参加；举办法律培训班66个，2703人参加。

积极开展法律服务和法律援助工作，维护残疾人合法权益。截至2014年底，成立残疾人法律救助工作协调机构145个，建立残疾人法律救助工作站144个，办理案件245件，建立残疾人法律援助中心（工作站）184个，办理案件829件，有力地推动了法律救助和法律援助工作。

残疾人参政议政工作得到加强。各级残联协助人大代表、政协委员提出议案、建议、提案71件，办理议案、建议、提案37件。

无障碍建设法规、标准进一步完善。共出台了45个省、地市、县级无障碍建设与管理法规、规章和规范性文件；182个市、县、区系统开展无障碍建设；开展无障碍建设检查105次，无障碍培训585人次；为1932个贫困残疾人家庭实施了无障碍改造；为17534名残疾人发放了残疾人机动轮椅车燃油补贴。

各级残联共处理残疾人群众来信984件，接待残疾人群众来访6135人次，其中集体访23批次、209人次。

八、残疾人组织更加健全

2014年，11个地市级残联在领导班子中配备了残疾人理事长或副理事长；172个县级残联机关配备了残疾人干部；已建乡镇（街道）残联2281个，已建率达到100%，选聘残疾人专职委员2283名；已建社区（村）残协51474个，已建率达到100%，选聘残疾人专职委员51474名。

省市县乡残联实有人员已达5575人。各级残联共举办培训班1487期，培训机关干部、协会干部及残疾人专职委员23899人次。

共建立省级以下各类残疾人专门协会916个，市级专门协会已建比例为100%；县级专门协会已建比例为99.53%。全省共建立助残社会组织16个，其中在民政部门注册的为13个，以残联为业务主管单位的6个。

九、综合服务设施建设

截至2014年底，全省已竣工并投入使用的各级残疾人综合服务设施145个，总建设规模144125平方米，总投资27198元；已竣工并投入使用的各级残疾人康复设施7个，总建设规模33979平方米，总投资8178元；已竣工并投入使用的各级残疾人托养服务设施9个，总建设规模50619平方米，总投资11410元。

十、信息化建设

残疾人信息化建设队伍不断壮大。全系统共有专、兼职统计人员241名，其中137人有统计从业资格证书，占统计人员总数的56.8%；统计人员业务素质培养普遍得到重视，举办省级培训班1期，52名统计人员接受了培训；举办市级统计培训班13期，526名统计人员接受了培训。

全面推进信息化建设。全省各级残联共有283名专业技术人员从事信息化工作，举办信息化工作培训班18期，552人次参加了培训；全省残联系统共建成门户网站35个，其中省级1个、市级10个、县级24个；省级网站当年发稿4369篇。各级残联本年度信息化建设投入各种经费343万元。

2014 年山西省残疾人事业发展统计公报

2014 年，全省残疾人工作按照省委、省政府的部署和中国残联的要求，科学谋划，突出重点，着眼于促进残疾人服务托住底、补短板，加快推进残疾人社会保障体系和服务体系建设，扎实开展“基础管理年活动”，各项任务圆满完成。

一、康复工作

（一）社区康复。在 23 个市辖区和 90 个县（市）开展了社区康复工作，累计已建社区康复站的社区总数 5080 个，配备 18742 名社区康复协调员。88 个县的 107 个医疗卫生机构陆续开展残疾儿童筛查工作，年度新诊断 0-6 岁残疾儿童 935 人。

（二）视力残疾康复。开展视力残疾康复机构总数达到 40 个，完成白内障复明手术 20017 例；为 4960 名贫困白内障患者免费施行复明手术；为 3669 名低视力患者配用助视器，培训低视力儿童家长 1414 名，有效开展家庭康复训练。对 5851 名盲人进行定向行走训练。

（三）听力语言残疾康复。推进听力语言康复机构规范化管理，完善基层服务网络。已建设省级听力语言康复机构 1 个、基层听力语言康复机构 43 个。年度新收训聋儿 404 名，在训聋儿 659 名；规范聋儿家长学校，开展家庭训练，共培训聋儿家长 1714 名；开展各级各类听力语言康复专业技术人员培训，共培训专业人员 339 人。

（四）肢体残疾康复。开展肢体残疾康复训练服务机构达 39 个，其中：省级康复机构 2 个、地市级 11 个、县级康复机构 26 个；培训各级各类肢体残疾康复人员 351 人次；全省共对 5259 名肢体残疾者实施康复训练；实施救助项目资助 380 名脑瘫儿童进行机构康复训练，资助 245 名贫困肢体残疾儿童实施矫治手术。积极开展宣传普及教育，为麻风患者回归社会营造良好社会氛围。

（五）智力残疾康复。开展智力残疾康复训练服务的机构 38 个，其中，省级康复机构 2 个，地市级 10 个、县级康复机构 26 个；培训各级各类智力残疾康复人员 157 人次；全省共对 2033 名智力残疾人进行康复训练。

（六）精神病防治康复和孤独症儿童康复。大力推广“社会化、综合性、开放式”精神病防治康复工作。在 65 个市县开展精神病防治康复工作，27053 名精神病患者接受了治疗，13137 名精神病患者进行了康复训练，监护率达到 90%，显好率达到 60%，社会参与率达到 50%；解除关锁 206 人；对 17733 名贫困精神病患者进行医疗救助。

建立了 2 个省级孤独症儿童康复训练机构；311 名孤独症儿童在各级机构进行了康复训练。

（七）辅助器具服务。加强残疾人辅助器具服务体系建设，深入开展辅助器具供应服务，为残疾人减免费用供应辅助器具 22875 件，其中：装配假肢 436 例、矫形器 280 例，验配助视器 4881 件。

二、教育工作

2014 年，实施残疾人事业专项彩票公益金助学项目，为 260 人次家庭经济困难的残疾儿童享受普惠性学前教育提供资助。

全省共有特殊教育普通高中班（部）5 个，在校生 975 人；其中聋生 816 人；盲生 159 人。残疾人中等职业学校（班）1 个，在校生 286 人，毕业生 67 人，其中 67 人获得职业资格证书。有 246 名残疾人被普通高等院校录取。

三、就业工作

（一）就业。2014 年，残疾人就业规模总体保持稳定。城镇新就业残疾人 6816 人，其中：集中就业残疾人 1947 人、按比例安排残疾人就业 911 人、公益性岗位就业 290 人、个体就业及其它形式灵活就业 3090 人、辅助性就业 578 人。城镇就业人数 113621 人；372706 名农村残疾人在业，其中 268005 名残疾人从事农业生产劳动。

（二）职业培训。残疾人职业培训基地达到 588

个，其中残联兴办 326 个，依托社会机构兴办 262 个，其中 7497 人次城镇残疾人接受了职业培训。

（三）盲人按摩。盲人按摩事业稳定发展，按摩机构迅速增长。全省保健按摩机构达到 442 个，医疗按摩机构达到 53 个；2014 年度共培训盲人保健按摩人员 729 名、盲人医疗按摩人员 326 名；在专业技术职务资格评审中，分别有 17 人和 72 人通过盲人医疗按摩人员中级和初级职称评审。

四、扶贫工作

2014 年，残疾人扶贫开发成效显著，贫困残疾人生产生活状况得到进一步改善。81000 名贫困残疾人得到扶持，其中 38533 人通过扶贫开发实现脱贫；接受实用技术培训的残疾人达到 13625 人次。

康复扶贫贴息贷款扶持 2461 名农村残疾人，残疾人扶贫基地达到 216 个，安置 3640 名残疾人就业，扶持带动残疾人户 5092 户。

完成 9 户农村贫困残疾人危房改造，各地投入危房资金 99950 元，13 名残疾人受益。

基层党组织助残扶贫项目帮扶 2017 名农村贫困残疾人，其中首次接受帮扶 1806 人。“万村千乡市场工程”助残扶贫项目安置 140 名贫困残疾人就业，帮扶贫困残疾人创办 37 个村级农村店。

五、社会保障工作

（一）社会保险。2014 年新型农村和城镇居民社会养老保险统一合并实施，已有 956378 名城乡残疾居民参保，参保率 90%，在 60 岁以下的参保残疾人中有 136826 名重度残疾人，其中 132243 人得到了政府的参保扶助，代缴补贴比例达到 97%。有 63389 名非重度残疾人也享受了全额或部分代缴的优惠政策。领取养老金待遇的人数达到 485110 人。

城镇残疾职工参加养老保险 82061 人，参加医疗保险 82209 人，城镇 67815 名和农村 243463 名残疾人纳入最低生活保障范围；城镇集中供养残疾人和农村五保供养残疾人分别达到 1316 名和 25418 名；46414 名和 52911 名符合条件的城乡残疾人分别享受了稳定的生活补贴和护理补贴。66271 名城乡残疾人得到了其他救助救济。

（二）托养服务。残疾人托养服务工作规范推进，残疾人托养服务机构达到 64 个，共为 14801 名残疾人提供了托养服务。其中：寄宿制托养服务机构 22 个、日间照料机构 9 个、综合性托养服务机构 33 个。

在以上机构中，共有 25 名残疾人实现辅助性就业，23 名残疾人实现了支持性就业。机构之外接受居家托养服务的残疾人达到 13801 人。全年共有 622 名托养服务管理和服务人员接受了各级各类专业培训，其中接受国家级培训 29 人。

六、宣传文化工作

截至 2014 年底，共有省级残疾人专题广播节目 1 个，电视手语新闻栏目 1 个；地市级残疾人专题广播节目 3 个，电视手语新闻栏目 1 个。

截至 2014 年底，省、市、县三级公共图书馆共设立盲文及盲人有声读物阅览室 8 个，共开展残疾人文化周活动 15 场次，共举办残疾人文化艺术类比赛及展览 2036 次，共有各类残疾人艺术团体 575 个。

七、体育工作

各地深入开展残疾人体育工作。组织省级残疾人群众体育健身活动 2 次，360 人次参加；省级残疾人群众体育活动示范点达到 30 个；培训省级残疾人体育健身指导员 549 人；组织省级残疾人体育比赛 1 次，参赛运动员达 405 人次；组织地市级残疾人体育健身活动 54 次，1982 人次参加；设立地市级残疾人群众体育活动示范点 40 个；培训地市级残疾人体育健身指导员 282 人。

八、维权工作

2014 年，制定或修改保障残疾人权益的规范性文件地市级 1 件、县级 8 件。县级以上人大进行《残疾人保障法》执法检查和专题调研 29 次；政协进行视察和专题调研 22 次。开展普法宣传教育活动 173 次，36203 人参加；举办法律培训班 51 期，3224 人参加。

截至 2014 年底，全省各级成立残疾人法律救助工作协调机构 17 个，建立残疾人法律救助工作站 8 个，办理案件 96 件；建立残疾人法律援助中心（工作站）83 个，办理案件 255 件，有力地推动了法律救助和法律援助工作。

残疾人参政议政工作得到加强，各级残联协助人大代表、政协委员提出议案、建议、提案80件，办理议案、建议、提案51件。

无障碍建设法规、标准进一步完善。省、市、县级共出台了9个无障碍建设与管理法规、规章和规范性文件；68个市、县、区系统开展了无障碍建设；全省各级开展无障碍建设检查46次，无障碍培训606人次。

全省共为1719个贫困残疾人家庭实施了无障碍改造；为7253名残疾人发放了残疾人机动轮椅车燃油补贴。

各级残联共处理残疾人群众来信977件，接待残疾人群众来访13343人次，其中集体访68批次、1221人次。

九、组织联络工作

2014年，8个市级残联在领导班子中配备了残疾人理事长或副理事长；90个县级残联机关配备了残疾人干部；已建乡镇（街道）残联1476个，已建率达到99%，选聘残疾人专职委员1393名；已建社区（村）残协22799个，已建率达到84%，选聘残疾人专职委员23812名。

省、市、县、乡残联实有人员已达4686人。各级残联共举办培训班265期，培训机关干部、协会干部及残疾人专职委员9140人次。

全省共建立省级以下各类残疾人专门协会629个，市级专门协会已建比例为100%；县级专门协会已建比例为97%。全省共建立助残社会组织9个，其中在民政部门注册的为8个，以残联为业务主管单位的5个。

十、基础设施建设工作

截至2014年底，全省已竣工并投入使用的各级残疾人综合服务设施51个，总建设规模107118.71平方米，总投资28589.83万元；已竣工并投入使用的各级残疾人康复设施32个，总建设规模74856.07平方米，总投资18438.35万元；已竣工并投入使用的各级残疾人托养服务设施1个，总建设规模2000平方米，总投资400万元。

十一、信息化建设工作

各级残联对网上政务公开、网上服务，无障碍等方面更加重视，总体建设水平有了明显提升，省残联网站完成了信息无障碍改造。截至2014年底，省级、11个市级、74个县级残联已开通网站。

2014 年内蒙古自治区残疾人事业发展统计公报

2014 年，自治区残联按照自治区党委、政府和中国残联的总体部署，积极落实党的十八大关于“健全残疾人社会保障和服务体系，切实保障残疾人权益”的要求，认真贯彻自治区“8337”发展思路和中国残联及自治区残联第六次代表大会精神，全面实施残疾人事业“十二五”发展纲要和残疾人工作专项工程，促进残疾人事业与经济社会协调发展，各项事业取得了重要进展。

一、康复工作

2014 年，我区按照社区康复、视力残疾康复、听力语言康复、智力残疾康复、肢体残疾康复、精神病防治康复、残疾人辅助器具服务、儿童残疾预防、残疾人康复人才建设 9 项实施方案和实施办法积极开展各项康复工作，截至 2014 年底，102 个县的 37 个医疗卫生机构陆续开展残疾儿童筛查工作，新诊断 0-6 岁残疾儿童 760 人。

开展视力残疾康复机构总数达到 21 个，完成白内障复明手术 9825 例；为 6063 名贫困白内障患者免费施行复明手术；为 2669 名低视力患者配用助视器，培训低视力儿童家长 578 名，有效开展家庭康复训练。对 2474 名盲人进行定向行走训练。

推进听力语言康复机构规范化管理，完善基层服务网络。已建设省级听力语言康复机构 1 个，基层听力语言康复机构 23 个。本年度新收训聋儿 369 名，在训聋儿 536 名；规范聋儿家长学校，开展家庭训练，共培训聋儿家长 825 名；开展各级各类听力语言康复专业技术人员培训，共培训专业人员 59 人。

开展肢体残疾康复训练服务机构达 35 个，培训各级各类肢体残疾康复人员 126 人次；实施救助项目资助 444 名脑瘫儿童进行机构康复训练，资助 158 名贫困肢体残疾儿童实施矫治手术。

开展智力残疾康复训练服务的机构 33 个，其中，省级康复机构 1 个，地市级、旗县级康复机构 32 个；培训各级各类智力残疾康复人员 194 人次；实施救助项目资助 487 名智力残疾儿童进行机构康复训练，同时培训儿童家长。

大力推广“社会化、综合性、开放式”精神病防治康复工作。全区 98 个旗县（市区）开展精神病防治康复工作，对 67596 名重性精神病患者进行综合防治康复，监护率达到 80.51%，显好率达到 61.01%，社会参与率达到 51.46%，肇事率 0.19%；解除关锁 54 人；对 3231 名贫困精神病患者进行医疗救助。

建立了 1 个省级孤独症儿童康复训练机构；516 名孤独症儿童在各级机构进行了康复训练。

加强残疾人辅助器具服务体系建设，深入开展辅助器具供应服务，为残疾人减免费用供应辅助器具 18325 件，其中装配假肢 709 例、矫形器 173 例，验配助视器 3086 件。

二、教育工作

2014 年，配合教育厅制定出台了《内蒙古自治区特殊教育提升计划（2014—2016 年）》。实施残疾人事业专项彩票公益金助学项目，为 356 人次家庭经济困难的残疾儿童享受普惠性学前教育提供资助。各地也积极多渠道争取资金支持，对 3 名残疾儿童给予学前教育资助。

全区共有特殊教育普通高中班（部）7 个，在校生 116 人；其中聋生 109 人；盲生 7 人。残疾人中等职业学校（班）8 个，在校生 145 人，毕业生 198 人，其中 143 人获得职业资格证书，239 名残疾人被普通高等院校录取。

三、就业工作

2014 年，我区残疾人就业规模总体保持稳定。城镇新就业残疾人 6295 人，其中，集中就业残疾人 1268 人，按比例安排残疾人就业 1026 人，公益性岗位就业 335 人，个体就业及其它形式灵活就业 3353 人，辅助性就业 313 人。城镇就业人数 112187

人；266200名农村残疾人在业，其中215869名残疾人从事农业生产劳动。

截止2014年底，残疾人职业培训基地达到68个，其中残联兴办21个，依托社会机构兴办47个，其中10881人次城镇残疾人接受了职业培训。

盲人按摩事业稳定发展，按摩机构迅速增长。2014年度培训盲人保健按摩人员237名、盲人医疗按摩人员125名；保健按摩机构达到287个，医疗按摩机构达到51个；在专业技术职务资格评审中，分别有13人和24人通过盲人医疗按摩人员中级和初级职称评审。

四、扶贫工作

2014年，残疾人扶贫开发成效显著，贫困残疾人生产生活状况得到进一步改善。41311名贫困残疾人得到扶持，接受实用技术培训的残疾人达到16891人次。

康复扶贫贴息贷款扶持3549名农村残疾人，残疾人扶贫基地达到108个，安置2101名残疾人就业，扶持带动3286名残疾人。

完成7033户农村贫困残疾人危房改造，各地投入危房资金5455.22万元，8005名残疾人受益。

基层党组织助残扶贫项目帮扶855名农村贫困残疾人，其中首次接受帮扶137人。“万村千乡市场工程”助残扶贫项目安置40名贫困残疾人就业，帮扶贫困残疾人创办8个村级农村店。

五、社会保障工作

2014年新型农村和城镇居民社会养老保险统一合并实施，已有286367名城乡残疾居民参保，参保率66.80%，在60岁以下的参保残疾人中有56301名重度残疾人，其中50798人得到了政府的参保扶助，代缴补贴比例达到90.23%。有33222名非重度残疾人也享受了全额或部分代缴的优惠政策。领取养老金待遇的人数达到123417人。

城镇残疾职工参加养老保险43533人，参加医疗保险51886人，城镇94304人和农村212555人残疾人纳入最低生活保障范围；城镇集中供养残疾人和农村五保供养残疾人分别达到2635名和18055名；212843名和233716名符合条件的城乡残疾人分别享受了稳定的生活补贴和护理补贴。131351名城乡残疾人得到了其他救助救济。

残疾人托养服务工作规范推进，残疾人托养服务机构达到111个，共为2794名残疾人提供了托养服务。其中寄宿制托养服务机构74个；日间照料机构7个；综合性托养服务机构30个。在以上机构中，共有43名残疾人实现辅助性就业，39名残疾人实现了支持性就业。机构之外接受居家托养服务的残疾人达到16305人。全年共有366名托养服务管理和服务人员接受了各级各类专业培训，其中接受国家级培训25人。

六、宣传文化工作

截至2014年底，共有省级电视手语新闻栏目1个，播出公益广告1个；地市级残疾人专题广播节目10个，电视手语新闻栏目7个，播出公益广告4个。

截至2014年底，省地县三级公共图书馆共设立盲文及盲人有声读物阅览室45个，共开展残疾人文化周活动87场次，共举办残疾人文化艺术类比赛及展览29次，共有各类残疾人艺术团体15个。

七、体育工作

2014年，全区各地深入开展残疾人体育工作。组织省级残疾人群众体育健身活动3次，150人次参加；建设省级残疾人群众体育活动示范点达到6个；培训省级残疾人体育健身指导员达到14人；组织省级残疾人体育比赛7次，参赛运动员达25人次；省级残疾人体育训练基地已达2个，组织地市级残疾人体育健身活动19次，1171人次参加；设立地市级残疾人群众体育活动示范点24个；培训地市级残疾人体育健身指导员148人。

八、维权工作

2014年，我区制定或修改保障残疾人权益的规范性文件地市级1件、县级2件。县级以上人大进行《残疾人保障法》执法检查和专题调研16次；政协进行视察和专题调研9次。开展普法宣传教育活动205次，17662人参加；举办法律培训班53个，2313人参加。

截至2014年底，成立残疾人法律救助工作协调机构 54 个，建立残疾人法律救助工作站 38 个，办理案件 79 件，建立残疾人法律援助中心（工作站）100 个，办理案件 348 件，有力地推动了法律救助和法律援助工作。

残疾人参政议政工作得到加强，各级残联协助人大代表、政协委员提出议案、建议、提案 74 件，办理议案、建议、提案 30 件。

无障碍建设法规、标准进一步完善。共出台了 5 个省、地市、县级无障碍建设与管理法规、规章和规范性文件；64 个市、县、区系统开展无障碍建设；开展无障碍建设检查 198 次，无障碍培训 162 人次；为 5739 个贫困残疾人家庭实施了无障碍改造；为 25370 名残疾人发放了残疾人机动轮椅车燃油补贴。

全区各级残联共处理残疾人群众来信 884 件，接待残疾人群众来访 3491 人次，其中集体访 5 批次、44 人次。

九、组织建设

2014 年，全区 11 个盟市残联在领导班子中配备了残疾人理事长或副理事长；57 个旗县（市区）级残联机关配备了残疾人干部；已建乡镇（街道）残联 1145 个，已建率达到 100.00%；全区选聘残疾人专职委员 14676 名。

全区各级残联实有人员已达 3174 人，各级残联共举办培训班 580 期。

共建立省级以下各类残疾人专门协会 561 个，盟市级专门协会已建比例为 100.00%；有国家行政批复的旗县专门协会已建比例为 100.00%。全国共建立助残社会组织 30 个，其中在民政部门注册的为 14 个，以残联为业务主管单位的 15 个。

十、服务设施工作

截至 2014 年底，已竣工并投入使用的各级残疾人综合服务设施 71 个，总建设规模 89139 平方米，总投资 20617 万元；已竣工并投入使用的各级残疾人康复设施 4 个，总建设规模 4194 平方米，总投资 510 万元；已竣工并投入使用的各级残疾人托养服务设施 8 个，总建设规模 11234 平方米，总投资 1659 万元。

十一、信息化工作

截至 2014 年底，各级残联全面推进网站建设，除自治区级残联开通了门户网站外，有 7 个盟市残联网站和 38 个县级残联开通门户网站。2014 年各级残联开设网站技术培训班 15 期，培训各级残联信息员达 330 人次。各级残联共有 151 名专业技术人员从事信息化工作。

2014 年辽宁省残疾人事业发展统计公报

2014 年，在省委、省政府重视关怀和中国残联悉心指导下，辽宁省残联坚持以科学发展观统领全局，紧紧围绕保障和改善残疾人民生，促进残疾人平等参与与全面发展这条主线，以提高残疾人满意度和幸福指数为出发点和落脚点，积极进取，务实创新，全面推进残疾人各项业务工作的深入开展。

一、康复

2014 年，全省有 62 个市辖区、44 个县（市）开展了社区康复服务。社区康复协调员 13345 名，本年新增 1417 名。已建社区康复站的社区 10382 个，本年新增 102 个。全省共 1182353 人建立了社区康复服务档案，占全省残疾人总数的 57.4%。433764 名残疾人接受了社区康复服务，本年度新增接受社区康复服务 29664 人。

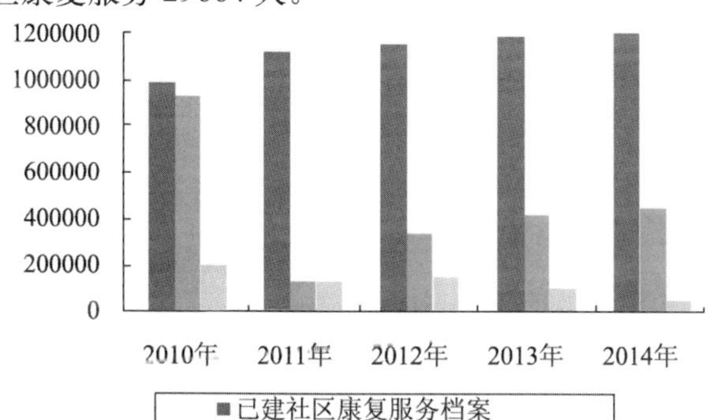

图 1 2014 年度与 2010-2013 年度社区康复情况（单位：人）

全省实施白内障复明手术 17929 例，其中，免费施行白内障复明手术的贫困患者 5287 名，占全年白内障手术总数的 29.5%。低视力患者配用助视器人数为 7136 名，培训低视力儿童家长 1467 名，为 4853 名盲人进行定向行走训练。

全省新收训聋儿 507 名，其中，机构训练 444 名，占新收训聋儿总数的 87.6%，家庭训练 63 名，占新收训聋儿 12.4%。在训聋儿 1000 名，培训聋儿家长 1209 名，比上年度增长 30%，培训专业人员 312 人，比上年度增长 9.9%。接受地方项目救助 39 人，为 702 名成年人提供听力语言康复技术服务。听力语言康复机构 46 个，在岗专业人员共 604 名。

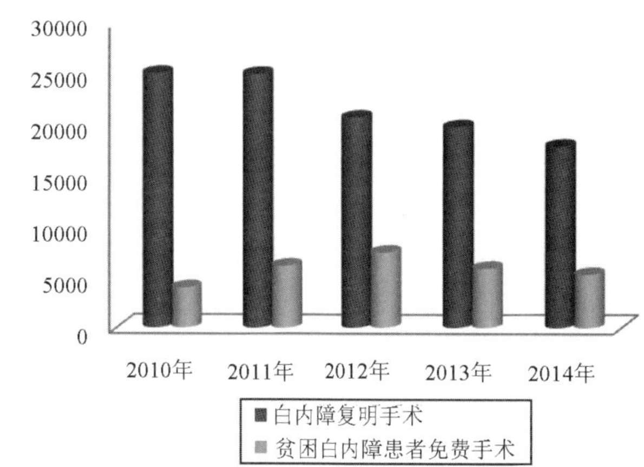

图 2 2014 年度与 2010-2013 年度白内障复明手术情况（单位：例）

肢体残疾康复训练服务机构 71 个，各级残联办机构在岗人员 194 名。肢体残疾康复训练 15778 人，其中，脑瘫儿童系统康复训练 763 人，肢体残疾儿童社区、家庭康复训练 878 人，成年肢体残疾人社区、家庭康复训练 14137 名。贫困肢体残疾儿童矫治手术 371 例，比上年度增长 12.1%。

智力残疾康复 4555 人，其中，智力残疾儿童机构康复训练 640 人，智力残疾儿童社区、家庭康复 2834 人，成年智力残疾人社区、家庭康复 1081 人。培训康复管理、技术人员 1176 人次。智力残疾康复训练服务机构 62 个，残联办机构在岗人员 166 人，比上年度增长 20.3%。

全省 107 个县（市、区）开展精神病防治康复工作，对 270316 名精神病患者进行综合防治康复，监护率 89.2%，显好率 66.1%，社会参与率 51.3%，肇事率 0.01%，接受治疗的精神病患者 58600 人，接受康复训练 35806 人，对 23787 名贫困精神病患者进行医疗救助。全省精神康复机构 151 个，精神病人数为 20367 名。培训精防康复管理、技术人员 1229 名。全省孤独症儿童康复训练机构 49 个，在训儿童 580 名。

深入开展辅助器具供应服务，累计建立辅助器具供应服务机构 108 个，为残疾人免费供应 87128 件各类辅助器具，比上年度增加了 122.1%。其中，装配假肢2514例、矫形器730例、其他83884件。

注重康复人才培养。全省各级康复机构在岗人员12038人，比上年度增长8.5%。举办康复管理人员培训班97期，培训1908人。举办康复业务人员培训班108期，培训2631人。举办社区康复协调员培训班172期，培训8178人。

二、教育

健全残疾人教育服务体系，提高残疾人受教育水平。全省残疾人事业专项彩票公益金助学项目资助960名家庭经济困难的残疾儿童，专项彩票公益金助学项目资助新入园儿童457人。

特殊教育普通高中学校（班）10个，在校生51人。残疾人中等职业学校（班）8个，招生62名，在校生279人，毕业生55人，其中，获得职业资格证书43人。

2014年，经省政府批准，成立辽宁特殊教育师范高等专科学校，是我省高等特殊教育独立院校，其前身为辽宁省残疾人中等职业技术学校。今年共录取专科（高职）生95人，其中，盲人考生41人，聋人考生54人。

全省共有241名残疾考生被普通高等院校录取。录取本科生116人，其中，盲人考生11人，聋人考生19人，肢残考生86人。录取专科（高职）考生125人，其中，盲人考生8人，聋人考生15人，肢残考生100人，其他2人。

三、就业

2014年，就业机制不断创新，与省委组织部等八部门联合下发《辽宁省关于促进残疾人按比例就业的实施意见》，大力推动党政机关、人民团体、事业单位和国有企业按比例安置残疾人就业。本年城镇新增就业8800人，其中，集中就业残疾人2217人，按比例安排残疾人就业2168人，个体及其他形式就业3845人，公益性岗位就业497人，辅助性就业73人。农村残疾人就业人数稳定增长，有399413名残疾人实际就业，其中，从事农业生产劳动290835人，其他形式就业为108578人。

大力开展职业技能培训，提升培训效率，促进就业，并以赛代训，组织残疾人职业技能竞赛。残疾人职业培训基地163个，其中，残联开办62个，依托社会机构开办101个，培训城镇残疾人16217人次。本年度培训保健按摩人员550名，培训医疗按摩人员168名，盲人保健按摩人员和医疗按摩人员就业人数分别为418人和60人，扶持82名特困盲人按摩师就业。

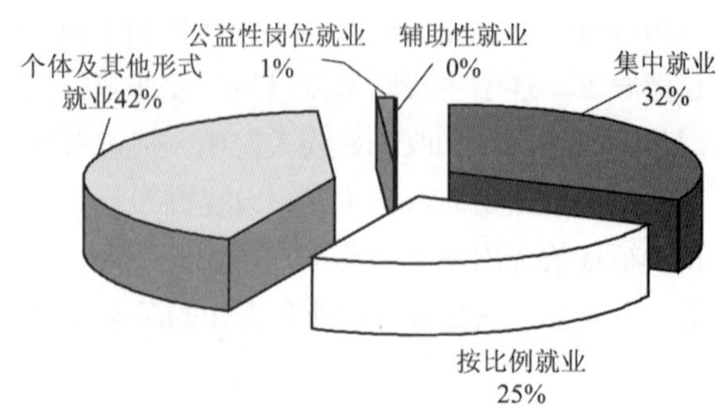

图3　2014年度全省城镇残疾人就业情况

四、 社会保障

2014年，新型农村和城镇居民社会养老保险统一合并实施，已有519595名城乡残疾居民参保，参保率82.7%，在60岁以下的参保残疾人中有96434名重度残疾人，其中，89767人得到了政府的参保扶助，代缴补贴比例达到93.1%。有190869名非重度残疾人也享受了全额或部分代缴的优惠政策。领取养老金待遇的人数达到147611人。城镇残疾职工参加养老保险236637人，参加医疗保险229017人。

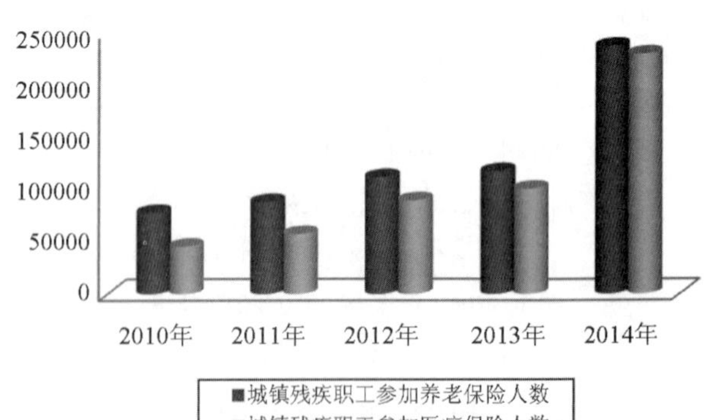

图4　2014年度与2010-2013年度全省城镇残疾职工参加社会保险情况（单位：人）

城镇纳入最低生活保障残疾人161338名，集中供养人数为5235名，其他救助救济人数为20522名。农村纳入最低生活保障残疾人183548名，五保供养24487人，其他救助救济31499人。全省享受生活补贴的人数为1446名，享受护理补贴的人数为1679名。

残疾人托养服务机构日趋完善。全省共有托养机构203个，为7107名残疾人提供托养服务。其中，寄宿制托养服务机构72个，日间照料机构101个，综合托养服务机构 30 个。共有 28733 名残疾人享受居家托养服务。

五、扶贫

2014 年，全省共有 63608 名贫困残疾人得到扶持，其中，33693 人通过扶贫开发实际脱贫，接受实用技术培训的残疾人 15679 名，地方投入培训经费 382.8 万元。

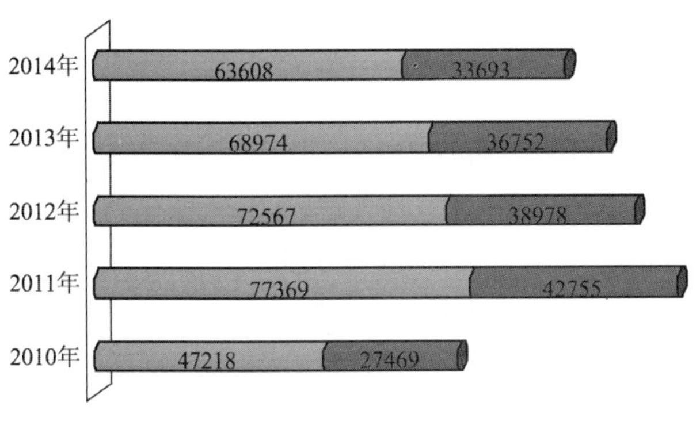

图 5　2014 年度与 2010-2013 年度全省贫困残疾人扶持情况（单位：人次）

省级财政投入扶贫资金 560 万元。康复扶贫贴息贷款实际落实 4640 万元，项目贷款扶持 1349 人，到户贷款扶持 599 人。结对帮扶贫困残疾人的单位和个人分别达到 3476 个和 20152 人。本年度危房改造实际完成 3074 户,危房改造项目受益残疾人 3341 名，投入资金 3810.9 万元。建立残疾人扶持基地 42 个，安排残疾人就业 1400 名,扶持带动 1878 户贫困残疾人就业。

六、宣传文化

打造立体化宣传文化格局，残疾人事业发展环境不断优化。中央级媒体采用稿件 28 件，省级主要新闻媒体刊播稿件 420 件,报纸专版有 18 个，广播电台残疾人专题节目 1 个，电视手语栏目 1 个。

市级主要新闻媒体刊播稿 6316 件,报纸专版 44 个，广播电台残疾人专题节目 6 个，电视手语栏目 10 个，电视公益广告片 1 个，报纸公益广告 3 个。

截至 2014 年底，省地县三级公共图书馆共设立盲文及盲人有声读物阅览室 64 个，共开展残疾人文化周活动 493 场次，共举办残疾人文化艺术类比赛及展览 168 次，共有各类残疾人艺术团体 26 个。

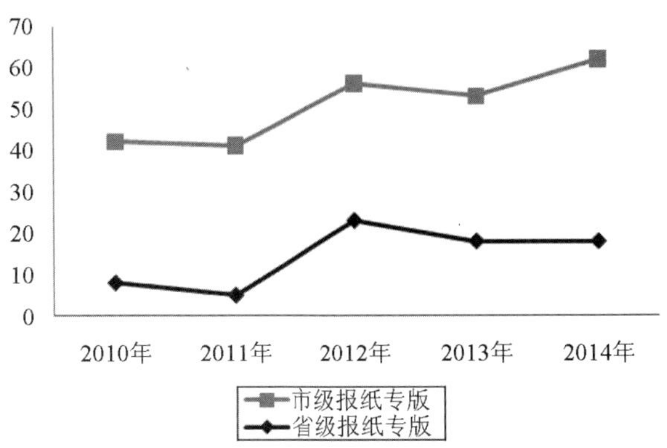

图 6　2014 年度与 2010-2013 年度全省报纸专版情况（单位：个）

七、体育

2014 年，全省建立省级残疾人体育训练基地 28 个，在编工作人员 50 人，聘任教练员 25 人，残疾人体育比赛 1 次，参赛运动员 556 人次。市级组织残疾人体育活动 98 次，53570 人次参加，残疾人群众体育活动示范点 57 个，体育健身指导员 629 人。

八、维权

我省残疾人法规体系建设逐步完善。全省开展普法宣传教育活动 194 次，21035 人参加；举办法律培训班 53 个，5768 人参加。

截至 2014 年底，成立残疾人法律救助工作协调机构 66 个，建立残疾人法律救助工作站 68 个，办理案件 375 件，建立残疾人法律援助中心（工作站）115 个，办理案件 787 件，有力地推动了法律救助和法律援助工作。

残疾人参政议政工作得到加强，各级残联协助人大代表、政协委员提出议案、建议、提案 46 件，办理议案、建议、提案 47 件。

表 1　2014 年度全省残疾人法律救助情况

级别	法律救助协调机构（个）	法律救助		法律援助	
		工作站（个）	办理案件(件)	工作站（个）	办理案件（件）
省级	1	1	8	1	1
地市级	13	13	102	14	149
县级	52	54	265	100	637
总计	66	68	375	115	787

表 2 2014 年度全省残疾人参政议政情况

级别	人大		
	人大代表（人）	协助人大代表提出议案、建议（件）	办理人大建议（件）
省级	2	1	3
地市级	11	8	12
县级	70	6	3
总计	83	15	18
级别	政协		
	政协委员（人）	协助政协委员提出议案、建议（件）	办理政协提案（件）
省级	2	2	11
地市级	33	12	12
县级	151	17	6
总计	186	31	29

无障碍建设法规、标准进一步完善。共出台了6个省、地市、县级无障碍建设与管理法规、规章和规范性文件；5个市、县、区系统开展无障碍建设；开展无障碍建设检查579次，无障碍培训5290人次；为13767个贫困残疾人家庭实施了无障碍改造，比上年度增长61.3%；为15515名残疾人发放了残疾人机动轮椅车燃油补贴。

各级残联共处理残疾人群众来信715件，接待残疾人群众来访14309人次，其中集体访161批次、3127人次。

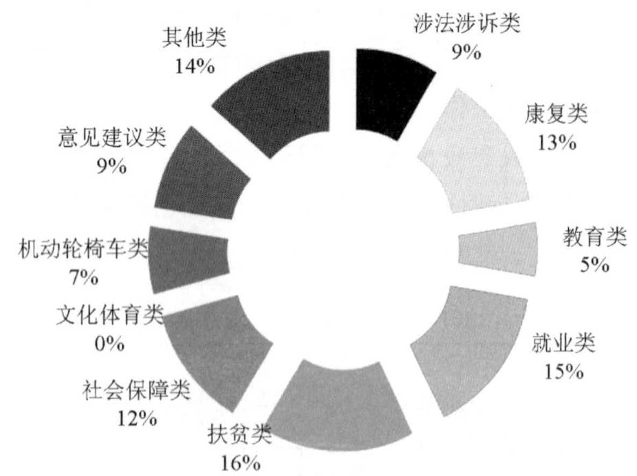

图 7 2014 年度全省残疾人维权（来信）情况

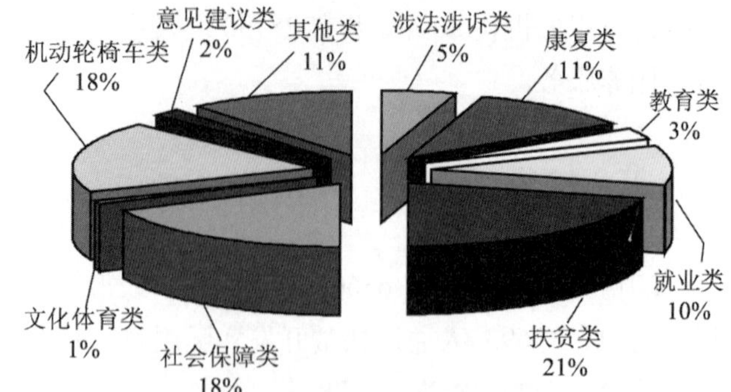

图 8 2014 年度全省残疾人维权（来访）情况

九、组织建设

2014年，省及14个市残联理事会已配备残疾人领导干部21人，县（市、区）配备残疾人干部113人。已建乡镇（街道）残联1516个，已建率达到100.00%，选聘残疾人专职委员1612名；已建社区（村）残协15445个，已建率达到100.00%，选聘残疾人专职委员15425名。

省市县乡残联实有人员已达4232人。各级残联共举办培训班1376期，培训机关干部、协会干部及残疾人专职委员37038人次。

共建立省级以下各类残疾人专门协会590个，市级专门协会已建比例为100%；县级专门协会已建比例为102%。全国共建立助残社会组织18个，其中在民政部门注册的为17个。

十、服务设施

截至2014年底，全省已竣工并投入使用的各级残疾人综合服务设施126个，总建设规模264831.6平方米，总投资91995.2万元；已竣工并投入使用的各级残疾人托养服务设施20个，总建设规模35773.5平方米，总投资12632.8万元；已竣工并投入使用的各级残疾人康复设施14个，总建设规模62927平方米，总投资13507.4万元。

十一、信息化建设

2014年，全省有129名专、兼职统计人员从事残疾人事业统计工作。各级残联非常重视统计人员业务培养工作，省级举办1期培训班，20人参训，市级举办16期培训班，309人参训。

我省加大残联网站的建设力度，已建立省级门户网站 1 个，市级 14 个，县级 53 个。省及各市举办信息工作培训班 21 期，645 人参训。省级网站全年发稿量 4796 篇。

图 9 2014 年度与 2010-2013 年度省级网站发稿量(单位：篇)

着力推进残联信息化平台建设，提升管理能力和水平。省本级 积极争取资金 500 余万元，进一步推进和完善省残疾人服务管理平台建设。

2015 年是“十二五”残疾人事业发展规划的收官之年，也是科学谋划“十三五”发展规划，稳步推进残疾人同步小康进程的关键之年。全省残疾人工作将认真贯彻落实党的十八届四中全会精神，认真按照中国残联及省委省政府的工作部署和要求，紧紧瞄准残疾人同步小康目标，扎实推进各项业务工作的深入开展，不断提升残疾人幸福指数，努力开创全省残疾人事业发展新局面。

2014 年吉林省残疾人事业发展统计公报

2014 年，吉林省各级残联积极抢抓残疾人事业发展机遇，注重完善残疾人保障制度，强化残疾人帮扶措施，认真落实省政府确定的民生实事任务，深入实施各类助残工程（项目），不断加强残疾人基本公共服务，着力改善残疾人的生产生活状况，全省残疾人工作取得了新的进展。

一、康复工作

2014 年，通过继续推进康复服务体系建设，组织实施国家残疾人事业专项彩票公益金康复项目和各类康复救助工程（项目），全省残疾人康复工作全面开展。

（一）视力残疾康复。全年完成白内障复明手术 1.5 万例；为 3,326 名贫困白内障患者免费施行复明手术，全年为 3,038 名低视力患者配用助视器，培训低视力儿童家长 1,400 名，有效开展家庭康复训练。对 4,254 名盲人进行定向行走训练。

（二）听力语言康复。推进听力语言康复机构规范化管理，完善基层服务网络。现有省级听力语言康复机构 1 个，基层听力语言康复机构 19 个。年度新收训聋儿 362 名，在训聋儿 457 名；规范聋儿家长学校，开展家庭训练，共培训聋儿家长 1100 名；开展各级各类听力语言康复专业技术人员培训，共培训专业人员 271 人。

听力语言残疾儿童训练后走向所占比例为普小 3.6 %，普幼 60.0 %，特教学校（聋校）14.5 %，其他 21.8 %。

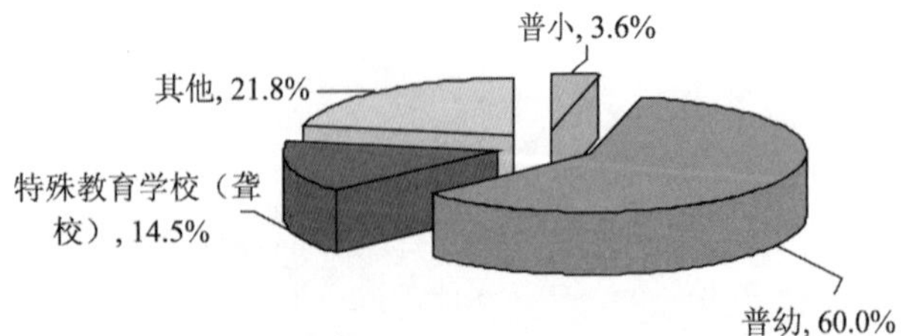

图 1　2014 年吉林省听力语言残疾儿童训练后走向

（三）精防康复和孤独症儿童康复。大力推广“社会化、综合性、开放式”精神病防治康复工作。2014 年，在 69 个市县开展精神病防治康复工作，对 16.2 万名精神病患者进行综合防治康复，监护率达到 96.84%，显好率达到 69.69%，社会参与率达到 57.63%；解除关锁 4 人；对 17,812 名贫困精神病患者进行医疗救助。

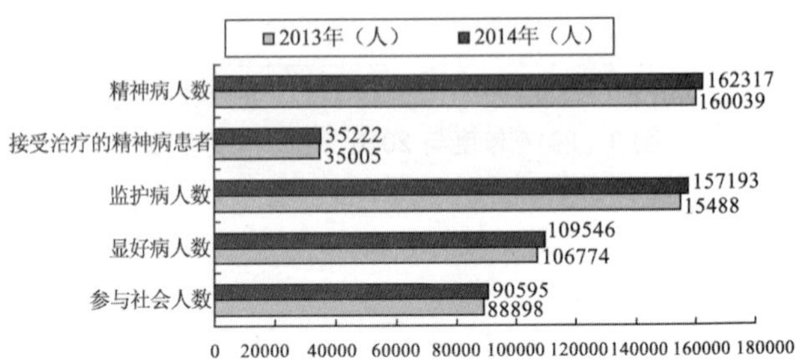

图 2　2013 年与 2014 年吉林省精防康复情况对比

全省共有孤独症儿童康复训练机构 45 个，其中省级 1 个，地市级及以下 44 个，机构内在训儿童 567 名。有 537 名贫困孤独症儿童得到了康复救助。据测算，还有大量贫困家庭孤独症儿童没有条件接受正规机构训练。

（四）肢体与智力残疾康复。全年开展肢体残疾康复训练服务的机构达到 119 个，其中，省级康复机构 1 个，地市级、县级康复机构 118 个；培训各级各类肢体残疾康复人员 825 人次；全省共对 5,320 名肢体残疾者实施康复训练，其中：脑瘫儿童系统康复训练 489 人，肢体残疾儿童社区、家庭康复 80 人，成年肢体残疾人社区、家庭康复 4751 人；资助 150 名贫困肢体残疾儿童实施矫治手术。

（五）全年开展智力残疾康复训练服务的机构达到 36 个，其中省级 1 个，地市级及以下 35 个，培训各类康复管理、技术人员 196 人次；对 1,977 名智力残疾人进行了康复训练，不同程度地开展了智力残疾儿童早期康复训练与服务。

（六）辅助器具供应服务。强化残疾人辅助器具服务体系建设，加大开展辅助器具供应服务力度，全年减免费用提供各类辅助器具 102,749 件，其中装配假肢 397 例、矫形器 223 例，发放其他辅助器具 10,1895 件，适配贫困残疾儿童辅助器具 707 件。

（七）社区康复服务。在 30 个市辖区（含开发区）和 41 个县（市）开展了社区康复工作，累计建立社区康复站 2,875 个，配备 9,122 名社区康复协调员。开展家长学校工作的残疾人康复机构达到 61 家，比上年新增 22 家，培训家长 5,761 人次，比上年增加 2,012 人次。

（八）康复人才。截止 2014 年底，全省康复机构在岗人数为 8,304 人，全年由各地残联主办的各类培训班 238 期，培训 7,810 名各类康复人才。

二、教育情况

2014 年，实施残疾人事业专项彩票公益金助学项目，260 名残疾儿童接受助学项目资助。

共有特殊教育普通高中班（部）4 个，在校生 34 人，均为聋生。残疾人中等职业学校（班）6 个，在校生 662 人，毕业生 153 人，其中 119 人获得职业资格证书。有 162 名残疾人被普通高等院校录取。

未入学适龄残疾儿童少年总数 2,498 人，其中视力残疾 64 人，听力残疾 110 人，言语残疾 124 人，肢体残疾 785 人，智力残疾 917 人，精神残疾 236 人，多重残疾 262 人。未入学儿童总人数比照上年减少 398 人。

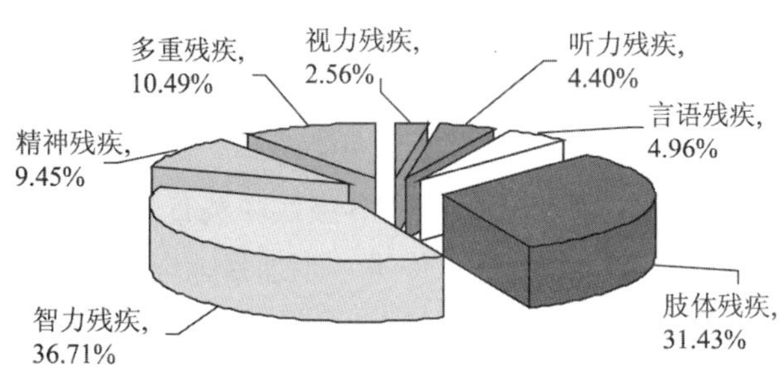

图 3　2014 年吉林省残疾未入学儿童少年情况

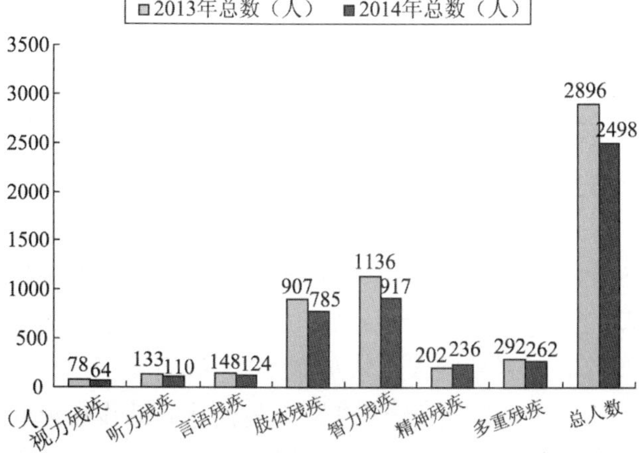

图 4　2013 年与 2014 年残疾儿童少年未入学情况对比

三、就业培训

（一）城乡残疾人就业情况。2014 年，残疾人就业规模总体保持稳定。城镇新就业残疾人 8,670 人。其中，集中就业残疾人 1,583 人，按比例安排残疾人就业 779 人，公益性岗位就业 635 人，个体及其它形式就业 5,178 人，辅助性就业 651 人，全省城镇实际在业残疾人 15.8 万人。30.6 万农村残疾人实现稳定就业，其中从事农业生产劳动 25.4 万人。全省共建立残疾人职业培训基地 199 个，其中残联兴办 54 个，依托社会机构兴办 145 个，本年度城镇职业培训人数 1.2 万人次。

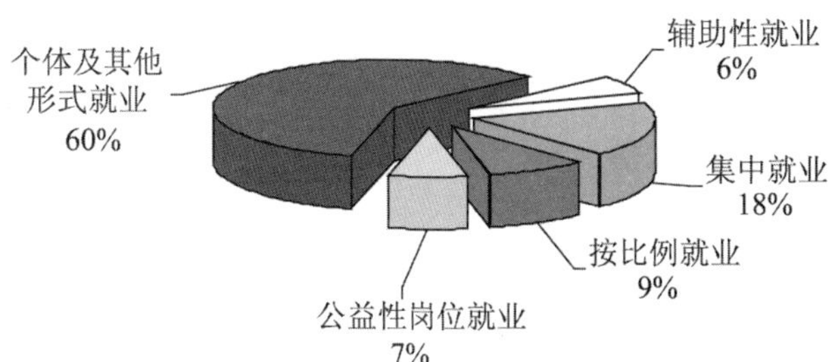

图 5　2014 年城镇残疾人新增就业情况

（二）盲人按摩。本年度培训盲人保健按摩人员 1,080 人；培训医疗按摩人员 265 人，医疗按摩机构 34 个，保健按摩机构达到 442 个；有 978 名盲人按摩人员实现就业，其中保健按摩人员 835 人，医疗按摩人员 143 人；全省各级残联扶持 254 名特困盲人按摩师实现就业。

四、社会保障

（一）社会保险。2014 年新型农村和城镇居民社会养老保险统一合并实施，已有 25.3 万名城乡残疾居民参保，参保率 78.83%，在 60 岁以下的参保残疾人中有 7.3 万名重度残疾人，其中 6.7 万人得到了政府的参保扶助，代缴补贴比例达到 92.42%。有 5.4 万名非重度残疾人也享受了全额或部分代缴的优惠政策。领取养老金待遇的人数达到 6.9 万人。

城镇残疾职工参加养老保险 6.5 万人，参加医疗保险 5.9 万人。城镇 12.7 万人和农村 16.0 万残疾人纳入最低生活保障范围；城镇集中供养残疾人和农村五保供养残疾人分别达到 0.4 万名和 1.3 万名。1.5 万名城乡残疾人得到了其他救助救济。

（二）社会救助。2014 年全省共有城镇 12.7 万人和农村 16.0 万残疾人纳入最低生活保障范围；城镇集中供养残疾人和农村五保供养残疾人分别达到 0.4 万名和 1.3 万名。3 万名城乡残疾人得到了其他救助救济。

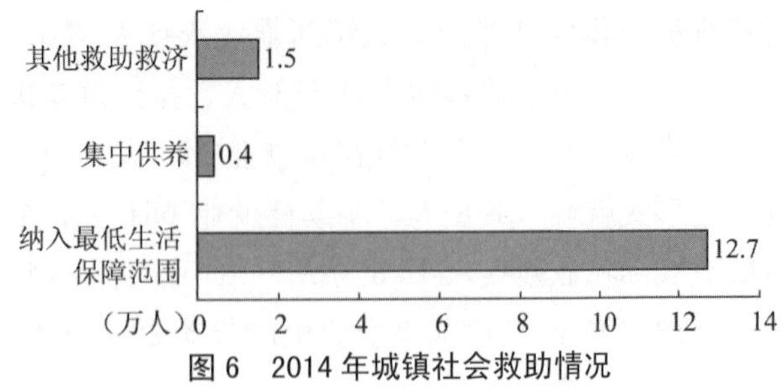

图 6　2014 年城镇社会救助情况

城镇已纳入最低生活保障 12.7 万人，集中供养 0.4 万人，其他救助救济 1.5 万人

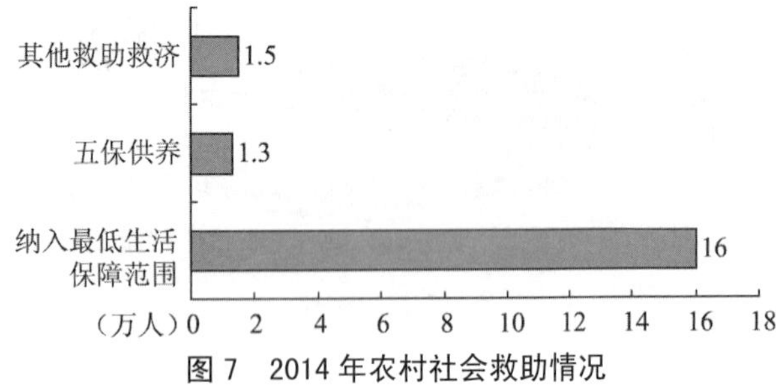

图 7　2014 年农村社会救助情况

农村已纳入最低生活保障 16 万人，农村五保供养 1.3 万人，其他救助救济 1.5 万人

（三）托养服务。残疾人托养服务工作规范推进，残疾人托养服务机构达到 18 个，共为 1.7 万名残疾人提供了托养服务。其中寄宿制托养服务机构 8 个；日间照料机构 2 个。机构之外接受居家托养服务的残疾人达到 1.6 万人。全年共有 211 名托养服务管理和服务人员接受了各级各类专业培训。

五、扶贫情况

2014 年，残疾人扶贫开发成效显著，贫困残疾人生产生活状况得到进一步改善。1.8 万户贫困残疾人得到扶持，其中 2.2 万人通过扶贫开发实现脱贫；接受实用技术培训的残疾人达到 2.6 万人次。

完成 143 户农村贫困残疾人危房改造，各地投入危房资金 152.1 万元，153 名残疾人受益。

开展社会帮扶活动，其中结对帮扶单位 1,649 个，结对帮扶个人 4,218 人；投入康复扶贫贴息贷款扶持 1909 名农村残疾人，残疾人扶贫基地达到 259 个，安置 3861 名残疾人就业，扶持带动 8520 名残疾人脱贫致富。

六、法律维权

（一）残疾人法规政策及执法检查。2014 年，县级以上制定或修改保障残疾人权益的规范性文件 11 件。县级以上人大进行《残疾人保障法》执法检查和专题调研 6 次；政协进行视察和专题调研 7 次。

（二）残疾人法制宣传与法律救助。全年开展普法宣传教育活动 160 次，1.5 万人参加；举办法律培训班 62 个，3,491 人参加。建立残疾人法律救助协调机构 41 个；建立残疾人法律救助工作站 35 个，办理案件 62 件；建立残疾人法律援助中心（工作站）66 个，办理案件 320 件。

（三）残疾人参政议政。全省残联协助各级人大代表、政协委员提出议案、建议、提案 32 件，办理议案、建议、提案 15 件。

（四）无障碍建设与残疾人机动轮椅车燃油补贴。截止 2014 年底，全省各级政府成立无障碍建设领导协调组织 25 个；贫困残疾人家庭无障碍改造 686 户，无障碍检查 30 次，无障碍培训 353 人次；为 1.5 万名残疾人发放了残疾人机动轮椅车燃油补贴。

（五）残疾人信访。2014 年，全省各级残联共处理残疾人群众来信 401 件，接待残疾人群众来访 5,825 人次，其中集体访 80 批次，2,328 人次。

七、组织建设

（一）残联组织。全省各级残联实有人员 2,865 人。残疾人干部配备工作进一步加强，全省县级以上残联领导班子中配备了 12 名残疾人领导干部；县级以上残联机关配备了 58 名残疾人干部。各级残联共举办培训班 581 期，培训机关干部、协会干部及残疾人专职委员 11,901 人次。

（二）残疾人专职委员。全省有 908 个乡镇（街道）选聘残疾人专职委员 973 名；9,475 个社区（村）选聘残疾人专职委员 11,068 名。

（三）残疾人专门协会。全省共建立各类残疾人专门协会 367 个，其中盲人协会 74 个、聋人协会 73 个、肢残人协会 74 个、智力残疾人及亲友协会 73 个、精神残疾人及亲友协会 73 个。

（四）助残社会组织。全省共建立助残社会组织 57 个，其中在民政部门注册的为 49 个，以残联为业务主管单位的 26 个。

（五）志愿者助残。全省助残志愿者活动蓬勃发展，涌现一大批扶残助残先进集体和个人。截止 2014 年底，全省助残志愿者登记数已达 18.7 万人，受助残疾人达到 130.8 万人次。

八、宣传文化

（一）宣传。截至 2014 年底，中央级媒体刊播我省残疾人事业稿件 31 件，省和地市级主要新闻媒体刊播稿件 2,256 件，报刊专版 36 个，残疾人专题广播节目 6 个,电视手语新闻栏目 10 个,投放各类公益广告 12 个。

（二）文化。截至 2014 年底，全省 53 个县级以上公共图书馆全部设立盲文及盲人有声读物阅览室；全省共举办残疾人文化周活动 136 场（次），举办残疾人文化艺术类比赛及展览 20 个，全省成立了 6 个残疾人艺术团队。

九、残疾人体育

全省深入开展残疾人体育工作。组织省级残疾人群众体育健身活动 3 次，2,300 人次参加；建设省级残疾人群众体育活动示范点达到 50 个，培训省级残疾人体育健身指导员达到 264 人；组织省级残疾人体育比赛 1 次，参赛运动员达 378 人次；省级残疾人体育训练基地已达 16 个；组织地市级残疾人体育健身活动 80 次，6,447 人次参加；设立地市级残疾人群众体育活动示范点 193 个；培训地市级残疾人体育健身指导员 853 人。

十、服务设施

截至 2014 年底，已竣工并投入使用的各级残疾人综合服务设施 46 个，总建设规模 7.7 万平方米，总投资 19,057.9 万元；已竣工并投入使用的各级残疾人康复设施 8 个，总建设规模 2.8 万平方米，总投资 10,356 万元；已竣工并投入使用的各级残疾人托养服务设施 2 个，总建设规模 7,300 平方米，总投资 2,052 万元。

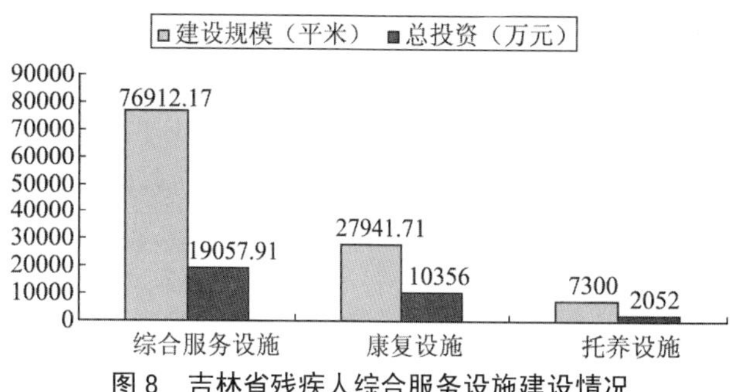

图 8 吉林省残疾人综合服务设施建设情况

十一、信息化建设

全省各级残联全面推进信息公开，目前省残联及各市州残联全面开通了公众网站，36 个县级残联开通网站。全省各级残联共有 132 名专兼职技术人员从事信息化工作。举办信息工作培训班 13 期，培训各级残联信息员 495 人次。吉林省第一个全面实现“无障碍”浏览的公众网站——“省残联无障碍门户网站”于 10 月 15 日“世界盲人日”期间正式上线，网站全年发稿 1,753 件，开通互动交流栏目，积极探索网上信息服务能力。

继续开展残疾人状况监测工作，科学分析残疾人小康进程，为推进各项业务工作提供依据。

2014 年黑龙江省残疾人事业发展统计公报

2014 年，在省委、省政府领导和中国残联的具体指导下，认真学习贯彻党的十八大和十八届三中、四中全会精神，全面落实中国残联“六代会”的任务要求，以推进省委省政府确定的民生实事为重点，落实残疾人同步小康年度任务，圆满完成了年初制定的各项任务目标。

一、康复

2014 年，围绕残疾人“人人享有康复服务”的工作目标，实施“十二五”残疾人康复项目，各类残疾人得到不同程度的康复。

全省在 57 个市辖区和 62 个县（市）的 3080 个社区（村）开展了社区康复服务工作；累计已建社区康复站的社区 1397 个，配备社区康复协调员 3873 名，其中，已接受过培训的社区康复协调员 3582 人；为 312257 人建立了社区康复服务档案，累计接受社区康复服务的残疾人 128161 人。

全省视力残疾康复机构 24 个，全年完成白内障复明手术 10673 例，为 4280 名贫困白内障患者免费施行复明手术；为 11756 名低视力患者配用助视器，培训低视力儿童家长 1434 名，有效开展家庭康复训练，对 4578 名盲人进行定向行走训练。

推进听力语言康复机构规范化管理，完善基层服务网络。已建设省级听力语言康复机构 1 个，地市级听力语言康复机构 13 个，县级听力语言康复机构 15 个；年度新收训聋儿 309 名，在训聋儿 525 名；规范聋儿家长学校，开展家庭训练，共培训聋儿家长 651 名；开展各级各类听力语言康复专业技术人员培训，共培训专业人员 195 人。

全省肢体残疾康复训练服务机构 48 个，其中，省级 1 个，地市级 22 个，县级 25 个；培训各级肢体残疾康复管理、技术人员 226 人次；对 6194 名肢体残疾者实施康复训练，其中脑瘫儿童机构康复训练 554 人，肢体残疾儿童社区、家庭康复训练 303 人，成年肢体残疾人社区、家庭康复训练 5337 人；全年共完成贫困肢体残疾儿童矫治手术 162 例。

全省智力残疾康复训练服务的机构 47 个，其中，省级康复机构 1 个，地市级康复机构 20 个，县级康复机构 26 个；培训各级智力残疾康复管理、技术人员 118 人次；对 3399 名智力残疾人进行康复训练，其中智力残疾儿童机构康复训练 838 人，智力残疾儿童社区、家庭康复训练 2105 人，成年智力残疾人社区、家庭康复训练 456 人。

大力推广“社会化、综合性、开放式”精神病防治康复工作。全省在 125 个县（市、区）开展精神病防治康复工作，对 182066 名精神病患者进行综合防治康复，监护率达到 80.7%，显好率达到 64.0%，社会参与率达到 39.8%，肇事率 0.03%；解除关锁 6 人；全省精神康复机构 39 个，机构中接受康复服务的精神病人 5067 名；对 5687 名贫困精神病患者进行医疗救助。全年培训精防康复管理、技术人员 55 人。全省孤独症儿童康复训练机构 45 个，机构内有 318 名从事孤独症儿童康复训练的教师，516 名孤独症儿童在机构内接受康复训练，全年有 255 名贫困孤独症儿童得到康复救助。

加强残疾人辅助器具服务体系建设，深入开展辅助器具供应服务，为残疾人减免费用供应辅助器具 27125 件，其中装配假肢 458 例、矫形器 317 例，验配助视器 16292 件。

全省有 56 个县（市、区）的 31 个医疗卫生机构陆续开展残疾儿童筛查工作，2014 年全年新诊断 0-6 岁残疾儿童 654 人；全省共举办举办儿童残疾预防宣传活动 60 次，发放儿童残疾预防宣传材料 33285 份；全省共有残疾儿童家长学校 10 个，全年开展家长学校活动 10 次，参与的残疾儿童家长 91 人。

注重康复人才培养，全年举办康复管理人员培训班 32 期，培训康复管理人员 260 人；举办康复业务人员培训班 38 期，培训康复业务人员 446 人；举办社区康复协调员培训班 95 期，培训社区康复协调员 1945 人。

二、教育

2014年，为300名家庭经济困难的残疾儿童享受普惠性学前教育提供资助。

全省共有特殊教育普通高中学校（班）1个，残疾人中等职业学校（班）7个；有155名残疾人被普通高等院校录取。

截止2014年底，全省有未入学学龄残疾儿童少年1073人，其中视力残疾39人，听力残疾52人，言语残疾33人，肢体残疾320人，智力残疾408人，精神残疾92人，多重残疾129人。

三、就业

截止2014年底，全省城镇残疾人就业人数127348人。本年度新增城镇就业残疾人9325人，其中集中就业残疾人2608人，按比例安排残疾人就业1611人，公益性岗位就业582人，个体就业及其它形式灵活就业4337人，辅助性就业187人；农村残疾人实际就业241925人，其中196595名农村残疾人从事农业生产劳动，45330名农村残疾人从事其他形式就业；全省残疾人职业培训基地102个，其中残联兴办32个，依托社会机构兴办70个，全年共有11835人次的城镇残疾人接受了职业培训。

盲人按摩事业稳定发展。2014年，培训盲人保健按摩人员435名，盲人医疗按摩人员186名；保健按摩机构达到247个，医疗按摩机构达到58个；在专业技术职务资格评审中，分别有56人和64人通过盲人医疗按摩人员中级和初级职称评审。

四、社会保障

2014年新型农村和城镇居民社会养老保险统一合并实施，截止2014年底，全省残疾居民参加城乡社会养老保险符合参保条件的有407387人，其中重度残疾人69661人，实际参保的有250593名，参保率61.5%，领取养老金待遇的人数达到120739人。全省60岁以下参保的残疾居民129854人，其中重度残疾人32459人，有27393人得到了政府的参保扶助（获得全额代缴9537人，获得部分代缴17856人），代缴补贴比例达到84.4%。有23267名非重度残疾人也享受了优惠政策（获得全额代缴4402人，获得部分代缴18865人）。

城镇残疾职工参加养老保险77856人，参加医疗保险64667人；全省有162269名城镇残疾人和140705名农村残疾人纳入最低生活保障范围，城镇集中供养残疾人3716人，农村五保供养残疾人10620人；全年有16939名城镇残疾人和29954名农村残疾人得到了其他救助救济；全年城镇残疾人和农村残疾人符合条件享受稳定生活补贴的有8085人，享受稳定护理补贴的有31630人。

残疾人托养服务工作规范推进，全省残疾人托养服务机构达到93个，其中寄宿制托养服务机构33个，日间照料机构5个，综合性托养服务机构55个，共为3902名残疾人提供了托养服务。在以上机构中，共有10名残疾人实现辅助性就业，8名残疾人实现了支持性就业。机构之外接受居家托养服务的残疾人达到15614人。全年共有414名托养服务管理和服务人员接受了各级各类专业培训，其中有5人接受了国家级培训。

五、扶贫

2014年，全省共扶持贫困残疾人户17344户，扶持贫困残疾人18303人，其中13599人通过扶贫开发实现脱贫，接受实用技术培训的残疾人达到16139人次，投入培训经费115.8万元。

通过康复扶贫贴息贷款扶持农村残疾人1134人，共有结对帮扶单位2629个，结对帮扶个人3800人。截止2014年底，全省建立残疾人扶贫基地156个，安置残疾人就业5033人，扶持带动残疾人7415人。全年完成1290户农村贫困残疾人危房改造，投入危房改造资金1236万元，有1327名残疾人受益。

六、宣传文化

2014年，省级宣传文化工作中，中央级媒体采用稿件20件，主要新闻媒体刊播稿件80件，报纸专版10个，共有省级残疾人专题广播节目1个，电视手语新闻栏目1个，播出公益广告2个；地市级主要新闻媒体刊播稿件625件，报纸专版62个，残疾人专题广播节目8个，电视手语新闻栏目7个，播出公益广告4个。

全省各级建立公共图书馆盲文及盲人有声读物阅览室57个，开展残疾人文化周活动214场次，残疾人文化活动参与人数 7925 人次，举办残疾人文化艺术类比赛及展览 108 次，有各类残疾人艺术团体 24 个。

七、体育

深入开展残疾人体育工作。组织省级残疾人群众体育健身活动 3 次，参加人数 270 人；建设省级残疾人群众体育活动示范点达到 43 个；培训省级残疾人体育健身指导员达到 420 人；组织省级残疾人体育比赛 5 次，参赛运动员达 340 人次；省级残疾人体育训练基地已达 5 个。组织地市级残疾人体育健身活动 19 次，参加人数 3890 人次；建设地市级残疾人群众体育活动示范点 11 个；培训地市级残疾人体育健身指导员 279 人。

八、维权

全省制定或修改关于残疾人的专门法规、规章 2 个；制定或修改保障残疾人权益的规范性文件省级 1 件、地市级 1 件、县级 1 件。县级以上人大进行《残疾人保障法》执法检查和专题调研 15 次；政协进行视察和专题调研 17 次。开展普法宣传教育活动 136 次，参加人数 13093 人；举办法律培训班 31 个，参加人数 1110 人。

截至 2014 年底，成立残疾人法律救助工作协调机构 3 个，建立残疾人法律救助工作站 2 个，办理案件 4 件，建立残疾人法律援助中心（工作站）117 个，办理案件 586 件，有力地推动了法律救助和法律援助工作。

残疾人参政议政工作得到加强，各级残联协助人大代表、政协委员提出议案、建议、提案 35 件，办理议案、建议、提案 42 件。

无障碍建设法规、标准进一步完善。全省共出台 4 个无障碍建设与管理法规、规章和规范性文件；有 36 个市、县、区系统开展了无障碍建设；全省开展无障碍建设检查 25 次，无障碍培训 7 人次；全年共为 3125 户贫困残疾人家庭实施了无障碍改造；全年发放残疾人机动轮椅车燃油补贴 18159 名。

全省各级残联共处理残疾人群众来信 1416 件，接待残疾人群众来访 5362 人次，其中集体访 65 批次、892 人次。

九、组织建设

2014 年，全省有 10 个地市级残联在领导班子中配备了残疾人理事长或副理事长，35 个县级残联机关配备了残疾人干部。全省已建乡镇（街道）残联 1329 个，已建率达到 97.5%，选聘残疾人专职委员 1876 名；已建社区（村）残协 9139 个，已建率达到 89.9%，选聘残疾人专职委员 5853 名。

全省建立省级以下各类残疾人专门协会 731 个，市级、县级专门协会已建比例为 100%。全省共建立助残社会组织 26 个，其中在民政部门注册的为 9 个，以残联为业务主管单位的 5 个。

全省省、市、县、乡残联实有人员已达 2948 人。为提高残联系统干部队伍素质，各级残联共举办培训班 555 期，培训机关干部、协会干部及残疾人专职委员 11910 人次。全省助残志愿者登记总数为 314074 人，受助残疾人达 712947 人次。

十、服务设施

截至 2014 年底，全省已竣工并投入使用的各级残疾人综合服务设施 101 个，总建设规模 114575.5 平方米，总投资 37030.9 万元；已竣工并投入使用的各级残疾人康复设施 4 个，总建设规模 5464.8 平方米，总投资 600.8 万元；已竣工并投入使用的各级残疾人托养服务设施 3 个，总建设规模 10817 平方米，总投资 3346 万元。

十一、信息化

全省各级残联共有 154 名专、兼职统计人员从事残疾人事业统计工作，其中 16 人有统计从业资格证书。2014 年全省残联系统共举办统计人员培训班 3 期，参加培训人数 110 人次。

全面推进网站建设，截止 2014 年底，全省建设残联门户网站 31 个，其中省级残联 1 个、地市级残联 7 个、县级残联 23 个。2014 年全省省级发稿量 818 篇，各级残联举办信息工作培训班 4 期，参加培训人数 67 人次。

全省建立省级局域网 1 个，各级残联系统拥有计算机 916 台，拥有信息化专业人才 175 人，全年信息化建设投入 76.6 万元，用于信息化安全投入 4.4 万元。

2014 年上海市残疾人事业发展统计公报

2014 年是加快推进残疾人“两个体系”建设和圆满完成残疾人事业“十二五”发展纲要的关键一年。本年度，上海市残联深入学习贯彻十八大和十八届三中、四中全会精神，以改革创新的思路，不断健全残疾人权益保障，突出发展重点，注重制度保障，动员社会力量，建立长效机制，残疾人生产生活状况持续改善，努力向残疾人同步小康迈进。2014 年，本市新领证残疾人 24576 人，持证残疾人总数合计 401318 人，其中视力残疾 74040 人，听力残疾 39399 人，言语残疾 4111 人，肢体残疾 177259 人，智力残疾 56032 人，精神残疾 45577 人，多重残疾 4900 人。

一、康复工作

2014 年，“为 1 万名残疾人补贴提供个性化辅助器具适配服务”再次纳入市政府实事项目。截至 2014 年底，该项目共完成适配人数 19535 人，适配辅助器具件数 233728 件。同时，国家科技惠民计划项目《上海市残障人群康复辅助器具技术集成及应用示范》向纵深推进，在本市 3 个示范区、20 个示范点的带动下，项目推广后惠及 100 万人以上。2014 年，上海、宁波、苏州三地残联共同签订了辅助器具技术服务和合作协议，沪甬苏辅助器具服务全面合作，聚焦残障人群的辅助器具多元需求，运用国家科技惠民项目成果，辐射长三角并影响全国，使辅具服务科技创新取得最大化效果。

为切实改善残疾人的生活质量，本市积极协调市民政局、市财政局，出台了以下相关政策，有力保障了残疾人的康复权益。一是调整本市残疾人养护床位补贴标准，由原 500 元/床/年提高到 1000 元/床/年；二是调整本市残疾人养护床位一次性建设经费补贴政策，由原来的每张床位 5000 元提高到 10000 元；三是调整残疾人居家养护补贴标准，由原来 10 元/小时调整为 20 元/小时，四是提高“阳光心园”相关经费补贴等，进一步提高了残疾人养护服务水平。市残联与市卫生计生委联合出台《关于为社区康复患者提供辅助器具服务的通知》（沪残联〔2014〕129 号），为社区有需求的康复患者提供专业、规范、便捷的辅助器具服务。市残康办协调市残疾人辅助器具资源中心、上海市盲童学校、上海市眼病防治中心，成立上海市辅助器具适配视力分中心，出台了《关于成立上海市辅助器具适配视力分中心的通知》（沪残康办〔2014〕16 号），对符合条件的市盲童学校学生提供视力辅助器具适配和租赁服务。探索了老年盲、聋残疾人及老携残疾子女提供特殊托养服务的途径，满足了这一群体残疾人的特殊养护需求。

根据残疾人个性化需求，全面开展常见遗传性耳聋致病基因检测工作，为育龄听障残疾人或听障残疾人直系亲属进行常见遗传性耳聋致病基因检测，并提供遗传咨询、婚育指导和产前诊断等服务，2014 年共检测 200 人。

为积极推进实施上海市示范型“阳光心园”、上海市残疾人示范型辅助器具服务社创建工作，截至 2014 年年底，全市共创建了 41 家示范型残疾人辅助器具服务社、53 家示范型阳光心园。通过开展康复示范创建工作，有序推进本市康复服务规范化建设。

为营造康复科研学术氛围，全面提高康复人才队伍水平，组织开展了残疾人康复管理与康复技术成果奖评工作，评出康复事业管理及康复服务技术成果一、二、三等奖共 18 项。启动“上海市残联系统康复人才培养三年行动计划”，确定了 5 名优秀学科带头人及 10 名优秀青年人才作为培养对象。开展 2014 年度残疾人康复科研课题立项工作，确定 40 个科研入围项目，40 个科研鼓励项目。组织专家完成 2012 年度科研入围项目的结题验收工作。积极举办康复学术论坛，提高残疾人康复的社会影响力。在 2014 国际康复无障碍生活博览会期间，主办国际康复无障碍生活博览会儿童康复论坛、国际康复无障碍生活博览会之脏器康复等。

2014 年全市 17 个区（县）均开展残疾儿童筛查工作，建立各级残疾儿童家长学校 103 家。截至

2014年底，累计建立社区康复服务档案366121人，接受社区康复服务累计达358591人。2014年度共完成白内障复明手术62433例，其中贫困白内障免费手术4439例。低视力者配用助视器7262名，培训低视力儿童家长1078人，盲人定向行走训练2065人。新收训聋儿136人，其中机构训练80人、家庭训练56人，在训聋儿374人，开展成年听力语言康复技术服务数10366人次。成年肢体残疾人社区、家庭康复3780人，脑瘫儿童康复训练1019人。智力儿童机构康复训练1574人，成年智力残疾人社区、家庭康复7616人。监护精神病人112395人，其中显好病人数为110905人，医疗救助贫困精神病患者13063人、孤独症儿童康复救助340人。全年完成辅助器具适配服务231799件，其中假肢装配875例、矫形器装配45926例、其他辅助器具184998件。

二、教育工作

2014年，本市继续开展未入学适龄残疾儿童少年调查工作，对发现的未入学适龄残疾儿童少年及时响应、及时妥善解决就学困难。据统计，2014年未入学适龄残疾儿童少年18人。全市特殊教育普通高中教育、中等职业教育相比2013年教育机构数未发生变化，在校残疾学生总数略有浮动。

三、就业培训工作

2014年，本市的残疾人就业工作,已经形成以分散按比例就业和集中就业为主、以非正规就业和自主创业为辅，多种就业形式并存的格局。本市现有的残疾人就业保障政策主要包括：一是对分散就业中超比例的给予奖励，未按比例安排残疾人就业征收残疾人就业保障金；二是对集中安排残疾人就业的福利企业，根据国家税务总局规定实施退减税政策；三是对残疾人非正规就业和自主创业，分别实施阳光职业康复援助基地庇护性就业和个体工商户扶持等举措；四是残疾人职业技能培训等为提高残疾人就业竞争力的扶持政策。2014年出台了分散安排残疾人就业岗位补贴、残疾人职业技能培训补贴，福利企业实施残疾人集中就业社会保险费补贴，调整了残疾人个体工商户开办费补贴、超比例安排残疾人就业单位奖励标准，完善了“阳光之家”相关经费补贴、阳光职业康复援助基地相关经费补贴等政策。这些政策的出台，填补和提高了多项政策空白点和补贴标准，强化了残疾人就业扶持力度，健全了本市残疾人就业促进政策框架体系。2014年，城镇残疾人在业人数66575人,其中集中就业14532人,按比例就业37017人,个体及其他形式就业6631人，公益性岗位就业4979人，辅助性就业3416人。农村残疾人实际就业25709人，其中从事农业生产劳动5317人，其他形式就业20392人。

四、社会保障

2014年，本市各类残疾人社会救助、社会保险和社会福利政策实施平稳。本市完成了重残人员参加城乡居民基本养老保险城镇与农村的并轨，并代缴重度残疾人城乡居民基本养老保险个人缴费。继续为城镇重残人员代缴城镇居民基本医疗保险、为农村困难残疾人提供新型农村合作医疗缴费补贴，全市城乡残疾人的社会养老、医疗保险制度全覆盖。全市残疾人城乡最低生活保障、重残无业人员生活补助、一户多残家庭困难生活补助等社会救助政策不断完善，做到应保尽保。城镇已纳入最低生活保障14999人，集中供养87人，其他救助救济42853人。农村已纳入最低生活保障2657人，五保供养312人，其他救助救济11041人。重残无业人员生活补助总计救助42509人。

深入开展残疾人托养服务。寄宿制机构托养残疾人5357人，日间照料机构托养智力残疾人6184人、精神残疾人3270人，居家托养服务残疾人13019人。

五、组织联络工作

经人社部、中国残联及国家表彰奖励办公室研究决定，本市吴建寅、韩颖、黄胜利、金婉、王志冲等5人被评为“全国自强模范”；莫晓东被评为“全国残联系统先进工作者”；嘉定区嘉定镇街道阳光彩虹社工事务所、上海海阳老年事业发展服务中心、奉贤区农业技术学校等3家单位被评为“全国助残先进集体”；陈东珍、郭海瑛、黄吉人等3人被评为“全国助残先进个人”；宝山区罗店镇“阳光家园”、静安区“阳光家园”、青浦区练塘镇大新村残疾人协会等3家单位被评为“残疾人之家”。

全面开展本市全国残疾人基本服务状况和需求专项调查工作。按照专项调查统一标准，对各区县师资及街镇骨干共700余人进行了集中培训，21个试点街镇开展了入户调查登记工作。

2014年，本市残疾人专职委员队伍人数为5849人。市残联继续组织实施全市残疾人专职委员新三年轮训规划（2014—2016年），对全市残疾人专职委员开展社会工作专业知识专题培训和网络在线学习培训工作，帮助残疾人专职委员进一步了解业务知识，提升工作能力。

市残联、市志愿者协会联合搭建助残志愿者工作服务平台，建立了市、区县、街镇的助残志愿者登记注册管理系统，实现了助残志愿者网上招募与注册管理。12月3日，市残联召开“2013—2014年度上海市助残志愿服务先进集体、先进个人”表彰大会，共表彰42个志愿助残先进集体、92名志愿助残先进个人，推动了上海助残志愿服务事业的发展。

六、维权工作

维权工作着力规范初信初访办理，从源头上预防新增重复信访，在“事清案结”上下功夫，确保信访矛盾的有效化解，全年受理来信1113件；接待来访266人次；《上海市实施<中华人民共和国残疾人保障法>办法》正式实施，从立法层面上为保障残疾人权益提供依据。加强区县残疾人法律救助站建设，完善全市残疾人法律救助网络，推进残疾人法律援助和法律救助工作，增加服务内容、扩大服务范围，切实降低了残疾人享受法律服务门槛。积极开展残疾人法律援助、救助服务，先后为294人次提供法律服务，维护了残疾人的合法权益。从保障残疾人最直接的利益出发，认真做好惠及残疾人的实事项目，及时发放残疾人机动轮椅车燃油补贴，惠及14241人；残疾人家庭无障碍改造共惠及1063户残疾人家庭。结合本市与市民生活密切相关的重大工程和民生工程，做到前期介入，开展现场检查，全年共组织市和区县督导队现场检查151次。为推动《无障碍环境建设条例》实施，提高督导队员素质，组织区县残联专职干部、督导队长及部分队员开展各类培训，共2332人次参加。

七、宣传文体

2014年，宣传工作稳步推进，全年本市主要媒体共播出电视广播报道50余条，文字和图片报道共计700余篇，积极营造了残疾人事业可持续发展的良好舆论氛围。文化工作捷报频传，嘉定区、松江区荣获“全国残疾人文化体育建设示范区”称号，黄浦区、徐汇区荣获“上海市残疾人文化体育建设示范区”称号，以点带面推动全市残疾人文体建设。无障碍电影列入市政府实事项目，全市20个影院开设无障碍电影放映专场，全年放映了现场解说的《安德的游戏》、《爸爸去哪儿》等12部国内外最新影片，累计放映192场，受益残疾人达2万人次。上海盲童合唱团在北京举办的第十二届中国国际合唱节中荣获金奖。“读书•圆梦”上海残疾人读书活动被市振兴中华读书指导委员会评为“经典传承项目”。信息无障碍工作持续发展，依托上海图书馆建成了无障碍数字图书馆，上海“两会”开幕式电视直播进行手语播报。

2014年，上海残疾人事业发展成果得到中央及市级媒体的关注，其中中央级媒体采用上海稿件数10件，本市各级主要新闻媒体刊播稿件数668件，其中专版及专题98个，刊播残疾人事业电视广播公益广告1个。2014年“上海市残疾人文化月”期间，市级举办残疾人文化活动16场，区县级举办残疾人文化活动266场。2014年新促会召开换届大会，正式更名为“上海市残疾人事业宣传文化促进会”，促进残疾人宣传文化工作协调发展。

体育方面以参加亚洲残运会、备战第九届全国残运会暨第六届全国特奥会为重点，大力开展群众体育工作，做好国家队集训工作。进一步深入开展基层社区残疾人体育事业，借助残疾人体育健身点为平台，使残疾人能就近参与各类体育活动。在全社会关心支持下，全市常年参与体育活动的残疾人保持在11万余人，全年开展市级残疾人群众体育健身活动14次，残疾人群众体育健身活动参加人次2455次，残疾人群众体育活动示范点达到273个，聘任各类体育项目教练员160人，组织全市性残疾人体育赛事22次，参加各类残疾人体育赛事运动员达到4600人次，培养市级残疾人体育健身指导员351人。

2014年江苏省残疾人事业发展统计公报

2014年，全省残联系统认真贯彻落实党的十八大、十八届三中、四中全会和省委十二届六次全会精神，全面落实中国残联和省残联第六次代表大会部署，以实现残疾人与全省人民同步小康为目标，攻坚克难，开拓进取，全面完成了年初确定的工作任务，省“十二五”残疾人事业发展纲要确定的各项目标任务进展良好，残疾人事业实现了新发展。

一、康复

2014年，全省残疾人康复工作紧紧围绕残疾人“人人享有基本康复服务”目标，继续完善残疾人康复政策顶层设计，扩大康复制度保障范围，出台儿童康复系列政策，建立贫困精神残疾人基本免费用药机制，继续推进康复项目进医保工作；同时健全康复服务网络，完善各级康复中心建设，提升康复服务能力和水平，扎实抓好重点康复项目，提高救助标准，扩大受益面，推进政府购买康复服务，调整康复项目补助方式，残疾人康复工作迈上新台阶。

全省在59个市辖区和44个县（市）开展了社区康复工作；在19821个社区（村）中，已开展社区康复服务的社区（村）有16843个，占85.0%；累计建立社区康复站14937个，配备18159名社区康复协调员；共有75个残疾人康复机构开展家长学校工作，全年共培训家长8060人次。

全省开展视力残疾康复机构总数达64个，巩固白内障无障碍省创建成果，全省白内障无障碍“发现一例、复明一例”机制成熟运行，全年完成白内障复明手术60404例，为16840名贫困白内障患者免费施行复明手术，为6408名低视力患者配用助视器，对7706名盲人进行定向行走训练。

推进听力语言康复机构规范化管理，完善基层服务网络；加强省级聋儿康复机构建设，完善聋儿康复网络；已建省级听力语言康复机构1个，基层听力语言康复机构64个；全省共对2706名聋儿进行听力语言康复训练，接受地方项目救助的聋儿有862名。培训各类专业人员343人。全年共开展成年听力语言康复技术服务2125人次。共筛查听障儿童500余名，年度人工耳蜗项目已完成手术35人，全年组织家长培训7期，培训家长138人。

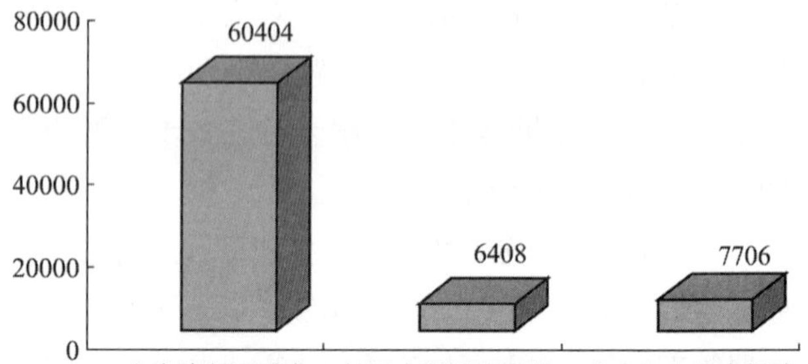

图1-1　2014年白内障复明手术、低视力康复、盲人定向行走训练开展情况（单位：例、人）

大力推广“社会化、综合性、开放式”精神病防治康复工作。在103个县（市、区）开展精神病防治康复工作，对52.0万名精神病患者进行综合防治康复，监护率达到79.7%，显好率达到60.0%，社会参与率达到50.9%，肇事率0.01%，解除关锁35人，对4.2万名贫困精神病患者进行医疗救助，截至2014年底全省共有108个精神康复机构。

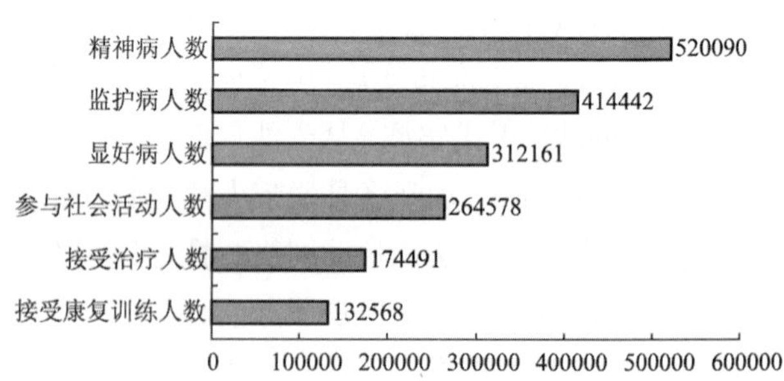

图1-2　2014年精神病人监护和救助情况（单位：人）

建立1个省级孤独症儿童康复训练机构，20名孤独症儿童在其中进行康复训练；基层共有93个孤独症儿童康复训练机构，在训孤独症儿童共计1303人。

全年开展肢体残疾康复训练服务的机构达到123个，对36256名肢体残疾人进行康复训练，其中：脑瘫儿童机构康复训练5845人，肢体残疾儿童社区、家庭康复训练2055人，成年肢体残疾人社区、家庭康复训练28356人，全年共完成贫困肢体残疾儿童矫治手术220例。

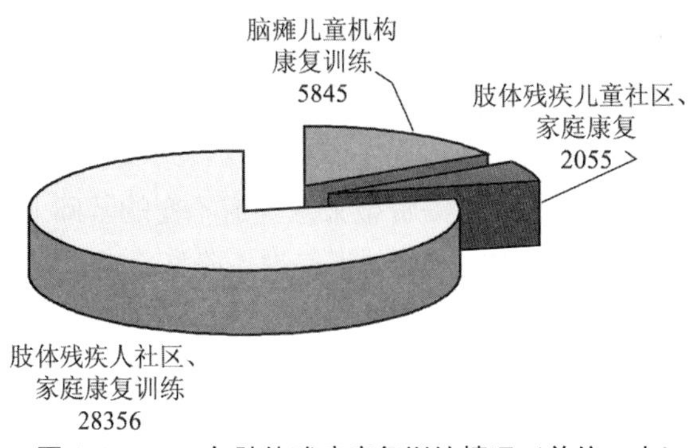

图 1-3　2014 年肢体残疾康复训练情况（单位：人）

全年开展智力残疾康复训练服务的机构达到 96 个，对 11994 名智力残疾儿童进行康复训练，其中为 3011 名智力残疾儿童开展机构康复训练，为 4540 名智力残疾儿童开展社区、家庭康复，为 4443 名成年智力残疾人开展社区、家庭康复，不同程度地开展了智力残疾儿童早期康复训练与服务；全年各类智力残疾康复管理、技术人员培训达 1668 人次。

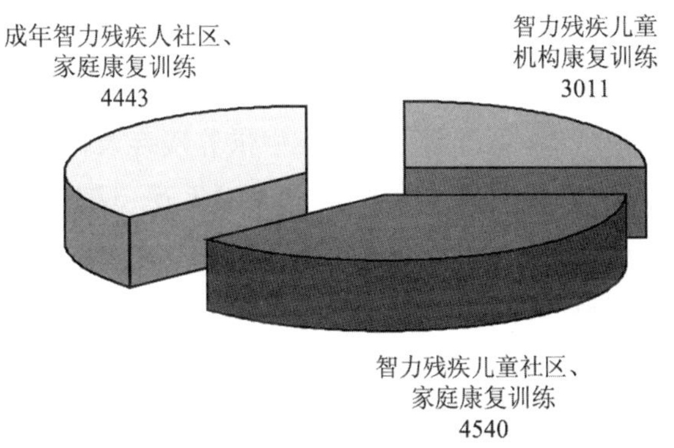

图 1-4　2014 年智力残疾康复训练开展情况（单位：人）

深入开展辅助器具供应服务，全面推进普及型假肢装配，截止到 2014 年底，累计建立辅助器具供应服务机构 61 个，为残疾人减免费用装配普及型假肢 1475 例，供应辅助器具达 250 种，供应各类辅助器具 11.5 万件，装配矫形器 1917 例；完成 2700 万元辅助器具和家庭无障碍产品的招标采购工作，为 5 万余户残疾人适配辅助器具和家庭无障碍环境改造。

全省共有 103 个县（市、区）和 129 个医疗卫生机构开展残疾儿童筛查工作，全省录入数据库救助的 0－6 岁残疾儿童有 13924 名，7－14 岁脑瘫、孤独症儿童 1208 名，其中 2014 年全年新诊断 0-6 岁残疾儿童 4598 名，并提高了部分残疾儿童救助标准。全省共举办 291 次儿童残疾预防宣传活动，发放儿童残疾预防宣传材料 20.5 万份；全省共有 62 个残疾儿童家长学校，全年共开展 174 次家长学校活动，残疾儿童家长参与人数达 7469 人次。

截至 2014 年底，全省共有康复机构在岗人员 11210 人，全年共举办康复管理人员培训班 90 期，培训康复管理人员 1591 人；举办康复业务人员培训班 113 期，培训康复业务人员 3979 人；举办康复社区康复协调员培训班 148 期，培训社区康复协调员 12041 人。

二、教育

2014 年，残疾人受教育权进一步得到保障，全面实施了残疾人义务教育免费和高中教育免学费、残疾人大学生免收学费政策。省政府办公厅转发了省教育厅等部门制定的《关于进一步加快特殊教育事业发展的意见》，明确提出实施残疾儿童少年十五年免费教育政策，并从 2014 年开始免除残疾人大学生学费，继续实施向残疾人高中生、大学生发放特殊教育补贴政策。

全年共有 720 名儿童接受残疾人事业彩票公益金助学项目资助，其中 294 名儿童受资助新入园。全省各地多渠道争取资金支持，对 93 名残疾儿童给予学前教育资助。

全省已开办特殊教育普通高中 4 所，在校生 422 人。残疾人中等职业教育机构 15 个，在校生 1023 人，2014 年度毕业生 280 人，其中获得职业资格证书 231 人。高等特殊教育学院 3 所，有 363 名残疾人被普通高等院校录取，242 名残疾人进入特殊教育学院学习。

截止到 2014 年底，全省有未入学适龄残疾儿童少年 1300 人，其中视力残疾 46 人，听力残疾 152 人，言语残疾 13 人，肢体残疾 362 人，智力残疾 612 人，精神残疾 37 人，多重残疾 78 人。

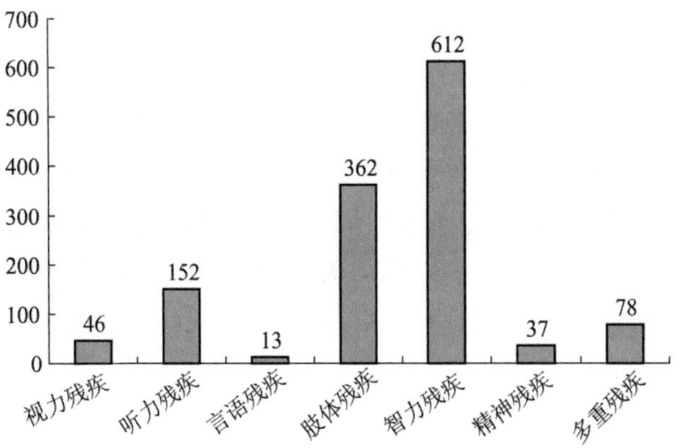

图 2-1　2014 年未入学学龄残疾儿童情况（单位：人）

三、就业

2014年全省“千企万岗”助残招聘活动成效明显。全国助残日期间，省残联会同省人社厅、国资委、教育厅在全省联动举办招聘会，省及各市、县1505家单位推出13565个岗位，15064名残疾人参加招聘活动，3296名残疾人签约就业；各地采取多种形式促进就业，努力扩大残疾人就业规模，切实加大按比例安排残疾人就业力度。省残联等七部门制定下发了关于促进残疾人按比例就业的实施意见，省政府残工委召开全体（扩大）会议，专题研究部署推动党政机关和事业单位及国有企业带头按比例安排残疾人就业有关工作，全省事业单位率先开展试点招录工作；贯彻落实《江苏省用人单位按比例安排残疾人就业补贴和超比例奖励办法（试行）》，全省发放用人单位奖补资金约800多万元。2014年全省城镇新安排1.9万名残疾人就业，其中，集中就业残疾人5797人，按比例安排残疾人就业7071人，个体及其它形式就业4616人，公益性岗位就业250人，辅助性就业1286人，全省城镇实际在业人数28.4万人；67.8万农村残疾人实现稳定就业，其中从事农业生产劳动50.5万人。

启动残疾人就业基地建设工作，要求各地依托本地已有的各类残疾人培训、实习、转移就业基地，利用已实践成熟的培训、创业就业模式，开发就业岗位，积极安置残疾人就业，并在此基础上发展和新建基地，进一步推动残疾人在基地就业。全省残疾人职业培训基地达234个，其中残联兴办80个，依托社会机构兴办154个。抓好残疾人就业培训工作，全年共有2.1万城镇残疾人接受职业培训。

进一步推动盲人保健按摩行业规范化管理。培训盲人保健按摩人员891名，培训盲人医疗按摩人员216名，保健按摩机构达到995个，医疗按摩机构达到19个；在专业技术职务资格评审中，分别有56人和108人通过医疗按摩人员中级和初级职称评审。全年共有1087名盲人保健按摩人员和65名盲人医疗按摩人员就业，扶持275名特困盲人按摩师就业。

四、社会保障

全省残疾人保障水平持续提高。在各级残联的共同努力和有关部门的支持配合下，平稳交接了特殊困难残疾人生活救助工作。低保外无业重残人员生活补助发放工作实施主体由民政转到残联，在保证原有政策落实所需资金来源渠道不变的基础上，确保受惠人员不减少、待遇标准不降低，受惠近33万残疾人。低保外重残及一户多残、依老养残生活救助、低保内重残补贴、保险补贴、无业重残人员护理补贴等政策得到全面落实，基本实现了全覆盖的目标。

新型农村和城镇居民社会养老保险统一合并实施，已有130.4万城乡残疾居民参保，参保率75.6%，在60岁以下的参保残疾人中有18.8万重度残疾人，其中17.2万得到政府的参保扶助，代缴补贴比例达到91.4%。有14.1万非重度残疾人享受全额或部分代缴的优惠政策。领取养老金待遇的人数达到67.0万人。

城镇残疾职工参加基本养老和医疗保险人数稳定在23万左右，城镇8.2万和农村22.5万残疾人纳入最低生活保障范围；城镇集中供养残疾人和农村五保供养残疾人分别达到0.6万和2.3万；32.1万和11.6万符合条件的城乡残疾人分别享受稳定的生活补贴和护理补贴。13.2万城乡残疾人得到其他救助救济。

全省已建成各类托养服务机构1123个，其中寄宿制托养服务机构36个，日间照料托养服务机构312个，综合托养服务机构775个，共有2841名残疾人实现辅助性就业，713名残疾人实现支持性就业。全省共托养残疾人6.1万人，其中寄宿制机构中托养残疾人0.1万人，日间照料机构中托养残疾人0.5万人，综合托养服务机构中托养残疾人1.6万人，机构之外接受居家托养服务的残疾人达到3.9万人。全年共有3749名托养服务管理和服务人员接受各级各类专业培训，其中接受国家级培训126人。

五、扶贫开发

残疾人扶贫工作扎实推进。认真组织全国首次“扶贫日”活动，开展《农村残疾人扶贫开发纲要（2011－2020）》执行情况检查，积极争取将残疾人纳入各地扶贫部门建档立卡对象，落实帮扶措施，加强农村残疾人实用技术培训，继续推进残疾人扶贫基地建设。全年共扶持贫困残疾人户2.2万户，扶持残疾人3.0万人，脱贫2.2万人次，接受实用技术培训的残疾人达1.8万人次，投入培训经费1126.8万元。

全省共有结对帮扶单位1870个，结对帮扶个人1.1万人。建立残疾人扶贫基地457个，安置残疾人就业11622人，扶持带动残疾人1.6万人。完成682户农村贫困残疾人危房改造，投入危房资金239.2万元，受益残疾人785人。

六、宣传文化

加强涉及残疾人事务社会热点、重大政策、困难诉求等方面的新闻报道，创新举办“我梦最美”全省残疾人微电影、公益广告歌曲大赛，收到全省自创微电影28部、公益广告和歌曲29部，举办全省优秀残疾人征文评选，组团参加“内地与澳门残疾人展能艺术墟”活动。

截至2014年底，省级宣传文化工作中，中央媒体采用稿件12件，主要新闻媒体刊播稿件数307件，省级共开辟报刊专版3个，残疾人专题广播节目1个，电视手语新闻栏目2个，电视公益广告片3个，报纸公益广告12个，省级残疾人事业新闻宣传促进会1个；地市级主要新闻媒体刊播稿件数2765件，共开辟地市级报刊专版137个，残疾人专题广播节目15个，电视手语新闻栏目14个，电视公益广告片23个，报纸公益广告79个，建立地市级新促会9个。

省级、地市级和县级公共图书馆设立盲文及盲人有声读物阅览室分别达到1个、17个和73个，共举办5个省级、81个地市级和369个县级残疾人文化周，共举办7次省级、73次地市级和157次县级残疾人文化艺术类比赛及展览；全年残疾人文化活动参与数量达3.5万人次。

七、体育

圆满承办了全国游泳锦标赛，申报16家残疾人自强健身示范点，我省残疾人运动健儿在仁川亚洲残运会上共夺得金牌33枚、银牌15枚、铜牌3枚，打破1项世界纪录，金牌和奖牌总数均位居全国各省区市第一。组织省级残疾人群众体育健身活动6次，参加人数2980人，建设残疾人群众体育活动示范点16个，配备残疾人体育健身指导员224人，组织省级残疾人体育比赛3次，参与的残疾人运动员278人次，省级残疾人体育训练基地2个，聘任教练员达32人。

各地深入开展残疾人体育工作。地市级组织残疾人体育活动96次，参加人数9081人次，设立残疾人体育示范点98个，配备残疾人体育健身指导员93人。

八、维权

认真做好《江苏省残疾人保障条例》的宣传贯彻，制定下发了《江苏省省级残疾人法律救助基金管理办法》和《残疾人法律救助工作站规范化建设指导意见》；省残疾人法律救助工作站正式开展法律咨询服务，开设了咨询热线。

全省有1个地市制定或修改了保障残疾人权益的规范性文件；全省县级以上人大执法检查或专题调研34次，政协视察和专题调研37次；全省开展普法宣传教育活动406次，参加人数4.1万人；举办法律工作者培训班79次，参加人数5346人。

截止到2014年底，全省建立残疾人法律救助协调机构79个；　建立残疾人法律救助工作站77个，办理案件136件；建立残疾人法律援助中心（工作站）110个，办理案件799件，有力地促进了法律救助和法律援助工作。

残疾人参政议政工作得到加强，各级残联协助人大代表、政协委员提出议案、建议、提案61件，办理议案、建议、提案101件。

无障碍建设法规、标准进一步完善。全省共有11个地市、12个县（市、区）出台了无障碍建设与管理办法；省本级、11个市、61个县（市、区）成立了无障碍建设领导协调组织；57个县（市、区）系统开展无障碍建设；为16884户贫困残疾人家庭实施了无障碍改造，全省开展无障碍检查159次，无障碍培训3661人次；为3.7万残疾人发放残疾人机动轮椅车燃油补贴。

各级残联共处理残疾人群众来信837件，接待残疾人群众来访7288人次，其中集体来访128批次、2467人次。

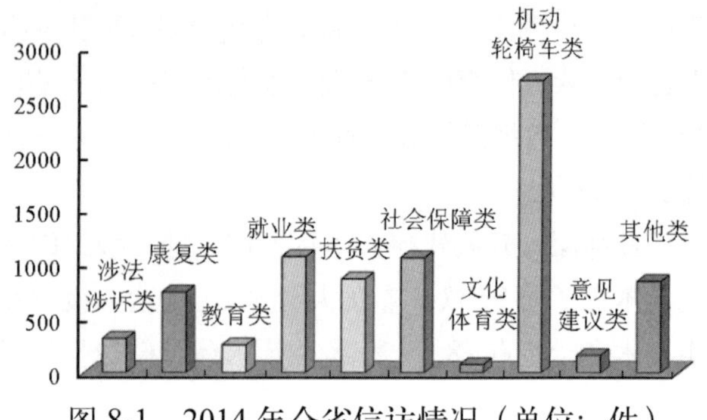

图 8-1　2014 年全省信访情况（单位：件）

九、组织建设

基层残疾人组织规范化建设进一步深入，残疾人工作者队伍建设力度进一步加大，城乡社区残疾人组织建设不断规范。认真开展了“基础管理建设年”活动，举办了两期全省残联理事长业务培训班，乡镇（街道）残联专职理事长配备率达到 80%，完成残联系统专兼职工作者状况和残联组织财物管理状况专项调查；完成省肢残协会和盲人协会法人注册登记工作。

全省 13 个地市级残联中，8 个领导班子配备了残疾人理事长或副理事长；105 个县级残联中，56 个县级残联机关配备了残疾人干部；在残疾人专职委员选聘方面，1344 个乡镇（街道）选聘残疾人专职委员 1469 名；15718 个村（含农村社区）和 4688 个城市社区选聘残疾人专职委员 20260 名。

全省省市县乡残联实有人员已达 4904 人。干部培训工作取得新进展，各级残联共举办培训班 351 期，培训机关干部、协会干部及残疾人专职委员 1.3 万人次，对提高残联系统干部队伍素质起到了重要作用。

全省共建立省级以下各类残疾人专门协会 570 个，其中盲人协会 116 个、聋人协会 116 个、肢残人协会 116 个、智力残疾人及亲友协会 106 个、精神残疾人及亲友协会 106 个，智力和精神残疾人及亲友协会合一的协会 10 个，各级各类残疾人专门协会活动日益活跃。

全省共建立助残社会组织 247 个，其中在民政部门注册的为 219 个，以残联为业务主管单位的 155 个。

十、服务设施建设

残疾人服务设施建设得到全面发展。截至 2014 年底，全省已竣工并投入使用的各级残疾人综合服务设施 75 个，总建设规模 44.0 万平方米，总投资 14.8 亿元；已竣工并投入使用的各级残疾人康复设施 50 个，总建设规模 12.0 万平方米，总投资 3.1 亿元；已竣工并投入使用的各级残疾人托养服务设施 48 个，总建设规模 22.8 万平方米，总投资 7.7 亿元。

十一、信息化建设

残疾人事业信息化建设得到加强。残疾人事业统计和状况监测工作科学规范，残疾人就业服务网、助残志愿者网站建设加快，残疾人工作业务信息数据库不断完善，为政策制定和执行评估提供了可靠依据；残疾人事业现代化研究取得新的成果。

2014 年全年省残联门户网站共录入信息 2317 条，大力宣传残疾人事业发展成就，加强政府信息公开工作。残疾人事业统计队伍建设进一步加强，全省各级残联共有 139 名专、兼职统计人员从事残疾人事业统计工作，统计人员业务素质培养普遍得到重视，省级残联举办培训班 1 期，30 人参加培训；地市级举办培训班 13 期，359 人参加了培训。

地方残联全面推进网站建设，目前省级残联、13 个地市级残联和 96 个县级残联已全部开通了公众服务网站，为残联系统网站集群服务奠定了基础，残联系统网上信息服务正在逐步覆盖全省；地方残联也积极举办各类信息工作培训班，2014 年省级及地市级残联共开设网站技术培训班 28 期，培训各级残联信息员达 1487 人次，各级残联共有 213 名专业技术人员从事信息化工作。

2014年浙江省残疾人事业发展统计公报

2014年是全面落实省残联六代会目标任务的开局之年。全省残联组织认真学习贯彻党的十八届三中、四中全会和省委全会精神，全面落实省委、省政府和中国残联、省残联主席团部署的重点任务，主动作为，扎实工作，改革创新，事业发展迈出新步伐，残疾人民生得到新实惠。

一、康复

2014年，通过实施一批重点康复工程，使22.2万名残疾人得到不同程度的康复服务。

截至2014年底，全省有33个市辖区和57个县（市）开展了社区康复工作，累计已建社区康复站的社区总数10082个，配备11345名社区康复协调员。全省已建社区康复示范站181个。

全省开展视力残疾康复机构总数达到21个，完成白内障复明手术34103例，其中为21518名贫困白内障患者提供资助；为1481名低视力患者配用助视器，培训低视力儿童家长391名，有效开展家庭康复训练。对2541名盲人进行定向行走训练。

全省开展听力语言康复机构共有28个，其中省级1个，地市级、县级27个。年度新收训聋儿581名，在训聋儿1050名；培训聋儿家长1194名；培训专业人员160人。

全省开展肢体残疾康复训练服务机构共有51个，其中，省级1个，地市级、县级50个；培训各级各类肢体残疾康复人员6296人次；共对6449名肢体残疾人实施康复训练；实施救助项目，资助601名脑瘫儿童进行机构康复训练，资助130名贫困肢体残疾儿童实施矫治手术。

全省开展智力残疾康复训练服务的机构共有47个，其中，省级1个，地市级、县级46个；培训各级各类智力残疾康复服务人员2249人次；共对2811名智力残疾人进行康复训练；实施救助项目，资助838名智力残疾儿童进行机构康复训练。

全省开展孤独症儿童康复训练机构共有67个，其中省级1个，地市级及以下66个；全省共有471名孤独症儿童在各级机构进行康复训练。

全省为残疾人减免费用供应辅助器具共28003件，其中装配假肢1206例、矫形器123例。

此外，全省共有50个县（市、区）的120个医疗卫生机构陆续开展残疾儿童筛查工作，年度新诊断0-6岁残疾儿童990人。

二、教育

2014年，积极推进《浙江省特殊教育提升计划（2014-2016）》的制定实施，残疾人得到更好的教育保障。全省有924名家庭困难的学龄前残疾儿童享受学前教育资助，其中有500名享受中央和省级专项资助。

全省已开办特殊教育普通高中学校（班）4个，在校生191人。残疾人中等职业学校（班）8个，在校生261人，毕业生124人，其中43人获得职业资格证书。全省有1034名在省内外就读的残疾大学生享受到学费、住宿费资助，其中，浙江特殊教育职业学院351名，省级财政安排资金836.9万元。全省有257名残疾人被普通高等院校录取，其中单招单考135人。浙江特殊教育职业学院正式建院，设大专27个班，中专10个班，当年毕业305人，目前在校生有862人。

三、就业

2014年，全省新增残疾人就业10854人，其中，新增集中就业1839人，新增按比例就业3811人，新增公益性岗位就业937人，个体就业及其它形式灵活就业3311人，新增辅助性就业956人。截至2014年底，全省城镇就业人数205933人；323903名农村残疾人在业，其中214765名残疾人从事农业生产劳动。

截至2014年底，全省共有残疾人职业培训基地333个，其中残联兴办114个，依托社会机构兴办219个。

四、社会保障

2014年新型农村和城镇居民基本养老保险统一合并实施，已有441342名城乡残疾居民参保，参保率85.00%，在60岁以下的参保残疾人中有104983名重度残疾人，其中95510人得到了政府的参保扶助，代缴补贴比例达到90.98%。有70064名非重度残疾人也享受了全额或部分代缴的优惠政策。领取养老金待遇的人数达到191877人。

城镇残疾职工参加养老保险172158人，参加医疗保险172415人，城镇27857人和农村153132人残疾人纳入最低生活保障范围；城镇集中供养残疾人和农村五保供养残疾人分别达到2058名和7540名；224038名和85086名符合条件的城乡残疾人分别享受了稳定的生活补贴和护理补贴。93270名城乡残疾人得到了其他救助救济。

残疾人托养服务工作规范推进，残疾人托养服务机构达到841个，共为22105名残疾人提供了托养服务。其中寄宿制托养服务机构388个；日间照料机构174个；综合性托养服务机构279个。全省已建庇护中心792家，16481人得到庇护照料服务。在以上机构中，共有3162名残疾人实现辅助性就业，237名残疾人实现了支持性就业。机构之外接受居家托养服务的残疾人达到74469人。全年共有3997名托养服务管理和服务人员接受了各级各类专业培训，其中接受国家级培训24人。

2014年，全省有116495名残疾人得到了无固定收入生活补助。

五、扶贫开发

2014年，全省有104234名贫困残疾人得到帮扶，接受实用技术培训的残疾人达19742人次。

康复扶贫贴息贷款扶持894名农村残疾人，残疾人扶贫基地达到1242个，安置8981名残疾人就业，扶持带动23378名残疾人。

完成3802户农村贫困残疾人危房改造，各地投入危房资金4631.87万元，4347名残疾人受益。

开展农村基层党组织助残扶贫帮扶工作，全省25万名低收入残疾人得到结对帮扶。其中“万村千乡市场工程”助残扶贫项目安置155名贫困残疾人就业，帮扶贫困残疾人创办63个村级农村店。

六、宣文体育

截至2014年底，共有省级电视手语新闻栏目1个，播出公益广告4个；地市级残疾人专题广播节目10个，电视手语新闻栏目10个，播出公益广告12个。

截至2014年底，省地县三级公共图书馆共设立盲文及盲人有声读物阅览室86个，共开展残疾人文化周活动219场次，共举办残疾人文化艺术类比赛及展览145次，共有各类残疾人艺术团体61个。

各地深入开展残疾人体育工作。组织省级残疾人群众体育健身活动4次，1230人次参加；建设省级残疾人群众体育活动示范点达到7个；培训省级残疾人体育健身指导员达到240人；组织省级残疾人体育比赛3次，参赛运动员达705人次；省级残疾人体育训练基地已达7个，组织地市级残疾人体育健身活动26次，6179人次参加；设立地市级残疾人群众体育活动示范点183个；培训地市级残疾人体育健身指导员1000人。

七、维权

2014年，制定或修改了关于残疾人的专门法规、规章省级1件、地市级1件；制定或修改保障残疾人权益的规范性文件省级1件、地市级8件、县级35件。县级以上人大进行《残疾人保障法》执法检查和专题调研52次；政协进行视察和专题调研70次，其中省政协开展残疾人就业专题调研1次。开展普法宣传教育活动248次，42312人参加；举办法律培训班73个，4716人参加。

截至2014年底，成立残疾人法律救助工作协调机构81个，建立残疾人法律救助工作站82个，办理案件390件，建立残疾人法律援助中心（工作站）95个，办理案件858件，有力地推动了法律救助和法律援助工作。

残疾人参政议政工作得到加强，各级残联协助人大代表、政协委员提出议案、建议、提案187件，办理议案、建议、提案187件。

无障碍建设法规、标准进一步完善。26个市、县、区系统开展无障碍建设；开展无障碍建设检查

379 次，无障碍培训 2101 人次；为 10079 个贫困残疾人家庭实施了无障碍改造；为 11912 名残疾人发放了残疾人机动轮椅车燃油补贴。

各级残联共处理残疾人群众来信 1399 件，接待残疾人群众来访 10484 人次，其中集体访 73 批次、795 人次。

八、组织建设

2014 年，全省有 10 个地市级残联在领导班子中配备了残疾人理事长或副理事长；62 个县级残联机关配备了残疾人干部；已建乡镇（街道）残联 1320 个，已建率达到 99.70%，选聘残疾人专职委员 1498 名；已建社区（村）残协 22948 个，已建率达到 93.60%，选聘残疾人专职委员 20775 名。

省市县乡残联实有人员 4594 人。各级残联共举办培训班 1240 期，培训机关干部、协会干部及残疾人专职委员 31270 人次。

共建立省级以下各类残疾人专门协会 454 个，市级专门协会已建比例为 85.45%；县级专门协会已建比例为 88.35%。

九、服务设施建设

截至 2014 年底，已竣工并投入使用的各级残疾人综合服务设施 84 个，总建设规模 476209 平方米，总投资 175065 万元；已竣工并投入使用的各级残疾人康复服务设施 25 个，总建设规模 145403 平方米，总投资 43480 万元；已竣工并投入使用的各级残疾人托养服务设施 18 个，总建设规模 101854 平方米，总投资 36977 万元。

十、信息化建设

2014 年，各级残联共有 97 名专、兼职统计人员从事残疾人事业统计工作。省级残联举办培训班 2 期，参加培训的人员共 112 人次；地市级举办培训班 19 期，参加培训的人员共 626 人次。

全省已开通 11 个地市级残联网站和 83 个县级残联网站。2014 年省级及地市级残联举办网站技术培训班 9 期，培训各级残联信息员达 590 人次。

综上所述，与 2013 年全省残疾人事业统计数据相比，2014 年全省残疾人康复工程完成情况较上年略有下降，其中人工耳蜗康复项目只完成了任务数的 78%，主要是由于我省人工耳蜗手术定点医院减少引起；残疾人助学工作成效显著，实际完成既定任务的 215.7%，这与省政府出台免除残疾大学生学费、住宿费政策密切相关；全面落实政府责任书要求，全省城镇残疾人新增就业数为 10521 人，超出任务数 23.8%；我省残疾人服务设施的建设规模和资金投入力度在全国走在前列，已竣工并投入使用的各级残疾人综合服务设施、康复服务设施、托养服务设施的总建设规模均占全国总数的 10%以上，但距离我省残疾人事业“十二五”规划目标（在全省建设 70 家康复和托养机构，新增床位 6000 张）还有一定的差距。

2014年安徽省残疾人事业发展统计公报

2014年，在省委、省政府的坚强领导下，在中国残联的大力支持下，省残联系统干部职工认真学习贯彻党的十八届、十八届三中、四中全会精神，全面落实中国残联“六代会”任务，努力为残疾人解难事、办好事，各项工作在新起点上取得了重要进展。

一、康复

2014年，我省残联深入开展残疾人康复工作，通过继续实施一批重点康复工程，使各类别残疾人得到不同程度的康复；加大残疾人康复服务机构建设力度；积极推进残疾人社区康复工作；大力宣传和普及康复知识。

在44个市辖区和57个县（市）开展了社区康复工作，累计已建社区康复站的社区总数4604个，配备12864名社区康复协调员。

73个县（市、区）的40个医疗卫生机构陆续开展残疾儿童筛查工作，年度新诊断0-6岁残疾儿童3524人。

全年完成白内障复明手术36657例；为14653名贫困白内障患者免费施行复明手术；为5552名低视力患者配用助视器，培训低视力儿童家长2048名，有效开展家庭康复训练。对11622名盲人进行定向行走训练。

推进听力语言康复机构规范化管理，完善基层服务网络。已建设省级听力语言康复机构1个，基层听力语言康复机构64个。年度新收训聋儿1802名，在训聋儿2697名；规范聋儿家长学校，开展家庭训练，共培训聋儿家长3719名；开展各级各类听力语言康复专业技术人员培训，共培训专业人员323人。

开展肢体残疾康复训练服务机构79个，其中，省级康复机构1个，地市级、县级康复机构78个；共对26722名肢体残疾者实施康复训练；实施救助项目资助2093名脑瘫儿童进行机构康复训练，资助491名贫困肢体残疾儿童实施矫治手术。

开展智力残疾康复训练服务机构75个，其中，省级康复机构1个，地市级、县级康复机构74个；培训各级各类智力残疾康复人员144人次；共对7427名智力残疾人进行康复训练；实施救助项目资助1937名智力残疾儿童进行机构康复训练，同时培训儿童家长。

大力推广“社会化、综合性、开放式”精神病防治康复工作。在94个市县开展精神病防治康复工作，对281248名精神病患者进行综合防治康复，监护率达到83.67%，显好率达到58.56%，社会参与率达到47.33%，肇事率0.02%；解除关锁26人；对73549名贫困精神病患者进行医疗救助。

建立了1个省级和77个基层孤独症儿童康复训练机构；1070名孤独症儿童在各级机构进行了康复训练。

加强残疾人辅助器具服务体系建设，深入开展辅助器具适配服务，为残疾人免费提供辅助器具28797件，其中装配假肢742例、矫形器1039例，验配助视器11700件。

二、教育

2014年，残疾人教育工作进展平稳，受特殊教育程度不断提高，受教育权得到了更好保障，进一步提高了残疾人素质和平等参与社会的能力。

我省实施残疾人事业专项彩票公益金助学项目，为300人次家庭经济困难的残疾儿童享受普惠性学前教育提供资助。另各地积极多渠道争取资金支持，对108名残疾儿童给予学前教育资助。

共有特殊教育普通高中学校3个，在校生503人；其中聋生493人；盲生10人。残疾人中等职业学校6个，在校生562人，毕业生196人，其中120人获得职业资格证书。有446名残疾人被普通高等院校录取。

三、就业

2014年，残疾人就业规模总体保持稳定。城镇新就业残疾人 8364 人，其中，集中就业残疾人 1604 人，按比例安排残疾人就业 1752 人，公益性岗位就业 226 人，个体就业及其它形式灵活就业 4558 人，辅助性就业 224 人。城镇就业人数 153006 人；763958 名农村残疾人在业，其中 628052 名残疾人从事农业生产劳动。

残疾人职业培训基地达到 82 个，其中残联兴办 23 个，依托社会机构兴办 59 个，其中 11697 人次城镇残疾人接受了职业培训。

盲人按摩事业稳定发展，按摩机构迅速增长。2014 年度培训盲人保健按摩人员 1214 名、盲人医疗按摩人员 119 名；保健按摩机构达到 411 个，医疗按摩机构达到 126 个；在专业技术职务资格评审中，分别有 38 人和 63 人通过盲人医疗按摩人员中级和初级职称评审。

四、社会保障

2014 年新型农村和城镇居民社会养老保险统一合并实施，已有 101.3 万名城乡残疾居民参保，参保率达 66.69%。在 60 周岁以下的参保残疾人中有 22.34 万名重度残疾人，其中 20.79 万人得到了政府的参保扶助，代缴补贴比例达到 93.06%。有 3.5 万名非重度残疾人也享受了全额或部分代缴的优惠政策。领取养老金待遇的人数达到 40.20 万人。

城镇残疾职工参加养老保险 7.26 万人，参加医疗保险 7.18 万人，城镇 12.66 万名和农村 43.24 万名残疾人纳入最低生活保障范围；城镇集中供养残疾人和农村五保供养残疾人分别达到 5787 名和 39243 名；545810 名和 7485 名符合条件的城乡残疾人分别享受了贫困残疾人生活补贴和重度残疾人护理补贴。55649 名城乡残疾人得到了其他救助救济。

残疾人托养服务工作规范推进，残疾人托养服务机构达到 84 个，共为 2394 名残疾人提供了托养服务。其中寄宿制托养服务机构 15 个，在以上机构中，共有 185 名残疾人实现辅助性就业，64 名残疾人实现了支持性就业。接受居家托养服务的残疾人达到 15551 人。全年共有 809 名托养服务管理和服务人员接受了各级各类专业培训，其中接受国家级培训 162 人。

五、扶贫开发

2014 年，残疾人扶贫开发成效显著，贫困残疾人生产、生活状况得到进一步的改善。152207 名贫困残疾人得到扶持，其中 31813 人通过扶贫开发实现脱贫；接受实用技术培训的残疾人达到 22685 人次。

康复扶贫贴息贷款扶持 1286 名农村残疾人,残疾人扶贫基地达到 122 个,安置 1998 名残疾人就业，扶持带动 2569 名残疾人。完成 6644 户农村贫困残疾人危房改造，各地投入危房资金 3712.70 万元，8104 名残疾人受益。

基层党组织助残扶贫项目帮扶 1031 名农村贫困残疾人，其中首次接受帮扶 552 人。“万村千乡市场工程”助残扶贫项目安置 266 名贫困残疾人就业，帮扶贫困残疾人创办 143 个村级农村店。

六、宣传文化

2014 年，全省残疾人事业宣文工作，紧紧围绕平等参与、融合发展的目标，精心组织以残疾人为主体、以助残为主题的系列大型活动，并进行密集报道，成绩显著。突出“保护听力、儿童优先”主题，组织开展第 15 次爱耳日宣教活动，龙舒宴集团等爱心企业捐赠款物 200 多万元，发送公益短信 300 万条，省领导陈先森以及卫生、民政、教育等部门负责同志一同出席现场活动。突出“比学赶帮、促进就业 ”主题，举办第七届残疾人职业技能大赛，又一批技术能手脱颖而出，副省长杨振超，省人社、民政、财政、教育、体育、统计和工青妇等部门负责同志陪同出席颁奖活动并观看才艺展示。突出“全民阅读、我不掉队”主题，联合静安集团举办首届残疾人“读书达人”竞赛，省领导童怀伟、王鹤龄等应邀为获奖选手亲自颁奖、鼓劲加油。突出“关心帮助残疾人，实现美好中国梦”主题，组织开展第 24 次助残日活动，全省 200 多名各级党政领导参加当天活动，送温暖、解难题、做表率。突出“自强不息、助残为乐”主题，组织全国自强模范与助残先进代表，开展省内巡回演讲，当地党政领导亲切看望各位成员，两千余名各界人士现场聆听报告会，乐观进取、催人泪下的故事引起社会积极反响。突出“爱我中华、挑战自我”为主题，协办第八届海峡两岸四地残疾人登黄山活动，数百名残疾人均由两倍以上青年志愿者全程陪护，游客驻足叹为观止，媒体蜂拥竞相报道，残健融合温暖两岸。

截至2014年底，我省共有省级电视手语新闻栏目1个；地市级残疾人专题广播节目9个，电视手语新闻栏目10个，播出公益广告10个。

省地县三级公共图书馆共设立盲文及盲人有声读物阅览室58个，共开展残疾人文化周活动346场次，共举办残疾人文化艺术类比赛及展览94次，共有各类残疾人艺术团体25个。

七、体育

2014年，我省首次与省运会一起在安庆同城举办第六届全省残运会，省委李锦斌副书记宣布开幕，省政府梁卫国副省长致开幕辞，中国残联负责同志到会祝贺，全社会把赞叹和关爱的目光又一次聚焦在特殊群体身上，把残疾人体育工作推向高潮。2014年，各地深入开展残疾人体育工作。培训省级残疾人体育健身指导员达到558人；组织省级残疾人体育比赛1次，参赛运动员达686人次；省级残疾人体育训练基地1个，地市级残疾人体育训练基地12个，省级特奥训练基地6个。组织地市级残疾人体育健身活动937次，34729人次参加；设立地市级残疾人群众体育活动示范点58个；培训地市级残疾人体育健身指导员494人。

八、维权

2014年，各级残联维权组织建设得到加强，残疾人事业法律法规体系进一步完善，残疾人维权工作全面开展。

为贯彻中国残联六代会精神，省委省政府两办印发《关于促进残疾人家庭增收，加快实现小康步伐的意见》，并被国务院残工委全文转发。《意见》针对残疾人特殊困难，做出制度性特惠安排。

截至2014年底，我省共制定或修改保障残疾人权益的规范性文件地市级2件、县级3件。县级以上人大进行《残疾人保障法》执法检查和专题调研36次；政协进行视察和专题调研36次。开展普法宣传教育活动324次，20906人参加；举办法律培训班65个，2860人参加。

我省共成立残疾人法律救助工作协调机构19个，建立残疾人法律救助工作站6个，办理案件16件，建立残疾人法律援助中心（工作站）119个，办理案件1743件，有力地推动了法律救助和法律援助工作。

残疾人参政议政工作得到加强，各级残联协助人大代表、政协委员提出议案、建议、提案52件，办理议案、建议、提案57件。

无障碍建设法规、标准进一步完善。共出台了8个省、地市、县级无障碍建设与管理法规、规章和规范性文件；77个市、县（区）系统开展无障碍建设；开展无障碍建设检查144次，无障碍培训548人次；为1574个贫困残疾人家庭实施了无障碍改造；为27651名残疾人发放了残疾人机动轮椅车燃油补贴。

各级残联共处理残疾人群众来信1152件，接待残疾人群众来访12292人次，其中集体访10批次、106人次。

九、组织建设

2014年，我省10个地市级残联在领导班子中配备了残疾人理事长或副理事长；32个县级残联机关配备了残疾人干部；已建乡镇（街道）残联1522个，已建率达到83.53%，选聘残疾人专职委员1457名；已建社区（村）残协15699个，已建率达到93.88%，选聘残疾人专职委员17311名。

省市县乡残联实有人员已达3657人。各级残联共举办培训班1351期，培训机关干部、协会干部及残疾人专职委员31183人次。

全省共建立省级以下各类残疾人专门协会546个，市级专门协会已建比例为93.75%；县级专门协会已建比例为87.10%。全省共建立助残社会组织20个，其中在民政部门注册18个，以残联为业务主管单位的13个。

十、服务设施建设

2014年，残疾人服务设施建设得到全面发展。

截至2014年底，全省已竣工并投入使用的各级残疾人综合服务设施74个，总建设规模152812平方米，总投资30574万元；已竣工并投入使用的各级残疾人康复设施10个，总建设规模13924平方米，总投资 13331 万元；已竣工并投入使用的各级残疾人托养服务设施 5 个，总建设规模 12900 平方米，总投资 1881 万元。

十一、信息化建设

2014 年，信息化建设进一步加强。全省残疾人基础数据实现与中国残联二代证系统数据交换，并建立数据交换机制，定期进行数据更新，为我省开发惠残民生工程信息系统提供精确有效基础数据。

截至 2014 年底，全省共有 16 个地市、82 个县级残联开通网站，为向残疾人提供精准服务和实施网上政务信息公开提供支持和保障。

2014年福建省残疾人事业发展统计公报

2014年以来，全省残疾人工作在省委、省政府的正确领导和中国残联的精心指导下，紧紧围绕党中央、国务院和省委、省政府的工作大局及对残疾人事业的部署精神，坚持稳中求进，突出改革创新，积极推进残疾人事业科学发展跨越发展取得新成效，各项事业在新起点上取得了重要进展。

一、康复

2014年，通过实施中央和省级重点康复项目，以及各地实施的配套项目，使11.9万名残疾人得到康复服务，大力推进残疾人“人人享有康复服务”。

全年完成白内障复明手术1.58万例，其中为1.18万名贫困白内障患者免费施行复明手术。为827名低视力患者配用助视器；培训低视力儿童家长359名，有效开展家庭康复训练。对3515名盲人进行定向行走训练。

加强省级聋儿康复机构建设，完善聋儿康复网络。年度新收训聋儿552名，在训聋儿共935名；规范聋儿家长学校，开展家庭训练，共对820名聋儿进行了听力语言康复训练；规范聋儿家长学校，开展家庭训练，共培训聋儿家长1172名；加强聋儿康复人才队伍建设，培养各类专业人员129人。

大力推广“社会化、综合性、开放式”精神病防治康复工作。在84个市县开展精神病防治康复工作，对12.1万名重性精神病患者进行综合防治康复，监护率达到86.05%，显好率达到72.80%，社会参与率达到53.66%，肇事率0.08%；解除关锁64人；对1.18万名贫困精神病患者进行医疗救助。建立了1个省级孤独症儿童康复训练机构；1164名孤独症儿童在各级机构进行了康复训练。

深入开展辅助器具供应服务，全面推进普及型假肢装配。截止到2014年底，为残疾人减免费用供应辅助器具2.1万件，其中装配假肢436例、矫形器301例，验配助视器831件，为残疾人提供更趋个性化的服务。

全省开展肢体残疾康复训练服务的机构达78个，培训各级各类肢体残疾康复人员182人次；全省共对9113名肢体残疾人实施康复训练；实施救助项目资助1542名脑瘫儿童进行机构康复训练，资助135名贫困肢体残疾儿童实施矫治手术。

全年开展智力残疾康复训练服务的机构达61个；对2876名智力残疾儿童进行了康复训练，其中：智力残疾儿童机构康复训练900人，智力残疾儿童社区、家庭康复1414人。

在26个市辖区和56个县（市）开展了社区康复工作，累计已建社区康复站的社区总数3877个，配备10504名社区康复协调员。

积极配合卫生等部门开展残疾儿童筛查工作。2014年，全省新诊断0-6岁残疾儿童1262名。积极开展儿童残疾预防宣传，共发放宣传材料5.59万份。

二、教育

已开办特殊教育普通高中班（部）26个，在校生472人，其中聋生419人、盲生53人。残疾人中等职业学校（班）15个，在校生59人，毕业生21人，其中11人获得职业资格证书。

扎实做好适龄未入学残疾儿童实名统计，推动教育部门对1461名未入学残疾儿童少年落实“一人一案”。认真做好残疾考生高招录取工作，有291名残疾人被普通高等院校录取。

实施专项彩票公益金助学项目、交通银行残疾青少年助学计划、残疾青壮年人扫盲试点等，为8000多名残疾学生提供资助，义务教育入学率达90%以上；积极推动残疾儿童幼儿园建设，让残疾少年儿童享受同等教育权。

三、就业

全省城镇新增就业1.22万人。残疾人职业培训基地达到323个，其中残联兴办200个，依托社会机构兴办123个；实名培训近2.2万人，其中9421人次城镇残疾人接受了职业培训。全省残保金申报总额达 8.69 亿元（含厦门），年比增 9.16%。

开展城镇百万残疾人就业工程、“福乐种养基地”等项目，共有 1.8 万名残疾人获得就业支持，农村实用技术培训近 1.2 万人次。成功举办第五届全省残疾人职业技能竞赛；省人大、省政协均专题组织残疾人就业工作视察、调研，全省设区市人大内司委主任工作会专题研讨残疾人按比例就业工作，为我省首次。

盲人按摩事业稳定发展，按摩机构迅速增长。2014 年度培训盲人保健按摩人员 542 名、盲人医疗按摩人员 105 名。保健按摩机构达到 329 个，医疗按摩机构达到 10 个。在专业技术职务资格评审中，分别有 53 人和 74 人通过盲人医疗按摩人员中级和初级职称评审。

四、扶贫

2014 年，残疾人扶贫开发成效显著，贫困残疾人生产生活状况得到进一步改善。3.07 万名贫困残疾人得到扶持，其中 1.7 万人通过扶贫开发实现脱贫。接受实用技术培训的残疾人达到 1.57 万人次。

康复扶贫贴息贷款扶持 955 名农村残疾人，残疾人扶贫基地达到 199 个，安置 4413 名残疾人就业，扶持带动 4605 名残疾人。

基层党组织助残扶贫项目帮扶 1241 名农村贫困残疾人，其中首次接受帮扶 1028 人。“万村千乡市场工程”助残扶贫项目安置 935 名贫困残疾人就业，帮扶贫困残疾人创办 34 个村级农村店。

开展残疾人十年扶贫纲要执行情况检查；实施残疾人危房改造工程，为 4200 户贫困残疾人家庭提供补贴。

五、社会保障

建立了重度残疾人护理补贴制度，制定了实施办法。我省成为全国 8 个实现残疾人两项“补贴”制度全覆盖的省份之一。落实重度残疾人生活和医疗救助提标扩面，统一城乡补助标准，28.2 万人得到救助。

2014 年新型农村和城镇居民社会养老保险统一合并实施，已有 66.2 万名城乡残疾居民参保，参保率 92%。

残疾人托养服务工作规范推进，残疾人托养服务机构达到 125 个，共为 2839 名残疾人提供了托养服务。机构之外接受居家托养服务的残疾人达到 2.5 万人。全年共有 960 名托养服务管理和服务人员接受了各级各类专业培训，其中接受国家级培训 40 人。

六、宣传文化

开展第五次全省自强模范及助残先进评选表彰，举办 5 场自强模范和助残先进事迹报告会；采用多元化方式扩大残疾人事业宣传，在《福建日报》等各类媒体宣传报道残疾人事业 200 余篇；编印《福建省残疾人政策服务手册》2.5 万本，广泛宣传党和政府的惠残政策。

举办“第四届闽台残疾人文化周”，开展了研讨会、手工艺作品展、残疾人艺术团走进武夷山、上杭、厦门等地交流演出等系列活动，56 名台湾嘉宾赴闽参加；省残疾人艺术团开展全省公益巡演活动 12 场。

截至 2014 年底，省市县三级公共图书馆共设立盲文及盲人有声读物阅览室 44 个，开展残疾人文化周活动共 52 场次，举办残疾人文化艺术类比赛及展览共 60 次，有各类残疾人艺术团体 5 个。

七、体育

实施残疾人“自强健身工程”，发展残疾人群众性体育，成功举办第七届全省残疾人运动会。有 12 名残疾人运动员代表国家参加韩国仁川亚残运会，取得 9 金、4 银、5 铜及打破 1 项世界纪录、3 项亚洲纪录的历届最好成绩。

在全省范围建设“福乐健身站”，残疾人体育健身指导员、分级员等队伍得到发展，全省残疾人体育工作新机制已初步建立。组织省级残疾人群众体育健身活动 30 次，3000 人次参加；建设省级残疾人群众体育活动示范点达 30 个；培训省级残疾人体育健身指导员达到 212 人；省级残疾人体育训练基地已达 15 个，组织地市级残疾人体育健身活动 55 次，2719 人次参加；设立地市级残疾人群众体育活动示范点 43 个；培训地市级残疾人体育健身指导员 1397 人。

八、维权

各级残联维权组织建设得到加强，残疾人事业法律法规体系进一步完善，残疾人维权工作全面开展。

2014年，县级以上人大进行《残疾人保障法》执法检查和专题调研18次；政协进行视察和专题调研21次。开展普法宣传教育活动195次，1.27万人参加；举办法律培训班39个，5243人参加。

截至2014年底，成立残疾人法律救助工作协调机构46个，建立残疾人法律救助工作站45个，办理案件157件，建立残疾人法律援助中心（工作站）85个，办理案件578件，有力地推动了法律救助和法律援助工作。

残疾人参政议政工作得到加强，各级残联协助人大代表、政协委员提出议案、建议、提案50件，办理议案、建议、提案63件。

无障碍建设法规、标准进一步完善。共出台了24个省、地市、县级无障碍建设与管理法规、规章和规范性文件；48个市、县、区系统开展无障碍建设；开展无障碍建设检查214次，无障碍培训1375人次；为6196个贫困残疾人家庭实施了无障碍改造；为1.52万名残疾人发放了残疾人机动轮椅车燃油补贴。

各级残联共处理残疾人群众来信1095件，接待残疾人群众来访6431人次，其中集体访14批次、175人次。

九、组联

2014年，全部（9个）地市级残联在领导班子中配备了残疾人理事长或副理事长；已建乡镇（街道）残联1105个，选聘残疾人专职委员1197名；已建社区（村）残协1.6万个，选聘残疾人专职委员1.61万名。

省市县乡残联实有人员已达2654人。各级残联共举办培训班679期，培训机关干部、协会干部及残疾人专职委员1.74万人次。

共建立省级以下各类残疾人专门协会454个，市级专门协会已建比例为100%；县级专门协会已建比例为95.06%。

十、服务设施

制定省委、省政府为民办实事“福乐家园”建设项目实施方案，做好2014年10所省级公办“福乐家园”申报、评审工作。通过评选确定10个省级公办“福乐家园”建设项目，按项目进度下达省级补助资金1670万元。

截至2014年底，已竣工并投入使用的各级残疾人综合服务设施79个，总建设规模16.45万平方米；已竣工并投入使用的各级残疾人康复设施210个，总建设规模1.99万平方米；已竣工并投入使用的各级残疾人托养服务设施40个，总建设规模4.35万平方米。

十一、信息化建设

建立与中国残联残疾人二代证数据库的实时接口，继续推进福建省残联综合信息服务平台项目建设，省委、省政府为民办实事“助残工程”项目全部实现网上申报、网上审批，数据随时核查、统计。

注重加强与纵向、横向部门(单位)的沟通协作，实现数据交换共享。2014年，我省与省城乡居民养老保险中心实现了全省所有残疾人参加养老保险的数据交换，获得全省残疾人参保数据。

充分发挥省残联门户网站作用，省级发布信息2958条，网页年浏览量逾116万人次，在残疾人事业新闻宣传、政务公开、信息服务等方面发挥了重要作用。推行电子政务应用，发送政务短信6220条，通过政务邮箱向各级残联发送电子文件4972封。9个地市级残联网站和84个县级残联网站已全部开通，残联系统网上信息服务逐步覆盖全省。省、市级残联共开办网站技术培训班12期，培训各级残联信息员达331人次。

统计队伍建设进一步加强，各级残联共有109名专、兼职统计人员从事残疾人事业统计工作，统计人员业务素质培养普遍得到重视，省级残联举办培训班1期，参加培训的人员达到60人次；地市级举办培训班8期，参加培训的人员达到155人次。

2014 年江西省残疾人事业发展统计公报

2014 年，在省委省政府的正确领导下，全省残联认真学习贯彻党的十八届三中、四中全会、习总书记系列讲话和省委十三届九次、十次全会精神，围绕“发展升级、小康提速、绿色崛起、实干兴赣”十六字方针，较好地完成了本年度的工作任务，全省残疾人事业得到了快速发展。

一、残疾人康复工作稳步提升

在 23 个市辖区和 79 个县（市）开展了社区康复工作，累计已建社区康复站的社区总数 3951 个，配备 1.3 万名社区康复协调员。

28 个县的 41 个医疗卫生机构陆续开展残疾儿童筛查工作，年度新诊断 0-6 岁残疾儿童 2653 人。

开展视力残疾康复机构总数达到 10 个，完成白内障复明手术 1.9 万例；为 1418 名贫困白内障患者免费施行复明手术；为 2917 名低视力患者配用助视器，培训低视力儿童家长 680 名，有效开展家庭康复训练。对 4700 名盲人进行定向行走训练。　推进听力语言康复机构规范化管理，完善基层服务网络。已建设省级听力语言康复机构 1 个，基层听力语言康复机构 24 个。年度新收训聋儿 556 名，在训聋儿 837 名；规范聋儿家长学校，开展家庭训练，共培训聋儿家长 835 名；开展各级各类听力语言康复专业技术人员培训，共培训专业人员 103 人。

开展肢体残疾康复训练服务机构达 25 个，其中，省级康复机构 1 个，地市级、县级康复机构 24 个；培训各级各类肢体残疾康复人员 205 人次；全国共对 1 万肢体残疾人实施康复训练；实施救助项目资助 875 名脑瘫儿童进行机构康复训练，资助 170 名贫困肢体残疾儿童实施矫治手术。 开展宣传普及教育，为麻风患者回归社会营造良好社会氛围。

开展智力残疾康复训练服务的机构 20 个。其中，省级康复机构 1 个，地市级、县级康复机构 19 个；培训各级各类智力残疾康复人员 120 人次；全国共对 3354 名智力残疾人进行康复训练；实施救助项目资助 470 名智力残疾儿童进行机构康复训练，同时培训儿童家长。

大力推广“社会化、综合性、开放式”精神病防治康复工作。在 101 个市县开展精神病防治康复工作，对 18.3 万名重性精神病患者进行综合防治康复，监护率达到 80.32%，显好率达到 57.01%，社会参与率达到 42.27%，肇事率 1.06%；解除关锁 226 人；对 2.1 万名贫困精神病患者进行医疗救助。建立了 1 个省级孤独症儿童康复训练机构；395 名孤独症儿童在各级机构进行了康复训练。

加强残疾人辅助器具服务体系建设，深入开展辅助器具供应服务，为残疾人减免费用供应辅助器具 1.8 万件，其中装配假肢 926 例、矫形器 146 例，验配助视器 3666 件。

二、残疾人教育工作扶持力度打断加大

实施残疾人事业专项彩票公益金助学项目，为 300 人次家庭经济困难的残疾儿童享受普惠性学前教育提供资助。各地也积极多渠道争取资金支持，对 2 名残疾儿童给予学前教育资助。

共有特殊教育普通高中班（部）4 个，在校生 129 人。其中聋生 129 人。残疾人中等职业学校（班）3 个，在校生 91 人，毕业生 39 人，其中 36 人获得职业资格证书。有 242 名残疾人被普通高等院校录取。

三、残疾人就业工作循序渐进

2014 年，残疾人就业规模总体保持稳定。城镇新就业残疾人 1 万人，其中，集中就业残疾人 3132 人，按比例安排残疾人就业 950 人，公益性岗位就业 699 人，个体就业及其它形式灵活就业 5174 人，辅助性就业 214 人。城镇就业人数 15.3 万人；55.9 万名农村残疾人在业，其中 42 万名残疾人从事农业生产劳动。

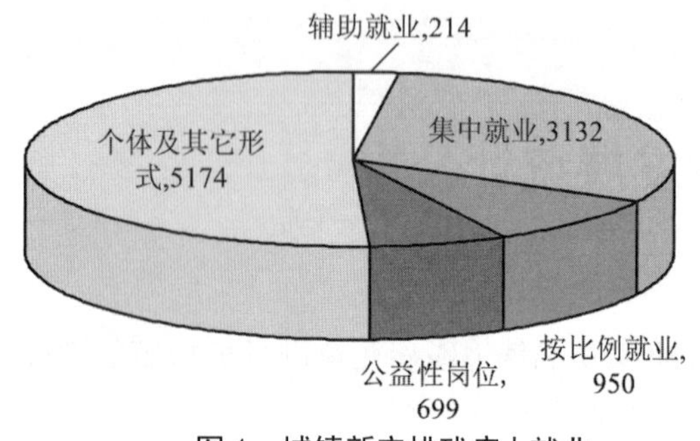

图 1　城镇新安排残疾人就业

残疾人职业培训基地达到 229 个，其中残联兴办 46 个，依托社会机构兴办 183 个，其中 4788 人次城镇残疾人接受了职业培训。

盲人按摩事业稳定发展，按摩机构迅速增长。2014 年度培训盲人保健按摩人员 747 名、盲人医疗按摩人员 291 名；保健按摩机构达到 542 个，医疗按摩机构达到 72 个；在专业技术职务资格评审中，分别有 43 人和 78 人通过盲人医疗按摩人员中级和初级职称评审。

四、残疾人社会保障进一步完善

2014 年新型农村和城镇居民社会养老保险统一合并实施，已有 58.2 万名城乡残疾居民参保，参保率 73.39%，在 60 岁以下的参保残疾人中有 7.4 万名重度残疾人，其中 7.4 万人得到了政府的参保扶助，代缴补贴比例达到 99.53%。有 5.9 万名非重度残疾人也享受了全额或部分代缴的优惠政策。领取养老金待遇的人数达到 30.6 万人。

城镇残疾职工参加养老保险 4.9 万人，参加医疗保险 4.9 万人，城镇 10.7 万人和农村 25.8 万人残疾人纳入最低生活保障范围；城镇集中供养残疾人和农村五保供养残疾人分别达到 1.1 万名和 2.6 万名；14.6 万名符合条件的城乡残疾人分别享受了稳定的生活补贴和护理补贴。5.4 万名城乡残疾人得到了其他救助救济。

残疾人托养服务工作规范推进，残疾人托养服务机构达到 21 个，共为 1454 名残疾人提供了托养服务。其中寄宿制托养服务机构 10 个；日间照料机构 3 个；综合性托养服务机构 8 个。在以上机构中，共有 407 名残疾人实现辅助性就业，375 名残疾人实现了支持性就业。机构之外接受居家托养服务的残疾人达到 1.4 万人。全年共有 3966 名托养服务管理和服务人员接受了各级各类专业培训，其中接受国家级培训 5 人。

五、残疾人扶贫工作显著提升

2014 年，残疾人扶贫开发成效显著，贫困残疾人生产生活状况得到进一步改善。4.1 万名贫困残疾人得到扶持，其中 4.7 万人通过扶贫开发实现脱贫；接受实用技术培训的残疾人达到 0.8 万人次。

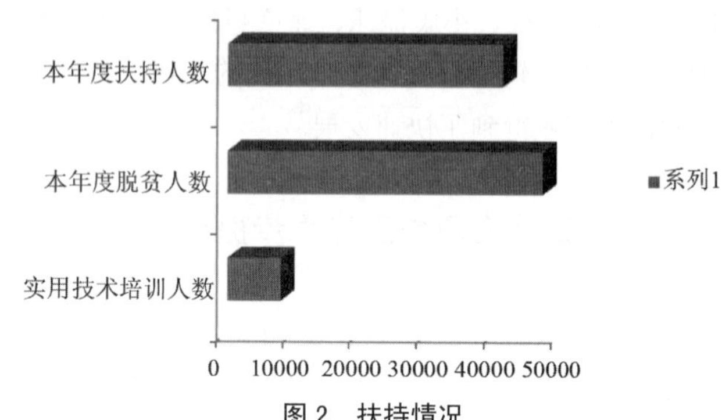

图 2　扶持情况

康复扶贫贴息贷款扶持 3517 名农村残疾人，残疾人扶贫基地达到 167 个，安置 2269 名残疾人就业，扶持带动 2927 名残疾人。

完成 2413 户农村贫困残疾人危房改造，各地投入危房资金 1225.4 万元，2498 名残疾人受益。

基层党组织助残扶贫项目帮扶 5038 名农村贫困残疾人，其中首次接受帮扶 1084 人。“万村千乡市场工程”助残扶贫项目安置 79 名贫困残疾人就业，帮扶贫困残疾人创办 30 个村级农村店。

六、残疾人维权工作推进力度加大

2014 年，制定或修改了关于残疾人的专门法规、规章地市级 2 件；制定或修改保障残疾人权益的规范性文件地市级 5 件、县级 11 件。县级以上人大进行《残疾人保障法》执法检查和专题调研 30 次；政协进行视察和专题调研 25 次。开展普法宣传教育活动 136 次，1 万人参加；举办法律培训班 42 个，2083 人参加。

截至 2014 年底，成立残疾人法律救助工作协调机构 34 个，建立残疾人法律救助工作站 33 个，办理案件 110 件，建立残疾人法律援助中心（工作站）97 个，办理案件 723 件，有力地推动了法律救助和法律援助工作。

残疾人参政议政工作得到加强，各级残联协助人大代表、政协委员提出议案、建议、提案62件，办理议案、建议、提案40件。

无障碍建设法规、标准进一步完善。共出台了7个省、地市、县级无障碍建设与管理法规、规章和规范性文件；72个市、县、区系统开展无障碍建设；开展无障碍建设检查33次，无障碍培训115人次；为1006个贫困残疾人家庭实施了无障碍改造；为2万名残疾人发放了残疾人机动轮椅车燃油补贴。

各级残联共处理残疾人群众来信883件，接待残疾人群众来访5617人次，其中集体访57批次、724人次。

七、宣传文化、体育工作进一步加强

截至2014年底，共有省级残疾人专题广播节目2个，电视手语新闻栏目1个；地市级残疾人专题广播节目3个，电视手语新闻栏目5个，播出公益广告9个。

省地县三级公共图书馆共设立盲文及盲人有声读物阅览室273个，共开展残疾人文化周活动82场次，共举办残疾人文化艺术类比赛及展览31次，共有各类残疾人艺术团体9个。

各地深入开展残疾人体育工作。组织省级残疾人群众体育健身活动3次，621人次参加；建设省级残疾人群众体育活动示范点达到35个；培训省级残疾人体育健身指导员达到936人；组织省级残疾人体育比赛1次，参赛运动员达210人次；省级残疾人体育训练基地已达2个，组织地市级残疾人体育健身活动15次，1045人次参加；设立地市级残疾人群众体育活动示范点4个；培训地市级残疾人体育健身指导员13人。

八、残疾人组织建设工作合理调配效果明显

8个地市级残联在领导班子中配备了残疾人理事长或副理事长；51个县级残联机关配备了残疾人干部；已建乡镇（街道）残联1632个，已建率达到98.19%，选聘残疾人专职委员3387名；已建社区（村）残协1.8万个，已建率达到99.48%，选聘残疾人专职委员1.4万名。

省市县乡残联实有人员已达4361人。各级残联共举办培训班1138期，培训机关干部、协会干部及残疾人专职委员1.7万人次。

共建立省级以下各类残疾人专门协会445个，市级专门协会已建比例为100.00%；县级专门协会已建比例为77.78%。全国共建立助残社会组织12个，其中在民政部门注册的为5个，以残联为业务主管单位的2个。

九、残疾人工作信息化建设积极推进

统计队伍逐年增强。各级残联共有132名专、兼职统计人员从事残疾人事业统计工作，统计人员业务素质培养得到大幅提升，省级残联举办培训班1期，培训人员30人次；地市级举办培训班13期，培训人员223人次。

地方残联全面推进网站建设。目前省残联已开通了公众服务网站，有6个设区市残联网站和37个县级残联网站也已开通，为今后残联系统网站集群服务奠定了基础，残联系统网上信息服务正在逐步覆盖全省。设区市残联积极举办各类信息工作培训班，2014年省残联及设区市残联开设网站技术培训班11期，培训各级残联信息员183人次。

各级残联共有163名专业技术人员从事信息化工作；省级残联共建立局域网1个，网上办公（OA）系统1个。

十、综合服务设施不断完善

截至2014年底，已竣工并投入使用的各级残疾人综合服务设施80个，总建设规模5.8万平方米，总投资1.4万元；已竣工并投入使用的各级残疾人康复设施4个，总建设规模3.2万平方米，总投资6940元；已竣工并投入使用的各级残疾人托养服务设施1个，总建设规模1.1万平方米，总投资3500元。

十一、民生工程投入逐年增加

2014年，我省残疾人民生工程的推进速度大幅提升，为12.7万名残疾人建立康复档案，为0.9万名残疾人配发了假肢等辅助器具，为2.1万名精神病患者提供了免费服药，为685名贫困残疾儿

童提供了抢救性康复救助，为 0.1 万名残疾人提供了免费白内障复明手术；全年共为 0.4 万名残疾人提供了公益性岗位，1.2 万名农家书屋残疾人管理员，为 0.8 万名残疾人提供了相应的职能技术培训服务。

2014年度山东省残疾人事业统计公报

2014年，全省各级残联组织以全面推进全省残疾人“整体赶平均、共同奔小康”行动计划为总抓手，开拓创新、积极作为，坚持不懈抓落实，立足长远打基础，圆满完成了各项工作任务。

一、康复

残疾儿童康复。继续抓好0－6岁残疾儿童抢救性康复救助政策的落实，实现了残疾儿童康复由项目化实施到制度性安排的根本性转变。全年完成聋儿听力语言康复训练1999人，脑瘫儿童机构康复训练3721人，智障儿童机构康复训练2580人。肢残儿童社区、家庭康复训练1668人，智障儿童社区、家庭康复训练4912人。对842名贫困肢残儿童实施矫治手术，孤独症儿童机构内在训1678人，救助贫困孤独症儿童611人。培训低视力儿童家长567人，聋儿家长2415人。全省139个医疗卫生机构开展了残疾儿童筛查工作，本年度新诊断0-6岁残疾儿童4028人。举办儿童残疾预防宣传活动533次，发放宣传材料26.5万份。残疾儿童家长学校98个，本年度开展各类活动182次，4932名残疾儿童家长参与了活动。

各类残疾康复项目。全年完成白内障复明手术5.1万例，为2.1万贫困白内障患者免费实施复明手术。低视力患者配用助视器5041人，盲人进行定向行走训练6451人。成年听力残疾人康复服务784人，成年肢体残疾人社区、家庭康复训练4.5万人，成年智力残疾人社区、家庭康复训练2417人。精神病患者通过服药、住院、家庭病床接受治疗19.8万人，其中2.9万贫困精神病患者得到医疗救助。供应各类辅助器具8.7万件，假肢装配1057例，矫形器装配589例。

康复机构和康复人才培养：截止2014年底，全省有视力残疾康复机构101个，听力语言康复机构83个，肢体残疾康复机构282个,智力残疾康复机构132个，孤独症儿童康复训练机构126个，辅助器具供应服务机构81个。全省158个县（市、区）（含开发区）开展社区康复工作，累计建立社区康复站4.2万个，配备社区康复协调员4.9万人。全省各级康复机构在岗人员2.7万人，本年度培训康复管理人员3269人，业务人员6659人，社区康复协调员1.9万人。

二、教育培训就业

义务教育：截止2014年底，全省未入学适龄残疾儿童少年总数5942人，其中视力残疾191人，听力残疾238人，言语残疾191人，肢体残疾1915人，智力残疾2210人，精神残疾332人，多重残疾865人。

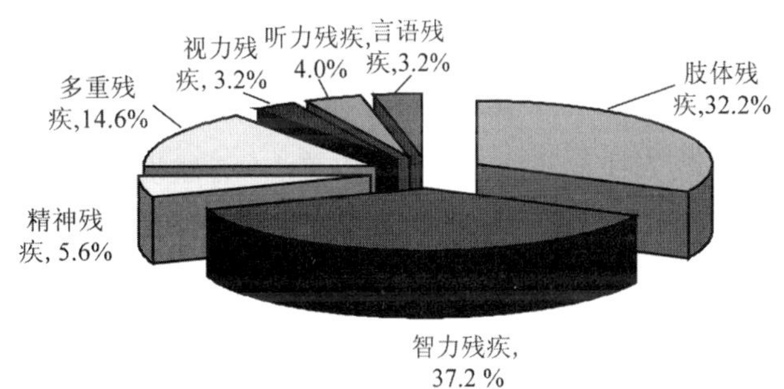

图1 2014年底全省未入学适龄各类残疾儿童分类

高中和高等教育：全省有特殊教育普通高中（班）23所，其中：盲普通高中（班）2所，聋普通高中（班）15所，其他普通高中（班）6所，在校生共567人。残疾人中等职业教育机构17个，在校生1719人，2014年新招生627人，毕业438人，其中有402人获得职业资格证书。2014年全省共有347名残疾学生高考达到大学录取分数线，被录取322人，其中：本科录取183人，专科（高职）录取139人。

就业:本年度全省城镇新安排残疾人就业17469人，其中：集中就业残疾人5119人，按比例安排残疾人就业6337人，个体及其它形式就业5166人，公益性岗位就业254人，辅助性就业593人。城镇实际在业残疾人24.0万人，农村138.7万残疾人实现稳定就业，其中从事农业生产劳动109.9万人。

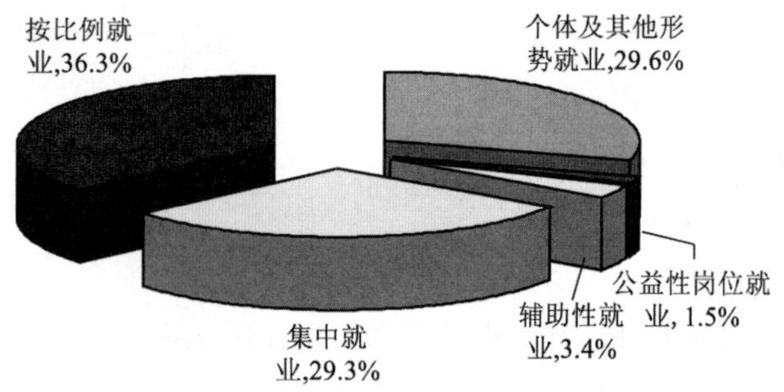

图 2　2014 年全省城镇新安排残疾人就业比例

职业培训：全省共有职业培训基地 845 个,其中残联兴办 107 个,依托社会机构兴办 738 个，本年度城镇职业培训 2.1 万人次。

盲人按摩：全省有盲人保健按摩机构 1236 个，医疗按摩机构 79 个。2014 年共培训盲人保健按摩人员 755 人、盲人医疗按摩人员 310 人。9 人通过医疗按摩人员中级职称评审，35 人通过初级职称评审。

三、扶贫和社会保障

扶贫：2014 年全省共扶持贫困残疾人户 8.7 万户，扶持贫困残疾人 13.7 万人，脱贫 6.3 万人。组建结对帮扶单位 10427 个，结对帮扶 20711 人。已建残疾人扶贫基地 782 个，安置 1.6 万残疾人就业，扶持带动了 3.7 万户残疾人。各级共投入经费 1405.4 万元，对 4.4 万残疾人进行实用技术培训。全年完成农村贫困残疾人危房改造 1986 户，受益残疾人 2271 人。

社会保障：全省城镇残疾职工参加养老保险 18.0 万人、医疗保险 17.1 万人。134.9 万残疾居民参加了城乡社会养老保险。城镇残疾人中，7.7 万人纳入最低生活保障，集中供养 7327 人，享受其他救助救济 2.3 万人。农村残疾人中，37.7 万人纳入最低生活保障，五保供养 3.1 万人，享受其他救助救济 7.3 万人。落实残疾人生活补贴和护理补贴制度，全省共有 26.7 万残疾人享受生活补贴，8.1 万人享受护理补贴。

托养：全省有残疾人托养服务机构 499 个，其中：寄宿制托养机构 192 个、日间照料托养机构 84 个、综合托养机构 223 个，共托养残疾人 1.7 万人。2.8 万残疾人享受居家托养服务。

四、政策法规与维权

法规、政策和执法：2014 年，市级制定或修改关于残疾人的专门法规、规章 1 个。市、县两级残联参与制定或修改保障残疾人权益的规范性文件 67 个。县级及以上人大开展执法检查或专题调研 58 次，政协视察和专题调研 35 次。

法制宣传：全省开展普法宣传教育活动 248 次，参加人数 1.9 万人次。开展法律培训班 124 次，培训 5743 人次。

法律救助：全省已建立残疾人法律救助协调机构 71 个。建立残疾人法律救助工作站 69 个，办理案件 171 件。 建立残疾人法律援助中心（工作站）143 个，办理案件 921 件。

无障碍建设：全省累计出台 31 个无障碍建设与管理法规或政府令，56 个市、县系统开展无障碍建设，开展无障碍专项检查 113 次。完成贫困残疾人家庭无障碍改造 1.1 万户。发放残疾人机动轮椅车燃油补贴 2.2 万人。

信访：各级残联共处理残疾人来信 1083 件次，接待残疾人来访 4735 人次，其中集体访 14 批、172 人次。

五、文化体育

宣传文化：截止 2014 年底，省、市两级共开播残疾人专题广播节目 12 个,电视手语新闻栏目 9 个，电视公益广告片 6 个，报纸公益广告 4 个，报纸专版 59 个。全省举办残疾人文化周活动 393 次，举办残疾人文化艺术类比赛及展览 187 次，成立残疾人艺术团 92 个。

体育：省级残疾人体育训练基地 4 个，聘任教练员 20 人。市级组织残疾人体育活动 81 次，参加人数 3149 人次，残疾人体育示范点 61 个，残疾人体育健身指导员 288 人。

六、组织建设

组织队伍：截止 2014 年底，省、市、县、乡四级残联机关和事业单位共有编制 4561 个，实有人员 6180 人。14 个市级残联领导班子配备残疾人，57 个县级残联机关配备残疾人干部。选聘乡镇（街道）残疾人专职干事 2073 人、村（社区）残疾人专职委员 6.3 万人。

干部培训：省、市两级残联举办综合类培训班

39 期、培训 1438 人次，举办残疾人干部培训班 20 期、培训 1348 人次。县、乡两级残联举办各类培训班 2662 期、培训 4.7 万人次。

参政议政：在县级及以上残疾人及其亲友和残疾人工作者中，共有人大代表 86 人、政协委员 177 人。残联系统协助人大代表、政协委员提出议案、建议、提案 88 件，办理建议、提案 107 件。

专门协会：省、市、县共建立各类残疾人专门协会 742 个，其中：盲人协会 159 个、聋人协会 154 个、肢残人协会 149 个、智力残疾人及亲友协会 140 个、精神残疾人及亲友协会 140 个。

七、信息化与统计

信息化建设：省和 17 个市、75 个县级残联开通了门户网站，省、市两级残联全面完成门户网站的信息无障碍改造。全年举办各类信息工作培训班 19 期，培训各级残联信息员 689 人次。各级残联信息化建设投入 300.5 万元，其中：硬件 165.1 万元、软件 96.6 万元、系统运行维护 38.8 万元。各级残联有 208 名专业技术人员从事信息化工作。

统计工作：各级残联有从事残疾人事业统计工作的专、兼职人员 164 人，全年举办统计业务培训班 19 期，培训 362 人次。在全省的 38 个样本县（市、区）开展残疾人状况监测工作，对 1826 名残疾人进行了入户监测。

2014年河南省残疾人事业发展统计公报

2014年，在河南省委、省政府的正确领导和中国残联的精心指导下，全省各级残联深入贯彻国家、省委、省政府关于残疾人事业发展的新部署新要求，坚持“重心下移，强基固本，努力创造残疾人幸福生活”的总体思路，开拓创新，务实奋进，年度残疾人工作取得新成绩，全省残疾人事业实现了新发展。

一、康复

残疾人康复服务持续加强，为基层残疾人提供康复服务的能力和水平进一步提升。在60个市辖区和104个县（市）开展了社区康复工作，累计已建社区康复站的社区总数5.4万个，配备社区康复协调员3.7万人。

13个县的5个医疗卫生机构陆续开展残疾儿童筛查工作，2014年新诊断0-6岁残疾儿童477人。

开展视力残疾康复机构总数达到28个，完成白内障复明手术8204例；为3190名贫困白内障患者免费施行复明手术；为6564名低视力患者配用助视器，培训低视力儿童家长3697名，有效开展家庭康复训练。对8721名盲人进行定向行走训练。

推进听力语言康复机构规范化管理，完善基层服务网络。已建设省级听力语言康复机构1个，基层听力语言康复机构79个。2014年新收训聋儿2466名，在训聋儿3411名；规范聋儿家长学校，开展家庭训练，共培训聋儿家长3298名；开展各级各类听力语言康复专业技术人员培训，共培训专业人员257人。

全省开展肢体残疾康复训练服务机构达77个，其中，省级康复机构1个，地市级、县级康复机构76个；培训各级各类肢体残疾康复人员71人次；全省共对15660名肢体残疾者实施康复训练；实施救助项目资助2634名脑瘫儿童进行机构康复训练，资助535名贫困肢体残疾儿童实施矫治手术。

全省开展智力残疾康复训练服务的机构57个，其中，省级康复机构1个，地市级、县级康复机构56个；培训各级各类智力残疾康复人员64人次；全省共对7147名智力残疾人进行康复训练；实施救助项目资助1281名智力残疾儿童进行机构康复训练，同时培训儿童家长。

大力推广“社会化、综合性、开放式”精神病防治康复工作。在156个市县开展精神病防治康复工作，对3.3万名重性精神病患者进行综合防治康复，监护率达到49.1%，显好率达到49.8%，社会参与率达到36.7%，肇事率0.2%；解除关锁612人；对51333名贫困精神病患者进行医疗救助。

全省建立省级孤独症儿童康复训练机构1个，建立市、县级康复机构107个；1193名孤独症儿童在各级机构进行了康复训练。

加强残疾人辅助器具服务体系建设，深入开展辅助器具供应服务，为残疾人减免费用供应辅助器具10.9万件，其中装配假肢1888例、矫形器739例，验配助视器8935件。

二、教育

2014年，残疾人教育工作取得新进展。实施残疾人事业专项彩票公益金助学项目，为780人次家庭经济困难的残疾儿童享受普惠性学前教育提供资助。各地也积极多渠道争取资金支持，对362名残疾儿童给予学前教育资助。

全省共有特殊教育普通高中班（部）5个，在校生220人；其中聋生197人；盲生23人。残疾人中等职业学校（班）9个，在校生429人，毕业生132人。有426名残疾人被普通高等院校录取，333名残疾人进入特殊教育学院学习。

三、就业

2014年，残疾人就业渠道不断拓展，全省大力开展“残疾人就业培训工程”，取得显著成效。残疾人就业规模总体保持稳定。城镇新就业残疾人3.0万人，其中，集中就业残疾人1.2万人，按比例安排残疾人就业0.6万人，公益性岗位就业808人，个体就业及其它形式灵活就业1.1万人，辅助性就业234人。

城镇在业人数 31.6 万人；19.0 万名农村残疾人在业，其中 15.3 万名残疾人从事农业生产劳动。

残疾人职业培训基地达到 251 个，其中残联兴办 53 个，依托社会机构兴办 198 个，其中 4.2 万人次城镇残疾人接受了职业培训。

盲人按摩事业稳定发展，按摩机构迅速增长。2014 年度培训盲人保健按摩人员 1798 名、盲人医疗按摩人员 511 名；保健按摩机构达到 707 个，医疗按摩机构达到 95 个；在专业技术职务资格评审中，分别有 12 人和 7 人通过盲人医疗按摩人员中级和初级职称评审。

四、扶贫

2014 年，全省残疾人扶贫开发成效显著，贫困残疾人生产生活状况得到进一步改善。16.9 万名贫困残疾人得到扶持，其中 7.9 万人通过扶贫开发实现脱贫；接受实用技术培训的残疾人达到 4.7 万人次。

康复扶贫贴息贷款扶持 1118 名农村残疾人，残疾人扶贫基地达到 341 个，安置 1.1 万名残疾人就业，扶持带动 1.5 万名残疾人。

全省完成 1636 户农村贫困残疾人危房改造，各地投入危房资金 364.42 万元，1820 名残疾人受益。

五、社会保障

2014 年新型农村和城镇居民社会养老保险统一合并实施，已有 296.4 万名城乡残疾居民参保，参保率 81.6%，在 60 岁以下的参保残疾人中有 59.4 万名重度残疾人，其中 53.7 万人得到了政府的参保扶助，代缴补贴比例达到 90.4%。有 2.2 万名非重度残疾人也享受了全额或部分代缴的优惠政策。领取养老金待遇的人数达到 123.7 万人。

城镇残疾职工参加养老保险 17.6 万人，参加医疗保险 17.5 万人，城镇 20 万人和农村 67.4 万残疾人纳入最低生活保障范围；城镇集中供养残疾人和农村五保供养残疾人分别达到 0.8 万名和 5.5 万名；31.4 万名和 0.3 万名符合条件的城乡残疾人分别享受了稳定的生活补贴和护理补贴。17.4 万名城乡残疾人得到了其他救助救济。

残疾人托养服务工作规范推进，残疾人托养服务机构达到 42 个，共为 2 万多名残疾人提供了托养服务。其中寄宿制托养服务机构 7 个；综合性托养服务机构 34 个。

六、宣传文化

截至 2014 年底，共有省级残疾人电视手语新闻栏目 1 个，报纸专版 4 个；地市级残疾人专题广播节目 9 个，电视手语新闻栏目 4 个，播出公益广告 2 个，报纸专版 32 个。

截至 2014 年底，省地县三级公共图书馆共设立盲文及盲人有声读物阅览室 51 个，共开展残疾人文化周活动 140 场次，共举办残疾人文化艺术类比赛及展览 74 次，共有各类残疾人艺术团体 5 个。

七、体育

各地深入开展残疾人体育工作。组织省级残疾人群众体育健身活动 1 次，1700 人次参加；培训省级残疾人体育健身指导员达到 50 人；组织省级残疾人体育比赛 1 次，参赛运动员达 800 人次；省级残疾人体育训练基地已达 6 个，组织地市级残疾人体育健身活动 63 次，7912 人次参加；设立地市级残疾人群众体育活动示范点 19 个；培训地市级残疾人体育健身指导员 2400 人。

八、维权

2014 年，制定或修改保障残疾人权益的规范性文件省级 1 件、地市级 5 件、县级 14 件。县级以上人大进行《残疾人保障法》执法检查和专题调研 42 次；政协进行视察和专题调研 27 次。开展普法宣传教育活动 249 次，4.6 万人参加；举办法律培训班 76 个，4991 人参加。

截至 2014 年底，成立残疾人法律救助工作协调机构 110 个，建立残疾人法律救助工作站 96 个，办理案件 204 件，建立残疾人法律援助中心（工作站）168 个，办理案件 585 件，有力地推动了法律救助和法律援助工作。

残疾人参政议政工作得到加强，各级残联协助人大代表、政协委员提出议案、建议、提案 11 件，办理议案、建议、提案 10 件。

无障碍建设法规、标准进一步完善。全省各级残联共出台了 31 个无障碍建设与管理法规、规章和规范性文件；58 个市、县、区系统开展无障碍建设；开展无障碍建设检查 171 次，无障碍培训 424 人次；为 2739 户贫困残疾人家庭实施了无障碍改造；为 6.6 万名残疾人发放了残疾人机动轮椅车燃油补贴。

各级残联共处理残疾人群众来信 625 件，接待残疾人群众来访 5259 人次，其中集体访 22 批次、291 人次。

九、组联

2014 年，全省 11 个地市级残联在领导班子中配备了残疾人理事长或副理事长；91 个县级残联机关配备了残疾人干部；已建乡镇（街道）残联 2379 个，已建率达到 100%，选聘残疾人专职委员 2553 名；已建社区（村）残协 4.3 万个，已建率达到 96.0%，选聘残疾人专职委员 4.9 万名。

省市县乡残联实有人员已达 8180 人。各级残联共举办培训班 1315 期，培训机关干部、协会干部及残疾人专职委员 2.1 万人次。

共建立省级以下各类残疾人专门协会 889 个，市级专门协会已建比例为 100%；县级专门协会已建比例为 100%。全省共建立助残社会组织 57 个，其中在民政部门注册的为 5 个，以残联为业务主管单位的 25 个。

十、服务设施

大力加强基层残疾人服务设施建设，截至 2014 年底，全省已竣工并投入使用的各级残疾人综合服务设施 137 个，总建设规模 18.8 万平方米，总投资 30214.3 万元；已竣工并投入使用的各级残疾人康复设施 9 个，总建设规模 6.4 万平方米，总投资 14104 万元；已竣工并投入使用的各级残疾人托养服务设施 5 个，总建设规模 1.5 平方米，总投资 3172 万元。

十一、信息化

2014 年统计队伍建设进一步加强，全省各级残联共有 196 名专、兼职统计人员从事残疾人事业统计工作，统计人员业务素质培养普遍得到重视，省级残联举办培训班 1 期，参加培训的人员达到 50 人次；地市级举办培训班 21 期，参加培训的人员达到 336 人次。

地方残联全面推进网站建设，目前 1 个省级残联已全部开通了公众服务网站，有 10 个地市级残联网站和 16 个县级残联网站也已开通。2014 年各级残联开设网站技术培训班 22 期，培训各级残联信息员达 440 人次。各级残联共有 232 名专业技术人员从事信息化工作。

2014 年湖北省残疾人事业发展统计公报

2014 年，是全省残联系统认真学习党的十八届三中、四中全会精神，深入贯彻省委关于残疾人事业的新部署新要求，全面落实省残联“六代会”任务的开局之年。一年来，在省委、省政府的坚强领导和中国残联的正确指导下，全省各级残联主动作为，广大残疾人和残疾人工作者共同努力，全省各项残疾人事业在新起点上实现了新突破。

一、康复

2014 年，湖北省残疾人康复工作抢抓机遇，趁势而上，紧紧围绕实现残疾人“人人享有康复服务”的目标，以实施重点康复项目工程为抓手，全力争创国家辅具华中区域中心，大力推进残疾人康复保障制度建设，着力构建残疾人康复服务体系，强力推动残疾人社区康复工作，努力探索残疾预防工作模式，湖北省残疾人康复工作继续保持良好的发展势头。

截至 2014 年底，全省共有康复机构 219 个，其中，残联系统康复机构 87 个，康复机构在岗人员总数达到 7757 人，其中业务人员 6618 人，管理人员 1139 人。

在 39 个市辖区和 59 个县（市）开展了社区康复服务工作，累计已建社区康复站的社区总数 4760 个，配备 7750 名社区康复协调员。

53 个县的 74 个医疗卫生机构陆续开展残疾儿童筛查工作，年度新诊断 0-6 岁残疾儿童 1968 人。依托各级各类残疾儿童康复机构建立儿童家长学校 9 个，开展家长学校活动 25 次，参与残疾儿童家长达 1090 人次。

开展视力残疾康复机构总数达到 20 个，完成白内障复明手术 30337 例；为 10161 名贫困白内障患者免费施行复明手术；为 5420 名低视力患者配用助视器，培训低视力儿童家长 10015 名，有效开展家庭康复训练。对 6000 名盲人进行定向行走训练。

推进听力语言康复机构规范化管理，完善基层服务网络。已建设省级听力语言康复机构 1 个，基层听力语言康复机构 38 个。年度新收训聋儿 829 名，在训聋儿 1023 名；规范聋儿家长学校，开展家庭训练，共培训聋儿家长 1128 名；开展各级各类听力语言康复专业技术人员培训，共培训专业人员 52 人；实施贫困聋儿人工耳蜗、助听器抢救性康复项目，资助 220 名聋儿免费植入人工耳蜗，资助 210 名聋儿免费配戴助听器；开展彩票公益金成年听力残疾人（助听器）康复项目，为 1368 名贫困成年听力残疾人免费验配助听器，各级康复机构共为 592 名成年听力残疾人提供技术服务。

开展肢体残疾康复训练服务机构达 54 个，其中，省级康复机构 1 个，地市级、县级康复机构 53 个；培训各级各类肢体残疾康复人员 228 人次；全省共对 2651 名肢体残疾者实施康复训练；实施救助项目资助 2651 名脑瘫儿童进行机构康复训练，资助 333 名贫困肢体残疾儿童实施矫治手术。

开展智力残疾康复训练服务的机构 56 个，其中，省级康复机构 1 个，地市级、县级康复机构 55 个；培训各级各类智力残疾康复人员 248 人次；全省共对 5481 名智力残疾人进行康复训练；实施救助项目资助 1379 名智力残疾儿童进行机构康复训练，同时培训儿童家长。

大力推广“社会化、综合性、开放式”精神病防治康复工作。在 93 个市县开展精神病防治康复工作，对 347389 名重性精神病患者进行综合防治康复，监护率达到 65.5 %，显好率达到 62.21%，社会参与率达到 47.82%，肇事率 0.11%；解除关锁 222 人；对 17785 名贫困精神病患者进行医疗救助。

建立了 37 个孤独症儿童康复训练机构；820 名孤独症儿童在各级机构进行了康复训练。

加强残疾人辅助器具服务体系建设，构建覆盖全省的服务网络，培育建设国家辅助器具华中区域中心，建设地市级服务机构 9 个，县级服务机构 32 个。深入开展辅助器具服务，组织实施系列辅助器具项目，全年共为残疾人减免费用供应辅助器具 32002 件，其中装配假肢 1597 件、矫形器 735 件，验配助视器 5651 件。

二、教育

2014 年，湖北省残联认真学习贯彻国务院办公厅下发的教育部等七部委制定的《特殊教育提升计划（2014-2016 年）》（国办发[2014]1 号），联合教育厅编制了《湖北省特殊教育提升计划（2014-2016 年）》，通过争取有利政策，不断加大对残疾学生的资助力度，残疾人受教育权得到了更好保障。

实施残疾人事业专项彩票公益金助学项目，为全省 500 名家庭经济困难的残疾儿童享受普惠性学前教育提供资助。各地积极多渠道争取资金支持，对 24 名残疾儿童给予学前教育资助。

全省共有特殊教育普通高中班（部）8 个，在校生 420 人；全为聋生。残疾人中等职业学校（班）9 个，在校生 262 人，毕业生 109 人，其中 79 人获得职业资格证书。全省有 369 名残疾人被普通高等院校录取.

三、就业

2014 年，残疾人就业规模总体保持稳定。城镇新就业残疾人 10865 人，其中，集中就业残疾人 3558 人，按比例安排残疾人就业 2753 人，公益性岗位就业 439 人，个体就业及其它形式灵活就业 3584 人，辅助性就业 531 人。全省城镇就业人数 220649 人；873649 人农村残疾人在业，其中 668392 名残疾人从事农业生产劳动。

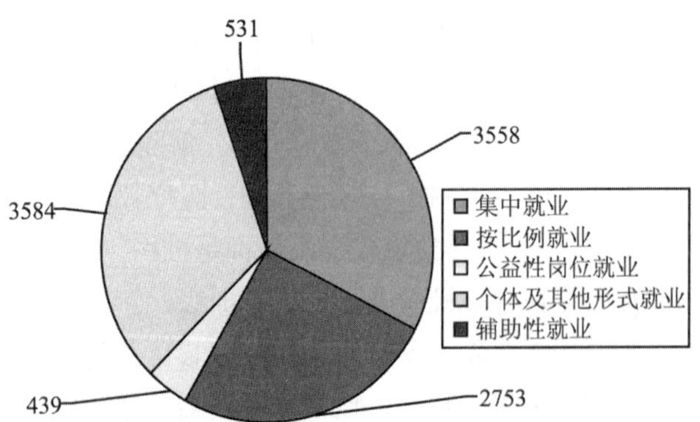

图 1　城镇新就业残疾人情况（总计 10865 人）

全省残疾人职业培训基地达到 277 个，其中残联兴办 205 个，依托社会机构兴办 72 个，11820 人次城镇残疾人接受了职业培训。

盲人按摩事业稳定发展，按摩机构迅速增长。2014 年度培训盲人保健按摩人员 1137 名、盲人医疗按摩人员 219 名；保健按摩机构达到 822 个，医疗按摩机构达到 51 个；在专业技术职务资格评审中，分别有 23 人和 99 人通过盲人医疗按摩人员中级和初级职称评审。

四、社会保障

2014 年新型农村和城镇居民社会养老保险统一合并实施，已有 104.6 万城乡残疾居民参保，参保率 64.86%，在 60 岁以下的参保残疾人中有 16.4 万重度残疾人，其中 15.3 万得到了政府的参保扶助，代缴补贴比例达到 93.04%。有 19.2 万非重度残疾人也享受了全额或部分代缴的优惠政策。

城镇残疾职工参加基本养老和医疗保险人数稳定在 29 万左右，城镇 17.7 万和农村 52.6 万残疾人纳入最低生活保障范围；城镇集中供养残疾人和农村五保供养残疾人分别达到 1.2 万和 4.0 万；24.1 万和 2.5 万符合条件的城乡残疾人分别享受了稳定的生活补贴和护理补贴。8.3 万城乡残疾人得到了其他救助救济。

残疾人托养服务工作规范推进，残疾人托养服务机构达到 219 个，共为 8699 名残疾人提供了托养服务。其中寄宿制托养服务机构 58 个；日间照料机构 114 个；综合性托养服务机构 47 个。在以上机构中，共有 239 名残疾人实现辅助性就业，53 名残疾人实现了支持性就业。机构之外接受居家托养服务的残疾人达到 14890 人。全年共有 1313 名托养服务管理和服务人员接受了各级各类专业培训，其中接受国家级培训 25 人。

五、扶贫开发

2014 年，12.9 万贫困残疾人得到扶持，其中 4.9 万人通过扶贫开发实现脱贫；接受实用技术培训的残疾人达到 3.0 万人次。

康复扶贫贴息贷款扶持 3789 名农村残疾人，残疾人扶贫基地达到 102 个，安置 2797 名残疾人就业，扶持带动 1.0 万残疾人户。

完成 513 户农村贫困残疾人危房改造，各地投入危房资金 138.6 万元，582 名残疾人受益。

六、宣传文化

中央级媒体采用稿件28件，主要新闻媒体刊播稿件3597件。组织推荐优秀新闻作品参加全国好新闻评选，共获得2个一等奖、1个二等奖、3个三等奖、1个优秀奖。截至2014年底，全省共有省级残疾人专题广播节目1个、电视手语栏目1个，播出公益广告2个；地市级残疾人专题广播节目16个、电视手语栏目5个，播出公益广告40个。

组织“牵手残疾人 走进图书馆”等公益文化活动。开展形式多样的残疾人文化活动。组织参加全国残疾人文化赛事，组织各地参加“中国梦•我的梦”全国残疾人网络摄影大赛。极大地丰富了残疾人的文化生活，进一步推动残疾人文化事业繁荣发展。截至2014年底，全省省地市县三级公共图书馆共设立盲文及盲人有声读物阅览室47个，共开展残疾人文化周活动113场次，共举办残疾人文化艺术类比赛及展览85次，全省共有各类残疾人艺术团体30个。

七、体育

全省累计培养了1240名残疾人体育健身指导员。在全省累计共资助建设自强健身示范点22个。为荆州、孝感地区各配发了1套健身器材，并纳入示范点统一管理；组队参加全国残疾人田径、游泳、举重、乒乓球锦标赛，共获得了7金、6银、15铜的优异成绩。组织3名运动员参加仁川亚残运会，共获得5枚金牌、2枚银牌，每个人都有金牌进账。1名运动员参加乒乓球世锦赛，获得1金1铜。

举办第十四届运动会暨第九届全省残疾人运动会，运动会共设立田径、举重、羽毛球、游泳、象棋、乒乓球六大项，231个小项，历时5个月，分别在5月、8月、10月分三个阶段举行，全省18支代表队，541名运动员、945名工作人员参加。

举办第四届残疾人健身周活动。 组织省级残疾人群众体育健身活动17次，2500人次参加；建设省级残疾人群众体育活动示范点达到25个；培训省级残疾人体育健身指导员达到1003人；组织省级残疾人体育比赛1次，参赛运动员达400人次；省级残疾人体育训练基地已达10个。组织地市级残疾人体育活动126次，17177人次参加；设立地市级残疾人群众体育活动示范点80个；培训地市级残疾人体育健身指导员237人。

八、维权

全省县级以上人大进行《残疾人保障法》执法检查和专题调研 32 次；政协进行视察和专题调研31次。全省开展普法宣传教育活动169次，3.9万人参加；举办法律培训班62个，2659人参加。

截至2014年底，全省成立残疾人法律救助工作协调机构98个，建立残疾人法律救助工作站60个，办理案件204件，建立残疾人法律援助中心（工作站）96个，办理案件1011件，有力地推动了法律救助和法律援助工作。

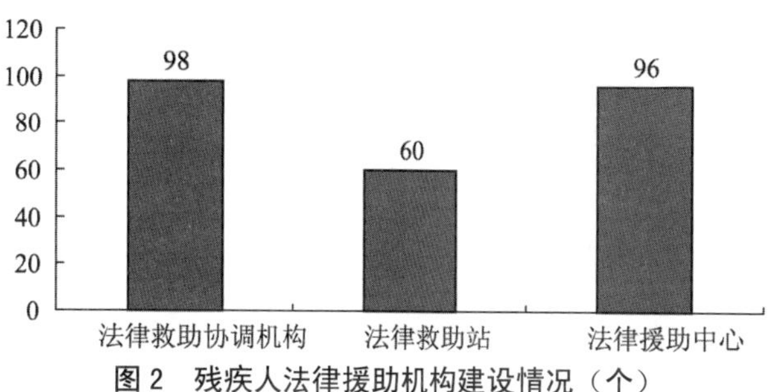

图2 残疾人法律援助机构建设情况（个）

残疾人参政议政工作得到加强，各地残联协助人大代表、政协委员提出议案、建议、提案103件，办理议案、建议、提案56件。

无障碍建设法规、标准进一步完善。全省共出台了7个地市、县级无障碍建设与管理法规、规章和规范性文件；76个市、县、区系统开展无障碍建设；全省开展无障碍建设检查119次，无障碍培训268人次；为2034户贫困残疾人家庭实施了无障碍改造；为4.4万残疾人发放了残疾人机动轮椅车燃油补贴。

全省各级残联共处理残疾人群众来信2397件，接待残疾人群众来访1.9万人次，其中集体访97批次、1145人次。

九、组织建设

截至2014年底，省级残联领导班子中配备了1名残疾人副理事长；6个市级残联在领导班子中配备了残疾人理事长或副理事长；41个县级残联机关配备了残疾人干部；已建乡镇（街道）残联1249个，已建率达到99.0%，选聘残疾人专职委员1796名；

已建社区（村）残协 23506 个，已建率达到 87.35%，选聘残疾人专职委员 18714 名。

全省省市县乡残联实有人员已达 4220 人。各级残联共举办培训班 1090 期，培训机关干部、协会干部及残疾人专职委员 1.8 万人次。

全省共建立省级以下各类残疾人专门协会 534 个，其中省级专门协会已建比例为 100%，市级专门协会已建比例为 100%，县级专门协会已建比例为 89.2%。全省共建立助残社会组织 1314 个，其中在民政部门注册的为 316 个。

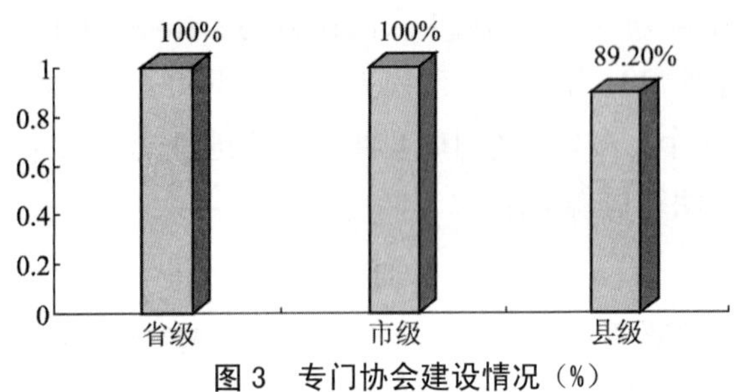

图 3　专门协会建设情况（%）

十、服务设施建设

残疾人服务设施建设得到全面发展。截至 2014 年底，全省已竣工并投入使用的各级残疾人综合服务设施 77 个，总建设规模 13.79 万平方米，总投资 25886 万元；已竣工并投入使用的各级残疾人康复设施 12 个，总建设规模 2.32 万平方米，总投资 4545 万元；已竣工并投入使用的各级残疾人托养服务设施 30 个，总建设规模 3.34 万平方米，总投资 5140 万元。

十一、信息化建设

截至 2014 年底，全省 1 个省级单位、12 个地市、43 个县级残联开通网站，比上年增加 4 个。全省各级残联共举办统计业务和信息工作培训班共 361 期，参加培训班接受培训人次共计 1233 人次。

2014年湖南省残疾人事业发展统计公报

2014年湖南省残疾人工作完成各项任务指标，残疾人各项工作全面发展，残疾人得到不同程度的服务和保障。综合2014年度残疾人事业统计数据及实际情况，公报如下：

一、康复

2014年我省残疾人康复工作全面提升，康复工作以围绕2015年初步实现“人人享有康复服务”为目标，以突破残疾儿童康复、辅助器具服务和残疾预防工作为重点，加快康复机构建设，并以康复机构为依托，认真实施各类康复救助项目，全面推进社区康复。

截止到2014年底，在全省14个市州所属125个县区13270个社区村开展社区康复服务，已建成5368个社区康复站，有13210名各级社区康复协调员，本年度新增社区康复协调员2611名。到2014年底全省共建立69所家长学校，已登记家长学员5176名，增强了社区康复力量。

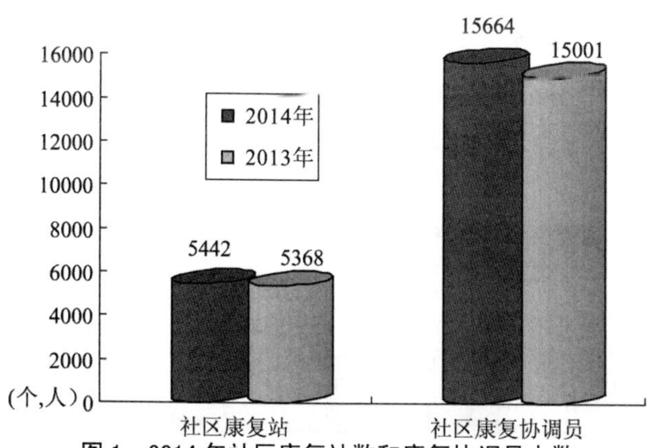

图1　2014年社区康复站数和康复协调员人数

2014年共完成白内障复明手术25919例，为12482名贫困白内障患者免费施行复明手术；为5746名低视力患者配用助视器，培训低视力儿童家长1963名。对5410名盲人进行定向行走训练。

全省共建立听力语言康复机构58个，新收训聋儿721名，在训聋儿1482名；规范聋儿家长学校，开展家庭训练，共培训聋儿家长1936名；开展各级各类听力语言康复专业技术人员培训，培训专业人员321人。

全省开展肢体残疾康复训练服务机构54个，培训各级各类肢体残疾康复专业人员337人次；共为13485名肢体残疾者实施康复训练，对515名脑瘫儿童实施国家康复救助项目，资助395名贫困肢体残疾儿童实施矫治手术。

开展智力残疾康复训练服务机构73个，比2013年增加23个。共为9034名智力残疾人实施康复训练；2626名智力残疾儿童得到了国家彩票公益金项目救助，110名智力残疾儿童得到地方救助项目救助。

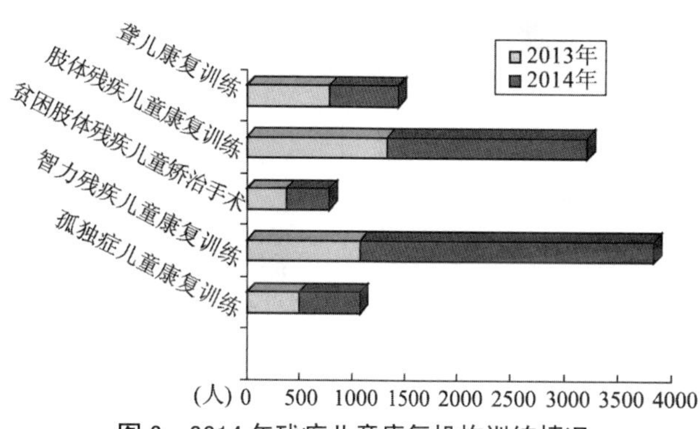

图2　2014年残疾儿童康复机构训练情况

全省120个县（市、区）开展精神病防治康复工作，覆盖总人口6455.66万人，73275名精神病贫困患者接受救助。2014年，加大了精神残疾康复机构建设，省残联共投入200万元，支持精神康复工、农、娱疗站的建设项目。现有各级精神康复机构92个，机构内精神病人19517名。建立孤独症儿童康复机构57个，563名孤独症儿童在各级机构接受康复训练，其中528名贫困孤独症儿童得到康复救助。

2014年，累计建立辅助器具供应机构98个，其中市级14个，县级84个，建成了省市县三级辅助器具配发服务网络。为残疾人减免费用供应辅助器具6.4万件，其中装配假肢1767例、矫形器1097例，验配助视器6230件。

二、教育

2014年，残疾人教育工作取得新进展，残疾人受教育权利得到了更好保障。

实施专项彩票公益金助学项目，资助学前残疾儿童 400 名，资助新入园儿童 274 名。

全省有特殊教育普通高中学校（班）9 个。残疾人中等职业学校（班）13 个，在校生 1129 人，411 人毕业，其中 182 人获得职业资格证书。全省有 318 名残疾人被普通高等院校录取，147 名残疾人进入特殊教育学院学习。

截止到 2014 年底，全省有未入学适龄残疾儿童少年 5012 名，其中视力残疾儿童 205 人，听力残疾儿童 186 人，言语残疾儿童 307 人，肢体残疾儿童 1766 人，智力残疾儿童 1509 人，精神残疾儿童 170 人，多重残疾儿童 869 人。

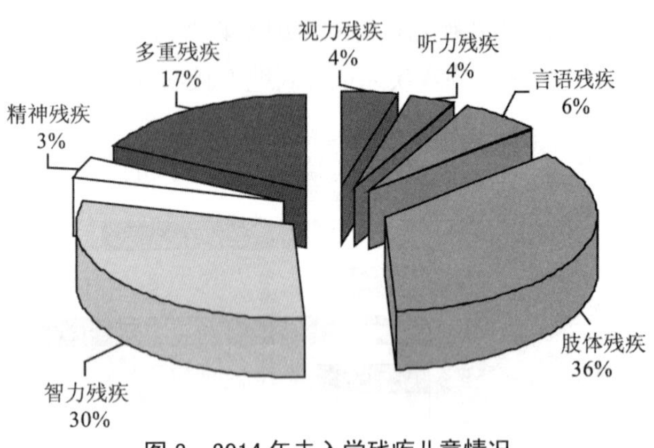

图 3　2014 年未入学残疾儿童情况

三、就业

残疾人就业稳步增长。2014 年，城镇新增 10950 名残疾人就业，其中，集中就业 3478 人，按比例就业 2232 人，个体及其他形式灵活就业 4110 人，公益性岗位就业 834 人，辅助性就业 299 人。全省城镇就业人数 27.99 万，94.93 万名农村残疾人实现就业，其中 69 万人从事农业生产劳动。

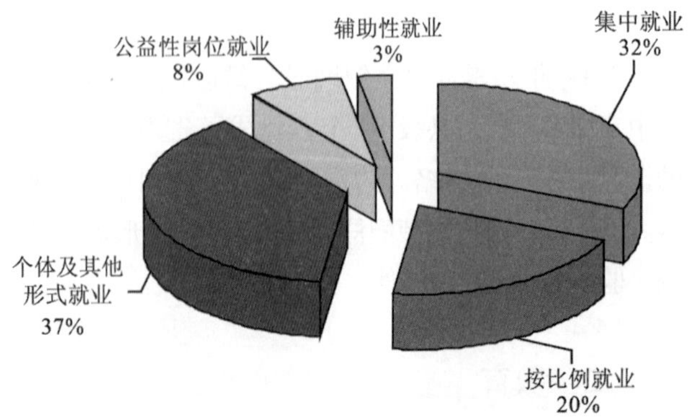

图 4　2014 年城镇残疾人新增就业情况

全省残疾人职业培训基地达到 243 个，6164 人次城镇残疾人接受了职业培训。

2014 年度培训盲人保健按摩和医疗按摩人员 1697 名，全省盲人保健按摩机构达到 597 个，盲人医疗按摩机构达到 24 个；在专业技术职务资格评审中，有 127 人通过医疗按摩人员初级职称评审。

四、扶贫开发

2014 年，残疾人扶贫开发进一步深化，贫困残疾人生产生活状况得到进一步改善。86483 名贫困残疾人得到扶持，其中 41359 人通过扶贫开发实际脱贫，接受实用技术培训的残疾人达 14451 人次。

康复扶贫贴息贷款实际到位 4586 万元，共扶持 1415 名农村残疾人。残疾人扶贫基地达到 196 个，安置 4834 名残疾人就业，扶持带动 11337 名残疾人。

对 6997 户农村贫困残疾人实施危房改造，各地投入危房改造资金 5680 万元，8285 名残疾人受益。

五、社会保障

2014 新型农村和城镇居民社会养老保险统一实施合并，已有 162.1 万城乡残疾居民参保。60 岁以下的参保残疾人中有 28.94 万重度残疾人，其中 27.17 万得到了政府全额代缴的扶助，有 6.11 万非重度残疾人也享受了全额或部分代缴的优惠政策。领取养老金待遇的人数达到 62.37 万人。

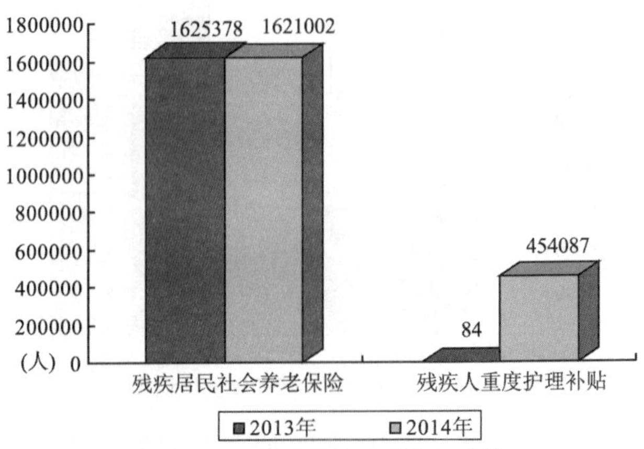

图 5　2014 年残疾人参加养老保险情况

城镇残疾职工参加基本养老和医疗保险人数 30.12 万人，城镇 20.53 万和农村 65.88 万残疾人纳入最低生活保障范围；城镇集中供养残疾人和农村五保供养残疾人分别达到 0.79 万和 6.94 万；16.94 万城乡残疾人得到了其他救助救济。2014 年出台了全省重度残疾人护理补贴政策，截止 2014 年 12 月 31 日，全省享受残疾人护理补贴人数达到454087人。

残疾人托养服务工作稳步推进。残疾人托养服务机构达到109个，为3356名残疾人提供托养服务。接受居家托养服务的残疾人达到18579人。

六、宣传文体

残疾人事业宣传紧密围绕事业大局，大力弘扬人道主义，营造了良好的舆论范围。2014年中央媒体采用稿件14件，开设电视手语栏目2个。省级公共图书馆及盲人有声读物图书室8个，举办全省第八届残疾人文艺汇演和全省残疾人文化周活动。

全年举办4次残疾人比赛，共1382名残疾人运动员参赛。举办全省第九届残运会，参加仁川亚运会。地市本年度举办138次残疾人体育活动，共有8858名残疾人参加体育活动。

七、维权

维护残疾人权益是残疾人工作的出发点和落脚点。2014年加大对残疾人保障法执法检查和监督力度，加强法律服务和法律救助，推动无障碍设施建设。

截止2014年底，全省共建立各级残疾人法律救助协调机构76个，残疾人法律救助工作站75个，共办理案件220件，残疾人法律援助中心119个，共办理案件655件。

各级残联协助人大代表、政协委员提出议案、建议、提案74件，办理议案、建议、提案51件。

全省共有6个市系统开展无障碍建设，共开展无障碍建设检查87次，无障碍培训390人次；为2926户贫困残疾人家庭实施了无障碍改造；为53771名残疾人发放了残疾人机动轮椅车燃油补贴。

2014年全省各级残联处理残疾人群众来信3847件，接待来访26003人次，其中集体上访130批次，个体上访24636人次，从数据上看，上访人数和上访批次比2013年呈下降趋势，上访原因主要集中在以下几方面：康复17%，教育7%，就业16%，扶贫15%，社会保障24%，机动轮椅车8%，数据体现残疾人在扶贫、社会保障、康复等方面还有很多问题迫切需要解决。

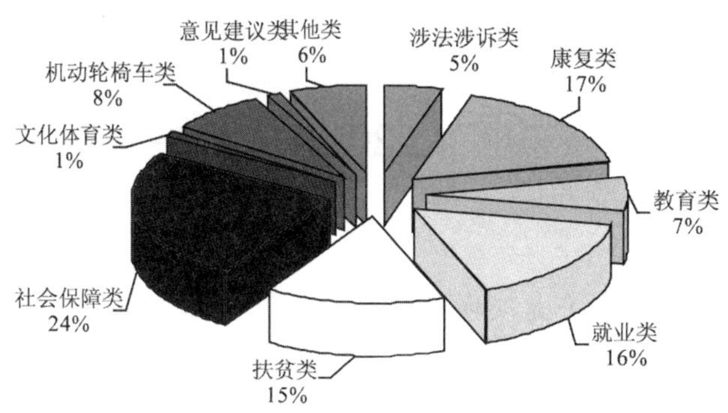

图6　2014年残疾人来访（人次）情况

八、组织

截止2014年底，市、县、乡残联实有工作人员5543人，14个市州、125个县市区建立残联，其中有10个市州残联配备残疾人领导干部，有73个县市区残联在编制内配备了残疾人干部。

全省2453个乡镇（街道）已有2420个成立残联，有2798名工作人员，有639个乡镇（街道）配备专职理事长，已建乡镇（街道）残联中有专职委员2343名，形成了比较完善、多层次的组织机构。

全省39527个村（社区）建立残疾人协会，配备了35148名残疾人专职委员，建立了22958个残疾人活动室。

全省共有注册志愿者12.54万人，受助残疾人达50.17万人次。

九、残疾人服务设施

残疾人服务设施建设得到全面发展。截至2014年底，全省已竣工并投入使用的各级残疾人综合服务设施93个，总建设规模12.16万平方米，总投资2.34亿元；已竣工并投入使用的各级残疾人康复设施32个，总建设规模1.66万平方米，总投资3245.5万元；已竣工并投入使用的各级残疾人托养服务设施18个，总建设规模2.86万平方米，总投资3384.1万元。

十、残疾人信息化

残疾人事业数据统计工作稳步推进，做到数据支撑有公信力，为出台残疾人政策决策提供可靠数据。全省各级有154名统计员，信息化专业人才188人，全省各级残联开通门户网站77个。

2014 年广东省残疾人事业发展统计公报

2014 年是实现残疾人事业“十二五”规划目标的关键年，一年来，在省委、省政府的领导和中国残联的指导下，全省各级残联共同努力，积极推进残疾人康复、教育、就业、社会保障、权益保障、信息助残等专项服务工作，残疾人事业发展取得了新的成绩。

一、残疾人康复

1. 残疾儿童筛查：截止 2014 年底，全省共 56 个县区，163 个医疗卫生机构开展残疾儿童筛查工作，年度新诊断 0-6 岁残疾儿童 3786 人，并进行了免费康复训练。

2. 社区康复：全省 63 个市辖区、62 个县（市）、15903 个村开展了社区康复工作，新增社区康复站 290 个，累计已建社区康复站的社区总数为 8154 个，配备社区康复协调员 1.92 万名。

3. 视力残疾康复：开展视力残疾康复机构总数达到 78 个，完成白内障复明手术 10.32 万例，为 4511 名低视力患者配用助视器，培训低视力儿童家长 273 人，盲人定向行走训练 6311 人。

4. 听力言语康复：开展听力语言康复机构 68 个，年度新收训聋儿 1222 人，在训聋儿 2496 人，培训聋儿家长 3208 人次，培训基层听力语言康复专业技术人员 1170 人次。

5. 肢体残疾康复：开展肢体残疾康复训练服务机构 257 个，康复训练肢体残疾人 37893 人，其中脑瘫儿童机构康复训练 3464 人，肢体残疾人社区家庭康复 34429 人。免费为 58 名贫困肢体残疾儿童实施矫治手术、装配矫形器并进行术后康复训练。培训基层肢体残疾康复训练人员 1622 人次。

6. 智力残疾康复：开展智力残疾康复训练服务的机构 261 个，康复训练智力残疾人 12293 人，其中智力残疾儿童机构康复训练 3421 人，智力残疾人社区家庭康复 8872 人。培训各级各类智力残疾康复管理、技术人员 710 人次。

7. 精神残疾康复：130 个县（市、区）开展精神病防治康复工作，对 37.92 万名精神病患者进行综合防治康复，监护率达到 81.63%，显好率达到 66.02%，社会参与率达到 51.67%，肇事率 0.06%。解除关锁精神残疾 722 人，救助贫困精神病患者 11.24 万人。

8. 孤独症儿童康复：各级孤独症儿童康复训练机构共 123 个，在训孤独症儿童 3559 人，其中救助贫困孤独症儿童 1904 人。

9. 辅助器具适配：全省省级以下辅助器具适配机构 80 个，为各类残疾人供应辅助器具 71637 件，其中免费装配假肢 1600 例、免费装配矫形器 4094 例、免费验配助视器 5040 件、免费其他辅助器具 4584 件。

二、残疾人教育

1. 学前教育阶段：本年度残疾人事业专项彩票公益金资助学前教育残疾儿童 550 人，其他助学项目资助学前教育残疾儿童 397 人。

2. 义务教育阶段：截止到 2014 年底，全省未入学适龄残疾儿童少年登记在册 3693 人，其中视力残疾 113 人、听力残疾 122 人、言语残疾 149 人、肢体残疾 987 人、智力残疾 1251 人、精神残疾 377 人、多重残疾 694 人。

3. 高中教育阶段：全省已办特殊教育普通高中班（部）8 个，在校生 151 人；已办残疾人中等职业学校（班）9 个，在校生 848 人；2014 年高中阶段教育毕业 372 人，其中 176 人获得职业资格证书。

4. 高等教育阶段：全省共 66 名残疾人进入特殊教育学院学习，327 名残疾人进入普通高等院校学习。

三、残疾人培训、就业与扶贫

1. 全省建立残疾人职业培训、就业、扶贫基地共 366 个。

2. 残疾人培训：全省城镇职业培训 1.09 万人，

培训盲人保健按摩人员745人，医疗按摩人员462人。

3. 残疾人就业：本年度城镇在业残疾人数20.40万，其中新安排残疾人就业1.36万；农村残疾人在业60.80万，其中49.69万残疾人从事农业生产劳动。

4. 残疾人扶贫：本年度扶持贫困残疾人5.09万人次，接受实用技术培训的残疾人达到1.38万人次；截止年底扶贫基地共安置残疾人就业3666人，扶持带动残疾人5614户。全年对1324户农村贫困残疾人危房改造，受益残疾人1377人。

四、残疾人社会保障与托养

1. 社会保障：2014年底城乡残疾居民参加社会养老保险61.46万人；城镇残疾职工参加养老保险10.84万人，城镇纳入最低生活保障8.45万人，城镇集中供养和其他救助救济残疾人3.41万人；农村纳入最低生活保障27.59万人，农村五保供养和其他救助救济残疾人5.25万人。全省141个县（市区）出台并实施残疾人生活补贴及重度残疾人护理补贴政策文件，40.57万残疾人享受了生活补贴，41.68万残疾人享受了护理补贴。

2. 残疾人托养：全省残疾人托养服务机构达到462个，共机构托养13535名残疾人。其中寄宿制托养服务机构21个，托养残疾人802人；日间照料机构400个，托养残疾人9874人；综合性托养服务机构41个，托养残疾人2859人。接受居家托养服务的残疾人达到1.77万人。

五、残疾人宣传文化与体育

1. 残疾人宣传：本年度省级主要新闻媒体刊播残疾人事业活动稿件90件，省级共有残疾人事业报刊专版4个，残疾人专题广播节目1个，电视手语新闻栏目1个，残疾人事业新闻宣传促进会1个；地级以上市主要新闻媒体刊播稿件2913件，地级以上市共有报刊专版57个，残疾人专题广播节目10个，电视手语新闻栏目9个，已建地级以上市新促会22个。

2. 残疾人文化：省级和地级以上市公共图书馆设立盲文及盲人有声读物阅览室已达到42个，举办残疾人文化周活动83次，举办残疾人文化艺术类比赛及展览35次，已成立残疾人艺术团队13个。

3. 残疾人体育：省级举办残疾人群众健身活动7次，残疾人参加活动920人次，举办残疾人体育比赛4次，残疾人运动员参加比赛250人次；地级以上市举办残疾人体育健身活动141次，参加人数1.7万人次。

六、残疾人法制建设与维权

1. 残疾人法规体系建设：2014年全省各级残联参与、制定、修改有关残疾人的法规、规章、政策性文件共13个；其中地级以上市5个，县区级8个。开展人大政协执法检查与专题调研22次；其中省1次，地级以上市12次，县区级9次。协助人大代表、政协委员提出议案、提案与建议共39件；其中地级以上市19件，县区级20件。

2. 残疾人法律宣传与救助：全省各级残联组织普法宣传教育活动248次，2.55万人次参加；组织残疾人工作者法律培训班49期，3979人次参加。地级以上市建立法律救助工作站和法律援助中心（工作站）29个，全年办理案件152件，县区级建立法律救助工作站和法律援助中心（工作站）129个，全年办理案件316件。

3. 无障碍建设：截止年底，全省各级残联共颁发无障碍建设与管理法规、政府令30个，21个市全部实现系统开展无障碍建设，系统开展无障碍县区110个；贫困残疾人家庭无障碍改造8525户；发放残疾人机动轮椅车燃油补贴29631人。

4. 残疾人信访工作：全年各级残联信访部门共处理残疾人来信3324件，其中省63件，地级以上市455件，县区级2806件；各级残联接待残疾人群众来访13844人次，其中集体访72批次、749人次。

七、残疾人事业组织建设

截止2014年底，省市县乡残联实有人员7418人。全省有13个地级以上市残联配备了残疾人领导，49个县（市、区）残联配备了残疾人干部；已建乡镇（街道）残联1616个，已建率达到99.75%，选聘残疾人专职委员1642名；已建社区（村）残协2.34万个，已建率达到94.78%，选聘残疾人专职委员2.31万名。各级残联共举办培训班1191期，培训残疾人干部20064人次。全省各级残联建立残疾人五大专门协会共704个，建设率为100%。

八、残疾人事业统计与信息化

截止2014年底，全省县区级以上残联有专兼职统计工作人员185人，其中有统计从业资格41人，占22.2%，地级以上市举办统计人员培训班25期，567人参加培训。全省共有各级残联门户网站83个，其中省1个、地级以上市21个、县区级61个；省级残联网站全年发稿量3554篇。2014年全省各级残联信息化建设共投入905万，其中硬件投入占50.4%、软件投入占33.7%、系统运行维护费占15.9%。各级残联共有信息化专业技术人员287名。

九、残疾人服务设施建设

截止2014年底，已竣工并投入使用的各级残疾人综合服务设施92个，总建设规模37.31万平方米，总投资10.31亿元；已竣工并投入使用的各级残疾人康复设施47个，总建设规模10.55万平方米，总投资3.21亿元；已竣工并投入使用的各级残疾人托养服务设施38个，总建设规模5.7万平方米，总投资1.1亿元。

2014年广西壮族自治区残疾人事业发展统计公报

2014年，广西残疾人工作深入贯彻落实中央、自治区关于促进残疾人事业发展重大部署，全面推进残疾人社会保障和服务体系建设，创新残疾人工作，夯实残疾人工作基础，促进残疾人事业迈上新台阶。

一、全面开展社区康复工作，大力推进城市和农村残疾人“人人享有康复服务”目标的实现

在37个市辖区和75个县（市）开展了社区康复工作，累计已建社区康复站的社区总数2371个，配备11710名社区康复协调员。

开展视力残疾康复机构总数达到7个，完成白内障复明手术23289例；为13241名贫困白内障患者免费施行复明手术；为6008名低视力患者配用助视器，培训低视力儿童家长531名，有效开展家庭康复训练。对2468名盲人进行定向行走训练。

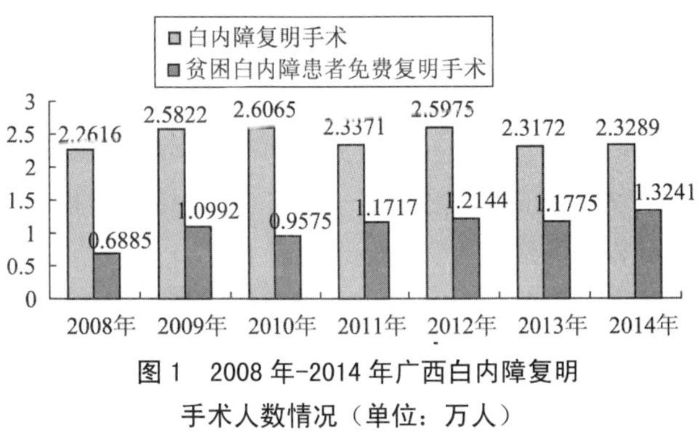

图1　2008年-2014年广西白内障复明手术人数情况（单位：万人）

推进听力语言康复机构规范化管理，完善基层服务网络。已建设省级听力语言康复机构1个，基层听力语言康复机构35个。年度新收训聋儿560名，在训聋儿916名；规范聋儿家长学校，开展家庭训练，共培训聋儿家长1153名；开展各级各类听力语言康复专业技术人员培训，共培训专业人员222人。

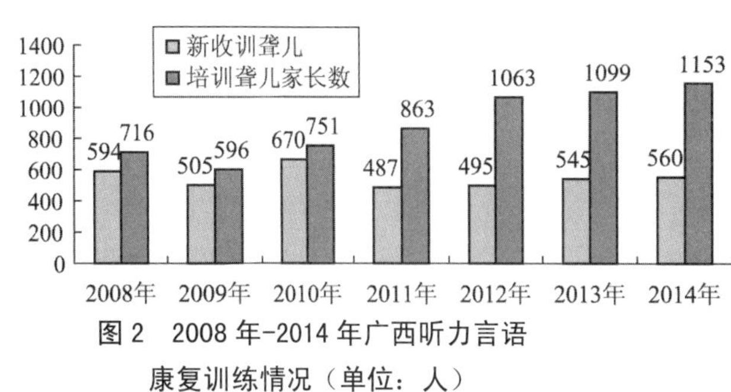

图2　2008年-2014年广西听力言语康复训练情况（单位：人）

大力推广“社会化、综合性、开放式”精神病防治康复工作。在94个市县开展精神病防治康复工作，对125833重性精神病患者进行综合防治康复，监护率达到79.47%，显好率达到63.54%，社会参与率达到52.12%，肇事率0.37%；解除关锁29人；对11642名贫困精神病患者进行医疗救助。

建立了1个省级孤独症儿童康复训练机构；289名孤独症儿童在各级机构进行了康复训练。

开展肢体残疾康复训练服务机构达25个，其中，省级康复机构1个，地市级、县级康复机构24个；培训各级各类肢体残疾康复人员108人次；全区共对7007肢体残疾者实施康复训练，其中肢体残疾儿童社区、家庭康复训练数为1622人、成年肢体残疾人社区、家庭康复训练数为4856人；实施救助项目资助529名脑瘫儿童进行机构康复训练，资助240名贫困肢体残疾儿童实施矫治手术。

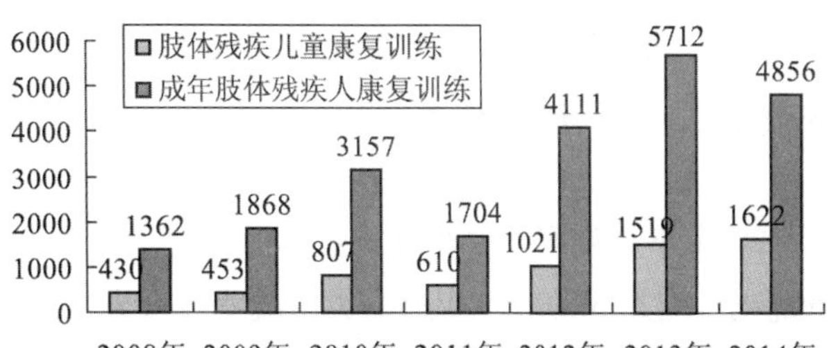

图3　2008年-2014年广西肢体残疾康复训练情况（单位：人）

开展智力残疾康复训练服务的机构24个，其中，省级康复机构1个，地市级、县级康复机构23个；培训各级各类智力残疾康复人员80人次；全区共对3416名智力残疾人进行康复训练；实施救助项目资助525名智力残疾儿童进行机构康复训练，同时培训儿童家长。

加强残疾人辅助器具服务体系建设，深入开展辅助器具供应服务，为残疾人减免费用供应辅助器具 20458 件，供应品种为 90 种，免费发放的辅助器具件数为 14747 件。全年装配假肢 941 例、矫形器 205 例，验配助视器 8748 件。

图 4　2008 年-2014 年广西辅助器具供应情况（单位：人）

53 个县的 138 个医疗卫生机构陆续开展残疾儿童筛查工作，年度新诊断 0-6 岁残疾儿童 1951 人。

二、以扶残助学为“引擎”，推动我区特殊教育事业上台阶

2014 年，实施残疾人事业专项彩票公益金助学项目，为 466 人次家庭经济困难的残疾儿童享受普惠性学前教育提供资助。各地也积极多渠道争取资金支持，对 135 名残疾儿童给予学前教育资助。

共有特殊教育普通高中班（部）10 个，在校生 273 人；其中聋高中 6 个，在校生 228 人；盲高中 3 个，在校生 45 人。残疾人中等职业学校（班）11 个，在校生 177 人，毕业生 26 人，其中 26 人获得职业资格证书。有 279 名残疾人被普通高等院校录取。

三、贯彻落实《残疾人就业条例》，促进就业工作迈出新步伐

2014 年，残疾人就业规模总体保持稳定。城镇新就业残疾人 5930 人，其中，集中就业残疾人 1162 人，按比例安排残疾人就业 1624 人，公益性岗位就业 176 人，个体就业及其它形式灵活就业 2863 人，辅助性就业 105 人。城镇就业人数 77938 人；650949 名农村残疾人在业，其中 519874 名残疾人从事农业生产劳动。

残疾人职业培训基地达到 70 个，其中残联兴办 26 个，依托社会机构兴办 44 个，其中 10055 人次城镇残疾人接受了职业培训。

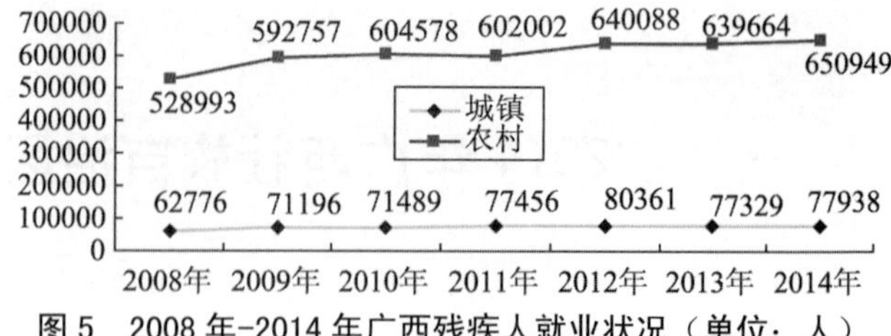

图 5　2008 年-2014 年广西残疾人就业状况（单位：人）

盲人按摩事业稳定发展，按摩机构迅速增长。2014 年度培训盲人保健按摩人员 662 名、盲人医疗按摩人员 30 名；保健按摩机构达到 181 个，医疗按摩机构达到 1 个；在专业技术职务资格评审中，有 2 人通过医疗按摩人员初级职称评审。

2014 年新型农村和城镇居民社会养老保险统一合并实施，已有 974129 名城乡残疾居民参保，参保率 65.82%，在 60 岁以下的参保残疾人中有 126566 名重度残疾人，其中 119451 人得到了政府的参保扶助，代缴补贴比例达到 94.38%。有 81073 名非重度残疾人也享受了全额或部分代缴的优惠政策。领取养老金待遇的人数达到 494578 人。

城镇残疾职工参加养老保险 40239 人，参加医疗保险 46772 人，城镇 67862 人和农村 398955 人残疾人纳入最低生活保障范围；城镇集中供养残疾人和农村五保供养残疾人分别达到 2218 名和 44278 名；9824 名和 316893 名符合条件的城乡残疾人分别享受了稳定的生活补贴和护理补贴。65208 名城乡残疾人得到了其他救助救济。

残疾人托养服务工作规范推进，残疾人托养服务机构达到 32 个，共为 1082 名残疾人提供了托养服务。其中寄宿制托养服务机构 3 个；日间照料机构 27 个；综合性托养服务机构 2 个。在以上机构中，共有 267 名残疾人实现辅助性就业，23 名残疾人实现了支持性就业。机构之外接受居家托养服务的残疾人达到 33222 人。全年共有 2339 名托养服务管理和服务人员接受了各级各类专业培训，其中接受国家级培训 1 人。

图 6　2008 年-2014 年广西残疾人纳入最低生活保障情况（单位：人）

四、以新农村建设为契机，探索扶贫工作新模式

2014年，残疾人扶贫开发成效显著，贫困残疾人生产生活状况得到进一步改善。59817名贫困残疾人得到扶持，其中38357人通过扶贫开发实际脱贫；接受实用技术培训的残疾人达到31528人次。

康复扶贫贴息贷款扶持1509名农村残疾人，残疾人扶贫基地达到128个，安置2427名残疾人就业，扶持带动14050名残疾人。

完成5848户农村贫困残疾人危房改造，各地投入危房资金5639.26万元，6109名残疾人受益。

基层党组织助残扶贫项目帮扶17813名农村贫困残疾人，其中首次接受帮扶15461人。“万村千乡市场工程”助残扶贫项目安置2名贫困残疾人就业，帮扶贫困残疾人创办 个村级农村店。

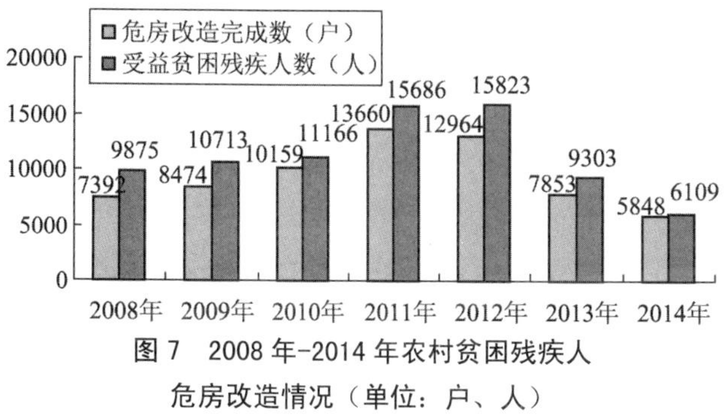

图7 2008年-2014年农村贫困残疾人危房改造情况（单位：户、人）

五、以丰富残疾人文化生活为出发点，提升宣传文体工作活力

截至2014年底，共有省级残疾人专题广播节目1个，电视手语新闻栏目1个；地市级残疾人专题广播节目3个，电视手语新闻栏目4个，播出公益广告3个。

截至2014年底，省地县三级公共图书馆共设立盲文及盲文有声读物阅览室35个，共开展残疾人文化周活动70场次，共举办残疾人文化艺术类比赛及展览81次，共有各类残疾人艺术团6个。

各地深入开展残疾人体育工作。组织省级残疾人群众体育健身活动1次，100人次参加；建设省级残疾人群众体育活动示范点达到3个；培训省级残疾人体育健身指导员达到284人；组织省级残疾人体育比赛1次，参赛运动员达546人次；省级残疾人体育训练基地已达1个，组织地市级残疾人体育健身活动26次，3449人次参加；设立地市级残疾人群众体育活动示范点16个；培训地市级残疾人体育健身指导员421人。

六、深入实施“扶残维权工程”，加强维权工作力度

2014年，制定或修改保障残疾人权益的规范性文件地市级2件、县级8件。县级以上人大进行《残疾人保障法》执法检查和专题调研6次；政协进行视察和专题调研4次。开展普法宣传教育活动211次，57087人参加；举办法律培训班43个，2950人参加。

截至2014年底，成立残疾人法律救助工作协调机构39个，建立残疾人法律救助工作站42个，办理案件99件，建立残疾人法律援助中心（工作站）118个，办理案件438件，有力地推动了法律救助和法律援助工作。

残疾人参政议政工作得到加强，各级残联协助人大代表、政协委员提出议案、建议、提案27件，办理议案、建议、提案20件。

无障碍建设法规、标准进一步完善。共出台了11个省、地市、县级无障碍建设与管理法规、规章和规范性文件；125个市、县、区系统开展无障碍建设；开展无障碍建设检查403次，无障碍培训500人次；为3611个贫困残疾人家庭实施了无障碍改造；为17187名残疾人发放了残疾人机动轮椅车燃油补贴。

各级残联共处理残疾人群众来信1337件，接待残疾人群众来访15130人次，其中集体访18批次、305人次。

七、规范基层残疾人组织建设

2014年，12个地市级残联在领导班子中配备了残疾人理事长或副理事长；46个县级残联机关配备了残疾人干部；已建乡镇（街道）残联1244个，已建率达到100.00%，选聘残疾人专职委员1397名；已建社区（村）残协15970个，已建率达到100.00%，选聘残疾人专职委员16154名。

省市县乡残联实有人员已达3167人。各级残联共举办培训班818期，培训机关干部、协会干部及

残疾人专职委员15078人次。

共建立省级以下各类残疾人专门协会631个，市级专门协会已建比例为100.00%；县（含县级市）级专门协会已建比例为100.18%。全国共建立助残社会组织14个，其中在民政部门注册的为8个，以残联为业务主管单位的6个。

八、基础服务设施建设力度进一步加大

截至2014年底，全国已竣工并投入使用的各级残疾人综合服务设施97个，总建设规模139939.1平方米，总投资24084.7万元；已竣工并投入使用的各级残疾人康复设施1个，总建设规模660平方米，总投资125万元；已竣工并投入使用的各级残疾人托养服务设施2个，总建设规模920平方米，总投资70.2万元。

九、信息化建设稳步推进

进一步完善残联统计系统网站建设评价指标，通过对省级及计划单列市残联网站开展测评，反映出省级网站对网上政务公开、网上服务，无障碍等方面更加重视，总体建设水平有了明显提升。截止2014年底，全区1个省级、15个地市级、101个县级残联开通网站。各级残联共有197名专业技术人员从事信息化工作；省级残联共建立局域网1个，网上办公（OA）系统1个。

统计队伍建设进一步加强，各级残联共有135名专、兼职统计人员从事残疾人事业统计工作，统计人员业务素质培养普遍得到重视，省级残联举办培训班1期，参加培训的人员达到150人次。

2014 年海南省残疾人事业发展统计公报

2014 年,在海南省委、省政府的领导下，在中国残联的指导下，省残联以残疾人为本，以落实党的十八届三中、四中全会和中国残联六代会以及省残联六代会精神统领残疾人事业发展全局。各级残联结合党的群众路线教育实践活动，密切联系群众，以全新的面貌，务实清廉的作风，完成残疾人各民生项目，推动全省残疾人事业再上新的台阶。

一、康复服务

围绕残疾人“人人享有康复服务”目标，加强残疾预防与康复工作，通过实施国家、省康复项目工程，使各类残疾人得到不同程度的康复。

截止 2014 年底，已在全省各市县、乡镇开展了社区康复工作，累计已建立 628 个社区康复站，配备了 1373 名社区康复协调员，有 7112 名残疾人得到不同程度的康复服务。

全省 4 个医疗卫生机构陆续开展残疾儿童筛查工作，年度新诊断 0-6 岁残疾儿童 333 人。在全社会的积极参与下，全省实施白内障复明手术 2628 例；其中，为贫困白内障患者免费手术 2463 例；为 937 名低视力患者配用助视器，开展家庭康复训练，培训低视力儿童家长 200 名；对 1519 名盲人进行定向行走训练。继续推进听力语言康复机构建设，累计已建听力语言康复机构省级 1 个，县级 3 个；本年度新收训聋儿 60 名，在训聋儿 108 名，培训聋儿家长 108 名；实施贫困聋儿人工耳蜗、助听器抢救性康复项目，完成国家“七彩梦”聋儿抢救性康复“人工耳蜗”26 名、“助听器”30 名的项目任务。完成 2014 年省委省政府为民办实事适应症贫困残疾儿童人工耳蜗植入手术 34 例，开展“成人助听行动”，为 465 名成年人免费验配助听器。开展肢体残疾康复训练服务机构达 6 个,对 2151 名肢体残疾者实施康复训练。实施救助项目资助 105 名脑瘫儿童进行机构康复训练，资助 38 名贫困肢体残疾儿童实施矫治手术。开展智力残疾康复训练服务省级机构 9 个,对 1332 名智力残疾人进行康复训练；实施救助项目资助 135 名智力残疾儿童进行机构康复训练，同时培训儿童家长。大力推广“社会化、综合性、开放式”精神病防治康复试点工作。在 18 个市县开展精神病防治康复工作，对 18207 名重性精神病患者进行综合防治康复，监护率达到 65.42%，显好率达到 18.39%，社会参与率达到 13.32%，肇事率 0.03%；解除关锁 25 人；对 3035 名贫困精神病患者进行医疗救助。新增了 6 个省级孤独症儿童康复训练机构；172 名孤独症儿童在各级机构进行了康复训练。深入开展辅助器具供应服务，为残疾人减免费用供应辅助器具 9014 件，其中装配假肢 64 例、矫形器 233 例，验配助视器 1053 件。

二、教育助学

加大残疾人受教育的保障力度。全省已开办特殊教育普通高中班（部）1 个，在校生 70 人；其中聋生 70 人；残疾人中等职业学校（班）2 个，在校生 88 人，毕业生 72 人，其中 72 人获得职业资格证书。有 69 名残疾人被普通高等院校录取。接受残疾人事业专项彩票公益金助学项目资助的残疾儿童有 111 人次;开展各教育阶段残疾学生或贫困残疾人子女学生资助工作。

三、就业培训

采取优惠和扶持保护措施，多渠道、多层次、多种形式促进残疾人实现就业。2014 年，全省城镇新增 878 名残疾人就业。其中，集中就业残疾人 88 名，按比例安排残疾人就业 389 名，公益性岗位安排就业残疾人 15 名，个体就业及其它形式灵活就业残疾人 356 名,辅助性就业 30 人；全省城镇实际在业人数 1.1 万人；有 6.9 万名残疾人在农村实现就业，其中，5.8 万人从事农业生产劳动。截止 2014 年底，全省残疾人职业培训基地有 10 个，其中残联自办 3 个，依托社会机构创办 7 个，全年有 1969 人次城镇残疾人接受了职业培训。2014 年度培训盲人保健按摩人员387名、盲人医疗按摩人员30名；保健按摩机构达到166个，医疗按摩机构达到3个；出台《海南省盲人医疗按摩人员从事医疗按摩资格证书管理实施细则》，全年为36名盲人按摩人员进行保健按摩师资格鉴定。

四、扶贫开发

残疾人扶贫工作有所进展，贫困残疾人生产生活状况得到进一步改善。2014年，6481台贫困残疾人得到扶持，其中2189人通过扶贫开发实际脱贫；接受实用技术培训的残疾人达到7437人次。在三亚、琼中、保亭等市县建立残疾人扶贫基地6个，安置101名残疾人就业，扶持带动258户残疾人家庭发展生产。残疾人居住环境不断改善，完成318户农村贫困残疾人危房改造，各地投入危房资金430万元，624名残疾人受益。基层党组织助残扶贫项目帮扶435名农村贫困残疾人，其中首次接受帮扶424人。

五、社会保障

我省残疾人社会保障状况明显改善。残疾人新型农村和城镇居民社会养老保险工作继续推进。由于我省残疾人社会保障工作起步晚，残疾人社会保障在供给与需求上矛盾仍然突出。2014年，全省有17.0万城镇残疾人参加了城镇居民社会养老保险，参保率77.15%。60岁以下的参保残疾人中有3.64万重度残疾人，其中3.60万名得到了政府的参保扶助，代缴补贴比例达到98.98%。有0.14万名非重度残疾人也享受了全额或部分代缴的优惠政策。领取养老金待遇的人数达到6.45万人。城镇残疾职工参加养老保险0.55万人，参加医疗保险0.54人，城镇1.53万人和农村4.58万人残疾人纳入最低生活保障范围；城镇集中供养残疾人和农村五保供养残疾人分别达到0.03万名和0.24万名；0.25万名和3.92万名符合条件的城乡残疾人分别享受了稳定的生活补贴和护理补贴。1.71万名城乡残疾人得到了其他救助救济。残疾人托养服务工作规范推进，残疾人托养服务机构达到6个，共为582残疾人提供了宿制托养托养服务，接受居家托养服务的残疾人达到1.43万人。

六、法制维权

各级残联维权组织建设得到加强，残疾人事业法律法规体系进一步完善，残疾人维权工作全面开展。2014年全省县级以上人大进行《残疾人保障法》执法检查和专题调研1次；政协进行视察和专题调研1次。开展普法宣传教育活动19次，2269万人参加；举办法律培训班2个，120人参加。截至2014年底，成立残疾人法律救助工作协调机构5个，建立残疾人法律救助工作站5个，办理案件3件，建立残疾人法律援助工作站15个，办理案件43件，各级残联协助人大代表、政协委员提出议案、建议、提案7件，办理议案、建议、提案4件。2014年全省有609户贫困残疾人家庭得到无障碍改造；为9382名残疾人发放残疾人机动轮椅车燃油补贴。全省各级残联共处理残疾人群众来信309余件，接待残疾人群众来访2725人次,其中集体访6批次、130人次。

七、宣文体育

大力宣传残疾人事业，反映残疾人生活，宣传扶残助残先进典型，全省共刊播残疾人事业新闻稿件共1381篇（条），大力营造有利于残疾人事业发展的社会环境。搭建“海南省公共卫生联播网残疾人事业宣传平台”，加大了扶残助残宣传力度，普及残疾预防等知识。截至2014年底，省地县三级公共图书馆共设立盲文及盲人有声读物阅览室2个，共开展残疾人文化周活动10场次，共举办残疾人文化艺术类比赛及展览5次，共有各类残疾人艺术团体1个。开展残疾人体育工作，组织开展省级残疾人体育健身活动4次，参加人数250人；培训残疾人体育健身指导员115人；举办全省性残疾人体育比赛1次，参与的残疾人运动员350人次。省级残疾人体育训练基地已达10个，组织地市级残疾人体育健身活动2次，80人次参加；设立地市级残疾人群众体育活动示范点3个；培训地市级残疾人体育健身指导员4人。

八、组织建设

残疾人基层组织规范化建设进一步完善，全省已建乡镇（街道）残联 228 个，已建率达到 99.56%，选聘残疾人专职委员 243 名；已建社区（村）残协 0.26 万个，已建率达到 85.21%，选聘残疾人专职委员 0.27 万名。各级残联队伍不断充实，工作队伍人数已达 0.06 万人。加强残联干部培训工作，举办各式各样培训班共 105 期，培训机关干部、协会干部及残疾人专职委员 1482 人次，残联系统干部队伍素质有所提升。全省乡（镇、街道）和村（社区）志愿者实名登记注册人数有 6890 人。截止 2014 年底，成立的省级以下各类残疾人专门协会达 89 个，市级专门协会已建比例为 100%，县（含县级市）级专门协会已建比例为 70.48%。全国共建立助残社会组织 7 个，其中在民政部门注册的为 6 个，以残联为业务主管单位的 2 个。

九、信息化建设

统计队伍建设进一步加强，各级残联共有 23 名专、兼职统计人员从事残疾人事业统计工作。统计人员业务素质培养普遍得到重视，省级残联举办培训班 1 期，参加培训的人员达到 35 人次。各级残联全面推进网站建设，省残联门户网站同时进行无障碍改造，为更多的残疾人提供信息服务。2014 年省残联开设网站技术培训班 1 期，培训各级残联信息员达 50 人次。

十、综合服务设施

各级残疾人综合服务设施项目建设有所进展，但部分已建成的残疾人综合服务设施存在局限性，如建筑面积不足、功能单一、硬件设施陈旧等，还不具备综合服务能力。截止 2014 年底，全省已投入使用和累计投入使用的项目有 8 个，总建设规模 10306 平方米，总投资 3831 元。

2014 年重庆市残疾人事业发展统计公报

2014 年，在重庆市委、市政府的正确领导和中国残联的关心指导下，全市残联系统深入学习贯彻党的十八届四中全会和习近平总书记关于残疾人事业发展系列讲话精神，按照市委四届四次、五次、六次全会和中国残联“基础管理建设年”总体安排部署，务实推进年初提出的从“六个方面取得突破”各项工作，着眼于加快残疾人奔小康进程，着眼于让残疾人生活更加殷实、精神更加丰富、人格更有尊严，把保障和改善残疾人民生摆在更加突出位置，密切联系残疾人，办成了一批残疾人普遍受益、社会广泛赞誉、利于残疾人事业长远发展的大事、实事、好事。

一、残疾人康复工作

推进“人人享有康复服务”工作，在全市 40 个区县开展了社区康复工作，累计已建社区康复站的社区总数 3313 个，配备 11073 名社区康复协调员。

全市 123 个医疗卫生机构陆续开展残疾儿童筛查工作，年度新诊断 0-6 岁残疾儿童 2086 人。

开展视力残疾康复机构 41 个，完成白内障复明手术 18947 例；为 7676 名贫困白内障患者免费施行复明手术；为 2193 名低视力患者配用助视器，培训低视力儿童家长 546 名。对 1177 名盲人进行定向行走训练。

推进听力语言康复机构规范化管理，完善基层服务网络。已建设市级听力语言康复机构 1 个，基层听力语言康复机构 13 个。年度新收训聋儿 349 名，在训聋儿 498 名；规范聋儿家长学校，开展家庭训练，共培训聋儿家长 1079 名。

开展肢体残疾康复训练服务机构 37 个；对 5987 肢体残疾者实施康复训练；实施救助项目资助 374 名脑瘫儿童进行机构康复训练，资助 325 名贫困肢体残疾儿童实施矫治手术。

开展智力残疾康复训练服务的机构 41 个；对 2921 名智力残疾人进行康复训练；实施救助项目资助 301 名智力残疾儿童进行机构康复训练，同时培训儿童家长。

大力推广“社会化、综合性、开放式”精神病防治康复工作。对 180559 名重性精神病患者进行综合防治康复，监护率达到 80.67%，显好率达到 81.51%，社会参与率达到 64.75%，肇事率 0.12%；解除关锁 52 人；对 14446 名贫困精神病患者进行医疗救助。

建立孤独症儿童康复训练机构 20 个，对 392 名孤独症儿童进行了康复训练。

加强残疾人辅助器具服务体系建设，深入开展辅助器具供应服务，为残疾人减免费用供应辅助器具 16675 件，其中装配假肢 240 例、矫形器 378 例，验配助视器 2720 件。

二、残疾人教育工作

残疾人接受特殊教育帮扶更加有效。2014 年中央彩票公益金助学项目，对 200 名学龄前贫困残疾儿童进行入园救助；各级残联多渠道争取资金支持，对 77 名残疾儿童给予学前教育资助。

全市现有特殊教育普通高中班 2 个，在校生 194 人。残疾人中等职业学校 5 个，在校生 261 人。有 166 名残疾人被普通高等院校录取，有 20 名残疾人被高等特殊教育机构录取。

三、残疾人就业工作

残疾人就业创业扶持帮扶更加给力。全年新增残疾人就业 4868 人，其中，集中就业残疾人 1327 人，按比例安排残疾人就业 1151 人，公益性岗位就业 95 人，个体就业及其它形式灵活就业 2004 人，辅助性就业 291 人。加大残疾人职业技能培训力度，残疾人职业培训基地达到 34 个， 5092 人次城镇残疾人接受了职业培训。开展了以“就业帮扶、真情相助”为主题的“就业援助月活动”，共入户走访困难残疾人家庭 2842 户，组织专场招聘会 134 次，帮助残疾登记失业人员实现就业 942 人。加强盲人按摩管理工作，推进实施《重庆市盲人按摩行业扶持办法》。2014 年度培训盲人保健按摩人员 798 名、盲人医疗按摩人员 85 名；保健按摩机构达到 735 个，医疗按摩机构达到 12 个；在专业技术职务资格评审中，分别有 4 人和 2 人通过盲人医疗按摩人员中级和初级职称评审。

四、社会保障工作

残疾人社会保障“兜底”力度进一步增强。出台了《关于提高参加城乡居民社会养老保险重度残疾人员政府代缴标准的通知》，对参加了城乡居民社会养老保险的一、二级重度残疾人员，将政府代缴的养老保险费标准由每人每年 40 元提高到 100 元。全市已有 45.12 万城乡残疾居民参加了城乡居民养老保险，参保率 74.84%，在 60 岁以下的参保残疾人中有 10.08 万名重度残疾人，其中 10.03 万人得到了政府的参保扶助，代缴补贴比例达到 99.49%。有 10.64 万名非重度残疾人也享受了全额或部分代缴的优惠政策。领取养老金待遇的人数达到 17.04 万人。城镇残疾职工参加养老保险 8.3 万人，参加医疗保险 8.6 万人，19.52 万名残疾人享受城乡居民最低生活保障；城镇集中供养残疾人和农村五保供养残疾人分别达到 0.4 万名和 2.1 万名；1.2 万名和 1.9 万名符合条件的城乡残疾人分别享受了稳定的生活补贴和护理补贴。8.5 万城乡残疾人得到了其他救助救济。

残疾人托养服务工作规范推进，残疾人托养服务机构达到 87 个，共为 1574 名残疾人提供了托养服务。其中寄宿制托养服务机构 22 个；日间照料机构 40 个；综合性托养服务机构 25 个。在以上机构中，共有 26 名残疾人实现辅助性就业，5 名残疾人实现了支持性就业。机构之外接受居家托养服务的残疾人达到 19742 人。

五、残疾人扶贫开发工作

残疾人扶贫帮扶整体合力进一步强化。全年共计扶持 49410 名贫困残疾人，其中 23327 人通过扶贫开发实现脱贫。开展农村实用技术培训，培训 21354 人次。

康复扶贫贴息贷款扶持 770 名农村残疾人，残疾人扶贫基地达到 91 个，安置 1130 名残疾人就业，扶持带动 1611 名残疾人。

实施农村贫困残疾人危房改造“阳光安居”工程，推行“一户一策”，完成农村贫困残疾人危房改造 3607 户，3681 名残疾人受益。

基层党组织助残扶贫项目帮扶 778 名农村贫困残疾人。“万村千乡市场工程”助残扶贫项目安置 30 名贫困残疾人就业，帮扶贫困残疾人创办 2 个村级农村店。

六、残疾人宣传文化体育工作

加大宣传工作力度。截至 2014 年底，共有市级残疾人专题广播节目 1 个，电视手语新闻栏目 1 个，播出公益广告 3 个；区级残疾人专题广播节目 7 个，电视手语新闻栏目 14 个，播出公益广告 14 个。

残疾人群众性文化体育活动更加丰富。全市公共图书馆共设立盲文及盲人有声读物阅览室 44 个，举办残疾人文化周 271 场，举办残疾人文化艺术类比赛及展览 49 次，成立各类残疾人艺术团体 9 个。

举办市级残疾人群众体育健身活动 5 次，参加人数 1600 人次，建设市级残疾人群众体育活动示范点 13 个，培训市级残疾人体育健身指导员 120 人，组织市级残疾人体育比赛 2 次，参赛的残疾人运动员 968 人次。举办区级残疾人体育健身活动 300 次，24807 人次参加，设立区级残疾人群众体育活动示范点 129 个，培训区级残疾人体育健身指导员 486 人。

七、残疾人维权工作

继续完善残疾人法律法规，开展法律服务、法律援助和法制宣传，维护残疾人合法权益。2014 年，全市制定或修改保障残疾人权益的规范性文件 16 件。县级以上人大进行《残疾人保障法》执法检查和专题调研 16 次；政协进行视察和专题调研 23 次。开展普法宣传教育活动 192 次，67841 人参加；举办法律培训班 60 个，3709 人参加。

截至 2014 年底，成立残疾人法律救助工作协调机构 27 个，建立残疾人法律救助工作站 27 个，办理案件 238 件，建立残疾人法律援助中心（工作站）41 个，办理案件 875 件，有力地推动了法律救助和法律援助工作。

残疾人参政议政工作得到加强，各级残联协助人大代表、政协委员提出议案、建议、提案63件，办理议案、建议、提案49件。

无障碍建设法规、标准进一步完善。截止目前，全市共出台了6个无障碍建设与管理法规、规章；38个区县系统开展无障碍建设；开展无障碍建设检查82次，无障碍培训2419人次；为2768个贫困残疾人家庭实施了无障碍改造；为4264名残疾人发放了残疾人机动轮椅车燃油补贴。

推出了专门针对残疾人的“爱心通”手机优惠套餐，已有500多名残疾人得到了实惠。开展下肢残疾人路桥费的减免工作，享受路桥减免的残疾人共有867人。

八、残疾人组织建设工作

残疾人基层组织体系建设更加完善。全市已建乡镇（街道）残联1018个，已建率达到100%，选聘残疾人专职委员1042名；已建社区（村）残协10552个，已建率达到100%，选聘残疾人专职委员10412名。

各级残联实有人员1960人。举办培训班1265期，培训机关干部、协会干部及残疾人专职委员44713人次。

九、残疾人综合服务设施建设

推进综合服务设施建设，引导鼓励多形式发挥服务设施作用。2014年，全市已竣工并投入使用的各级残疾人综合服务设施28个，总建设规模8.54万平方米；已竣工并投入使用的各级残疾人康复设施5个，总建设规模1.03万平方米；已竣工并投入使用的各级残疾人托养服务设施1个，总建设规模0.01万平方米。

十、残疾人事业统计与信息化建设

统计队伍建设进一步加强，全市共有47名专、兼职统计人员从事残疾人事业统计工作，统计人员业务素质培养普遍得到重视，举办培训班1期，参加培训的人员达到50人次。

全面推进网站建设，目前市残联和38个区县残联已开通网站。开设网站技术培训班1期，培训各级残联信息员达55人次。

2014年四川省残疾人事业发展统计公报

2014年，在省委、省政府的领导下，在中国残联的指导和支持下，在全社会的关爱下，我省残疾人事业继续依托“量体裁衣”式残疾人服务工作，延续了良好的发展势头，各方面工作取得了新进步、新成效，残疾人得到了更多的实惠。现根据我省2014年度残疾人事业统计数据和实际情况，进行分析，并公报如下:

一、康复

1. 积极推进残疾人社区康复工作。截止2014年底，在31个市辖区和103个县（市）开展了社区康复工作，累计已建社区康复站的社区总数7048个，配备15908名社区康复协调员。

2. 大力完善视力康复机构和人员，通过实施一批重点康复工程，使各类视力残疾人得到不同程度的康复。截止2014年底，全省视力残疾康复机构的总数为24个，完成白内障复明手术42302例；为26841名贫困白内障患者免费施行复明手术；为5368名低视力患者配用助视器，培训低视力儿童家长920名，有效开展家庭康复训练。对6910名盲人进行定向行走训练。

3. 加强全省听力语言康复网络建设，大力充实听力康复机构专业人员。已建设省级听力语言康复机构1个，基层听力语言康复机构31个。年度新收训聋儿855名，在训聋儿1224名；规范聋儿家长学校，开展家庭训练，共培训聋儿家长1260名；开展各级各类听力语言康复专业技术人员培训，共培训专业人员170人。

4. 肢体残疾康复工作成效显著。截止年底，全省开展肢体残疾康复训练服务机构达72个，培训各级各类肢体残疾康复人员1469人次；全国共对24731肢体残疾者实施康复训练；实施救助项目资助5365名脑瘫儿童进行机构康复训练，资助931名贫困肢体残疾儿童实施矫治手术。

5. 稳步推进智力残疾康复工作。截止年底，全省开展智力残疾康复训练服务的机构64个，其中，省级康复机构1个，地市级、县级康复机构63个；培训各级各类智力残疾康复人员807人次；全国共对6472名智力残疾人进行康复训练；实施救助项目资助1311名智力残疾儿童进行机构康复训练，同时培训儿童家长。

6. 大力推广“社会化、综合性、开放式”精神病防治康复工作。2014年，共在145个市县开展精神病防治康复工作，对407803名重性精神病患者进行综合防治康复，监护率达到78.07%，显好率达到62.33%，社会参与率达到35.58%，肇事率0.32%；解除关锁862人；对21983名贫困精神病患者进行医疗救助。

7. 加强残疾人辅助器具服务体系建设，深入开展辅助器具供应服务。全年共为残疾人减免费用供应辅助器具92843件，其中装配假肢1513例、矫形器571例，验配助视器4765件。

二、教育

2014年，我省残疾人受教育权得到了更好地保障，进一步提高了残疾人整体素质和平等参与社会的能力。

1. 本年度，残疾人事业专项彩票公益金助学项目共为我省家庭经济困难的残疾儿童享受普惠性学前教育提供资助901人次；全省各地也积极多渠道争取资金支持，对441名残疾儿童提供了学前教育资助。

2. 截止2014年底，全省特殊教育普通高中共有14所，在校生256人；残疾人中等职业教育机构共有10个，在校生272人，本年度毕业生74人，获得职业资格证书10人；全年共有415名残疾人被普通高等院校录取。

三、就业

1. 2014年，全省残疾人就业工作取得稳步进展。城镇新增2.7万名残疾人就业，其中：集中就业残疾人 9574 人，按比例安排残疾人就业 3983 人，公益性岗位就业 885 人，个体就业及其它形式灵活就业 12541 人，辅助性就业 768 人。

2. 截止 2014 年底，全省残疾人职业培训基地达到 424 个,其中残联兴办 144 个。本年度共有 3.4 万名城镇残疾人接受了职业培训。

3. 盲人按摩事业稳定发展，按摩机构迅速增长。全年共培训盲人保健按摩人员 1160 名、盲人医疗按摩人员 105 名;全省保健按摩机构达到 1491 个，医疗按摩机构达到 48 个。

四、社会保障

2014 年度,全省残疾人社会保障状况保持平稳，残疾人参加新型农村和城镇居民社会养老保险工作实现了全覆盖。

1. 新型农村和城镇居民社会养老保险统一合并实施，截止年底，已有 178.3 万名城乡残疾居民参保，参保率 77.83%，在 60 岁以下的参保残疾人中有 29.7 万名重度残疾人，其中 29.4 万人得到了政府的参保扶助，代缴补贴比例达到 98.78%。有 14.3 万名非重度残疾人也享受了全额或部分代缴的优惠政策。领取养老金待遇的人数达到 45.5 万人。

2. 截止年底，已有 96 万名城乡残疾人纳入最低生活保障范围；城镇集中供养残疾人和农村五保供养残疾人分别达到 8543 名和 5.6 万名；共有 9.5 万人享受了稳定的生活补贴，6.9 万人享受了护理补贴；22.3 万名城乡残疾人得到了其他救助救济。

3. 残疾人托养服务工作规范推进，残疾人托养服务机构达到 153 个，共为 4153 名残疾人提供了托养服务。通过托养机构共有 498 名残疾人实现辅助性就业，208 名残疾人实现支持性就业。机构之外接受居家托养服务的残疾人达到 4 万人。全年共有 1428 名托养服务管理和服务人员接受了各级各类专业培训。

五、扶贫开发

2014 年,全省残疾人扶贫开发工作进一步推进，贫困残疾人生产生活状况得到进一步改善。

1. 本年度共扶持贫困残疾人 21.2 万名，脱贫 14 万名；接受实用技术培训的残疾人共计 11.4 万人次。

2. 已建残疾人扶持基地增长至 378 个，全年共安置 9834 名残疾人就业，扶持带动残疾人 2 万名。

3. 2014 年，全省共投入危房改造资金 1763.3 万元，完成 2889 户农村贫困残疾人家庭危房改造，受益残疾人 3198 名。

4. 通过基层党组织助残扶贫项目，帮扶 8496 名农村贫困残疾人，其中首次接受帮扶 2888 人；通过“万村千乡市场工程”助残扶贫项目，安置 774 名贫困残疾人就业，帮扶贫困残疾人创办 87 个村级农村店。

六、维权

2014 年，全省残疾人维权组织建设得到加强，残疾人事业法律法规体系得以进一步完善。

1. 截至年底，县级以上人大进行《残疾人保障法》执法检查和专题调研 41 次；政协进行视察和专题调研 58 次。全年共开展普法宣传教育活动 683 次，参加人数 12.8 万名；开展法律培训班 111 次，参加人数 7883 名。

2.截至 2014 年底，全省已成立残疾人法律救助工作协调机构 80 个，建立残疾人法律救助工作站 67 个，建立残疾人法律援助中心（工作站）140 个，有力地推动了法律救助和法律援助工作。

3. 残疾人参政议政工作得到加强，本年度各级残联协助人大代表、政协委员提出议案、建议、提案 106 件，办理议案、建议、提案 88 件。

4. 无障碍建设法规、标准进一步完善。截止年底，已出台 25 个省、地市、县级无障碍建设与管理法规、规章和规范性文件，35 个市、县、区系统开展了无障碍建设；本年度为 2 万个贫困残疾人家庭实施了无障碍改造，为 2.8 万名残疾人发放了残疾人机动轮椅车燃油补贴。

5. 2014 年，全省各级残联共处理残疾人群众来信 3991 件，接待残疾人群众来访 3.3 万人次，其中集体访 34 批次、540 人次。

七、宣传文化

随着事业的发展，残疾人文化生活更加丰富活跃，残疾人受到社会广泛关注并更加全面地参与到社会生活当中。

1. 截至年底，共有地市级残疾人专题广播节目25个，电视手语新闻栏目4个，全年播出公益广告38个。

2. 截至年底，省地县三级公共图书馆共设立盲文及盲人有声读物阅览室81个，共开展残疾人文化周活动153场次，共举办残疾人文化艺术类比赛及展览203次，共有各类残疾人艺术团体19个。

八、体育

1. 2014年，共组织省级残疾人群众体育健身活动5次，3000人次参加；已建立省级残疾人群众体育示范点5个，培训省级残疾人体育健身指导员35名；组织全省残疾人体育比赛1次，参赛运动员达90人次；省级残疾人体育训练基地已达到13个。

2. 共组织地市级残疾人体育健身活动178次，1.3万人次参加；已建立地市级残疾人体育示范点177个，培训地市级残疾人体育健身指导员1686名。

九、组织建设

1. 截止2014年底，全省有10个地市级残联的领导班子配备了残疾人理事长或副理事长；有95个县级残联机关配备了残疾人干部。

2. 全省已建乡镇（街道）残联4363个，已建率达94.5%，选聘残疾人专职委员4436名；已建村（社区）残协4.5万个，已建率达87.6%，选聘残疾人专职委员3.5万名。

3. 全省省市县乡级残联实有人员已达9116名；残联干部综合培训工作取得较好成绩，全年共培训机关干部、协会干部及残疾人专职委员10.7万人次。

4. 截至年底，已建立省级以下各类残疾人专门协会935个，市级专门协会已建比例为100%；县级专门协会已建比例为90.2%。全国共建立助残社会组织88个，其中在民政部门注册的为80个，以残联为业务主管单位的19个。

十、信息化

1. 2014年，全省统计队伍建设进一步加强。全省各级残联共有185名专、兼职统计人员从事残疾人事业统计工作。

2. 全面推进网站建设。省残联已开通无障碍公众服务网站，有18个地市级残联网站和93个县级残联网站也已开通。

3. 截止2014年底，全省各级残联共有267名专业技术人员从事信息化工作。

十一、服务设施建设

全省残疾人服务设施建设得到全面发展。

截止到2014年底，已竣工并投入使用的各级残疾人综合服务设施共计87个，总建设规模19.3万平方米，总投资5.5亿元；

已竣工并投入使用的各级康复设施共计27个，总建设规模11.1万平方米，总投资5.7亿元；

已竣工并投入使用的各级托养设施共计12个，总建设规模2.2万平方米，总投资0.5亿元。

2014年贵州省残疾人事业统计公报

2014年，我省残疾人工作在省委、省政府的领导下，在中国残联的指导下，在省政府残工委成员单位及社会各界的支持下，认真落实《残疾人保障法》，不断健全残疾人权益保障制度，有力促进残疾人服务托住底、补短板工作，有效落实残疾人同步小康创业就业年度任务，有序推动政府购买残疾人服务试点工作，扎实提升残联组织的服务能力和管理水平，着力实施一系列民生项目，全面完成各项工作任务，残疾人事业迈出新步伐、取得新成就。根据残疾人事业统计数据和实际情况公报如下:

一、康复

在10个市辖区和75个县（市）开展了社区康复工作，完成白内障复明手术13385例,其中贫困白内障患者9292名，为2745名低视力患者配用助视器，培训低视力儿童家长297名，有效开展家庭康复训练。对2300名盲人进行定向行走训练。

推进听力语言康复机构规范化管理，完善基层服务网络。已建设省级听力语言康复机构1个，基层听力语言康复机构16个,年度新收训聋儿383名，在训聋儿540名，规范聋儿家长学校，开展家庭训练，共培训聋儿家长690名。

培训各级各类肢体残疾康复人员213人（次），共对1793肢体残疾者实施康复训练，实施救助项目资助374名脑瘫儿童进行机构康复训练，资助252名贫困肢体残疾儿童实施矫治手术；为麻风畸残者实施矫治手术89例，开展宣传普及教育，为麻风患者回归社会营造良好社会氛围。

培训各级各类智力残疾康复人员152人次，全省共对1092名智力残疾人进行康复训练，实施救助项目资助562名智力残疾儿童进行机构康复训练，同时培训儿童家长。

大力推广“社会化、综合性、开放式”精神病防治康复工作。在85个市县开展精神病防治康复工作，对67457名精神病患者进行监护，14262名精神病患者接受治疗，监护率达到85.32%，显好率达到67.86%，社会参与率达到56.38%，肇事率0.24%，解除关锁234人，对5774名贫困精神病患者进行医疗救助。

308名孤独症儿童在各级机构进行了康复训练。加强残疾人辅助器具服务体系建设，深入开展辅助器具供应服务，为残疾人减免费用供应辅助器具19118件，其中装配假肢654例、矫形器439例，验配助视器3671件。

二、教育就业

2014年，实施残疾人事业专项彩票公益金助学项目，为290人次家庭经济困难的残疾儿童享受普惠性学前教育提供资助；各地也积极多渠道争取资金支持，对45名残疾儿童给予学前教育资助。417名残疾人被普通高等院校录取。

2014年，全省启动实施残疾人同步小康创业就业行动，创建残疾人创业就业示范点340个，扶持1310户残疾人家庭创业,新增残疾人就业10800人，其中，集中就业残疾人1384人，按比例安排残疾人就业1572人，公益性岗位就业143人，个体就业及其它形式灵活就业7592人，辅助性就业109人。城镇残疾人就业人数88216人；747962名农村残疾人在业，其中595475名残疾人从事农业生产劳动。

残疾人职业培训基地达到40个,其中残联兴办17个，依托社会机构兴办23个。5142人次城镇残疾人接受了职业培训。

盲人按摩事业稳定发展，按摩机构迅速增长。2014年度培训盲人保健按摩人员496名、盲人医疗按摩人员48名；保健按摩机构达到433个，医疗按摩机构达到10个。

三、社会保障

2014年新型农村和城镇居民社会养老保险统一合并实施，已有542338名城乡残疾居民参保，参保率60.82%，在60岁以下的参保残疾人中有78990名重度残疾人，其中77254人得到了政府的参保扶助，代缴补贴比例达到97.80%。有24569名非重度残疾人也享受了全额或部分代缴的优惠政策。领取养老金待遇的人数达到 281521 人。城镇残疾职工参加养老保险 44796 人，参加医疗保险 46298 人。

城镇 52220 人和农村 433440 人残疾人纳入最低生活保障范围；城镇集中供养残疾人和农村五保供养残疾人分别达到 1839 名和 11197 名；68395 名城乡残疾人得到了其他救助救济。

残疾人托养服务工作规范推进，残疾人托养服务机构达到 11 个，其中寄宿制托养服务机构 3 个，日间照料机构 3 个，综合性托养服务机构 5 个，共为 543 名残疾人提供了托养服务。在以上机构中，共有 33 名残疾人实现辅助性就业。机构之外接受居家托养服务的残疾人达到 13937 人。全年共有 409 名托养服务管理和服务人员接受了各级各类专业培训，其中接受国家级培训 6 人。

四、扶贫

2014 年，残疾人扶贫开发成效显著，贫困残疾人生产生活状况得到进一步改善。91546 名贫困残疾人得到扶持，其中 59499 人通过扶贫开发实现脱贫；接受实用技术培训的残疾人达到 17020 人次。

康复扶贫贴息贷款扶持 419 名农村残疾人，残疾人扶贫基地达到 340 个，安置 1979 名残疾人就业，扶持带动 15133 户残疾人。完成 986 户农村贫困残疾人危房改造，各地投入危改资金 947.57 万元，1426 名残疾人受益。

基层党组织助残扶贫项目帮扶 2824 名农村贫困残疾人，其中首次接受帮扶 2230 人。“万村千乡市场工程”助残扶贫项目安置 120 名贫困残疾人就业，帮扶贫困残疾人创办 96 个村级农村店。

五、维权

2014 年，修订了《贵州省残疾人保障法》，制定或修改保障残疾人权益的规范性文件地市级 1 件、县级 5 件。县级以上人大进行《残疾人保障法》执法检查和专题调研 15 次；政协进行视察和专题调研 10 次。开展普法宣传教育活动 269 次，38342 人参加；举办法律培训班 31 个，3012 人参加。

截至 2014 年底，成立残疾人法律救助工作协调机构 38 个，建立残疾人法律救助工作站 27 个，办理案件 71 件，建立残疾人法律援助中心（工作站）74 个，办理案件 194 件，有力地推动了法律救助和法律援助工作。

残疾人参政议政工作得到加强，各级残联协助人大代表、政协委员提出议案、建议、提案 33 件，办理议案、建议、提案 19 件。

无障碍建设法规、标准进一步完善。26 个县（市、区）系统开展无障碍建设，开展无障碍建设检查 108 次，无障碍培训 142 人次，中央和省级资金为 650 户贫困残疾人家庭实施了无障碍改造；为 18771 名残疾人发放了残疾人机动轮椅车燃油补贴。各级残联共处理残疾人群众来信 1024 件，接待残疾人群众来访 7819 人次，其中集体访 27 批次、448 人次。

六、宣传文化

集中宣传残联系统学习贯彻党的十八大及十八届三中、四中全会精神；积极谋划，精心组织残疾人同步小康就业创业典型宣传活动；围绕重要的活动节点，不断扩大宣传的覆盖面和影响力；配合贵州省第五次全国自强模范与助残先进事迹巡回报告会系列宣传工作在全省引起了强烈反响；加强宣传工作机制建设，不断提升残疾人事业宣传工作水平。2014 年通过电视、广播、报纸、杂志、网络等媒体投放宣传稿件千余篇，形成了强大的宣传声势，使我省残疾人事业宣传工作在质和量上得到了保证，残疾人宣传工作的主阵地不断得到巩固完善，残疾人事业发展的良好社会氛围不断得到优化。

残疾人文化工作以贯彻落实中宣部等 11 部委下发的《关于加强残疾人文化建设的意见》和我省《实施意见》为抓手，以组织残疾人文化周活动开展为平台，以举办全国残疾人网络摄影大赛为工作重点，努力加强盲人语音图书室、文化进社区、特殊艺术人才培养等残疾人文化基础建设，积极推进我省残疾人文化工作全面开展，不断丰富残疾人精神文化生活。

七、体育

根据我省残疾人体育工作发展的新特点、新要求，切实加强残疾人群众体育工作，强化体育竞赛训练管理，确保优势项目运动成绩的提升，完善优秀残疾人运动员就学、就业保障，推动我省残疾人体育事业不断发展。圆满完成贵州省第五届残疾人运动会举办工作。参加亚洲残疾人运动会取得两枚金牌、一枚银牌的优异成绩。成功承办2014年全国残疾人羽毛球公开赛；参加全国单项锦标赛取得较好成绩；精心组织集训，积极备战2015年第九届全国残运会；特奥活动内容丰富，残疾人群体活动积极开展。

八、组织建设

截止2014年底，8个市州级残联在领导班子中配备了残疾人副理事长；68个县级残联机关配备了残疾人干部；已建乡镇（街道）残联1423个，组建率达到99.37%，选聘残疾人专职委员1395名；已建社区（村）残协14021个，组建率达到83.26%，选聘残疾人专职委员14657名。

省市县乡残联实有人员已达3237人。各级残联共举办培训班597期，培训机关干部、协会干部及残疾人专职委员13266人次。累计核发残疾人证954847本，发证率为40%。

九、基础设施

截至2014年底，已竣工并投入使用的各级残疾人综合服务设施62个，总建设规模55720平方米，总投资9173万元；已竣工并投入使用的各级残疾人康复设施3个，总建设规模11397平方米，总投资2520万元；已竣工并投入使用的各级残疾人托养服务设施1个，总建设规模1640平方米，总投资252万元。

十、信息化

按照省政府办公厅转发的《贵州省残疾人基础信息调查工作实施方案》要求，精心组织，周密安排，科学运作，开展残疾人基础信息调查工作，全面摸清我省残疾人基本情况，建立科学规范、系统完整的残疾人基础信息数据库，为残疾人同步小康精确制导提供数据支撑。截止12月31日，现场入户调查采集阶段全面完成，全省残疾人基础信息系统录入实名数据250万余条，圆满完成年初既定任务，全省各类残疾人的数量、结构、区域分布、基本需求等情况初步统计清楚，并基本建立了科学规范、系统完整的残疾人基础信息数据库，为省委、省政府及相关部门制定涉残政策提供决策支撑，为“十三五”的总体规划和各项政策出台作好了前期准备。

2014 年云南省残疾人事业发展统计公报

2014 年是云南省残联系统深入学习贯彻党的十八届三中、四中全会和省委九届八次、九次全会精神，全面落实云南省残联“六代会”任务的开局之年。一年来，在云南省委、省政府的坚强领导下，在新一届主席团的带领下，全省残联主动作为，积极创新，广大残疾人和残疾人工作者共同努力，各项事业在新起点上取得了新的成效。

一、残疾人康复

2014 年省政府将“残疾人扶助行动”和“光明工程”纳入 10 件惠民实事重要工作。省残联采取多项措施早安排、早落实，各项任务提前超额圆满完成。一是为 9841 名低视力者免费配发助视器，完成率达 120%。为 6270 名听障人士免费配发助听器，完成率达 156%。为 1247 名下肢缺肢者免费装配假肢，完成率达 125%；二是为全省 21639 名智力、精神和重度残疾人提供托养服务资助，完成率达 108%；三是配合省卫生计生委，为 33816 例白内障患者免费实施复明手术，完成率达 112%。

截止到 2014 年底，全省已有 11 个市辖区、117 个县（市）中的 13861 个社区开展了残疾人社区康复工作，全省共有 11923 名社区康复协调员接受培训，建立了 47.45 万人的康复服务档案，有 19.86 万人接受社区康复服务，上述数据相比 2013 年均有大幅增长，其中接受社区康复服务人数增长 37.73%，社区康复覆盖面进一步扩大。

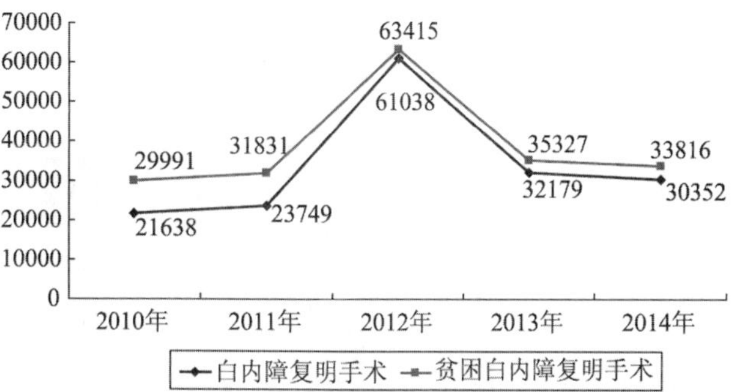

图 1　2010-2014 年云南省白内障复明手术完成情况(例)

围绕初步实现残疾人“人人享有康复服务”的目标。将常规康复工作与康复重点项目有机融合，将对外合作交流康复项目融入到常规康复工作中，统筹安排，不断扩大残疾人康复的受益面。全省培训社区康复员 11923 名；对 2688 名盲人进行盲人定向行走训练；对 7860 名成年肢体残疾人开展社区家庭康复训练；为 15204 名贫困精神病人提供医疗救助，监护精神病患者 102628 名。完成辅助器具配发 50938 件，为 2314 名残疾人装配假肢、矫形器。

加强省级聋儿康复机构建设，完善聋儿康复网络。共对 699 名聋儿进行了听力语言康复训练，规范聋儿家长学校，开展家庭训练，共培训聋儿家长 1047 名。

大力推广“社会化、综合性、开放式”精神病防治康复工作。2014 年，在全省 123 个市县开展精神病防治康复工作，覆盖人口 4588.61 万人，共掌握 15.3 万人精神病患者，其中对 4.02 万人进行综合防治康复；监护数 10.26 万人，监护率达到 67.06%；显好数 6.35 万人，显好率达到 41.50%；社会参与人数 5.11 万人，精神病人肇事率 0.13%；发现关锁病人 79 人，解除关锁病人 43 人；对 15204 名贫困精神病患者进行医疗救助。

深入开展辅助器具供应服务，全面推进普及型假肢装配，截止到 2014 年底，累计建立辅助器具供应服务机构 50 个，为残疾人免费供应辅助器具 50938 件。

全年开展肢体残疾康复训练服务的机构达到 31 个,对 509 名贫困肢体残疾儿童实施矫治手术；对 9858 名肢体残疾人进行了康复训练，其中：脑瘫儿童机构康复训练 472 人,肢体残疾儿童社区、家庭康复 1526 人，成年肢体残疾人社区、家庭康复 7860 人。

全年开展智力残疾康复训练服务的机构达到 21 个，康复训练人数 4110 人；对 3296 名 0-14 岁的智力残疾儿童进行了不同程度的机构康复训练和社区、家庭康复训练；对 814 名成年智力残疾人开展了不同程度的康复训练与服务。

二、残疾人教育

2014 年，残疾儿童少年义务教育稳步发展。特教学校发展到 59 所，在校接受义务教育的残疾学生达 2 万余人，残疾儿童入学率达 90%。《云南省特殊教育提升计划（2014—2016 年）》出台，规划了云南省特殊教育发展。5 月 8 日，省残联与云南开放大学共建特殊教育学院在省华夏中专正式挂牌，并于 9 月份招收 4 个专业 92 名学生。远程开放模式申报登记了 3 个专业 43 人基本信息，将于 2015 年春季学期进行学籍注册和授课，实现残疾人足不出户即可就读大学的梦想。云南开放大学特殊教育学院的成立，不仅填补了云南省没有针对残疾特殊人群高等教育和终身教育体系的空白，而且为全省 288.3 万残疾人提供了公平、终身学习的机会。有力促进了基础教育均衡发展、保障残疾人接受平等教育的权利，为更多的残疾人接受优质教育奠定了基础。云南省华夏中专搬迁新建项目一期建设完工，待验收后投入使用。

2014 年云南省未入学适龄残疾少年儿童总数 4690 人，其中视力残疾 268 人，听力残疾 287 人，言语残疾 392 人，智力残疾 1164 人，肢体残疾 1509 人，精神残疾 90 人，多重残疾 980 人。

2014 年全省有 480 名残疾学生达到普通高等院校录取分数线，其中录取 437 人，录取率为 91.04%。

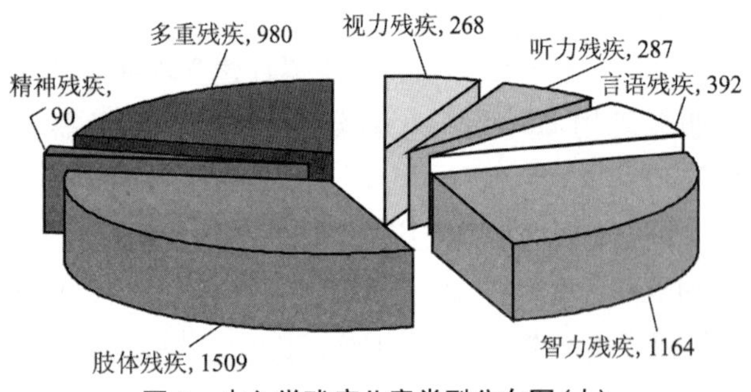

图 2　未入学残疾儿童类型分布图（人）

全省残疾人中等职业教育机构有 5 个，在校生 625 人，招生 234 人，毕业生 155 人，其中获得职业资格证书 39 人。

三、残疾人就业与扶贫

2014 年云南省残疾人就业扶贫实现新突破。一是《云南省残疾人就业规定》经省政府第 44 次常务会议通过，于 2014 年 10 月 1 日起施行。《规定》进一步明确了安排残疾人就业的具体比例，细化了有关部门和用人单位的主体责任，完善了促进残疾人就业的保障措施；二是省残联会同省人社厅、省财政厅印发了《云南省残疾人职业技能竞赛组织管理暂行办法》，明确规定参加残疾人职业技能竞赛获得各竞赛项目第一名的选手，由各级人力资源和社会保障部门授予"技术能手"称号。获得各竞赛项目前三名并通过相应理论知识考试者，由各级人力资源和社会保障部门按有关资格条件审定后，晋升职业资格。获得未纳入国家职业技能标准职种各项目前五名的选手，由各级人力资源和社会保障部门按有关资格条件审定后，授予相应专项职业能力证书；三是省委组织部等七部委共同出台了《关于促进云南省残疾人按比例就业的意见》，明确了党政机关、事业单位及国有企业应当依照有关法律、法规履行扶持残疾人就业的责任和义务；四是全省全年征收残疾人保障金 3.7 亿元。完成培训 34568 人次，城镇残疾人新增就业 4938 人，城镇残疾人实际在业 77133 人；农村残疾人从事农业生产劳动 854495 人，其他形式就业 131536 人。

开展盲人保健按摩培训 20 期共 595 人次，进一步拓展了残疾人就业渠道；医疗按摩人员培训 49 人；保健按摩机构达到 714 个，医疗按摩机构达 11 个；有 8 人通过医疗按摩人员初级职称评审;盲人保健按摩师就业人数 410 人，其中扶持特困盲人按摩师就业 303 人。

城镇残疾职工参加养老保险人数 5.17 万人，参加医疗保险人数 5.24 万人；城乡残疾居民参加城乡社会保险人数 78.95 万人；城乡 65.97 万名残疾人纳入最低生活保障范围。其中已纳入最低生活保障城镇残疾人 8.0 万人，享受集中供养和其他救助受助形式城镇残疾人 2.1 万人；已纳入最低生活保障农村残疾人 57.97 万人，享受五保供养和其他救助受助形式农村残疾人 14.77 万人。

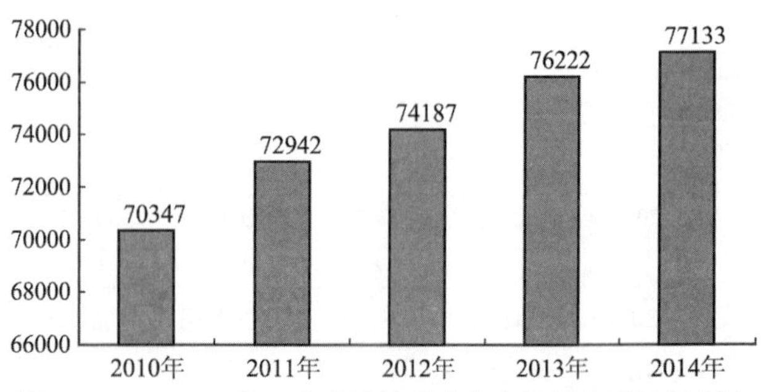

图 3　2010-2014 年云南省城镇残疾人实际就业情况图（人）

寄宿制托养服务机构16个，托养残疾人768人；日间照料托养服务机构8个，托养残疾人235人，综合托养机构合计20个，托养残疾人427人；本年度享受居家托养服务残疾人21279人。

2014年云南省残疾人扶贫呈现新局面。康复扶贫贷款贴息全面落实，共扶持残疾人2130人。残疾人扶贫示范基地建设发展迅速。已建立各级残疾人扶贫培训示范基地175个，累计培训和扶持残疾人1.7万余人次。农村实用技术培训效果明显，全省投入资金475万元，共培训1万余名农村贫困残疾人。危房改造项目继续推进，有效解决了贫困残疾人住房困难。专项助残扶贫项目特点突出。在省委组织部和省商务厅等单位的支持下，在全省开展了“基层党组织助残扶贫项目”和“万村千乡市场工程助残扶贫项目”，并接受中组部、中国残联的专项督查，得到充分肯定。

2014年度扶持农村贫困残疾人户54479户，扶持7.45万人，脱贫3.09万人，返贫1.46万人，接受实用技术培训的农村贫困残疾人4.37万人次。

结对帮扶单位2339个，结对帮扶个人24035人；建立残疾人扶贫基地175个，安置残疾人就业1943人，扶持带动残疾人7847人。

完成2395户农村贫困残疾人危房改造，受益残疾人3063人。

四、残疾人宣传文化体育

2014年全省各级残联广泛依托省、州（市）级报刊、广播电台、电视台、网站等公共媒体，广泛宣传残疾人事业，为残疾人“两个体系”建设营造良好的社会环境。以“全国助残日”、“国际残疾人日”等为契机，精心组织协调主要媒体开展系列主题宣传活动。2014年省残联与曲靖市残联联合开展第二十四次“全国助残日”活动。邀请中国残联艺术团到曲靖演出，为省第十届残运会暨第四届特奥会营造良好氛围。

2014年云南省残联完成《云南残疾人事业发展报告（2013年卷）》编制工作，全面反映和宣传了残疾人事业的发展状况，并向省委、省政府、26个残工委成员单位进行赠阅，扩大了残疾人事业的影响力。

2014年省级主要新闻媒体刊播残疾人事业稿件数241件，报刊专版15个，电视手语新闻栏目1个，建立省级新促会1个；地市级主要新闻媒体刊播稿件数1533件，报刊专版67个，残疾人专题广播栏目5个，电视手语新闻栏目7个，建立地市级新促会9个。

省级、地市级和县级公共图书馆设立盲文及盲人有声读物阅览室已达到29个，举办残疾人文化周295场次，举办残疾人文化艺术类比赛及展览62次，已成立残疾人艺术团队41个。

省级开展残疾人群众体育健身活动2次，参加人数57人，残疾人群众体育活动示范点8个，残疾人体育健身指导员12人，聘任教练员20人。地市级残联开展残疾人体育健身活动65次，参加人次7916人，建立残疾人体育示范点21个，培训残疾人体育健身指导员495人。

五、残疾人维权

2014年省残联不断完善领导接访制度，开展信访律师坐班制度，关口前移、排查化解矛盾，不断提高为残疾人服务的能力，没有发生一起群体性残疾人上访事件。

2014年省残联积极指导各州（市）健全维权机构。243名残疾人、残疾人亲友和残疾人工作者进入县级以上人大、政协参政议政，共提出议案提案42件，办理议案提案24件。认真办理省人大代表建议、省政协委员的提案和其他信访案件，争取残疾人合理诉求得到满足。全省批准建立1个省级、4个州（市）级、4个县（区）级残疾人法律救助站。完成云南省2014年度全国残疾人状况监测相关工作。州（市）级安排完成60户贫困残疾人家庭无障碍改造；县（区）级完成146户贫困残疾人家庭无障碍改造。

2014年全省各级残联开展普法宣传教育活动296次，参加人数3.05万人；开展法律培训班42次，参加人数1879人。

国家批准建立在我省的法律救助工作站，2014年办理案件10件；全省累计建立残疾人法律援助中心（工作站）134个，2014年办理案件715件。

截至2014年全省累计颁布无障碍建设与管理规定、政府令18个，成立无障碍建设领导协调组织36个，系统开展无障碍建设市、县达74个。

2014 年全省共完成贫困残疾人家庭无障碍改造 1378 户，开展无障碍建设检查 161 次；2014 年各地共向 19502 名残疾人发放残疾人机动轮椅车燃油补贴。

2014 年全省各级残联共受理残疾人群众来信 3254 件，接待残疾人群众来访 1.83 万人次，其中集体访 20 批次 501 人次。

六、残疾人组织建设

全省 2014 年各级残联共有工作人员 3672 人；所有的县级残联均已计划单列并实现规范化建设达标；全省建有乡镇（街道）残联 1382 个，共配备乡镇（街道）残联专职（兼职）理事长 1082 人，选聘乡镇(街道)残疾人专职委员数 1355 人；建立 12556 个农村残协和 1492 个社区残协，选聘基层残疾人专职委员 13358 人。

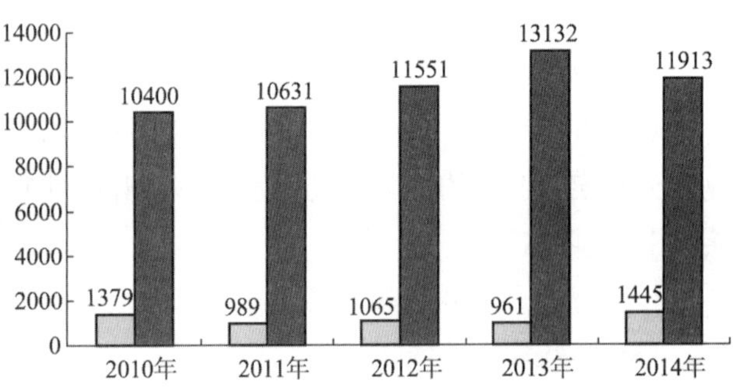

图 4　2010-2014 年城乡社区(村)专职委员聘用情况(人)

全省共建立各类残疾人专门协会 702 个，其中盲人协会 143 个、聋人协会 143 个、肢残人协会 143 个、智力残疾人及亲友协会 137 个、精神残疾人及亲友协会 135 个。全省建立省级助残社会组织 6 个，州（市）级助残社会组织 7 个，县级助残社会组织 9 个。

七、信息化建设工作

2014 年启动了云南省残联信息化建设规划和一期项目可研报告编制工作，在充分调研残联业务工作，摸清系统基本需求的基础上前后数易其稿，编制完成了省残联信息化建设规划和一期项目可研报告。2015 年 1 月底一期项目可研报告由云南省工信委组织进行了专家评审论证，获得原则性通过。

云南省残联门户网站改版及信息无障碍改造工作，网站呈现版面新颖、信息内容丰富、时效性较强、信息无障碍应用较好等特点。

统计队伍建设进一步加强，2014 年全省各级残联共有 155 名专职、兼职统计人员从事残疾人事业统计工作，统计人员业务素质培养普遍得到重视，云南省残联举办培训班 1 期，参加培训人员 50 人次；地市级举办培训班 15 期，参加人员 222 人次。

全省各级残联全面推进网站建设，截止到 2014年底,全省各级残联共计建设网站50个。2014年，全省各级残联共举办网站技术培训班 16 期，培训人员 372 人次。各级残联共有 212 名专业技术人员从事信息化工作。截止 2014 年底，各级残联配备了 1906 台计算机，投入信息化建设经费达 366.35 万元。

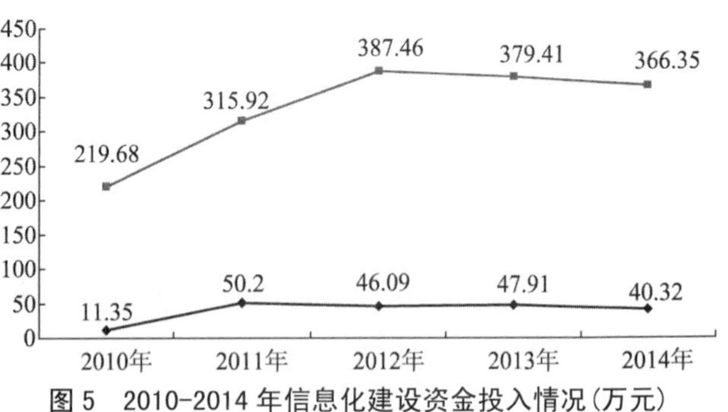

图 5　2010-2014 年信息化建设资金投入情况(万元)

2014 年，虽然全省残疾人工作取得了较大的进展，但是与广大残疾人的需求相比，仍然存在很大的差距。推动我省残疾人事业迈上新台阶的任务还十分繁重，挑战巨大。从总体上看，各级残联组织充分发挥了“代表、管理、服务”的职能，但面对最需要帮助的残疾人群体，我们的政策支持力度还不大，离残疾人的实际需求还有较大的差距；从具体服务能力看，一、全省普遍存在残疾人服务设施建设进展不理想的问题；二、信息化建设工作急需加强，以适应残疾人事业发展需要；从政策支持看，我省的重度残疾人护理补贴政策虽经深入调研论证，多方面协调基本一致，但最终未能按计划出台。这些问题，都有待我们在今后的工作中努力加以解决。

2015 年是全面深化改革的关键之年，是全面推进依法治国的开局之年，也是完成“十二五”规划的收官之年。我省残疾人工作总的要求是：以邓小平理论、“三个代表”重要思想、科学发展观为指导，深入学习贯彻习近平总书记系列重要讲话精神，按照党的十八大、十八届三中、四中全会，省委九届八次、九次会议精神和省委、省政府关于残疾人事业的新部署新要求，加快推进残疾人小康进程，全力完成“十二五”规划任务，精心编制“十三五”发展规划，积极开展“基础管理提升年”活动，努力为促进广大残疾人共享我省经济社会发展成果做出新的贡献、带来更多的福祉。

2014 年度西藏自治区残疾人事业发展统计公报

2014 年，是贯彻落实党的十八大、十八届二中、三中全会精神，贯彻落实习近平总书记一系列重要讲话精神，贯彻落实西藏自治区党委、政府的统一部署和中国残联的工作安排，全力实施《西藏自治区残疾人事业“十二五”发展纲要》的重要一年，西藏残疾人事业发展有了新的突破，残疾人工作有了新的进展，残疾人状况有了新的改善。

一、康复

围绕《西藏自治区残疾人康复“十二五”实施方案》任务，全面开展各类残疾人康复服务工作。

截至 2014 年底。在全区 21 个县（区）开展社区康复服务工作，配备接受过培训的社区康复协调员 58 人。全年完成白内障复明手术 1396 例，其中 1235 例为免费手术；为 18 名低视力患者配用助视器;对 281 名盲人进行了定向行走训练;

对 533 肢体残疾者实施康复训练；实施救助项目，资助 122 名脑瘫儿童进行机构康复训练，资助 84 名贫困肢体残疾儿童实施矫治手术。对 205 名智力残疾人进行康复训练；资助 10 名智力残疾儿童进行机构康复训练。

加强残疾人辅助器具服务体系建设，深入开展辅助器具供应服务，为残疾人减免费用供应辅助器具 1727 件，其中装配假肢 56 例、矫形器 96 例，验配助视器 18 件

。

二、教育

开展残疾人特殊教育和残疾儿童随班就读工作，保障残疾学生和残疾家庭子女接受教育。开展“彩票公益金助学项目”，落实资金 9 万元，资助 30 名残疾儿童接受学前教育。筹集资金 8 万元，资助 4 名盲人大学生就学。加大特殊教育师资培训力度，为拉萨、山南、日喀则、那曲、昌都等特校培训特教师资 35 名。积极协助教育厅完成 2014 年度残疾人考生高等院校录取工作，共有 10 名残疾人被普通高等院校录取。组织开展“交通银行特教园丁奖”和“交通银行残疾大学生励志奖”的推荐、评选和奖励工作。

三、就业、扶贫

贯彻落实《西藏自治区实施<残疾人就业条例>办法》，积极开展残疾人就业援助月活动，举办 16 次残疾人专场招聘会、1 期区直系统雇主培训班和 1 场盲人音乐演出会。做好各类残疾人就业服务工作，进行职业指导 182 人次、职业介绍 112 人，开展残疾人就业实名制录入工作，录入残疾人 29371 人，扶持 120 名残疾人自主创业。建设自治区残疾人职业能力测评室，为 60 名残疾人进行职业能力评估测评，组织开展西藏自治区第三届残疾人职业技能竞赛，共有 37 名残疾人参加了缝纫、唐卡绘画、家具彩绘、盲人按摩等 4 个项目的竞赛。加大残疾人职业培训力度，拓展培训内容，培训残疾人 197 人，提高了残疾人的就业能力。2014 年度培训盲人保健按摩人员 17 名、盲人医疗按摩人员 10 名；保健按摩机构达到 17 个；在专业技术职务资格评审中，分别有 9 人通过盲人医疗按摩人员中级评审，6 人通过盲人医疗按摩人员初级职称。

开展“三大节日”慰问活动，发放慰问金 12.82 万元。贫困残疾人生产生活状况得到进一步改善。700 名贫困残疾人得到扶持，其中 120 人通过扶贫开发实现脱贫;接受实用技术培训的残疾人达到 203 人次。完成 28 户农村贫困残疾人危房改造，投入危房资金 5.00 万元，36 名残疾人受益。

四、宣文、体育、维权

开展残疾人文体活动，活跃残疾人文体生活。组织开展“文化助残”图书捐赠仪式，为残疾人捐赠各类图书 1000 册，满足残疾人的精神文化需求，保障残疾人的基本文化权益。

做好全国第九次残疾人运动会暨全国第六次特

奥会的各项前期准备工作，为20名残疾人运动员完成注册工作，组建自治区首个残疾人轮椅篮球队，举办 2014 年特奥国家级教练员培训班，培训学员 21 名。

为 210 个贫困残疾人家庭实施了无障碍改造；为 2094 名残疾人发放了残疾人机动轮椅车燃油补贴。各级残联共处理残疾人群众来信 253 件，接待残疾人群众来访 120 人次。

五、组织建设

2014 年，2 个地市级残联在领导班子中配备了残疾人理事长或副理事长；7 个县级残联机关配备了残疾人干部；省市县乡残联实有人员已达 427 人。已建立助残社会组织 5 个，各类残疾人专门协会 3 个。

六、信息化建设和事业统计

利用残联门户网站和残联微博等电子信息手段，不断加大残疾人工作信息宣传力度，信息量有了大幅度增长，信息质量显著提升，公开发布信息 23 条，扩大了残疾人工作影响面；　统计队伍建设进一步加强，各级残联共有 10 名专、兼职统计人员从事残疾人事业统计工作，统计人员业务素质培养普遍得到重视，省级残联举办培训班 1 期，参加培训的人员达到 20 人次；地市级举办培训班 1 期，参加培训的人员达到 14 人次。

2014 年陕西省残疾人事业统计公报

2014 年，省残联坚持以“科学发展、富民强省”为主题，认真贯彻落实党的十八大精神，按照“三个依托、两个整合”的总体思路，扎实推进残疾人“两个体系”建设，全面完成了年度目标任务，全省残疾人事业呈现出重点突破、协调推进、全面发展的良好势头，在全面建成小康社会进程中迈出了新步伐。

一、康复

2014 年，通过实施一批重点康复工程，为残疾人提供了有效的康复服务。大力加强残疾人社区康复示范站建设；积极推进残疾人康复机构规范化建设；加强康复人才队伍建设，大力宣传和普及康复知识。

在 28 个市辖区和 83 个县（市）开展了社区康复工作，累计已建社区康复站的社区总数 1350 个，配备 8833 名社区康复协调员。

27 个县的 25 个医疗卫生机构陆续开展残疾儿童筛查工作，年度新诊断 0-6 岁残疾儿童 979 人。

开展视力残疾康复机构总数达到 65 个，全年完成白内障复明手术 11613 例；为 8631 名贫困白内障患者免费施行复明手术，全年为 9294 名低视力患者配用助视器，培训低视力儿童家长 40 名；对 3700 名盲人进行定向行走训练。

推进听力语言康复机构规范化管理，完善基层服务网络。已建设省级听力语言康复机构 1 个，基层听力语言康复机构 35 个。年度机构新收训聋儿 564 名，在训聋儿 876 名；规范聋儿家长学校，开展家庭训练，共培训聋儿家长 1197 名；开展各级各类听力语言康复专业技术人员培训，共培训专业人员 130 人。

开展肢体残疾康复训练服务机构达 157 个，其中，省级康复机构 4 个，地市级、县级康复机构 153 个；培训各级肢体残疾康复管理、技术人员 162 人次；全省共对 9828 名肢体残疾者实施康复训练；实施救助项目资助 858 名脑瘫儿童进行机构康复训练，资助 637 名贫困肢体残疾儿童实施矫治手术。

开展智力残疾康复训练服务的机构达到 36 个，其中，省级康复机构 2 个，地市级、县级康复机构 34 个；培训各级智力残疾康复管理、技术人员 298 人次；全省共对 4258 名智力残疾人进行康复训练；实施救助项目资助 1902 名智力残疾儿童进行机构康复训练。

大力推广“社会化、综合性、开放式”精神病防治康复工作。全省精神病防治康复工作已经实现全覆盖，对 20.46 万名重性精神病患者进行综合防治康复，监护率达到 57.40%，显好率达到 67.10%，社会参与率达到 56.24%，肇事率 0.07%；解除关锁病人 86 人；对 16763 名贫困精神病患者进行了医疗救助。

建立了 2 个省级孤独症儿童康复训练机构，省级机构对 459 名孤独症儿童进行了康复训练。

深入开展辅助器具供应服务，为残疾人减免费用供应辅助器具 60073 件，其中装配普及型假肢 1267 例，装配矫形器 177 例，验配助视器 11021 件。其中扎实实施“关爱重残 共享阳光”重度残疾人辅助器具适配项目，为 5000 名重度残疾人适配了 20674 件辅助器具。

二、教育

实施残疾人事业专项彩票公益金助学项目，为家庭经济困难的残疾儿童享受普惠性学前教育提供资助 200 人次。各地也积极多渠道争取资金支持，对 25 名残疾儿童给予学前教育资助。

已开办特殊教育普通高中班（部）3 个，在校生 106 人；其中聋高中 2 个，在校生 98 人；盲高中 1 个，在校生 8 人。残疾人中等职业学校（班）6 个，在校生 1374 人，毕业生 722 人，其中 383 人获得职业资格证书。有 272 名残疾人被普通高等院校录取，30 名残疾人进入特殊教育学院学习。

三、就业

2014年，残疾人就业规模总体保持稳定。城镇新就业残疾人6117人，其中，集中就业残疾人1454人，按比例安排残疾人就业1783人，公益性岗位就业494人，个体就业及其它形式灵活就业2192人，辅助性就业194人。城镇就业人数106043人；652542名农村残疾人在业，其中490174名残疾人从事农业生产劳动。

残疾人职业培训基地达到372个，其中残联兴办134个，依托社会机构兴办238个，其中12637人次城镇残疾人接受了职业培训。

盲人按摩事业稳定发展，按摩机构迅速增长。2014年度培训盲人保健按摩人员752名、盲人医疗按摩人员54名；保健按摩机构达到351个，医疗按摩机构达到65个；在专业技术职务资格评审中，分别有26人和20人通过盲人医疗按摩人员中级和初级职称评审。

四、社会保障

2014年新型农村和城镇居民社会养老保险统一合并实施，已有438704名城乡残疾居民参保，参保率35.29%，在60岁以下的参保残疾人中有82958名重度残疾人，其中79531人得到了政府的参保扶助，代缴补贴比例达到95.87%。有128272名非重度残疾人也享受了全额或部分代缴的优惠政策。领取养老金待遇的人数达到135831人。

城镇残疾职工参加养老保险74702人，参加医疗保险74196人，城镇77269人和农村304969人残疾人纳入最低生活保障范围；城镇集中供养残疾人和农村五保供养残疾人分别达到3244名和20201名；747928名和603名符合条件的城乡残疾人分别享受了稳定的生活补贴和护理补贴。375390名城乡残疾人得到了其他救助救济。

残疾人托养服务工作规范推进，残疾人托养服务机构达到132个，共为7016名残疾人提供了托养服务。其中寄宿制托养服务机构67个；日间照料机构16个；综合性托养服务机构49个。在以上机构中，共有221名残疾人实现辅助性就业，146名残疾人实现了支持性就业。机构之外接受居家托养服务的残疾人达到20536人。全年共有1299名托养服务管理和服务人员接受了各级各类专业培训，其中接受国家级培训29人。

五、扶贫开发

2014年，残疾人就业规模总体保持稳定。城镇新就业残疾人6117人，其中，集中就业残疾人1454人，按比例安排残疾人就业1783人，公益性岗位就业494人，个体就业及其它形式灵活就业2192人，辅助性就业194人。城镇就业人数106043人；652542名农村残疾人在业，其中490174名残疾人从事农业生产劳动。

残疾人职业培训基地达到372个，其中残联兴办134个，依托社会机构兴办238个，其中12637人次城镇残疾人接受了职业培训。

盲人按摩事业稳定发展，按摩机构迅速增长。2014年度培训盲人保健按摩人员752名、盲人医疗按摩人员54名；保健按摩机构达到351个，医疗按摩机构达到65个；在专业技术职务资格评审中，分别有26人和20人通过盲人医疗按摩人员中级和初级职称评审。

2014年，残疾人就业规模总体保持稳定。城镇新就业残疾人6117人，其中，集中就业残疾人1454人，按比例安排残疾人就业1783人，公益性岗位就业494人，个体就业及其它形式灵活就业2192人，辅助性就业194人。城镇就业人数106043人；652542名农村残疾人在业，其中490174名残疾人从事农业生产劳动。

残疾人职业培训基地达到372个，其中残联兴办134个，依托社会机构兴办238个，其中12637人次城镇残疾人接受了职业培训。

盲人按摩事业稳定发展，按摩机构迅速增长。2014年度培训盲人保健按摩人员752名、盲人医疗按摩人员54名；保健按摩机构达到351个，医疗按摩机构达到65个；在专业技术职务资格评审中，分别有26人和20人通过盲人医疗按摩人员中级和初级职称评审。

2014年，残疾人扶贫开发成效显著，贫困残疾人生产生活状况得到进一步改善。215250名贫困残疾人得到扶持，其中82671人通过扶贫开发实现脱贫；接受实用技术培训的残疾人达到15475人次。

康复扶贫贴息贷款扶持14562名农村残疾人，

残疾人扶贫基地达到 226 个，安置 4404 名残疾人就业，扶持带动 10314 户残疾人。

完成 3168 户农村贫困残疾人危房改造，各地投入危房资金 4419.90 万元，3588 名残疾人受益。

基层党组织助残扶贫项目帮扶 5066 名农村贫困残疾人，其中首次接受帮扶 3655 人。“万村千乡市场工程”助残扶贫项目安置 79 名贫困残疾人就业，帮扶贫困残疾人创办 23 个村级农村店。

六、宣传文化

省残联首次联合省文化厅举办全省残疾人文化建设培训会，提出了“一纳入三依托”的工作思路，即将残疾人文化工作纳入全省文化工作范围同步实施，依托全省文化资源优势发展残疾人文化事业、依托全省文化机构阵地健全残疾人文化服务网络、依托社会力量开展残疾人各项文化活动。省残联联合省教育厅、省民政厅、省文化厅、省广播电影电视局举办第八届全省残疾人文艺汇演，300 多名残疾人演员进行了 4 类 72 个节目的展示，艺术形式之广泛、演出质量之高堪为历届之最。我省代表团在第八届全国残疾人艺术汇演中荣获一等奖、二等奖各三个，三等奖六个，团体总分二等奖，创历届最好成绩。省残联协调省广播电视台首次对省“两会”进行了电视手语同步直播。

省级中央媒体采用稿件 227 件，主要新闻媒体刊播稿件 419 件，电视手语新闻栏目 1 个，省级残疾人事业新闻宣传促进会 1 个。

地市级主要新闻媒体刊播稿件数 800 件，报刊专版 6 个，残疾人专题广播节目 2 个，电视手语新闻栏目 9 个，建立地市级新促会 3 个。

截至 2014 年底，省地县三级公共图书馆共设立盲文及盲人有声读物阅览室 48 个，共开展残疾人文化周活动 128 场次，共举办残疾人文化艺术类比赛及展览 33 次，共有各类残疾人艺术团体 14 个。

七、体育

各地深入开展残疾人体育工作。组织省级残疾人群众体育健身活动 41 次，4000 人次参加；建设省级残疾人群众体育活动示范点达到 30 个；培训省级残疾人体育健身指导员达到 390 人；组织省级残疾人体育比赛 15 次，参赛运动员达 220 人次；省级残疾人体育训练基地已达 28 个，组织地市级残疾人体育健身活动 51 次，4181 人次参加；设立地市级残疾人群众体育活动示范点 32 个；培训地市级残疾人体育健身指导员 186 人。

八、维权

各级残联维权组织建设得到加强，残疾人事业法律法规体系进一步完善，残疾人维权工作全面开展。配合省发改委省财政厅起草并报请省政府印发了《陕西省基本公共服务体系规划（2013-2020）残疾人基本公共服务专章》。

2014 年，制定或修改保障残疾人权益的规范性文件省级 2 件、县级 1 件。县级以上人大进行《残疾人保障法》执法检查和专题调研 10 次；政协进行视察和专题调研 11 次。开展普法宣传教育活动 143 次，16397 人参加；举办法律培训班 28 个，1579 人参加。

截至 2014 年底，成立残疾人法律救助工作协调机构 77 个，建立残疾人法律救助工作站 64 个，办理案件 107 件，建立残疾人法律援助中心（工作站）107 个，办理案件 428 件，有力地推动了法律救助和法律援助工作。

残疾人参政议政工作得到加强，各级残联协助人大代表、政协委员提出议案、建议、提案 22 件，办理议案、建议、提案 36 件。

无障碍建设法规、标准进一步完善。共出台了 13 个省、地市、县级无障碍建设与管理法规、规章和规范性文件；43 个市、县、区系统开展无障碍建设；开展无障碍建设检查 27 次，无障碍培训 129 人次；为 1509 个贫困残疾人家庭实施了无障碍改造；为 18320 名残疾人发放了残疾人机动轮椅车燃油补贴。

各级残联共处理残疾人群众来信 968 件，接待残疾人群众来访 10934 人次，其中集体访 6 批次、258 人次。

九、组织建设

2014 年，9 个地市级残联在领导班子中配备了残疾人理事长或副理事长；60 个县级残联机关配备了残疾人干部；已建乡镇（街道）残联 1490 个，已建率达到 90.58%，选聘残疾人专职委员 1653 名；已建社区（村）残协 28437 个，已建率达到 99.45%，选聘残疾人专职委员 28844 名。

省市县乡残联实有人员已达 4608 人。各级残联共举办培训班 1561 期，培训机关干部、协会干部及残疾人专职委员 40413 人次。

共建立省级以下各类残疾人专门协会 595 个，市级专门协会已建比例为 100.00%；县级专门协会已建比例为 99.08%。共建立助残社会组织 22 个，其中在民政部门注册的为 15 个，以残联为业务主管单位的 16 个。

十、服务设施建设

截至 2014 年底，已竣工并投入使用的各级残疾人综合服务设施 77 个，总建设规模 147956 平方米，总投资 31500 万元；已竣工并投入使用的各级残疾人康复设施 31 个，总建设规模 47204 平方米，总投资 7153 万元；已竣工并投入使用的各级残疾人托养服务设施 47 个，总建设规模 109383 平方米，总投资 13461 万元。

十一、事业统计与信息化建设

统计队伍建设进一步加强，各级残联共有 135 名专、兼职统计人员从事残疾人事业统计工作，统计人员业务素质培养普遍得到重视，省级残联举办培训班 2 期，参加培训的人员达到 33 人次；地市级举办培训班 9 期，参加培训的人员达到 152 人次。

全面推进网站建设。全省残联系统已开通公众服务网站 63 个，其中，省级、地市级及杨陵区、韩城市残联全部开通网站,县级残联开通网站 52 个。各级残联共有 165 名专业技术人员从事信息化工作。2014 年省级及地市级残联开设网站技术培训班 12 期，培训各级残联信息员达 474 人次。

2014 年甘肃省残疾人事业发展统计公报

2014 年在省委省政府的坚强领导下，在中国残联的有力指导及有关部门的大力支持下，各级残联深入贯彻中央和省上关于残疾人事业的新部署新要求，全省残疾人工作呈现出领导重视程度高、助残民生项目实、经费支持力度大、大型活动效果好、各地特色亮点多、残疾人收益面广等特点，残疾人事业在新的起点上取得显著成绩、迈上新台阶。

一、康复

2014 年，全省 40.24 万残疾人得到了社区康复服务(图 1)。86 个县（区、市）的 5653 个村（社区）开展了社区康复工作，累计建成社区康复站 1275 个，社区康复协调员达到 8366 人。

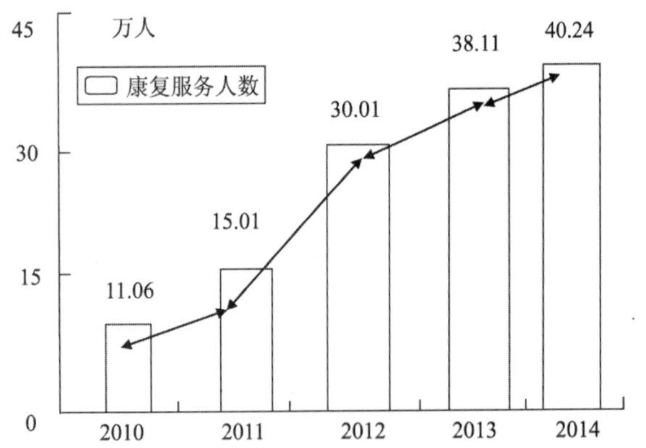

图 1　2010-2014 年接受社区康复服务残疾人数及增长速度

开展视力残疾康复机构总数达 21 个，完成白内障复明手术 13330 例，其中为贫困白内障患者免费手术 8338 例 (图 2)；为 3574 名低视力患者配用了助视器，培训低视力儿童家长 338 名；对 2199 名盲人进行了定向行走训练。

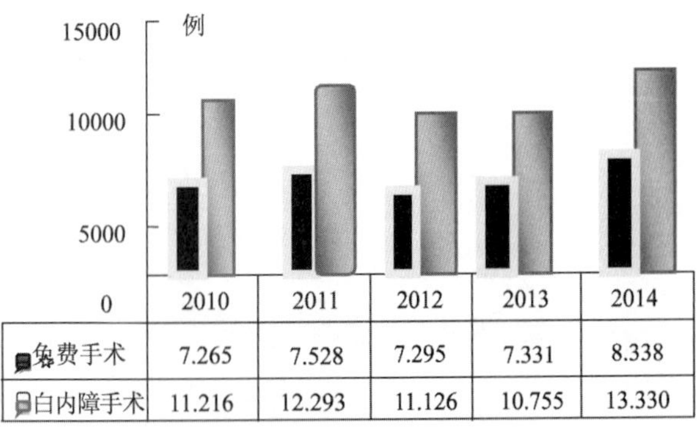

	2010	2011	2012	2013	2014
免费手术	7.265	7.528	7.295	7.331	8.338
白内障手术	11.216	12.293	11.126	10.755	13.330

图 2　2010-2014 年全省实施白内障手术数量

已建省级听力语言康复机构 1 个，市、县级听力语言康复机构 16 个。年度新收训聋儿 478 名，在训聋儿 569 名；全年培训聋儿家长 518 名。

开展肢体残疾康复训练机构 28 个，实施肢体残疾儿童矫治手术 509 人，有 5090 名肢体残疾人接受了康复训练。肢体残疾儿童社区、家庭康复 670 人，成年肢体残疾人社区、家庭康复 3905 人。

开展智力残疾康复训练机构 28 个，对 2225 名智力残疾人进行了康复训练，其中有 665 名智力残疾儿童得到康复机构训练，1475 名智力残疾儿童、85 名成年智力残疾人得到了社区、家庭康复训练。

有 62 个县（区、市）开展了精神病防治康复工作，对 14343 名精神病患者进行了综合防治康复,对 3394 名精神病患者进行了康复训练；对 21925 名贫困精神病患者进行医疗救助。

建立了 23 个孤独症儿童康复训练机构， 194 名孤独症儿童在康复机构进行了训练。

建立了辅助器具服务机构 64 个，全年共为残疾人减免费用供应辅助器具 26311 件。其中装配假肢 1059 例、装配矫形器 282 例，验配助视器 3838 件。（表 1）

表 1　2014 年康复训练服务机构（个）

级　别	类别				
	视力	听力语言	肢体	智力	辅助器具
省　级	1	1	1	1	1
市州级	5	10	8	12	7
县　级	15	6	19	15	56
合　计	21	17	28	28	64

二、教育

272 名残疾儿童得到了普惠性学前教育资助；173 名残疾儿童得到了其他学前教育助学项目资助。

全年未入学学龄残疾儿童少年有 3618 人（图 3），其中视力残疾 192 人，比上年减少 1%；听力残疾 206 人，比上年增加 11%；言语残疾 177 人，比上年增加4%；肢体残疾1194人，比上年增加8%；智力残疾1026人，比上年增加24%；精神残疾136人，比上年增加11%；多重残疾687人，比上年增加30%。

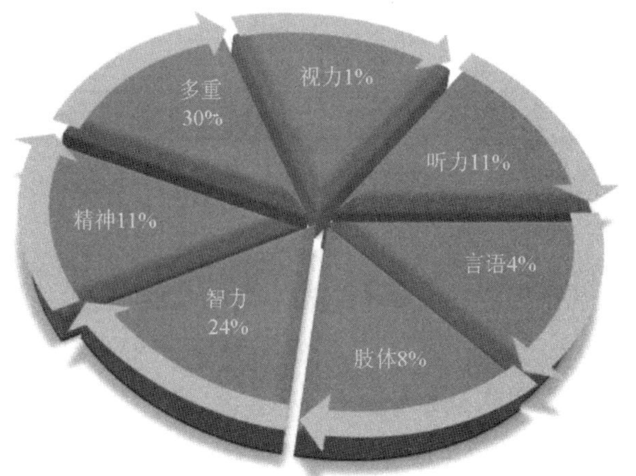

图3　2014年全省未入学适龄残疾儿童类别比例

全省有特殊教育普通高中学校（班）6个，在校生327人。残疾人中等职业学校（班）5个，在校生49人，获得职业资格证书4人。全省有243名残疾考生被普通高等院校录取。

三、就业

认真贯彻《甘肃省残疾人就业办法》，2014年全省残疾人就业工作取得新进展，全省城镇在业残疾人达到10.7万人。本年度新增8523人，其中集中就业1273人，按比例就业1097人，个体及其他形式就业3737人，公益性岗位就业1505人，辅助性就业911人（图4）。农村残疾人就业53.3万人。其中从事农业生产劳动44.2万人。

全省有残疾人职业培训基地50个，其中残联兴办25个，依托社会机构兴办25个。接受了职业培训的残疾人达21659人。

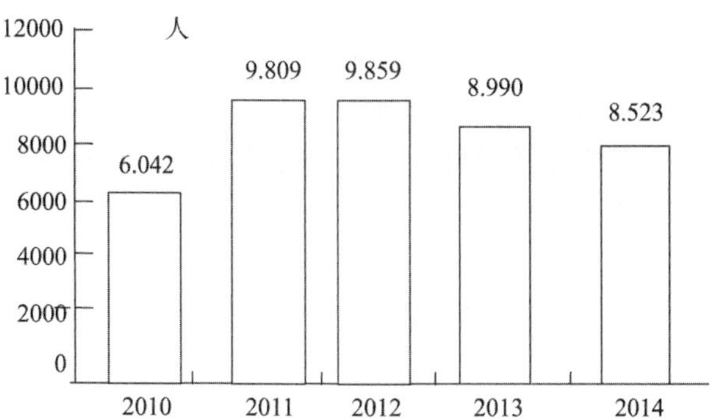

图4　2010-2014年城镇残疾人新增就业人数

全省有医疗按摩机构29个，培训盲人医疗按摩人员116名；有保健按摩机构230个，培训保健按摩人员339名；盲人医疗按摩就业43人，盲人保健按摩就业255人。在专业技术职务资格评审中有8人通过了中级职称评审，13人通过了初级职称评审。

四、社会保障

2014年，残疾人农村和城镇居民社会养老保险统一合并实施，已有92.6万城镇残疾居民参加了城镇居民社会养老保险，参保率达到86%。60岁以下的参保残疾人中，有21.4万重度残疾人享受了政府全额或部分代缴的优惠政策。

4.8万城镇残疾职工参加养老保险，5万残疾职工参加医疗保险。

城镇6.8万和农村35.5万残疾人纳入最低生活保障。（图5）

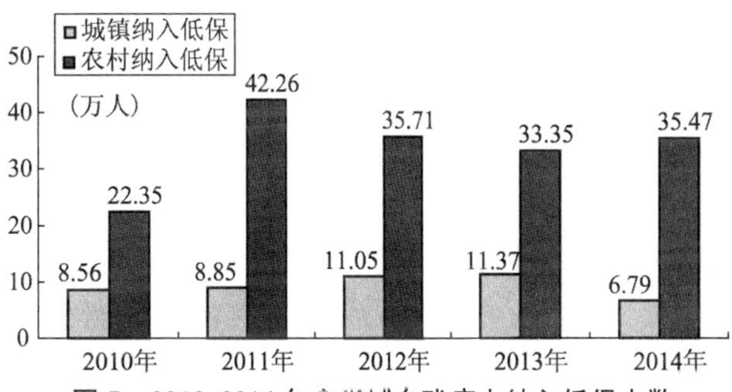

图5　2010-2014年全省城乡残疾人纳入低保人数

城镇集中供养残疾人和农村五保供养残疾人分别为1024人和18203万人；城镇和农村残疾人获得其他救助救济分别为12968万人和88501万人；享受了生活补贴和护理补贴分别为85630人和66125人。

残疾人托养机构达到50个，为20479名残疾人提供了托养服务。其中寄宿制托养服务机构23个；日间照料机构7个；综合托养服务机构20个。接收居家托养服务的残疾人达到17402人。

五、扶贫

扶贫攻坚模式在精准发力中得到新转变。全年12.7万贫困残疾人得到扶持，其中96925名贫困残疾人实际脱贫；4.4万人次接受实用技术培训。落实中央康复扶贫贷款项目资金3857万元，有1007名残疾人得到项目贷款扶持。

已建残疾人扶贫基地 99 个，扶持带动残疾人户 3540 户，单位结对帮扶残疾人 71109 人。

全省共投入资金 9086 万元，实施农村贫困残疾人危房改造 1.5 万户。

六、宣传文体

宣传文化：全年省市主要新闻媒体刊播残疾人事业稿件 4063 条，专题广播节目 47 个，电视手语栏目 14 个。举办残疾人文化艺术比赛及展览 125 场次。全省共建盲人有声读物图书室 43 个。有 1 个省级、2 个市级、7 个县级残疾人艺术团队。

体育：培养省级残疾人健身指导员 507 人,市级残疾人健身指导员 221 人。建立省级群众体育活动示范点 18 个,市州级残疾人体育活动示范点 18 个。组织省级残疾人群众体育健身活动 2 次，参加人数 1200 人次，组织地市级残疾人体育活动人数 7.8 万人次。举办省级体育比赛 2 次，参赛运动员 697 人次。

七、维权

权益保障工作在政策落实中获得新提升。全省共计制定或修改了关于残疾人的专门法规、规章 6 个，共计制定或修改保障残疾人权益的规范性文件 38 件。全省各级人大执法检查 39 次，政协专题调研 37 次，举办普法活动 164 次。

残疾人参政议政工作得到加强，各级残联协助人大代表、政协委员提出议案、建议及提案 57 件。

全省共出台 39 个无障碍建设和管理法规、规章和规范性文件； 101 个省市县开展无障碍建设，进行 49 次无障碍建设检查，举办 368 次无障碍培训。为 2229 户贫困残疾人家庭进行了无障碍改造，为 2.3 万残疾人发放机动轮椅车燃油补贴。

全省各级残联接待残疾人来信 1742 件，来访 6241 人次，其中集体访 11 批次、96 人次。

全省建立残疾人法律救助工作协调机构 102 个（表 2）。建立残疾人法律救助工作站 95 个，办理案件 310 件；建立残疾人法律援助中心 95 个，办理案件 566 件。

表 2　2014 年全省各级残疾人法律救助情况

级别	法律救助协调机构（个）	法律救助		法律援助	
		工作站（个）	办理案件（件）	工作站（个）	办理案件（件）
省　级	1	1	1	1	3
市州级	15	15	20	15	58
县　级	86	79	289	79	508
合　计	102	95	310	95	566

八、组织建设

省市残联领导班子配备残疾人理事长或副理事长 15 人。省市县残联机关配备残疾人干部 169 人。省市县乡残联实有人员 4020 人。已建乡镇（街道）残联 1372 个，已建村（社区）残协 17198 个，选聘残疾人专职委员 18650 人（图 6）。

全省各级残联举办培训班 239 期，培训机关干部、协会主席及残疾人专职委员 3342 人次。3084 名优秀残疾人被收入残疾人人才库。全省各级专门协会全部建立。

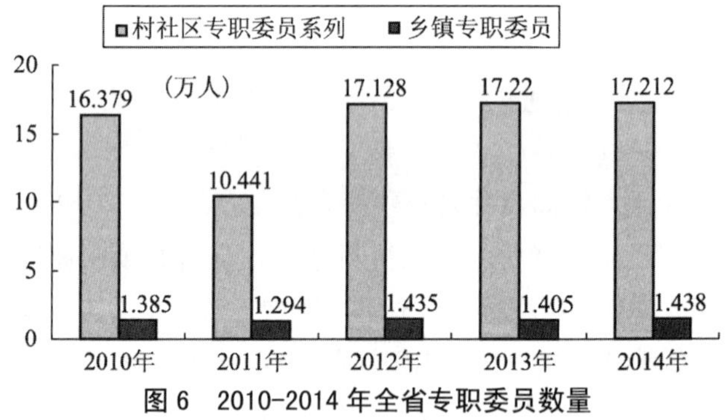

图 6　2010-2014 年全省专职委员数量

九、服务设施建设

残疾人服务设施得到全面发展。全省残疾人服务设施截止 2014 年底竣工并投入使用 90 个，建设规模 9.6 万平方米，总投资 3 亿元；已竣工并投入使用的各级残疾人康复设施 2 个，总建设规模 1300 平方米，总投资 347 万元；竣工并投入使用的各级残疾人托养服务设施 5 个，总建设规模 1.1 万平方米，总投资 3 亿元。

十、信息化建设

2014 年甘肃省残联网站年度访问量达到 67 万次。刊登残联系统信息稿件 3500 篇,较上年增长

31%。省市级残联举办各类信息统计、网络技术培训班 33 期，培训信息化工作干部 410 人。全年投入信息化建设资金 165 万元（图 7）。

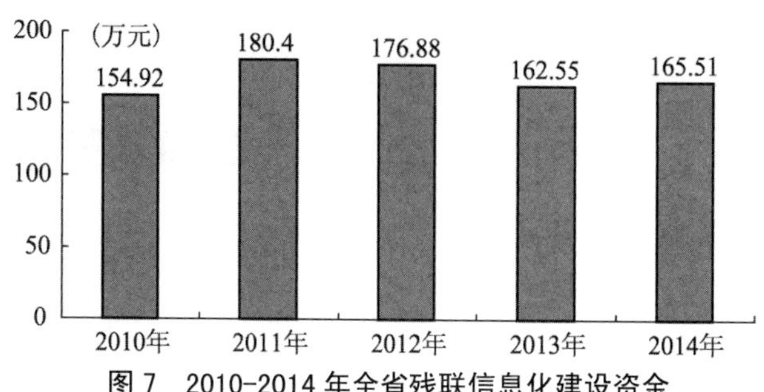

图 7　2010-2014 年全省残联信息化建设资金

2014 年青海省残疾人事业发展统计公报

2014 年，在省委、省政府的坚强领导和中国残联的有力指导下，青海省残联以残疾人社会保障和服务体系建设为核心任务，全力推进《青海省残疾人事业“十二五”规划》和年度计划，全面完成了各项业务指标，残疾人生产生活状况进一步改善，残疾人事业实现新发展。

一、康复

在 4 个市辖区和 42 个县（市）开展了社区康复工作，累计已建社区康复站的社区总数 485 个，配备 2249 名社区康复协调员。

21 个县的 30 个医疗卫生机构陆续开展残疾儿童筛查工作，年度新诊断 0-6 岁残疾儿童 421 人。

开展视力残疾康复机构总数达到 5 个，完成白内障复明手术 3735 例；为 3723 名贫困白内障患者免费施行复明手术；为 2438 名低视力患者配用助视器，培训低视力儿童家长 191 名，有效开展家庭康复训练。对 1137 名盲人进行定向行走训练。

推进听力语言康复机构规范化管理，完善基层服务网络。已建设省级听力语言康复机构 1 个，基层听力语言康复机构 5 个。年度新收训聋儿 69 名，在训聋儿 154 名；规范聋儿家长学校，开展家庭训练，共培训聋儿家长 217 名；开展各级各类听力语言康复专业技术人员培训，共培训专业人员 60 人。

开展肢体残疾康复训练服务机构达 14 个，其中，省级康复机构 1 个，地市级、县级康复机构 13 个；培训各级各类肢体残疾康复人员 227 人次；全国共对 1400 肢体残疾者实施康复训练；实施救助项目资助 177 名脑瘫儿童进行机构康复训练，资助 111 名贫困肢体残疾儿童实施矫治手术。

开展智力残疾康复训练服务的机构 11 个，其中，省级康复机构 1 个，地市级、县级康复机构 10 个；培训各级各类智力残疾康复人员 158 人次；全省共对 646 名智力残疾人进行康复训练；实施救助项目资助 184 名智力残疾儿童进行机构康复训练，同时培训儿童家长。

大力推广“社会化、综合性、开放式”精神病防治康复工作。在 34 个市县开展精神病防治康复工作，对 3893 名重性精神病患者进行综合防治康复，监护率达到 65.25%，显好率达到 45.91%，社会参与率达到 28.43%，肇事率 0.13%；解除关锁 2 人；对 1635 名贫困精神病患者进行医疗救助。

建立了 1 个省级孤独症儿童康复训练机构；161 名孤独症儿童在各级机构进行了康复训练。

加强残疾人辅助器具服务体系建设，深入开展辅助器具供应服务，为残疾人减免费用供应辅助器具 23505 件，其中装配假肢 448 例、矫形器 587 例，验配助视器 2155 件。

二、教育

2014 年，实施残疾人事业专项彩票公益金助学项目，为 70 人次家庭经济困难的残疾儿童享受普惠性学前教育提供资助。各地也积极多渠道争取资金支持，对 311 名残疾儿童给予学前教育资助。

共有特殊教育普通高中班（部）2 个，在校生 51 人；其中聋生 51 人。残疾人中等职业学校（班）2 个，在校生 21 人。有 82 名残疾人被普通高等院校录取。

三、就业

2014 年，残疾人就业规模总体保持稳定。城镇新就业残疾人 1367 人，其中，集中就业残疾人 546 人，按比例安排残疾人就业 159 人，公益性岗位就业 121 人，个体就业及其它形式灵活就业 531 人，辅助性就业 10 人。城镇就业人数 6766 人；51852 名农村残疾人在业，其中 44551 名残疾人从事农业生产劳动。

残疾人职业培训基地达到 31 个，其中残联兴办 16 个，依托社会机构兴办 15 个，其中 1762 人次城镇残疾人接受了职业培训。

盲人按摩事业稳定发展，按摩机构迅速增长。

2014 年度培训盲人保健按摩人员 276 名、盲人医疗按摩人员 83 名；保健按摩机构达到 216 个，医疗按摩机构达到 4 个；在专业技术职务资格评审中，分别有 4 人和 15 人通过盲人医疗按摩人员中级和初级职称评审。

四、扶贫

2014 年，残疾人扶贫开发成效显著，贫困残疾人生产生活状况得到进一步改善。14324 名贫困残疾人得到扶持，其中 8126 人通过扶贫开发实现脱贫；接受实用技术培训的残疾人达到 6025 人次。

康复扶贫贴息贷款扶持 650 名农村残疾人，残疾人扶贫基地达到 37 个，安置 457 名残疾人就业，扶持带动 444 名残疾人。

完成 2031 户农村贫困残疾人危房改造，各地投入危房资金 2532.15 万元，2100 名残疾人受益。

基层党组织助残扶贫项目帮扶 770 名农村贫困残疾人，其中首次接受帮扶 514 人。“万村千乡市场工程”助残扶贫项目安置 158 名贫困残疾人就业，帮扶贫困残疾人创办 98 个村级农村店。

五、社会保障

2014 年新型农村和城镇居民社会养老保险统一合并实施，已有 40149 名城乡残疾居民参保，参保率 69.95%，在 60 岁以下的参保残疾人中有 9553 名重度残疾人，其中 8720 人得到了政府的参保扶助，代缴补贴比例达到 91.28%。有 1818 名非重度残疾人也享受了全额或部分代缴的优惠政策。领取养老金待遇的人数达到 26587 人。

城镇残疾职工参加养老保险 6050 人，参加医疗保险 6154 人，城镇 5827 人和农村 22498 人残疾人纳入最低生活保障范围；城镇集中供养残疾人和农村五保供养残疾人分别达到 850 名和 800 名；47589 名和 1327 名符合条件的城乡残疾人分别享受了稳定的生活补贴和护理补贴。7441 名城乡残疾人得到了其他救助救济。

残疾人托养服务工作规范推进，残疾人托养服务机构达到 39 个，共为 546 名残疾人提供了托养服务。其中寄宿制托养服务机构 13 个；日间照料机构 8 个；综合性托养服务机构 18 个。在以上机构中，共有 5 名残疾人实现辅助性就业，15 名残疾人实现了支持性就业。机构之外接受居家托养服务的残疾人达到 17488 人。全年共有 92 名托养服务管理和服务人员接受了各级各类专业培训，其中接受国家级培训 2 人。

六、宣传文化

截至 2014 年底，共有省级残疾人专题广播节目 1 个，电视手语新闻栏目 1 个。

截至 2014 年底，省地县三级公共图书馆共设立盲文及盲人有声读物阅览室 17 个，共开展残疾人文化周活动 43 场次，共举办残疾人文化艺术类比赛及展览 22 次，共有各类残疾人艺术团体 4 个。

七、体育

各地深入开展残疾人体育工作。组织省级残疾人群众体育健身活动 12 次，2600 人次参加；建设省级残疾人群众体育活动示范点达到 5 个；培训省级残疾人体育健身指导员达到 70 人；组织省级残疾人体育比赛 6 次，参赛运动员达 850 人次；省级残疾人体育训练基地已达 1 个，组织地市级残疾人体育健身活动 5 次，353 人次参加；设立地市级残疾人群众体育活动示范点 1 个；培训地市级残疾人体育健身指导员 4 人。

八、维权

2014 年，制定或修改保障残疾人权益的规范性文件省级 1 件、县级 2 件。县级以上人大进行《残疾人保障法》执法检查和专题调研 5 次；政协进行视察和专题调研 12 次。开展普法宣传教育活动 79 次，6589 人参加；举办法律培训班 25 个，910 人参加。

截至 2014 年底，成立残疾人法律救助工作协调机构 32 个，建立残疾人法律救助工作站 25 个，办理案件 446 件，建立残疾人法律援助中心（工作站）51 个，办理案件 418 件，有力地推动了法律救助和法律援助工作。

残疾人参政议政工作得到加强，各级残联协助人大代表、政协委员提出议案、建议、提案 29 件，办理议案、建议、提案 14 件。

无障碍建设法规、标准进一步完善。11 个市、县、区系统开展无障碍建设；开展无障碍建设检查28次，无障碍培训4人次；为704个贫困残疾人家庭实施了无障碍改造；为11153名残疾人发放了残疾人机动轮椅车燃油补贴。

各级残联共处理残疾人群众来信302件，接待残疾人群众来访430人次。

九、组联

2014年，2个地市级残联在领导班子中配备了残疾人理事长或副理事长；14个县级残联机关配备了残疾人干部；已建乡镇（街道）残联404个，已建率达到100.00%，选聘残疾人专职委员514名；已建社区（村）残协4520个，已建率达到98.03%，选聘残疾人专职委员3137名。

省市县乡残联实有人员已达1239人。各级残联共举办培训班180期，培训机关干部、协会干部及残疾人专职委员5763人次。

共建立省级以下各类残疾人专门协会271个，市级专门协会已建比例为100.00%；县级专门协会已建比例为98.26%。全国共建立助残社会组织1个。

十、设施

截至2014年底，已竣工并投入使用的各级残疾人综合服务设施32个，总建设规模45830平方米，总投资14779万元；已竣工并投入使用的各级残疾人康复设施1个，总建设规模1485平方米，总投资380元；已竣工并投入使用的各级残疾人托养服务设施9个，总建设规模17235平方米，总投资4490元。

十一、信息化

统计队伍建设进一步加强，各级残联共有59名专、兼职统计人员从事残疾人事业统计工作，统计人员业务素质培养普遍得到重视，省级残联举办培训班1期，参加培训的人员达到84人次；地市级举办培训班11期，参加培训的人员达到176人次。

地方残联全面推进网站建设，目前1个省级残联已全部开通了公众服务网站，有4个地市级残联网站和4个县级残联网站也已开通。2014年省级及地市级残联开设网站技术培训班10期，培训各级残联信息员达169人次。

各级残联共有67名专业技术人员从事信息化工作；省级残联共建立局域网1个。

2014 年宁夏回族自治区残疾人事业发展统计公报

2014 年，在自治区党委、政府的正确领导下，在中国残联的精心指导下，在社会各界的关爱支持和全区广大残疾人工作者的共同努力下，残疾人事业发展取得重大进展。

一、康复

2014 年，通过实施一批重点康复工程，使各类别残疾人得到不同程度的康复。

1. 视力残疾康复。本年度完成白内障复明手术 2789 例，其中为 2406 名贫困白内障患者免费施行复明手术。全年为 1685 名低视力患者配用助视器，培训低视力儿童家长 358 名，有效开展家庭康复训练。对 1205 名盲人进行定向行走训练。

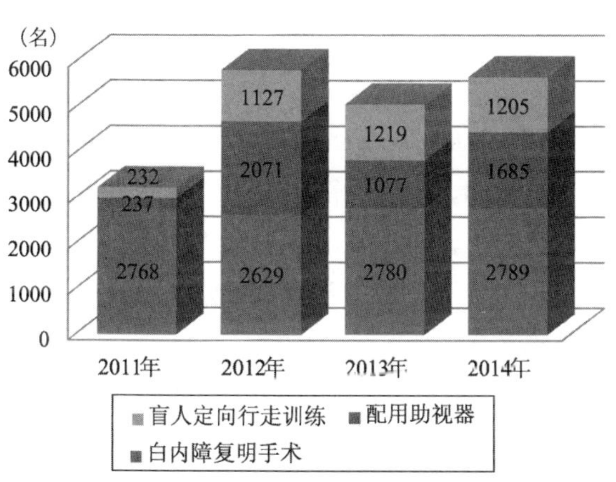

图 1　视力残疾康复状况

2. 听力言语残疾康复。建立各级聋儿康复机构建设 6 个，共对 123 名聋儿进行了听力语言康复训练。规范聋儿家长学校，开展家庭训练，共培训聋儿家长 114 名；培养各类专业人员 40 人。

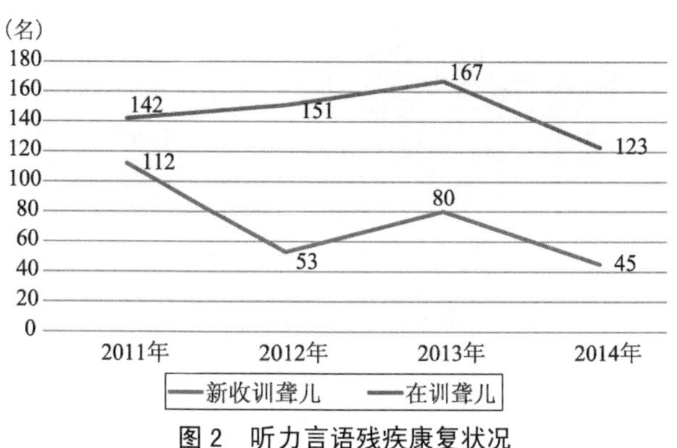

图 2　听力言语残疾康复状况

3. 肢体残疾康复。全年开展肢体残疾康复训练服务的机构达到 18 个,对 95 名贫困肢体残疾儿童实施矫治手术、装配了矫形器等辅助器具，进行了术后康复训练；对 5240 名肢体残疾人进行了康复训练，其中：脑瘫儿童机构康复训练 204 人,肢体残疾儿童社区、家庭康复 135 人，成年肢体残疾人社区、家庭康复 4901 人。

2014 年，深入开展辅助器具供应服务，为残疾人装配假肢 298 例、矫形器 297 例，供应各类辅助器具 10220 件。

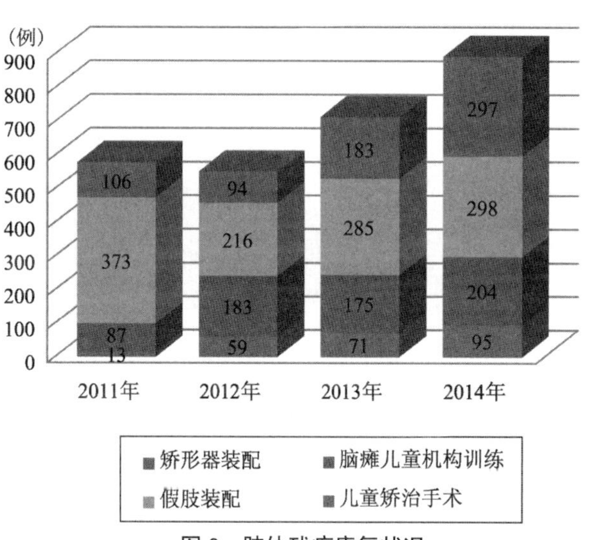

图 3　肢体残疾康复状况

4. 智力残疾康复。全年开展智力残疾康复训练服务的机构达到 18 个；对 845 名智力残疾儿童进行了康复训练，不同程度地开展了智力残疾儿童早期康复训练与服务。

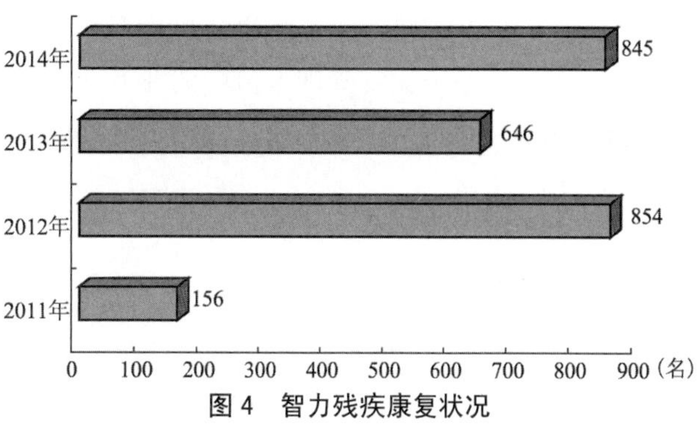

图 4　智力残疾康复状况

5. 精神残疾康复。大力推广"社会化、综合性、开放式"精神病防治康复工作。2014 年，在 21 个县（市、区）开展精神病防治康复工作，精神病人数达 3.4 万，监护病人数达 3.1 万，显好病人数达 2.2 万，参与社会总人数达 1.8 万。贫困精神病患者 1.1 万多人，其中接受医疗救助 5397 人、服药救助 4832 人、住院救助 560 人、其他项目救助 5 人。

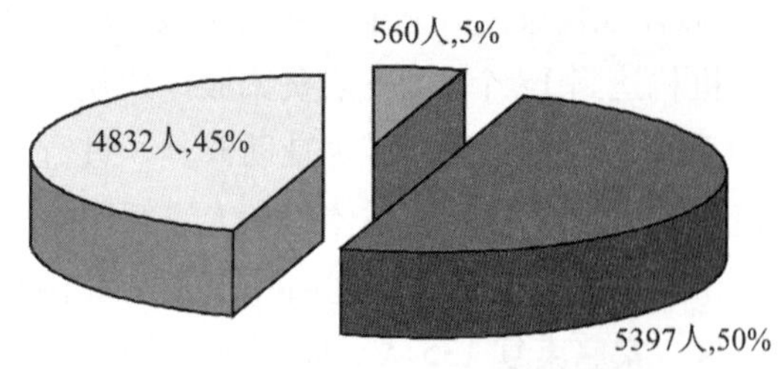

图 5　2014 年度贫困精神病患者救助状况

全区建立了 18 个孤独症儿童康复训练机构，机构内在训儿童 160 名，有 56 名贫困孤独症儿童得到了康复救助。

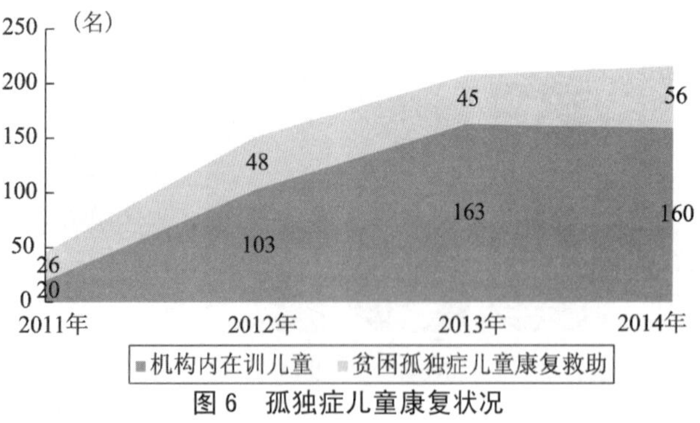

图 6　孤独症儿童康复状况

6. 社区康复。在 9 个市辖区和 13 个县（市）开展了社区康复工作，累计建立社区康复站 554 个，配备 1282 名社区康复协调员。

7. 儿童残疾预防。在 11 个县（市、区）开展残疾儿童筛查工作，本年度新诊断 0-6 岁残疾儿童 400 名，发放儿童残疾预防宣传材料 3 万多份，举办儿童残疾预防宣传活动 28 次。

8. 康复人才培训。区市县康复机构在岗人员 400 人，本年度举办康复管理人员培训班 6 期，康复业务人员培训班 5 期，社区康复协调员培训班 17 期，共培训 730 人。

二、教育

学前康复教育阶段，本年度接受残疾人事业专项彩票公益金助学项目资助 158 人、新入园 95 人；其他残疾儿童学前教育助学项目资助 63 人。

义务教育阶段，未入学适龄残疾儿童少年总数 1003 人，其中视力残疾 62 人，听力残疾 49 人，言语残疾 58 人，肢体残疾 261 人，智力残疾 372 人，精神残疾 38 人，多重残疾 163 人。

高中教育阶段，开办特殊教育普通高中学校 1 所，在校生 275 人；残疾人中等职业学校 1 所，在校生 15 人。

高等教育阶段，普通高等院校录取残疾考生 123 人。

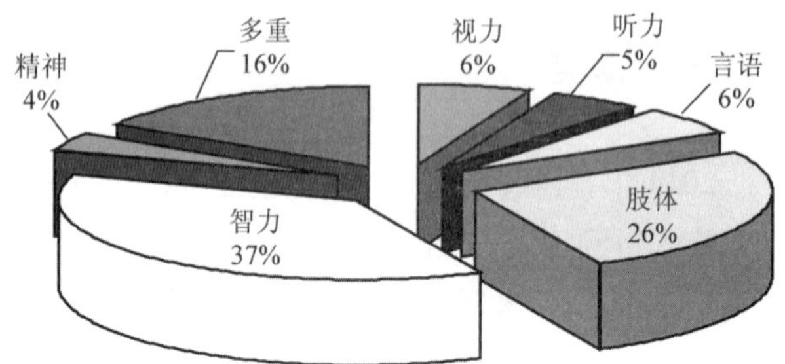

图 7　义务教育阶段未入学残疾儿童状况

三、就业

城镇残疾人就业状况。在业人数 26133 人，其中，集中就业 4003 人，本年度新增 214 人；按比例就业 9755 人，本年度新增 151 人；公益性岗位就业 653 人，本年度新增 130 人；个体及其它形式就业 11685 人，本年度新增 557 人；辅助性就业 37 人，本年度新增 7 人。

农村残疾人就业状况。实际就业 109395 人，其中从事农业生产劳动 94073 人，其他形式就业 15322 人。

残疾人职业培训。累计建立残疾人职业培训基地 37 个，其中残联兴办 6 个，依托社会机构兴办 31 个。本年度城镇职业培训 2232 人次。

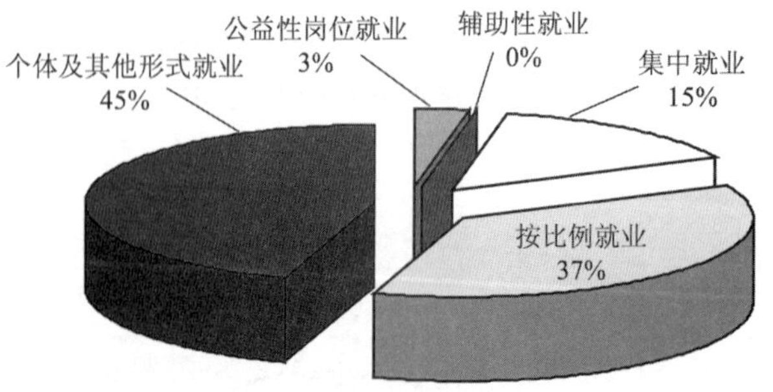

图 8　城镇残疾人就业状况

盲人按摩。本年度培训盲人保健按摩 121 人、医疗按摩 16 人；开办保健按摩机构达到 136 个，医疗按摩机构 2 个；有 9 人通过医疗按摩专业技术中级和初级资格评审。从事保健和医疗按摩就业 173 人。

四、社会保障

1. 社会保险。城镇残疾职工参加社会保险人数达到 29417 人，残疾居民参加城乡社会养老保险 187269 人，参保率为 81%。

2. 社会救助。城乡 93013 名残疾人纳入最低生活保障范围。城镇已纳入最低生活保障 15210 人、集中供养 393 人、其他救助救济 5743 人；农村已纳入最低生活保障 77803 人、五保供养 1679 人、其他救助救济 10871 人。

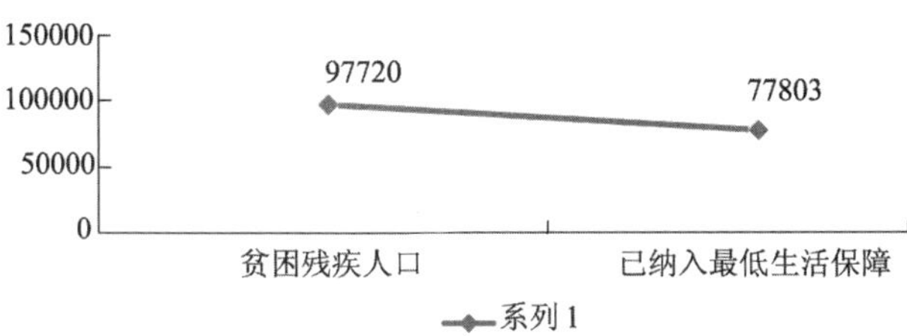

图 9 农村贫困残疾人享受低保状况

3. 社会福利。自治区出台生活补贴政策文件 1 个，有 1 个地市级和 16 个县级出台了生活补贴政策文件，本年度享受生活补贴的残疾人为 69042 人。

4. 托养服务。建立寄宿制托养服务机构 10 个，托养残疾人 328 人；兴办日间照料托养服务机构 38 个，托养残疾人 1342 人；建立综合托养服务机构 7 个，托养残疾人 284 人。本年度享受居家托养服务残疾人 14295 人。培训托养服务管理和服务人员 725 人。

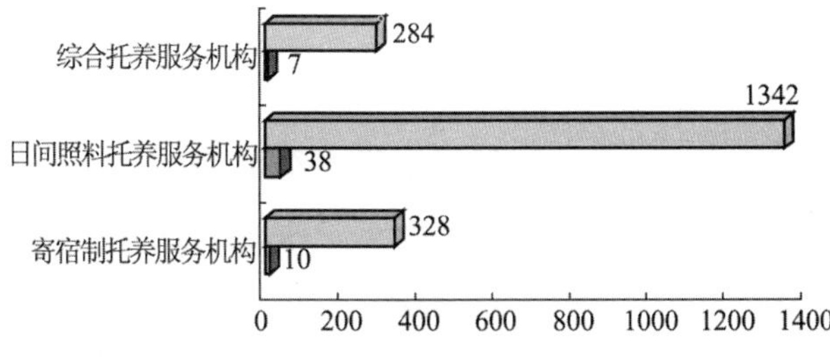

图 10 全区残疾人托养状况

五、扶贫

农村现有贫困残疾人户 80357 户，本年度扶持 14692 户，扶持率达 18%；农村现有贫困残疾人 97720 人，本年度扶持 16189 人，扶持率达 17%。本年度脱贫残疾人 12783 人，接受实用技术培训 7181 人次。

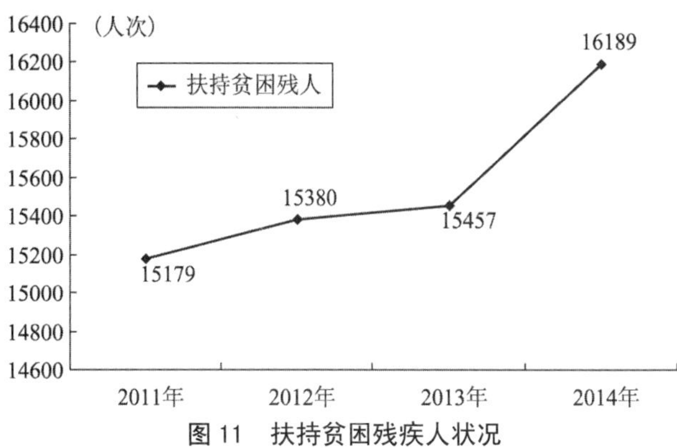

图 11 扶持贫困残疾人状况

建立结对帮扶单位 377 个，结对帮扶个人 1413 人；共建立残疾人扶持基地 32 个，安置残疾人就业 632 人，扶持带动残疾人 2169 户。

本年度康复扶贫贴息贷款 1890.8 万元，项目贷款扶持残疾人 1160 人，到户贷款扶持残疾人 386 人。

本年度完成农村贫困残疾人危房改造 75 户，投入危房改造资金 49.1 万元，受益残疾人 81 人。

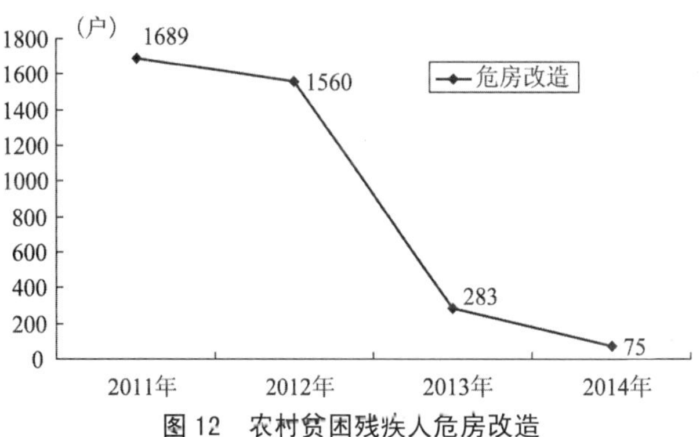

图 12 农村贫困残疾人危房改造

六、组织建设

2014 年，区市县乡残联实有人员 776 人，编制 504 人；5 个地市级残联中，有 4 个配备了残疾人领导干部；21 个县级残联，其中有 11 个县级残联配备了残疾人干部。

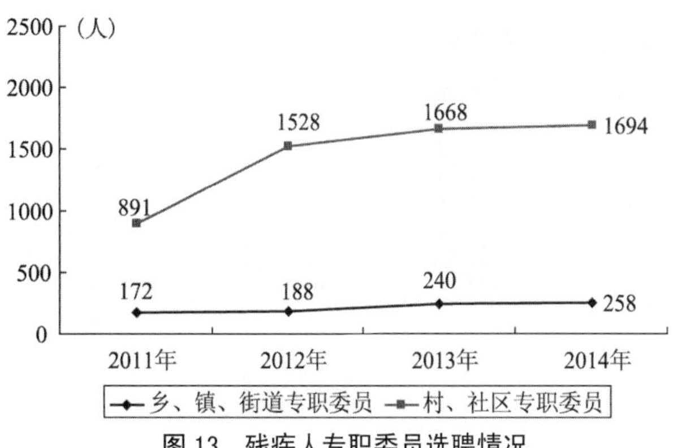

图 13 残疾人专职委员选聘情况

在残疾人专职委员选聘方面，228 个乡（镇、街道）中，选聘残疾人专职委员 258 名；2338 个村（社区）中，已建残疾人活动室 840 个，选聘残疾人专职委员 1694 名。

各级残联举办干部队伍培训班 151 期，参加培训 3087 人次，较往年有大幅度的提升。

区市县建立助残社会组织 14 个，登记注册助残志愿者 61959 名，受助残疾人 82864 人。

各市、县（区）应建立各类残疾人专门协会 140 个，已建各类残疾人专门协会 121 个，组建率达 86%。

七、维权

本年度地市级政府制定或修改了关于残疾人的专门法规、规章 1 个，县级以上人大执法检查或专题调研残疾人工作 3 次，政协视察和专题调研 5 次。

全区开展普法宣传教育活动 44 次，参加人数 2595 人；

举办法律培训班 21 个，参加人数 687 人；

建立残疾人法律救助工作协调机构 10 个；

建立残疾人法律救助工作站 8 个，办理案件 27 件；

建立残疾人法律援助中心（工作站）25 个，办理案件 96 件；残联协助人大代表、政协委员提出议案、建议、提案 18 件；残联办理建议、提案 19 件。

各级政府制定无障碍建设与管理法规、政府令 6 个；成立无障碍建设领导协调组织 15 个；系统开展无障碍建设市、县 23 个；开展贫困残疾人家庭无障碍改造 761 户，组织无障碍检查 31 次，无障碍培训 189 人次，发放残疾人机动轮椅车燃油补贴 19699 人。

县级残联共处理残疾人群众来信 67 件，比上年增加 24 件；接待残疾人群众来访 1636 人次，比上年减少 187 人次。

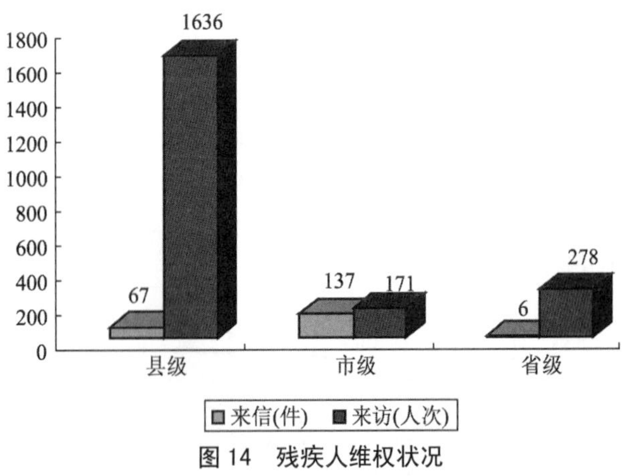

图 14　残疾人维权状况

地市级残联共处理残疾人群众来信 137 件，比上年增加 67 件；接待残疾人群众来访 171 人次，比上年减少 158 人次。

区残联共处理残疾人群众来信 6 件，比上年减少 5 件；接待残疾人群众来访 278 人次，比上年减少 129 人次。

八、宣传

自治区级主要新闻媒体刊播稿件 523 件，报纸专版 3 个，广播电台残疾人专题节目 1 个，电视手语栏目 1 个，自治区残疾人事业新闻宣传促进会 1 个。

地市级主要新闻媒体刊播稿件 347 件，报纸专版 12 个，广播电台残疾人专题节目 2 个，电视手语栏目 4 个。

九、文化

自治区公共图书馆设立盲文及盲人有声读物图书室 1 个，举办残疾人文化周 1 场次，参加人达 150 人次。

地市级公共图书馆设立盲文及盲人有声读物图书室 5 个，举办残疾人文化周 12 场次，举办残疾人文化艺术类的比赛及展览 15 次，成立残疾人艺术团队 2 个。

县级公共图书馆设立盲文及盲人有声读物图书室 5 个，举办残疾人文化周 16 场次，参加人达 590 人次。举办残疾人文化艺术类的比赛及展览 9 次，成立残疾人艺术团队 5 个。

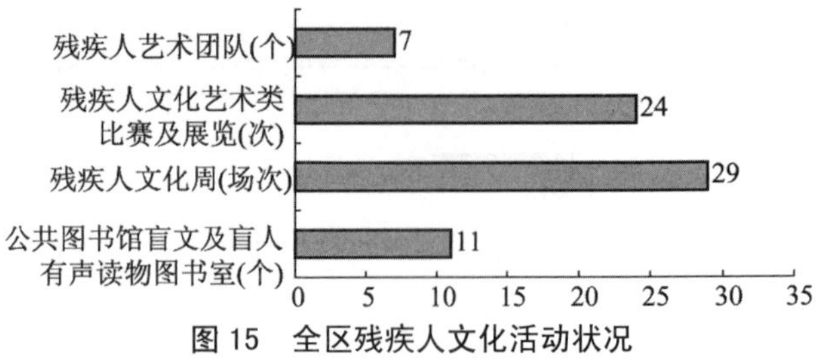

图 15　全区残疾人文化活动状况

十、体育

自治区举办残疾人群众体育健身活动 2 次，参加人数 2200 人；设立残疾人群众体育示范点 13 个，聘任残疾人体育健身指导员 107 人；建立残疾人体育训练基地 2 个，聘任教练员 3 人。

地市级举办残疾人体育健身活动 8 次，参加人数 232 人，设立残疾人群众体育示范点 19 个，聘任残疾人体育健身指导员 52 人。

十一、综合服务设施

截止到 2014 年底，已竣工并投入使用的各级残疾人综合服务设施共计 17 个，在建项目 3 个。其中已竣工并投入使用的各级残疾人综合服务设施总建设规模达 2.98 万平方米，总投资 6957.12 万元。

各级残疾人康复设施累计投入使用项目 1 个，在建项目共计 5 个，建设规模 6.06 万平方米，总投资 25647.98 万元。

各级残疾人托养设施在建项目 1 个，建设规模 2000 平方米，总投资 440 万元。

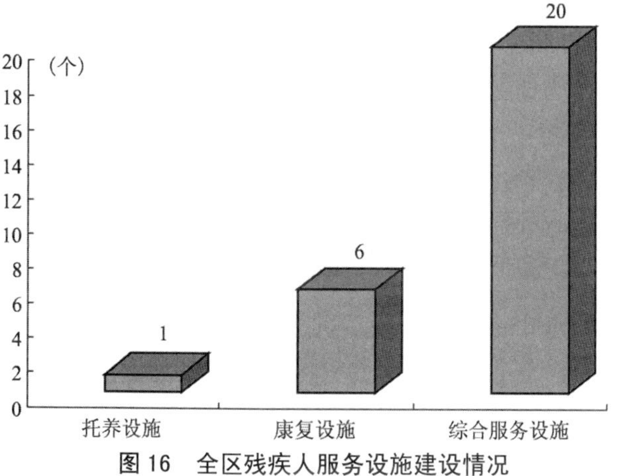

图 16 全区残疾人服务设施建设情况

十二、信息化

统计队伍建设进一步加强，各级残联共有 24 名专、兼职统计人员从事残疾人事业统计工作，其中有 8 名持有统计从业资格证书。统计人员业务素质培养普遍得到重视，本年度自治区残联举办统计业务培训 2 期，参加培训 120 人次；地市级举办业务培训 6 期，参加培训 182 人次。

各级残联全面推进网站建设。自治区残联建立局域网，全部开通了公众服务网站，网上信息服务覆盖全区。有 4 个地市级残联和 8 个县级残联开通网站，这为今后残联系统网站集群服务奠定了基础。

各级残联共有 35 名专业技术人员从事信息化工作。自治区及地市级残联举办信息工作培训班 6 期，培训各级残联信息员 147 人次，自治区残联网站本年度发稿量达 1500 多篇。

2014 年新疆维吾尔自治区残疾人事业发展统计公报

一年来，自治区残联围绕贯彻中央和自治区党委对残疾人事业的工作部署和重要指示精神，始终以社会稳定和长治久安为着眼点和着力点，坚持谋大谋深谋远，统筹谋划和推进残疾人康复、教育、就业、扶贫、维权、宣传文体等各项工作。自治区残联党组理事会牢固树立全心全意为残疾人服务的宗旨，全面履行“代表、服务、管理”职能，认真开展党的群众路线教育实践活动，转作风、带队伍、强服务，密切联系残疾人，紧紧依靠和带领全区各族残疾人工作者，努力改善残疾人生存发展状况，四项惠残民生工程全部完成，成功开展了第二十四次全国助残日、国际残疾人日等一系列活动，为推动我区残疾人事业健康发展做了大量卓有成效的工作。去年新疆残疾人身上发生了许多可喜变化：有的得到了周到的康复服务，有的住上了宽敞舒适的新房，有的靠扶贫基地带动改善了生活，有的在残联的帮助下通过培训、创业、就业和自己的努力找到了工作、有了固定的收入，有的残疾孩子还得到了学业上的帮助，通过学习知识来改变命运，等等，这些工作使残疾人生活得到改善，生活得更加有尊严，充分感受到党和政府的关怀，感受到社会的温暖，更加凝聚了人心，为推进社会稳定和长治久安做出了重要贡献。现根据 2014 年度残疾人事业统计数据和实际情况，进行分析，并公报如下：

一、康复

在 11 个市辖区和 80 个县（市）开展了社区康复工作，累计已建社区康复站的社区总数 1624 个，配备 3472 名社区康复协调员。

17 个县的 11 个医疗卫生机构陆续开展残疾儿童筛查工作，年度新诊断 0-6 岁残疾儿童 277 人。

开展视力残疾康复机构总数达到 35 个，完成白内障复明手术 12793 例；为 6010 名贫困白内障患者免费施行复明手术；为 4446 名低视力患者配用助视器，培训低视力儿童家长 161 名，有效开展家庭康复训练。对 1221 名盲人进行定向行走训练。

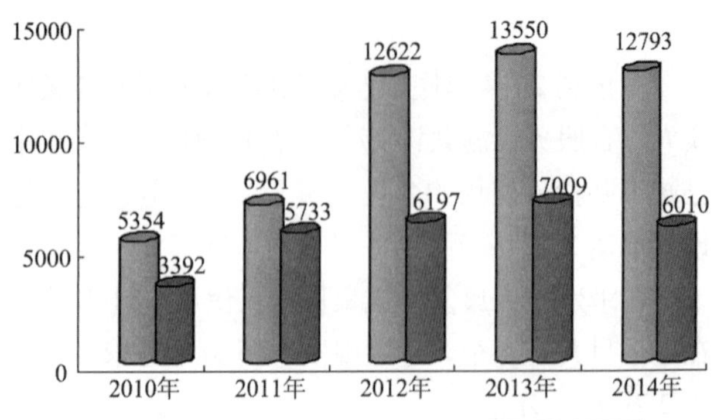

图 1-1 白内障患者复明手术开展情况（单位：例、人）

推进听力语言康复机构规范化管理，完善基层服务网络。已建设省级听力语言康复机构 1 个，基层听力语言康复机构 15 个。年度新收训聋儿 147 名，在训聋儿 314 名；规范聋儿家长学校，开展家庭训练，共培训聋儿家长 408 名；开展各级各类听力语言康复专业技术人员培训，共培训专业人员 15 人。

开展肢体残疾康复训练服务机构达 87 个（全部为：地市级、县级康复机构）；培训各级各类肢体残疾康复人员 425 人次；共对 6608 名肢体残疾者实施康复训练；实施救助项目资助 909 名脑瘫儿童进行机构康复训练，资助 80 名贫困肢体残疾儿童实施矫治手术。开展宣传普及教育，为麻风患者回归社会营造良好社会氛围。

开展智力残疾康复训练服务的机构 26 个，其中，省级康复机构 1 个，地市级、县级康复机构 25 个；培训各级各类智力残疾康复人员 43 人次；全区共对 2087 名智力残疾人进行康复训练；实施救助项目资助，对 430 名智力残疾儿童进行机构康复训练，同时培训儿童家长。

大力推广“社会化、综合性、开放式”精神病防治康复工作。在 69 个市县开展精神病防治康复工作，对 16040 名重性精神病患者进行监护，监护率达到 68.72%，显好率达到 47.54%，社会参与率达到 29.02%，肇事率 0.02%；解除关锁 18 人；对 5436 名贫困精神病患者进行医疗救助。

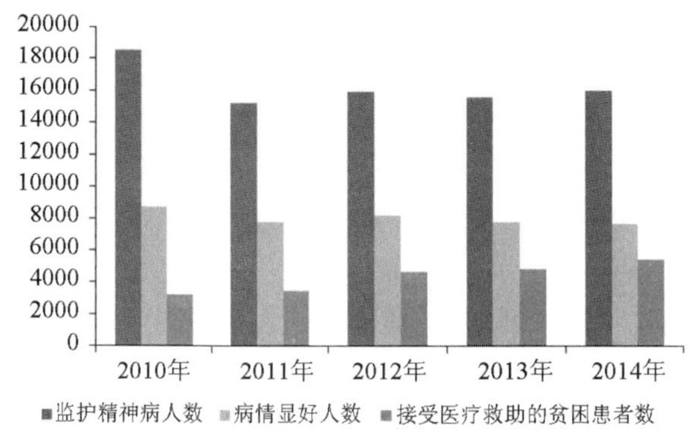

图 1-2　精神病防治康复工作情况（单位：人）

建立了 1 个省级孤独症儿童康复训练机构；465 名孤独症儿童在各级机构进行了康复训练。

加强残疾人辅助器具服务体系建设，深入开展辅助器具供应服务，为残疾人减免费用供应辅助器具 32772 件，其中装配假肢 607 例、矫形器 337 例，验配助视器 8101 件。

二、教育

2014 年，实施残疾人事业专项彩票公益金助学项目，为 200 人次家庭经济困难的残疾儿童享受普惠性学前教育提供资助。

共有特殊教育普通高中班（部）1 个，在校聋生 97 人；残疾人中等职业学校（班）2 个，在校生 440 人，毕业生 197 人，其中 172 人获得职业资格证书。有 273 名残疾人被普通高等院校录取。

截止到 2014 年底，有未入学适龄残疾儿童少年 3877 人，其中视力残疾儿童 216 人，听力残疾儿童 167 人，言语残疾儿童 258 人，智力残疾儿童 1238 人，肢体残疾儿童 1065 人，精神残疾儿童 208 人，多重残疾儿童 725 人。

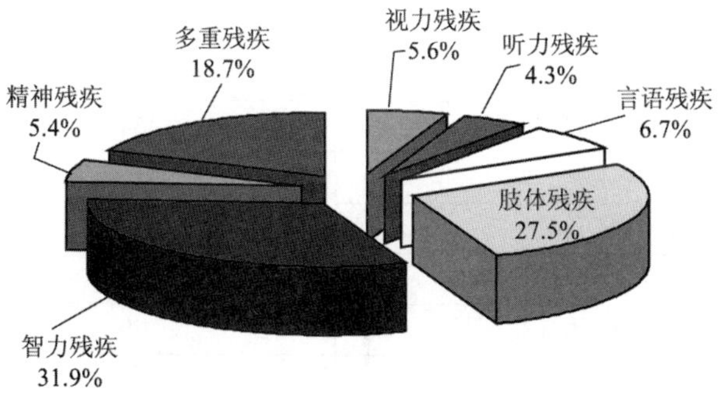

图 2-1　未入学残疾儿童中各类残疾儿童所占比例

三、就业

2014 年，残疾人就业规模总体保持稳定。城镇新就业残疾人 6130 人，其中，集中就业残疾人 1008 人，按比例安排残疾人就业 1694 人，公益性岗位就业 203 人，个体就业及其它形式灵活就业 2919 人，辅助性就业 306 人。城镇就业人数 76146 人；227026 名农村残疾人在业，其中 197159 名残疾人从事农业生产劳动。

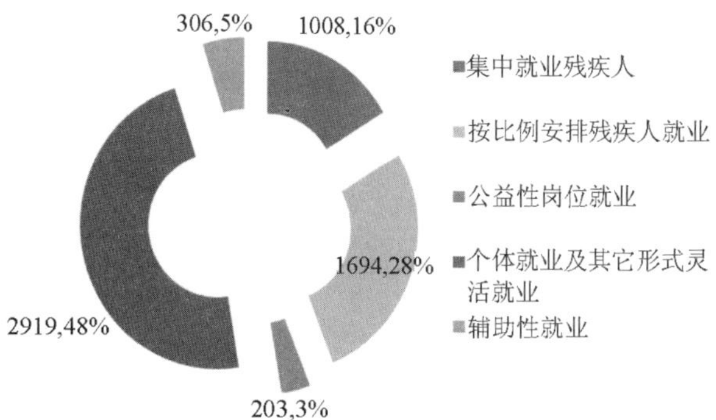

图 3-1 各类就业类别 2014 年新增就业人员情况（单位：人）

残疾人职业培训基地达到 417 个，其中残联兴办 110 个，依托社会机构兴办 307 个，其中 12714 人次城镇残疾人接受了职业培训。

盲人按摩事业稳定发展，按摩机构迅速增长。2014 年度培训盲人保健按摩人员 139 名、盲人医疗按摩人员 114 名；保健按摩机构达到 120 个，医疗按摩机构达到 18 个；在专业技术职务资格评审中，有 25 人通过盲人医疗按摩人员初级职称评审。

四、社会保障

2014 年新型农村和城镇居民社会养老保险统一合并实施，已有 282351 名城乡残疾居民参保，参保率 73.60%，在 60 岁以下的参保残疾人中有 51298 名重度残疾人，其中 47357 人得到了政府的参保扶助，代缴补贴比例达到 92.32%。有 88336 名非重度残疾人也享受了全额或部分代缴的优惠政策。领取养老金待遇的人数达到 84503 人。城镇残疾职工参加养老保险 53456 人，参加医疗保险 63487 人，城镇 64207 人和农村 156768 人残疾人纳入最低生活保障范围；城镇集中供养残疾人和农村五保供养残疾人分别达到 903 名和 2939 名；8976 名和 7953 名符合条件的城乡残疾人分别享受了稳定的生活补贴和护理补贴。17721 名城乡残疾人得到了其他救助救济。

残疾人托养服务工作规范推进，残疾人托养服务机构达到 126 个，共为 2287 名残疾人提供了托养服务。其中寄宿制托养服务机构 19 个；日间照料机构 97 个；综合性托养服务机构 10 个。在以上机构中，共有 4 名残疾人实现辅助性就业，2 名残疾人实现了支持性就业。机构之外接受居家托养服务的残疾人达到 30211 人。全年共有 518 名托养服务管理和服务人员接受了各级各类专业培训，其中接受国家级培训 22 人。

五、扶贫

2014 年，残疾人扶贫开发成效显著，贫困残疾人生产生活状况得到进一步改善。33049 名贫困残疾人得到扶持，其中 9744 人通过扶贫开发实现脱贫；接受实用技术培训的残疾人达到 19630 人次。

康复扶贫贴息贷款扶持 2714 名农村残疾人，残疾人扶贫基地达到 160 个，安置 3342 名残疾人就业，扶持带动 4891 名残疾人。

完成 5140 户农村贫困残疾人危房改造，各地投入危房资金 1954.81 万元，5188 名残疾人受益。

基层党组织助残扶贫项目帮扶 3917 名农村贫困残疾人，其中首次接受帮扶 2985 人。“万村千乡市场工程”助残扶贫项目安置 116 名贫困残疾人就业，帮扶贫困残疾人创办 81 个村级农村店。

六、宣传文化

截至 2014 年底，共有省级残疾人专题广播节目 1 个，电视手语新闻栏目 1 个，播出公益广告 2 个；地市级残疾人专题广播节目 5 个，电视手语新闻栏目 3 个，播出公益广告 3 个。

截至 2014 年底，省地县三级公共图书馆共设立盲文及盲人有声读物阅览室 14 个，共开展残疾人文化周活动 156 场次，共举办残疾人文化艺术类比赛及展览 9 次，共有各类残疾人艺术团体 7 个。

七、体育

各地深入开展残疾人体育工作。组织省级残疾人群众体育健身活动 1 次，1500 人次参加；组织省级残疾人体育比赛 1 次，参赛运动员达 570 人次；省级残疾人体育训练基地已达 5 个，组织地市级残疾人体育健身活动 22 次，2177 人次参加；设立地市级残疾人群众体育活动示范点 4 个；培训地市级残疾人体育健身指导员 160 人。

八、维权

自治区残联深入开展依法保护残疾人权益工作，做好自治区实施《残疾人保障法》办法、《残疾人就业条例》、《无障碍环境建设条例》等有关残疾人权益保障的法律法规的宣传贯彻工作。

2014 年，制定或修改保障残疾人权益的规范性文件县级 3 件。县级以上人大进行《残疾人保障法》执法检查和专题调研 11 次；政协进行视察和专题调研 8 次。开展普法宣传教育活动 215 次，59551 人参加；举办法律培训班 30 个，1589 人参加。

截至 2014 年底，成立残疾人法律救助工作协调机构 72 个，建立残疾人法律救助工作站 62 个，办理案件 116 件，建立残疾人法律援助中心（工作站）88 个，办理案件 554 件，有力地推动了法律救助和法律援助工作。

残疾人参政议政工作得到加强，各级残联协助人大代表、政协委员提出议案、建议、提案 31 件，办理议案、建议、提案 17 件。

无障碍建设法规、标准进一步完善。共出台了 10 个县级无障碍建设与管理法规、规章和规范性文件；2 个地市级单位开展无障碍建设；开展无障碍建设检查 78 次，无障碍培训 610 人次；为 1336 个贫困残疾人家庭实施了无障碍改造；为 21560 名残疾人发放了残疾人机动轮椅车燃油补贴。

各级残联共处理残疾人群众来信 3367 件，接待残疾人群众来访 9811 人次，其中集体访 6 批次、41 人次。

表 8-1 各级残联处理残疾人群众来访分类表（单位：件）

1. 涉法涉诉类	56
2. 康复类	2036
3. 教育类	464
4. 就业类	945
5. 扶贫类	1503
6. 社会保障类	961
7. 文化体育类	79
8. 机动轮椅车类	426
9. 意见建议类	158
10. 其他类	2663
合计	9811

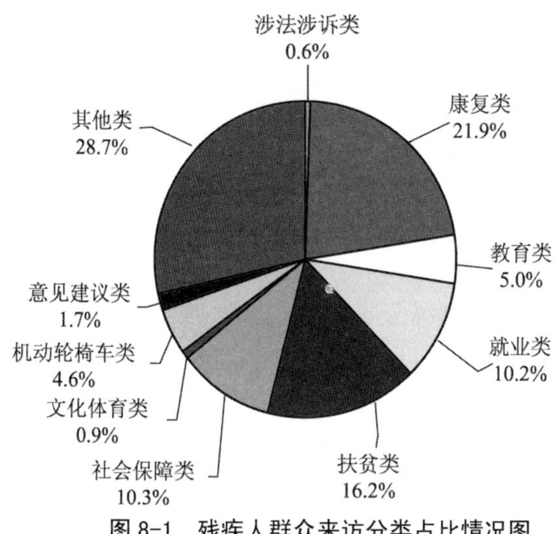

图 8-1 残疾人群众来访分类占比情况图

九、组织建设

2014 年，12 个地市级残联在领导班子中配备了残疾人理事长或副理事长；58 个县级残联机关配备了残疾人干部；已建乡镇（街道）残联 1035 个，已建率达到 96.55%，选聘残疾人专职委员 1288 名；已建社区（村）残协 8966 个，已建率达到 87.51%，选聘残疾人专职委员 4684 名。

省市县乡残联实有人员已达 2885 人。各级残联共举办培训班 592 期，培训机关干部、协会干部及残疾人专职委员 11747 人次。

共建立省级以下各类残疾人专门协会 524 个，市级专门协会已建比例为 98.57%；县级专门协会已建比例为 93.75%。全区共建立助残社会组织 14 个，其中在民政部门注册的为 11 个，以残联为业务主管单位的 9 个。

十、信息化

统计队伍建设进一步加强，各级残联共有 103 名兼职统计人员从事残疾人事业统计工作，统计人员业务素质培养普遍得到重视，省级残联举办培训班 1 期，参加培训的人员达到 50 人次；地市级举办培训班 14 期，参加培训的人员达到 393 人次。

地方残联全面推进网站建设，目前 1 个省级残联已开通了公众服务网站，省级网站发稿量 1610 篇；有 13 个地市级残联网站和 25 个县级残联网站也已开通。2014 年省级及地市级残联开设网站技术培训班 10 期，培训各级残联信息员达 303 人次。

十一、基础设施

截至 2014 年底，全疆已竣工并投入使用的各级残疾人综合服务设施 73 个，总建设规模 187638 平方米，总投资 51493 万元；已竣工并投入使用的各级残疾人康复设施 11 个，总建设规模 5535 平方米，总投资 1698 万元；已竣工并投入使用的各级残疾人托养服务设施 9 个，总建设规模 16766 平方米，总投资 3928 万元。

2014 年新疆兵团残疾人事业发展统计公报

2014 年，兵团残联系统认真学习贯彻落实党的十八届三中、四中全会、中央第二次新疆工作座谈会和兵团党委六届十三次全委（扩大）会议精神，深入贯彻落实科学发展观，以残疾人社会保障体系和服务体系建设为主线，以保障和改善残疾人民生为出发点和落脚点，围绕“托住底、补短板、保基本、广覆盖”， 多措并举，多管齐下，切实解决残疾人最关心、最直接、最现实的利益问题，统筹推进残疾人康复、教育、就业、扶贫和社会保障等工作协调发展，较好完成了“十二五”年度各项工作目标任务。现根据 2014 年度残疾人事业统计数据公报如下:

一、康复

通过实施一批重点康复工程，使各类别残疾人得到不同程度的康复。围绕“人人享有康复服务”的工作目标，充分发动和利用社会资源，积极推进社区康复示范团场创建活动。有 11 个师直单位和 132 个团场开展了社区康复工作，已建立社区康复站的社区有 144 个，配备 308 名社区康复协调员。开展残疾儿童筛查工作，年度新诊断 0-6 岁残疾儿童 44 人。

全年完成白内障复明手术 1751 例，为 909 名贫困白内障患者免费施行复明手术，为 687 名低视力患者配用助视器，培训低视力儿童家长 126 名，对 134 名盲人进行定向行走训练。

开展听力语言康复工作，年度新收训聋儿 27 人，在训聋儿 63 人，培训聋儿家长 82 名。

开展肢体残疾康复训练服务机构 3 个，其中，省级康复机构 1 个，地市级、县级康复机构 2 个,共对 2612 名肢体残疾患者实施康复训练，实施救助项目资助 20 名脑瘫儿童进行机构康复训练，资助 38 名贫困肢体残疾儿童实施矫治手术。

开展智力残疾康复训练服务的机构 1 个，其中，省级康复机构 1 个，对 810 名智力残疾患者进行不同程度的康复训练与服务，实施救助项目资助 15 名智力残疾儿童进行机构康复训练。

大力推广“社会化、综合性、开放式”精神病防治康复工作。在 6 个师开展精神病防治康复工作，对 9537 名重性精神病患者进行综合防治康复，监护率达到 73.27%，显好率达到 67.17%，社会参与率达到 52.22%，肇事率 0.09%，对 2139 名贫困患者进行医疗救助。

加强残疾人辅助器具服务体系建设，深入开展辅助器具供应服务，为残疾人减免费用供应辅助器具 3384 件，其中装配假肢 127 例、矫形器 50 例，验配助视器 858 件。

二、教育

2014 年，实施残疾人事业专项彩票公益金助学项目，为 30 人次家庭经济困难的残疾儿童享受普惠性学前教育提供资助。各地也积极多渠道争取资金支持，对 17 名残疾儿童给予学前教育资助。认真做好残疾学生残疾高考工作， 有 26 名残疾人被普通高等院校录取。

三、就业

2014 年，残疾人就业规模总体保持稳定。城镇新就业残疾人 1732 人，其中，集中就业残疾人 226 人，按比例安排残疾人就业 520 人，公益性岗位就业 40 人，个体就业及其它形式灵活就业 179 人，辅助性就业 767 人。城镇就业人数达 18170 人。

残疾人职业培训基地 2 个，其中残联兴办 1 个，依托社会机构兴办 1 个，其中 914 人次城镇残疾人接受了职业培训。

2014 年度培训盲人保健按摩人员 5 名、盲人医疗按摩人员 1 名。保健按摩机构达到 29 个，医疗按摩机构达到 7 个。在专业技术职务资格评审中，分别有 6 人和 3 人通过盲人医疗按摩人员中级和初级职称评审。

四、社会保障

2014 有 10475 名城乡残疾居民参保，参保率 63.66%，在 60 岁以下的参保残疾人中有 3787 名重度残疾人，其中 3231 人得到了政府的参保扶助，代缴补贴比例达到 85.32%。有 1865 名非重度残疾人也享受了全额或部分代缴的优惠政策。领取养老金待遇的人数达到 3158 人。

城镇残疾职工参加养老保险 16786 人，参加医疗保险 17245 人，城镇 20213 人残疾人纳入最低生活保障范围，城镇集中供养残疾人 174 名，300 名符合条件的城乡残疾人分别享受了稳定的生活补贴和护理补贴，8035 名城乡残疾人得到了其他救助救济。

残疾人托养服务工作规范推进，残疾人托养服务机构达到 29 个，共为 583 名残疾人提供了托养服务，其中寄宿制托养服务机构 24 个，日间照料机构 2 个，综合性托养服务机构 3 个。机构之外接受居家托养服务的残疾人达到 7226 人。全年共有 177 名托养服务管理和服务人员接受了各级各类专业培训。

五、扶贫开发

2014 年，残疾人扶贫开发成效显著，贫困残疾人生产生活状况得到进一步改善。15610 名贫困残疾人得到扶持，其中 1884 人次通过扶贫开发实现脱贫，接受实用技术培训的残疾人达到 11994 人次。

康复扶贫贴息贷款扶持 536 名残疾人，残疾人扶贫基地达到 22 个，安置 351 名残疾人就业，扶持带动 881 名残疾人。

2014 年完成 854 户贫困残疾人危房改造，各地投入危房资金 5307.60 万元，有 858 名残疾人受益。

基层党组织助残扶贫项目帮扶 895 名贫困残疾人，其中首次接受帮扶 86 人。“万村千乡市场工程”助残扶贫项目安置 34 名贫困残疾人就业。

六、宣传文化

截至 2014 年底，兵师团三级公共图书馆共设立盲文及盲人有声读物阅览室 1 个，共开展残疾人文化周活动 87 场次，共举办残疾人文化艺术类比赛及展览 10 次。

七、体育

各地深入开展残疾人体育工作。培训省级残疾人体育健身指导员 3 人，组织师级残疾人体育健身活动 15 次，1385 人次参加。设立地市级残疾人群众体育活动示范点 2 个，培训各级级残疾人体育健身指导员 87 人。

八、维权

开展普法宣传教育活动 178 次，19916 人参加。截至 2014 年底，成立残疾人法律救助工作协调机构 5 个，建立残疾人法律救助工作站 3 个，办理案件 17 件，建立残疾人法律援助中心（工作站）142 个，办理案件 437 件，有力地推动了法律救助和法律援助工作。为 176 个贫困残疾人家庭实施了无障碍改造。为 5329 名残疾人发放了残疾人机动轮椅车燃油补贴。各级残联共处理残疾人群众来信 236 件，接待残疾人群众来访 2247 人次。

九、组织建设

2014 年，有 1 个师级残联在领导班子中配备了残疾人理事长，兵师团残联实有人员 130 人，选聘残疾人专职委员 20 名。共建立省级以下各类残疾人专门协会 54 个，建立助残社会组织 2 个，其中在民政部门注册的为 2 个，以残联为业务主管单位的 1 个。

十、服务设施建设

截至 2014 年底，已竣工并投入使用的各级残疾人综合服务设施 10 个，总建设规模 6983 平方米，总投资 983 万元；已竣工并投入使用的各级残疾人康复设施 4 个，总建设规模 15003 平方米，总投资 5520 万元；投入使用的各级残疾人托养服务设施 27 个，总建设规模 45338 平方米，总投资 7210 万元。

十一、信息化建设

截至 2014 年底，兵团和八师（石河子市）残联开通了公众服务网站。

2014 年黑龙江垦区残疾人事业统计公告

2014 年是执行《中国残疾人事业“十二五”计划发展纲要和《黑龙江垦区残疾人事业“十二五”发展规划》的攻坚年，在农垦总局党委的高度重视下，在中国残联的正确领导下，在全垦区残疾人工作者和广大残疾人的共同努力下，垦区残联全面完成了年初制定的工作目标，在残疾人在康复、教育、就业、扶贫、文化等各个方面取得了较好成绩。

一、康复工作

围绕实施“人人享有基本康复服务”的目标，加强康复托养机构与基层卫生机构的合作，继续做好垦区三级康复网络的建设。截止 2014 年 12 月，全垦区社区康复协调员累计达 131 人，已建社区康复服务档案人数 37718 人，接受社区康复的人数累计达 2053 人，其中，本年度新增接受社区康复的人数为 279 人。

2014 年，全年完成白内障复明手术 464 例，为 43 名贫困白内障患者免费施行复明手术。低视力者配用助视器 140 人，培训低视力儿童家长 61 人，盲人定向行走训练 140 人。

大力推进精神病防治康复工作，显好精神病人数 2371 人。接受治疗的精神病患者 2538 人，精神病康复机构 2 家，在其中康复的精神病人数为 523 人。

积极开展智力残疾人康复救助工作，为 50 名智力残疾儿童提供机构康复训练，为 117 名轻度智力残疾儿童提供社区、家庭康复训练。

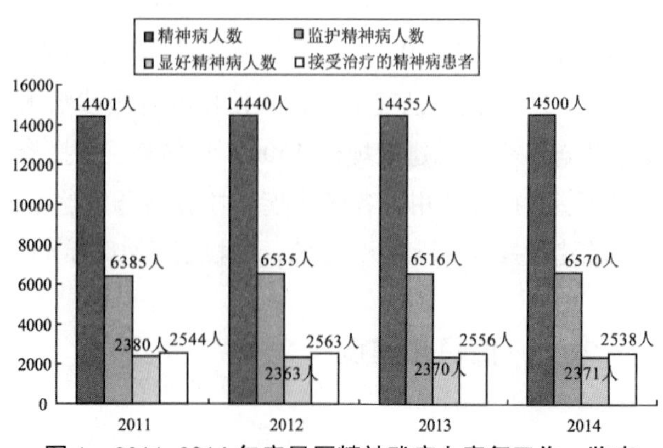

图 1　2011-2014 年度垦区精神残疾人康复工作一览表

加强肢体康复训练工作，共为 276 名肢体残疾人提供训练，其中肢体残疾儿童机构训练 25 人，肢体残疾人社区、家庭训练 250 人。

加强对听力残疾儿童的康复训练，2014 年为 10 名听力残疾儿童提供家庭康复训练，新培训听力残疾儿童家长 36 名。

2014 年为各类残疾人免费配发辅助器具 2181 件，使更多的残疾人得以恢复和改善肢体功能。

加大对残疾儿童的筛查和救助力度，目前有 103 个农场开展残疾儿童筛查工作，开展儿童筛查的医疗机构有 7 所，新诊断的 0-6 岁残疾儿童有 1 人。发放残疾儿康预防宣传材料 1435 份，举办残疾儿童预防宣传活动 16 次。

培训康复管理人员 41 人，康复业务人员 44 人，培训社区康复协调员 93 人，对康复理论知识、辅助器具适配建设、社区康复技术普及和实用康复技术等进行培训，提高工作人员业务素质及理论知识业务能力。

二、教育工作

未入学的学龄残疾儿童少年共 177 人，其中视力残疾人 2 人，听力残疾人 6 人，言语残疾 10 人，肢体残疾人 58 人，智力残疾人 79 人，精神残疾人 10 人，多重 12 人。20 名学龄前儿童接受彩票公益金助学资助。

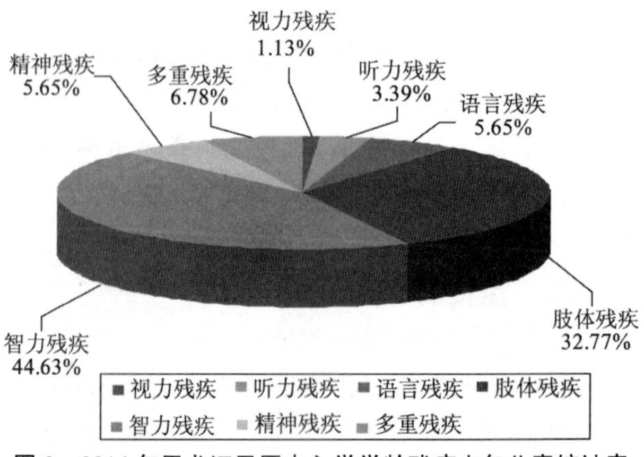

图 2　2014 年黑龙江垦区未入学学龄残疾少年儿童统计表

三、残疾人劳动就业和扶贫

采取集中和分散相结合的方式，大力推进按比例安排残疾人就业工作，鼓励有能力的残疾人自主创业。截至目前，残疾人就业人数 15836 人，其中集中就业 42 人，按比例就业 5494 人，个体及其他形式就业 9959 人，公益岗位就业 275 人。

为了更好的解决残疾人的实际困难，动员全社会的力量，开展“帮包带扶”工作。垦区目前有贫困残疾人 12232 人，低收入残疾人 16850 人。本年度扶持贫困残疾人 4302 户，共 5361 人，脱贫 1499 人。为 2965 名残疾人提供实用技术培训。为 350 户贫困残疾人进行危房改造。全年参与扶贫的结对帮扶单位 99 个，帮扶个人 646 人，物资和资金投入 28.8 万元。

盲人医疗按摩机构 1 个，保健按摩机构 2 个，盲人医疗按摩人员中级的 4 人，初级的 5 人，盲人保健按摩人员 5 人。

四、社会保障

残疾人社会保障工作是当前残疾人工作的重点，垦区出台贫困残疾人生活补贴和重度残疾人护理补贴制度，对每个贫困和重度残疾人均实行每月补贴 100 元，进一步改善了贫困和重度残疾人的生活状况。2014 年城镇残疾职工参加养老保险人数为 9827 人，城镇残疾职工参加医疗保险人数 14685 人。全年纳入最低生活保障范围的 30476 人，集中供养 111 人，其他救济 4145 人。机构托养残疾人 365 人，其中智力残疾 27 人，精神残疾 292 人，其他类别残疾人 46 人，享受居家托养服务残疾人 1132 人。

五、宣传文化

2014 年残疾人事业的社会宣传力度得到进一步加强，社会舆论环境得到进一步改善。在主要新闻媒体刊播稿件数 193 件，完善北大荒新月网站的各项工作，开设网上办公、法律援助、新月论坛、残疾人热线、整合残疾人数据库，建立覆盖垦区的电子数据传输平台为垦区残疾人事业的发展和残疾人工作者之间的交流提供了良好的平台。

六、维权

开展法律服务、法律援助和法制宣传，维护残疾人权益，为残疾人创造文明进步的无障碍环境。全年共开展普法宣传教育活动 64 次，参加人数 3103 人，为残疾人提供法律援助的案件 128 件。为 150 名贫困残疾人家庭进行无障碍改造。为 1618 名残疾人发放机动轮椅车燃油补贴。

信访工作的开展，有力的维护了残疾人的合法权益。全年共处理各类信访案件 174 件，其中康复类 20 件，教育类 7 件，就业类 16 件，扶贫类 44 件，社会保障类 70 件，机动车轮椅车类 2 件，意见见议类 11 件，其他类 4 件。全年接待来访 821 人次，无一起集体上访案件发生。整体上看，问题主要集中在社会保障政策和扶贫方面，这说明残疾人的仍然是我们迫切要解决的重大问题。

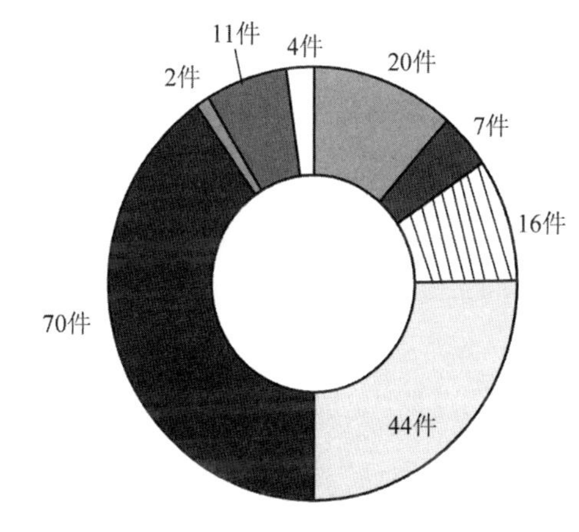

图 3　2014 年处理各类信访案件图表

七、组织建设

全垦区有专兼职残疾人工作者 219 人，其中行政编制 71 人，事业编制 136 人。配备残疾人专职委员 103 人。举办省级综合培训班 2 次，参加人数 234 人；地市级干部培训班 3 次，参加人数 126 人。

八、综合服务设施

截止到 2014 年底，已竣工并投入使用的各级残疾人综合服务设施共计 6 个，综合服务设施的投入使用将会给残疾人带来更大的方便。

九、信息化建设

统计队伍建设进一步加强，共有 113 名专、兼职统计人员从事残疾人事业统计工作，其中省级 1 人，地市级 9 人，县级 103 人。统计人员业务素质培养普遍得到重视，省级、管理局级统计人员均持证上岗。省级残联举办培训班 1 期，参加培训的人员 40 人次；地市级举办培训班 2 期，参加培训的人员达到 33 人次。

全面推进网站建设，有门户网站 1 个，信息化建设投入资金约 27 万余元，系统维护费 3.2 万元，信息化专业人才 127 人，为垦区残联信息化建设提供保障。

十、存在的问题和不足

2014 年，黑龙江农垦总局的残疾人工作较好地完成了各项计划任务，但由于经济和体制等原因，从工作整体来看，黑龙江农垦的残疾人事业发展与中国残联的要求还有一定的差距：一是贫困残疾人的医疗、康复、教育、就业、社会保障等方面还存在着一定的困难,不能完全满足残疾人的需求；二是改善残疾人社会保障体系还不够健全；三是残疾人无障碍建设环境还存在不足，尤其是信息无障碍建设还处在起步阶段。因此，2015 年垦区各级残联全面推进“两个体系”建设，提高服务能力和保障能力，在保障民生等方面加大扶持力度，完善工作机制，保障残疾人的基本需求。

附录

Appendix

关于使用 2010 年末全国残疾人总数及各类、不同残疾等级人数的通知

残联〔2012〕25 号

各省、自治区、直辖市及计划单列市残联，新疆生产建设兵团残联，黑龙江农垦总局残联:

根据第六次全国人口普查我国总人口数，及第二次全国残疾人抽样调查我国残疾人占全国总人口的比例和各类残疾人占残疾人总人数的比例，推算了 2010 年末我国残疾人总人数及各类、不同等级的残疾人数，现通知如下:

全国残疾人总数为 8502 万人。

各类残疾人的人数分别为: 视力残疾 1263 万人; 听力残疾 2054 万人; 言语残疾 130 万人; 肢体残疾 2472 万人; 智力残疾 568 万人; 精神残疾 629 万人; 多重残疾 1386 万人。

各残疾等级人数分别为: 重度残疾 2518 万人; 中度和轻度残疾人 5984 万人。

以上数据可在工作中使用并对外公开。

中国残疾人联合会
二〇一二年三月五日

第二次全国残疾人抽样调查残疾标准

（国务院 2005 年 11 月 4 日批准）

视力残疾标准

一、视力残疾的定义

视力残疾，是指由于各种原因导致双眼视力低下并且不能矫正或视野缩小，以致影响其日常生活和社会参与。

视力残疾包括盲及低视力。

二、视力残疾的分级

类别	级别	最佳矫正视力
盲	一级	无光感-＜0.02；或视野半径＜5 度
	二级	0.02-＜0.05；或视野半径＜10 度
低视力	三级	0.05-＜0.1
	四级	0.1-＜0.3

〔注〕

1. 盲或低视力均指双眼而言，若双眼视力不同，则以视力较好的一眼为准。如仅有单眼为盲或低视力，而另一眼的视力达到或优于 0.3，则不属于视力残疾范畴。

2. 最佳矫正视力是指以适当镜片矫正所能达到的最好视力或针孔视力。

3. 以注视点为中心，视野半径＜10 度者，不论其视力如何均属于盲。

听力残疾标准

一、听力残疾的定义

听力残疾，是指人由于各种原因导致双耳不同程度的永久性听力障碍，听不到或听不清周围环境声及言语声，以致影响日常生活和社会参与。

二、听力残疾的分级

听力残疾一级：

听觉系统的结构和功能方面极重度损伤，较好耳平均听力损失≥91 dB HL，在无助听设备帮助下，不能依靠听觉进行言语交流，在理解和交流等活动上极度受限，在参与社会生活方面存在极严重障碍。

听力残疾二级：

听觉系统的结构和功能重度损伤，较好耳平均听力损失在 81-90 dB HL 之间，在无助听设备帮助下，在理解和交流等活动上重度受限，在参与社会生活方面存在严重障碍。

听力残疾三级：

听觉系统的结构和功能中重度损伤，较好耳平均听力损失在 61-80 dB HL 之间，在无助听设备帮助下，在理解和交流等活动上中度受限，在参与社会生活方面存在中度障碍。

听力残疾四级：

听觉系统的结构和功能中度损伤，较好耳平均听力损失在 41-60dB HL 之间，在无助听设备帮助下，在理解和交流等活动上轻度受限，在参与社会生活方面存在轻度障碍。

言语残疾标准

一、言语残疾的定义

言语残疾，是指由于各种原因导致的不同程度的言语障碍，经治疗一年以上不愈或病程超过两年者,而不能或难以进行正常的言语交往活动，以致影响日常生活和社会参与（3 岁以下不定残）。

言语残疾包括：

1. 失语：是指由于大脑言语区域以及相关部位损伤所导致的获得性言语功能丧失或受损。

2. 运动性构音障碍：是指由于神经肌肉病变导致构音器官的运动障碍，主要表现为不会说话、说话费力、发声和发音不清等。

3. 器官结构异常所致的构音障碍：是指构音器官形态结构异常所致的构音障碍。其代表为腭裂以及舌或颌面部术后造成的构音障碍。主要表现为不能说话、鼻音过重、发音不清等。

4. 发声障碍（嗓音障碍）：是指由于呼吸及喉存在器质性病变导致的失声、发声困难、声音嘶哑等。

5. 儿童言语发育迟滞：指儿童在生长发育过程中其言语发育落后于实际年龄的状态。主要表现不会说话、说话晚、发音不清等。

6. 听力障碍所致的语言障碍：是指由于听觉障碍所致的言语障碍。主要表现为不会说话或者发音不清。

7. 口吃：是指言语的流畅性障碍。常表现为在说话的过程中拖长音、重复、语塞并伴有面部及其他行为变化等。

二、言语残疾的分级

言语残疾一级：

无任何言语功能或语音清晰度≤10%，言语表达能力等级测试未达到一级测试水平，不能进行任何言语交流。

言语残疾二级：

具有一定的发声及言语能力。语音清晰度在11%-25%之间，言语表达能力等级测试未达到二级测试水平。

言语残疾三级：

可以进行部分言语交流。语音清晰度在26%-45%之间，言语表达能力等级测试未达到三级测试水平。

言语残疾四级：

能进行简单会话，但用较长句或长篇表达困难。语音清晰度在46%-65%之间，言语表达能力等级测试未达到四级测试水平。

肢体残疾标准

一、肢体残疾的定义

肢体残疾，是指人体运动系统的结构、功能损伤造成四肢残缺或四肢、躯干麻痹（瘫痪）、畸形等而致人体运动功能不同程度丧失以及活动受限或参与的局限。

肢体残疾包括：

1. 上肢或下肢因伤、病或发育异常所致的缺失、畸形或功能障碍；

2. 脊柱因伤、病或发育异常所致的畸形或功能障碍；

3. 中枢、周围神经因伤、病或发育异常造成躯干或四肢的功能障碍。

二、肢体残疾的分级

肢体残疾一级：不能独立实现日常生活活动。

1. 四肢瘫：四肢运动功能重度丧失；

2. 截瘫：双下肢运动功能完全丧失；

3. 偏瘫：一侧肢体运动功能完全丧失；

4. 单全上肢和双小腿缺失；

5. 单全下肢和双前臂缺失；

6. 双上臂和单大腿（或单小腿）缺失；

7. 双全上肢或双全下肢缺失；

8. 四肢在不同部位缺失；

9. 双上肢功能极重度障碍或三肢功能重度障碍。

肢体残疾二级：基本上不能独立实现日常生活活动。

1. 偏瘫或截瘫，残肢保留少许功能（不能独立行走）；

2. 双上臂或双前臂缺失；

3. 双大腿缺失；

4. 单全上肢和单大腿缺失；

5. 单全下肢和单上臂缺失；

6. 三肢在不同部位缺失（除外一级中的情况）；

7. 二肢功能重度障碍或三肢功能中度障碍。

肢体残疾三级：能部分独立实现日常生活活动。

1. 双小腿缺失；

2. 单前臂及其以上缺失；

3. 单大腿及其以上缺失；

4. 双手拇指或双手拇指以外其他手指全缺失；

5. 二肢在不同部位缺失（除外二级中的情况）；

6. 一肢功能重度障碍或二肢功能中度障碍。

肢体残疾四级：基本上能独立实现日常生活活动。

1. 单小腿缺失；

2. 双下肢不等长，差距在5厘米以上（含5厘

米）;

3. 脊柱强（僵）直;

4. 脊柱畸形，驼背畸形大于 70 度或侧凸大于 45 度;

5. 单手拇指以外其他四指全缺失;

6. 单侧拇指全缺失;

7. 单足跗跖关节以上缺失;

8. 双足趾完全缺失或失去功能;

9. 侏儒症（身高不超过 130 厘米的成年人）;

10. 一肢功能中度障碍或两肢功能轻度障碍;

11. 类似上述的其他肢体功能障碍。

智力残疾标准

一、智力残疾的定义

智力残疾，是指智力显著低于一般人水平，并伴有适应行为的障碍。此类残疾是由于神经系统结构、功能障碍，使个体活动和参与受到限制，需要环境提供全面、广泛、有限和间歇的支持。

智力残疾包括：在智力发育期间（18 岁之前），由于各种有害因素导致的精神发育不全或智力迟滞；或者智力发育成熟以后，由于各种有害因素导致智力损害或智力明显衰退。

二、智力残疾的分级

级别	分级标准			
	发展商（DQ）0-6 岁	智商（IQ）7 岁及以上	适应性行为（AB）	WHO-DAS Ⅱ分值 18 岁以上
一级	≤25	<20	极重度	≥116 分
二级	26-39	20-34	重度	106-115 分
三级	40-54	35-49	中度	96-105 分
四级	55-75	50-69	轻度	52-95 分

精神残疾标准

一、精神残疾的定义

精神残疾，是指各类精神障碍持续一年以上未痊愈，由于存在认知、情感和行为障碍，以致影响其日常生活和社会参与。

二、精神残疾的分级

18 岁以上（含）的精神障碍患者根据《世界卫生组织残疾评定量表Ⅱ》（WHO-DASⅡ）分数和下述的适应行为表现，18 岁以下者依据下述的适应行为的表现，把精神残疾划分为四级：

精神残疾一级：

WHO-DASⅡ值≥116 分，适应行为严重障碍；生活完全不能自理，忽视自己的生理、心理的基本要求。不与人交往，无法从事工作，不能学习新事物。需要环境提供全面、广泛的支持，生活长期、全部需他人监护。

精神残疾二级：

WHO-DASⅡ值在 106-115 分之间，适应行为重度障碍；生活大部分不能自理，基本不与人交往，只与照顾者简单交往，能理解照顾者的简单指令，有一定学习能力。监护下能从事简单劳动。能表达自己的基本需求，偶尔被动参与社交活动；需要环境提供广泛的支持，大部分生活仍需他人照料。

精神残疾三级：

WHO-DASⅡ值在 96-105 分之间，适应行为中度障碍；生活上不能完全自理，可以与人进行简单交流，能表达自己的情感。能独立从事简单劳动，能学习新事物，但学习能力明显比一般人差。被动参与社交活动，偶尔能主动参与社交活动；需要环境提供部分的支持，即所需要的支持服务是经常性的、短时间的需求，部分生活需由他人照料。

精神残疾四级：

WHO-DASⅡ值在 52-95 分之间，适应行为轻度障碍；生活上基本自理，但自理能力比一般人差，有时忽略个人卫生。能与人交往，能表达自己的情感，体会他人情感的能力较差，能从事一般的工作，学习新事物的能力比一般人稍差；偶尔需要环境提供支持，一般情况下生活不需要由他人照料。

多重残疾

存在两种或两种以上残疾为多重残疾。多重残疾应指出其残疾的类别。多重残疾分级按所属残疾中最重类别残疾分级标准进行分级。

中国残联统计调查项目目录

审批项目一览表

统计调查项目名称	批准文号	有效期截止时间
中国残疾人事业统计年报报表制度	国统制[2014]76 号	2016-08
中国残疾人事业统计年报快报制度	国统制[2014]76 号	2016-08
中国残疾人事业统计台账制度	国统制[2014]76 号	2016-08

中国残疾人联合会文件

残联发[2006]1 号

关于印发《中国残联系统统计工作管理办法》的通知

各省、自治区、直辖市及计划单列市残联，新疆生产建设兵团残联、黑龙江农垦总局残联:

为了加强统计工作的管理,规范统计调查行为，提高统计调查的整体效益，充分发挥统计工作的服务和监督作用，中国残联依据《中华人民共和国统计法》、《中华人民共和国统计法实施细则》、《部门统计调查管理暂行办法》，结合工作实际，对原有的《中国残联系统统计工作暂行规定》、《中国残联系统专项业务统计调查项目管理暂行办法》、《中国残联机关统计资料管理暂行办法》等进行了修订和整合，制定了《全国残联系统统计工作管理办法》，现予以印发，请遵照执行。

中国残疾人联合会
二〇〇六年一月三日

中国残联系统统计工作管理办法

一、总 则

第一条 为了科学、有效地组织全国残联系统统计工作，规范统计调查行为，提高统计调查的整体效益，充分发挥统计工作的服务和监督作用，依据《中华人民共和国统计法》（以下简称《统计法》）、《中华人民共和国统计法实施细则》（以下简称《实施细则》）、《部门统计调查管理暂行办法》，结合工作实际，制定本办法。

第二条 全国残联系统统计工作的基本任务是：对全国残疾人事业的发展状况和残联系统的业务工作进行统计调查、统计分析、统计预测和统计监督，为国家和各级人民政府制定与残疾人事业相关的政策、法规提供依据，为领导运筹决策和残联系统工作的发展提供有效的服务。

第三条 全国残联系统统计工作由：中国残疾人事业统计年报制度、中国残疾人事业统计快报制度、中国残疾人事业基础统计台账制度、专项业务统计调查工作组成。

第四条 各级残联应加强统计现代化建设，积极利用信息技术手段，使残疾人事业统计数据更加科学、准确、及时，逐步实现残疾人事业统计数据的电子化和统计数据的社会共享与服务。

二、统计机构、职责和统计人员

第五条 全国残联系统统计工作实行统一领导、分级负责。中国残联负责全国残疾人事业统计工作的组织、协调与管理，并对地方残联统计工作进行指导，具体由中国残联设置的统计机构负责组织实施。地方各级残联的统计工作由地方各级残联设置的统计机构或统计主管部门负责管理和组织实施，并接受上级残联统计机构和同级人民政府统计部门的指导、监督与管理。

第六条 中国残联的统计机构设在中国残联信息中心，负责组织、协调和管理全国残联系统的统计工作。其主要职责是：制定残疾人事业统计调查计划和项目，制定统计标准；组织协调各级残联搜集、整理、提供统计资料，管理统计资料的发布，开展统计分析、统计预测和统计监督工作；指导、检查全国残联系统统计工作，组织统计业务经验交流，开展全国残联系统统计科学研究；做好统计人员培训工作；制订全国残联系统统计工作现代化规划。

各省级残联应设置统计机构或明确统计主管部门并设专职统计人员，负责指导本行政区域内各级残联统计工作，组织管理本级残联的统计工作。其主要职责是：在完成好中国残联和上级残联下达的各项统计调查工作的同时，为本级残疾人事业提供各项统计数据，并开展统计调查活动。

各地级市残联应明确统计主管部门并设专（兼）职统计人员，其主要职责是：在完成好中国残联和上级残联下达的各项统计调查工作的同时，为本级残疾人事业提供各项统计数据，并开展统计调查活动。

各县级残联应明确统计工作主管部门或主管负责人，确定兼职统计人员。其主要职责是：做好基础数据工作，建立统计台账，完成好中国残联和上级残联下达的统计调查任务，为本级残疾人事业提供各项统计数据，并开展统计调查活动。

第七条 各级残联统计人员应保持相对稳定。统计人员的调动，应当征得本级统计主管部门或统计工作负责人的同意；省级专职统计人员的调动，应当征得中国残联统计机构的同意。统计人员调动工作或离职，应当由经过统计业务培训、能够胜任统计业务工作的人员接替，并办理交接手续。各级残联的统计人员应取得同级人民政府统计机构颁发的统计上岗证，具有残联系统业务知识和计算机操作能力。

三、统计报表制度的编制、修改与审批

第八条 中国残疾人事业统计年报、快报制度和统计台账制度中的指标、指标涵义、调查范围、

分类目录、计算方法和统计报表表式、统计编码以及报送时间，由中国残联统一规定，按照国家统计局的要求报送国家统计局进行审批备案。按规定程序经国家统计局批准或备案的统计报表，在报表的右上角标明制表机关名称、表号、批准或备案机关名称及其批准文号。被调查的部门、人员应当准确、及时地按报表规定填报。

不符合前款规定的统计报表（包括以搜集数字为主的调查提纲）是非法报表，被调查的部门可以拒绝填报。

第九条 中国残疾人事业统计年报、快报和统计台账应根据中国残疾人事业发展的需要及时进行调整和补充。中国残联各业务部门因工作需要，调整和补充有关指标时，应进行充分论证并与中国残联统计管理部门联系与协商，经中国残联理事会批准后，报国家统计局批准或备案。

四、统计台账管理

第十条 为了规范中国残联系统统计工作，做到依法统计，发挥统计服务和监督作用，根据《中华人民共和国统计法》和国家相关统计工作的规定，中国残联将制定中国残疾人事业统计台账制度，加强统计台账的管理与数据的报送。

第十一条 中国残疾人事业统计台账（卡）充分利用电子网络化的方式、将科学合理、准确实用的动态管理，与中国残疾人事业统计报表制度相衔接。台账填写内容要符合法律法规政策的要求，填写对象真实、准确；先填卡，后建帐，做到由台账中提取统计数字。

第十二条 各级残联必须依据中国残疾人事业统计台账（卡）中的数据，报送中国残疾人事业统计快报、年报和各项专项业务统计调查的统计报表，做到填报统计报表的数据全面、准确、及时、数出一门。

第十三条 中国残疾人事业统计台账在统一格式、统一软件下实施，由各级地方残联统计人员协调业务部门和人员用计算机或纸质台账、台卡方式进行专门管理。统计人员发生变动时，要严格履行交接手续。

第十四条 省级、地（市）级残联都应建立电子化台账。有条件的县级残联也要实行电子化台账，各级残联应积极推动电子化台账建设，加强统计台账的管理工作。在没有实行全面电子化台账之前，将实行电子化台账和纸质台账、台卡的同时保存。

第十五条 中国残疾人事业统计台账、台卡按中国残疾人事业统计报表逐级汇总上报。

五、专项业务统计调查管理

第十六条 中国残联和地方各级残联开展的专项业务统计调查，以及残联各业务部门与其他部门或单位联合组织实施的统计调查，其调查的统计指标与中国残联年报、快报指标交叉重复或需要对外公布统计数据的统计调查，均属于专项业务统计调查管理范畴。

第十七条 中国残联系统各级统计机构统一管理和协调本级业务部门专项业务统计调查。

第十八条 专项业务统计调查项目必须符合国家统计局《部门统计调查项目管理暂行办法》的基本原则与要求。专项业务统计调查项目的立项必须有充分的理由。调查要有明确的目的和资料使用范围。调查项目应当与中国残联职能范围和各项业务工作相对应。

第十九条 中国残联系统各级统计机构通过建立审批备案制度、调查项目公布制度、跟踪检查制度、举报制度，对会内专项业务统计调查进行管理。

第二十条 专项业务统计调查项目中的统计标准和分类必须与政府综合统计机构规定使用的标准和分类相一致。涉及政府综合统计机构规定以外的专业标准和分类，要与国家有关标准或行业标准相一致。尚无国家标准和行业标准的，必须严格按照标准化及分类科学的原则进行归纳和设计，并在使用前征求政府综合统计机构的意见。

第二十一条 中国残联新增设的统计调查项目在制定好统计调查方案后，须提交中国残联统计机构审核，报国家统计局批准后统一组织实施。

地方残联新增设的统计调查项目，由本级残联统计机构统一管理，报上级残联统计机构和同级人民政府统计局批准后组织实施。地方残联制发的统计调查表内容、指标涵义、计算方法、完成期限等，均不得与中国残联制发的有关统计调查表相抵触。

六、统计资料的管理与发布

第二十二条　残联系统统计资料实行归口管理。全国性残联系统　统计资料，由中国残联统计机构统一管理；地方性残联系统统计资料，由地方残联统计机构或统计人员统一管理。统计机构和统计人员必须建立统计工作责任制和统计资料整理、审查、管理制度，不断提高工作质量和工作效率，保证残联系统统计资料的准确、及时。

各级残联的文件、报告、简报、情况反映、信息等引用综合性的统计数字，必须经本级统计机构或统计人员复核。对外提供和公布的统计资料，必须经本级统计机构或统计人员统一复核和办理并由主管理事长批准。任何部门和个人不得擅自公开和使用未经正式公布的残联系统统计资料。

第二十三条　各级残联统计机构、统计人员必须建立健全统计资料档案，对原始记录、统计台账和综合分析等统计资料，按有关规定保管，不得损坏。对于属于国家秘密的残联系统统计资料，要按照《中华人民共和国保守国家秘密法》、国家统计局《统计资料保密管理办法》等有关规定，妥善保管。

七、奖励和惩罚

第二十四条　各级残联对有下列表现之一的残联统计机构或者人员，给予表扬或奖励:

一、在改革和完善残联系统统计制度．统计方法等方面，有重要贡献的;

二、在完成规定的残联系统统计调查任务，保障残联系统统计资料的准确性、及时性方面，做出显著成绩的;

三、在进行残联系统统计分析、统计预测和统计监督方面取得重要成绩的;

四、在运用和推广现代化信息技术方面，有显著效果的;

五、在残联系统统计科学研究方面有所创新的;

六、坚持实事求是，依法办事，同违反统计法规和本办法的行为作斗争，表现突出的。

第二十五条　各级残联对有下列行为之一的机构或者人员，给予批评或处分:

一、虚报、瞒报、拒报残联系统统计资料的;

二、伪造、篡改残联系统统计资料的;

三、无故迟报残联系统统计资料的;

四、侵犯统计机构、统计人员行使统计法规及本办法所规定的职权或打击报复统计人员的;

五、违反统计法规及本办法，未经批准，自行编制发布残联系统统计报表的;

六、违反统计法规及本办法，未经核定批准，擅自对外提供或公布残联系统统计资料的。

八、附　则

第二十六条　本办法由中国残联负责解释。

第二十七条　本办法自发布之日起试行。

中华人民共和国统计法

（1983 年 12 月 8 日第六届全国人民代表大会常务委员会第三次会议通过 根据 1996 年 5 月 15 日第八届全国人民代表大会常务委员会第十九次会议《关于修改〈中华人民共和国统计法〉的决定》修正 2009 年 6 月 27 日第十一届全国人民代表大会常务委员会第九次会议修订）

第一章 总 则

第一条 为了科学、有效地组织统计工作，保障统计资料的真实性、准确性、完整性和及时性，发挥统计在了解国情国力、服务经济社会发展中的重要作用，促进社会主义现代化建设事业发展，制定本法。

第二条 本法适用于各级人民政府、县级以上人民政府统计机构和有关部门组织实施的统计活动。

统计的基本任务是对经济社会发展情况进行统计调查、统计分析，提供统计资料和统计咨询意见，实行统计监督。

第三条 国家建立集中统一的统计系统，实行统一领导、分级负责的统计管理体制。

第四条 国务院和地方各级人民政府、各有关部门应当加强对统计工作的组织领导，为统计工作提供必要的保障。

第五条 国家加强统计科学研究，健全科学的统计指标体系，不断改进统计调查方法，提高统计的科学性。

国家有计划地加强统计信息化建设，推进统计信息搜集、处理、传输、共享、存储技术和统计数据库体系的现代化。

第六条 统计机构和统计人员依照本法规定独立行使统计调查、统计报告、统计监督的职权，不受侵犯。

地方各级人民政府、政府统计机构和有关部门以及各单位的负责人，不得自行修改统计机构和统计人员依法搜集、整理的统计资料，不得以任何方式要求统计机构、统计人员及其他机构、人员伪造、篡改统计资料，不得对依法履行职责或者拒绝、抵制统计违法行为的统计人员打击报复。

第七条 国家机关、企业事业单位和其他组织以及个体工商户和个人等统计调查对象，必须依照本法和国家有关规定，真实、准确、完整、及时地提供统计调查所需的资料，不得提供不真实或者不完整的统计资料，不得迟报、拒报统计资料。

第八条 统计工作应当接受社会公众的监督。任何单位和个人有权检举统计中弄虚作假等违法行为。对检举有功的单位和个人应当给予表彰和奖励。

第九条 统计机构和统计人员对在统计工作中知悉的国家秘密、商业秘密和个人信息，应当予以保密。

第十条 任何单位和个人不得利用虚假统计资料骗取荣誉称号、物质利益或者职务晋升。

第二章 统计调查管理

第十一条 统计调查项目包括国家统计调查项目、部门统计调查项目和地方统计调查项目。

国家统计调查项目是指全国性基本情况的统计调查项目。部门统计调查项目是指国务院有关部门的专业性统计调查项目。地方统计调查项目是指县级以上地方人民政府及其部门的地方性统计调查项目。

国家统计调查项目、部门统计调查项目、地方统计调查项目应当明确分工，互相衔接，不得重复。

第十二条 国家统计调查项目由国家统计局制定，或者由国家统计局和国务院有关部门共同制定，报国务院备案；重大的国家统计调查项目报国务院审批。

部门统计调查项目由国务院有关部门制定。统计调查对象属于本部门管辖系统的，报国家统计局备案；统计调查对象超出本部门管辖系统的，报国家统计局审批。

地方统计调查项目由县级以上地方人民政府统计机构和有关部门分别制定或者共同制定。其中，由省级人民政府统计机构单独制定或者和有关部门共同制定的，报国家统计局审批；由省级以下人民政府统计机构单独制定或者和有关部门共同制定的，报省级人民政府统计机构审批；由县级以上地方人民政府有关部门制定的，报本级人民政府统计机构审批。

第十三条 统计调查项目的审批机关应当对调查项目的必要性、可行性、科学性进行审查，对符合法定条件的，作出予以批准的书面决定，并公布；对不符合法定条件的，作出不予批准的书面决定，并说明理由。

第十四条 制定统计调查项目，应当同时制定该项目的统计调查制度，并依照本法第十二条的规定一并报经审批或者备案。

统计调查制度应当对调查目的、调查内容、调查方法、调查对象、调查组织方式、调查表式、统计资料的报送和公布等作出规定。

统计调查应当按照统计调查制度组织实施。变更统计调查制度的内容，应当报经原审批机关批准或者原备案机关备案。

第十五条 统计调查表应当标明表号、制定机关、批准或者备案文号、有效期限等标志。

对未标明前款规定的标志或者超过有效期限的统计调查表，统计调查对象有权拒绝填报；县级以上人民政府统计机构应当依法责令停止有关统计调查活动。

第十六条 搜集、整理统计资料，应当以周期性普查为基础，以经常性抽样调查为主体，综合运用全面调查、重点调查等方法，并充分利用行政记录等资料。

重大国情国力普查由国务院统一领导，国务院和地方人民政府组织统计机构和有关部门共同实施。

第十七条 国家制定统一的统计标准，保障统计调查采用的指标涵义、计算方法、分类目录、调查表式和统计编码等的标准化。

国家统计标准由国家统计局制定，或者由国家统计局和国务院标准化主管部门共同制定。

国务院有关部门可以制定补充性的部门统计标准，报国家统计局审批。部门统计标准不得与国家统计标准相抵触。

第十八条 县级以上人民政府统计机构根据统计任务的需要，可以在统计调查对象中推广使用计算机网络报送统计资料。

第十九条 县级以上人民政府应当将统计工作所需经费列入财政预算。

重大国情国力普查所需经费，由国务院和地方人民政府共同负担，列入相应年度的财政预算，按时拨付，确保到位。

第三章 统计资料的管理和公布

第二十条 县级以上人民政府统计机构和有关部门以及乡、镇人民政府，应当按照国家有关规定建立统计资料的保存、管理制度，建立健全统计信息共享机制。

第二十一条 国家机关、企业事业单位和其他组织等统计调查对象，应当按照国家有关规定设置原始记录、统计台账，建立健全统计资料的审核、签署、交接、归档等管理制度。

统计资料的审核、签署人员应当对其审核、签署的统计资料的真实性、准确性和完整性负责。

第二十二条 县级以上人民政府有关部门应当及时向本级人民政府统计机构提供统计所需的行政记录资料和国民经济核算所需的财务资料、财政资料及其他资料，并按照统计调查制度的规定及时向本级人民政府统计机构报送其组织实施统计调查取得的有关资料。

县级以上人民政府统计机构应当及时向本级人民政府有关部门提供有关统计资料。

第二十三条 县级以上人民政府统计机构按照国家有关规定，定期公布统计资料。

国家统计数据以国家统计局公布的数据为准。

第二十四条 县级以上人民政府有关部门统计调查取得的统计资料，由本部门按照国家有关规定公布。

第二十五条 统计调查中获得的能够识别或者推断单个统计调查对象身份的资料，任何单位和个人不得对外提供、泄露，不得用于统计以外的目的。

第二十六条 县级以上人民政府统计机构和有关部门统计调查取得的统计资料，除依法应当保密的外，应当及时公开，供社会公众查询。

第四章 统计机构和统计人员

第二十七条 国务院设立国家统计局，依法组织领导和协调全国的统计工作。

国家统计局根据工作需要设立的派出调查机构，承担国家统计局布置的统计调查等任务。

县级以上地方人民政府设立独立的统计机构，乡、镇人民政府设置统计工作岗位，配备专职或者兼职统计人员，依法管理、开展统计工作，实施统计调查。

第二十八条 县级以上人民政府有关部门根据统计任务的需要设立统计机构，或者在有关机构中设置统计人员，并指定统计负责人，依法组织、管理本部门职责范围内的统计工作，实施统计调查，在统计业务上受本级人民政府统计机构的指导。

第二十九条 统计机构、统计人员应当依法履行职责，如实搜集、报送统计资料，不得伪造、篡改统计资料，不得以任何方式要求任何单位和个人提供不真实的统计资料，不得有其他违反本法规定的行为。

统计人员应当坚持实事求是，恪守职业道德，对其负责搜集、审核、录入的统计资料与统计调查对象报送的统计资料的一致性负责。

第三十条 统计人员进行统计调查时，有权就与统计有关的问题询问有关人员，要求其如实提供有关情况、资料并改正不真实、不准确的资料。

统计人员进行统计调查时，应当出示县级以上人民政府统计机构或者有关部门颁发的工作证件；未出示的，统计调查对象有权拒绝调查。

第三十一条 国家实行统计专业技术职务资格考试、评聘制度，提高统计人员的专业素质，保障统计队伍的稳定性。

统计人员应当具备与其从事的统计工作相适应的专业知识和业务能力。

县级以上人民政府统计机构和有关部门应当加强对统计人员的专业培训和职业道德教育。

第五章 监督检查

第三十二条 县级以上人民政府及其监察机关对下级人民政府、本级人民政府统计机构和有关部门执行本法的情况，实施监督。

第三十三条 国家统计局组织管理全国统计工作的监督检查，查处重大统计违法行为。

县级以上地方人民政府统计机构依法查处本行政区域内发生的统计违法行为。但是，国家统计局派出的调查机构组织实施的统计调查活动中发生的统计违法行为，由组织实施该项统计调查的调查机构负责查处。

法律、行政法规对有关部门查处统计违法行为另有规定的，从其规定。

第三十四条 县级以上人民政府有关部门应当积极协助本级人民政府统计机构查处统计违法行为，及时向本级人民政府统计机构移送有关统计违法案件材料。

第三十五条 县级以上人民政府统计机构在调查统计违法行为或者核查统计数据时，有权采取下列措施：

（一）发出统计检查查询书，向检查对象查询有关事项；

（二）要求检查对象提供有关原始记录和凭证、统计台账、统计调查表、会计资料及其他相关证明和资料；

（三）就与检查有关的事项询问有关人员；

（四）进入检查对象的业务场所和统计数据处理信息系统进行检查、核对；

（五）经本机构负责人批准，登记保存检查对象的有关原始记录和凭证、统计台账、统计调查表、会计资料及其他相关证明和资料；

（六）对与检查事项有关的情况和资料进行记录、录音、录像、照相和复制。

县级以上人民政府统计机构进行监督检查时，监督检查人员不得少于二人，并应当出示执法证件；未出示的，有关单位和个人有权拒绝检查。

第三十六条 县级以上人民政府统计机构履行监督检查职责时，有关单位和个人应当如实反映情况，提供相关证明和资料，不得拒绝、阻碍检查，不得转移、隐匿、篡改、毁弃原始记录和凭证、统计台账、统计调查表、会计资料及其他相关证明和资料。

第六章 法律责任

第三十七条 地方人民政府、政府统计机构或者有关部门、单位的负责人有下列行为之一的，由任免机关或者监察机关依法给予处分，并由县级以上人民政府统计机构予以通报：

（一）自行修改统计资料、编造虚假统计数据的；

（二）要求统计机构、统计人员或者其他机构、人员伪造、篡改统计资料的；

（三）对依法履行职责或者拒绝、抵制统计违法行为的统计人员打击报复的；

（四）对本地方、本部门、本单位发生的严重统计违法行为失察的。

第三十八条 县级以上人民政府统计机构或者有关部门在组织实施统计调查活动中有下列行为之一的，由本级人民政府、上级人民政府统计机构或者本级人民政府统计机构责令改正，予以通报；对直接负责的主管人员和其他直接责任人员，由任免机关或者监察机关依法给予处分：

（一）未经批准擅自组织实施统计调查的；

（二）未经批准擅自变更统计调查制度的内容的；

（三）伪造、篡改统计资料的；

（四）要求统计调查对象或者其他机构、人员提供不真实的统计资料的；

（五）未按照统计调查制度的规定报送有关资料的。

统计人员有前款第三项至第五项所列行为之一的，责令改正，依法给予处分。

第三十九条 县级以上人民政府统计机构或者有关部门有下列行为之一的，对直接负责的主管人员和其他直接责任人员由任免机关或者监察机关依法给予处分：

（一）违法公布统计资料的；

（二）泄露统计调查对象的商业秘密、个人信息或者提供、泄露在统计调查中获得的能够识别或者推断单个统计调查对象身份的资料的；

（三）违反国家有关规定，造成统计资料毁损、灭失的。

统计人员有前款所列行为之一的，依法给予处分。

第四十条 统计机构、统计人员泄露国家秘密的，依法追究法律责任。

第四十一条 作为统计调查对象的国家机关、企业事业单位或者其他组织有下列行为之一的，由县级以上人民政府统计机构责令改正，给予警告，可以予以通报；其直接负责的主管人员和其他直接责任人员属于国家工作人员的，由任免机关或者监察机关依法给予处分：

（一）拒绝提供统计资料或者经催报后仍未按时提供统计资料的；

（二）提供不真实或者不完整的统计资料的；

（三）拒绝答复或者不如实答复统计检查查询书的；

（四）拒绝、阻碍统计调查、统计检查的；

（五）转移、隐匿、篡改、毁弃或者拒绝提供原始记录和凭证、统计台账、统计调查表及其他相关证明和资料的。

企业事业单位或者其他组织有前款所列行为之一的，可以并处五万元以下的罚款；情节严重的，并处五万元以上二十万元以下的罚款。

个体工商户有本条第一款所列行为之一的，由县级以上人民政府统计机构责令改正，给予警告，可以并处一万元以下的罚款。

第四十二条 作为统计调查对象的国家机关、企业事业单位或者其他组织迟报统计资料，或者未按照国家有关规定设置原始记录、统计台账的，由县级以上人民政府统计机构责令改正，给予警告。

企业事业单位或者其他组织有前款所列行为之一的，可以并处一万元以下的罚款。

个体工商户迟报统计资料的，由县级以上人民政府统计机构责令改正，给予警告，可以并处一千元以下的罚款。

第四十三条 县级以上人民政府统计机构查处统计违法行为时，认为对有关国家工作人员依法应当给予处分的，应当提出给予处分的建议；该国家工作人员的任免机关或者监察机关应当依法及时作出决定，并将结果书面通知县级以上人民政府统计机构。

第四十四条 作为统计调查对象的个人在重大国情国力普查活动中拒绝、阻碍统计调查，或者提供不真实或者不完整的普查资料的，由县级以上人民政府统计机构责令改正，予以批评教育。

第四十五条 违反本法规定，利用虚假统计资料骗取荣誉称号、物质利益或者职务晋升的，除对其编造虚假统计资料或者要求他人编造虚假统计资料的行为依法追究法律责任外，由作出有关决定的单位或者其上级单位、监察机关取消其荣誉称号，追缴获得的物质利益，撤销晋升的职务。

第四十六条 当事人对县级以上人民政府统计机构作出的行政处罚决定不服的，可以依法申请行政复议或者提起行政诉讼。其中，对国家统计局在省、自治区、直辖市派出的调查机构作出的行政处罚决定不服的，向国家统计局申请行政复议；对国家统计局派出的其他调查机构作出的行政处罚决定不服的，向国家统计局在该派出机构所在的省、自治区、直辖市派出的调查机构申请行政复议。

第四十七条 违反本法规定，构成犯罪的，依法追究刑事责任。

第七章 附 则

第四十八条 本法所称县级以上人民政府统计机构，是指国家统计局及其派出的调查机构、县级以上地方人民政府统计机构。

第四十九条 民间统计调查活动的管理办法，由国务院制定。

中华人民共和国境外的组织、个人需要在中华人民共和国境内进行统计调查活动的，应当按照国务院的规定报请审批。

利用统计调查危害国家安全、损害社会公共利益或者进行欺诈活动的，依法追究法律责任。

第五十条 本法自 2010 年 1 月 1 日起施行。

部门统计调查项目管理暂行办法

（1999年10月27日国家统计局令第4号公布）

第一章 总 则

第一条 为加强对部门统计调查的管理和监督，规范部门统计调查行为，提高统计调查的整体效率，减轻被调查者负担，保障统计资料的准确性，提高共享性，根据《中华人民共和国统计法》及其实施细则，制定本办法。

第二条 本办法适用于国家机关、具有行政管理职能的事业单位、经授权代主管部门行使统计职能的国家级集团公司和工商领域联合会或协会、经国务院授权具有一定行政职能的人民团体开展的统计调查，以及上述部门和单位与其他部门联合组织实施的统计调查。法院、检察院组织实施的统计调查，参照本办法执行。

第三条 本办法所称的统计调查，是指部门搜集国民经济、社会和科技发展情况，用于政府管理目的的各类统计调查。包括以数字形式、文字形式或混合形式；以表格、问卷、电讯（电报、电话、传真等）、磁盘磁带、网络通讯（网络表格、电子邮件等）等为介质的普查、经常性调查、一次性调查、试点调查等。

第二章 部门统计调查项目的管理

第四条 政府综合统计机构统一管理和协调部门统计调查。国家统计局管理和协调国家一级部门制定的统计调查；县及县以上地方各级政府统计局管理和协调同级部门的统计调查。

第五条 部门的综合统计机构统一组织、管理和协调本部门各职能机构的统计调查活动，制定本部门的统计调查总体方案。部门内其它职能机构无权单独制定统计调查项目。

第六条 政府综合统计机构通过建立审批备案制度、有效期制度、调查项目公布制度、跟踪检查制度、举报制度，对部门统计调查进行管理。

第三章 制定统计调查项目的基本原则与要求

第七条 国家机关、具有行政管理职能的事业单位、经授权代主管部门行使统计职能的国家级集团公司和工商领域联合会或协会、经国务院授权具有一定行政职能的人民团体，可以制定与职能范围相对应的统计调查项目。

国务院临时机构，一般不得直接制定统计调查项目。工作需要的统计资料，应当向有关部门搜集、加工。确有需要调查的，须事先取得国家统计局的同意，方可制定统计调查。法院、检察院可制定业务情况统计调查项目。

第八条 统计调查项目的立项必须有充分的理由。调查要有明确的目的和资料使用范围。

第九条 统计调查的内容和调查范围必须与部门的职能相一致，必须符合既定的政府综合统计与部门统计的分工原则。

第十条 统计调查项目必须兼顾需要与可能，充分考虑基层调查人员和被调查对象的承受能力。必须符合精简、效能的原则。凡一次性调查能满足需要的，不搞定期调查；凡非全面调查能满足需要的，不搞全面调查。最大限度地减少调查频率，缩小调查规模，降低调查成本。

第十一条 调查项目中的报表表式和文字说明必须规范；指标解释和计算方法必须科学；调查内容要简明扼要，不能与其他调查重复、交叉、矛盾。

第十二条 调查项目中的统计标准和分类必须与政府综合统计部门规定使用的标准和分类相一致。涉及政府综合统计部门规定以外的专业标准和分类，要与有关国家标准或行业标准相一致。尚无国家标准和行业标准的，必须严格按照标准化科学及分类科学的原理进行归纳和设计，并在使用前征求政府综合统计部门的意见。

第十三条 所使用的调查方法要科学合理。要结合调查目的和要求选择最适当的调查方法，以获得最大的调查效益。避免由于调查方法使用不当给基层造成过重负担和产生数据质量问题。

第十四条 重大调查项目必须经过研究论证和试点，必须有完备的论证材料和试点材料。

第十五条 调查者必须依法使用调查资料，对属于国家秘密的统计资料，必须保密；对属于私人、家庭的单项调查资料和在统计调查中知悉的调查对象的商业秘密，负有保密义务。

第四章 审批及备案程序

第十六条 部门建立以系统内单位为对象的调查项目，须报同级政府综合统计机构备案；部门建立调查范围涉及到系统外单位的统计调查项目，必须报同级政府综合统计机构审批，在取得政府综合统计机构的同意或批准后方可组织实施。

系统内是指：与部门有直接隶属关系的单位及部门的派出机构；省及省以下与部门对口设立的管理机构；国家级集团公司所属企业。除此之外均属系统外。

第十七条 审批及备案程序的有关时间规定：

（一）政府综合统计机构在收到部门正式申请函及完整的相关资料后，在 20 个工作日内完成审批；在 5 个工作日内完成备案。完成时间以复函日期为准。

（二）部门收到复函后，在 20 个工作日内将布置调查的正式文件、调查方案和调查表式送达政府综合统计机构，以便及时在“部门统计调查项目库”中建立或更新记录，以及履行公文存档手续。

（三）对有关自然灾害、突发事件等不可预知、有特殊时效性要求的调查，政府综合统计机构将根据特事特办的原则，在最短的时间内完成审批工作，备案项目可事后补办。

第十八条 部门统计调查项目送审及备案时，须备齐以下文件：

（一）以部门名义发出的申请审批或备案的函。

（二）调查方案和表式。包括：总说明、报表目录、基层表式、综合表式、统计标准和分类目录、指标解释、逻辑关系及抽样方案（针对抽样调查）等。应明确表述调查目的、调查对象、统计范围、调查方法、调查频率、填报要求、报送渠道、时间要求等。

（三）相关文件。包括新建立该调查项目的背景材料、重大调查项目的研究论证材料及试点报告等。

第十九条 制定统计调查的部门，在将调查方案送审的同时，要认真填写《部门统计调查项目审批/备案登记表》。

第二十条 政府综合统计机构对送审的部门统计调查进行初审，提出修改意见和建议，部门应积极配合，及时作出说明和解释，并按照修改意见认真进行修改；如有不同意见，双方应进一步研究磋商达成一致。否则由国家统计局进行最终裁决，部门应按最终裁决意见进行修改。

政府综合统计机构对送备案的部门统计调查提出修改意见和完善建议。

第二十一条 政府综合统计机构对部门统计调查的具体审核工作完成之后，以统计局名义发函批复。批复分为：同意实施；不同意实施；建议暂缓实施三种。部门收到批复后，应严格按照批复执行。

第二十二条 部门收到同意实施的复文后，要及时印制调查方案和调查表式，起草布置实施的部门文件，部署调查工作。如遇特殊情况不能实施调查、延期实施调查或需调整变更调查方案的，须及时向政府综合统计机构报告说明。

第二十三条 调查范围涉及到省及省以下单位的部门调查，在将调查任务逐级布置时，应及时通知同级政府综合统计机构。

第二十四条 对部门内职能机构为监控生产经营活动的具体环节而建立的内容专一、分类至细、频率固定的业务统计项目，在其内容不与其它统计调查项目重复的前提下，可向政府综合统计机构提出申请，由政府综合统计机构研究同意后，授权部门的综合统计机构进行定期审批管理。部门的综合统计机构审批后，须将调查方案送政府综合统计机构，以便纳入“部门统计调查项目库”。

第五章 调查的法定标识和有效期

第二十五条 部门统计调查经政府综合统计机构批准或备案后，必须在报表的右上角标明法定标识。法定标识包括：（一）表号；（二）制表机关；

（三）批准机关/备案机关；（四）批准文号/备案文号；（五）有效期截止时间。

第二十六条 政府综合统计机构对部门统计调查实行有效期管理制度。批准的年度调查及其调查周期小于一年的定期调查的有效期为两年；普查、一次性调查、调查周期大于一年的定期调查，其有效期到该次调查的资料上报结束时止。备案的定期调查的有效期为三年；一次性调查的有效期到该次调查的资料上报结束时止。有效期皆以复函的日期为起点计算。

超过有效期的调查项目，一律自动废止。如需要继续执行，应当重新办理审批或备案手续。在有效期内发生变化的调查项目，应随时办理重新审批或备案手续。

第六章 监督与处罚

第二十七条 政府综合统计机构为了保护合法的部门统计调查项目顺利实施，采取以下监督措施：

（一）定期通过公共媒体向社会公布“部门统计调查项目目录”，以便建立全社会监督机制。“部门统计调查项目目录”的内容包括：

1、经过批准或备案的部门统计调查项目名称；

2、制定及组织实施该项调查的单位名称；

3、批准文号或备案文号及其日期；

4、调查项目的有效期。

同时公布经查实的违规调查项目和因超过有效期而被废止的调查项目。

（二）建立对违规调查的举报核实制度。在政府综合统计机构设立举报接待部门，根据举报线索，对违规调查的情况进行调查核实后予以公布。

第二十八条 为保护国家利益和被调查者的权益，减轻被调查者和各级数据加工部门的负担，政府综合统计机构对部门调查的资料使用情况、实施方案与批准方案的一致性进行监督，监督内容包括：

（一）检查调查取得的资料是否被正当使用。资料使用与调查目的是否一致；资料使用是否超出原定的范围；资料是否被私自用于营利目的；是否违反有关保密的规定；是否有其他损害国家利益和被调查者权益的行为。

（二）检查调查资料的有用性。对大部分内容使用频率不高、针对性不强的调查，建议修改、合并或停止实施。

（三）检查调查实施过程中是否严格按政府统计机构批准的方案执行，是否有擅自变更调查内容、调查范围、计算方法和报送频率等行为。

第二十九条 对违反本办法第十六条、第二十二条、第二十六条的规定，未履行法定的审批或者备案程序和擅自变更调查方案的部门统计调查，县级以上政府综合统计机构可以依法予以废止，并按照《统计法》及其实施细则的有关规定处理。

第七章 管理部门提供的服务

第三十条 为主动作好部门统计调查的管理工作，避免可能出现的问题，政府综合统计机构为制定统计调查的部门提供有关业务性咨询、调查方案设计指导。帮助部门掌握设计统计调查项目的基本方法，提高设计工作的效率和质量。

第三十一条 为了避免调查项目之间的重复、矛盾，政府综合统计机构建立并向部门开放“部门统计调查项目库”。部门在制定调查项目前可先进行查询，以达到避免重复调查，充分利用已有信息的目的。

第三十二条 对于部门利用已有资料，精简调查项目和调查内容的，政府综合统计机构给予充分支持和协助。对部门之间在利用对方资料中遇到障碍的，政府综合统计机构可出面协调。

第八章 附 则

第三十三条 对于政府综合统计机构与部门联合制定的统计调查项目，以政府综合统计机构为主制定的（使用政府统计机构的文号），参照政府综合统计机构调查审批程序办理；以部门为主制定的（使用部门的文号），参照部门调查审批程序办理，最后以会签文件作为实施依据。

第三十四条 本办法由国家统计局负责解释。

第三十五条 本办法自公布之日起施行。